LAW AND DEVELOPMENT IN EAST AND SOUTHEAST ASIA

During the 1980s and 1990s Asian 'developmental states' attracted much attention in political science and economics literature, but the role of law in their economic development was neglected. It was only after the Asian crisis of 1997 that many analysts began to focus on a lack of regulation and transparency as a major factor triggering the crisis. As a result, international financial institutions now tend to make further financial support for Asian economies dependent on improvements of the legal framework in which businesses operate. The crucial questions now are how successful the current reforms will be, and which features of the Asian approach to commercial law will be resistant to reform pressures.

This book examines the prospects for commercial law reform in Asia. Japan and Singapore, as frequently cited role models for Asian developmentalism, receive particular attention. Development related business laws in countries such as China, Korea, Indonesia, Malaysia, Vietnam and the Philippines are also examined. The book includes chapters on individual fields of commercial law such as intellectual property law, financial market regulation and labour law as well as chapters that explain the socio-legal background of Asian legal development. All are placed into the industrial policy framework of the countries concerned.

Christoph Antons is Senior Lecturer in the Faculty of Law and Centre for Southeast Asian Law at the Northern Territory University, Darwin, Australia.

RoutledgeCurzon-IIAS Asian Studies Series

Series Co-ordinator: Dick van der Meij
Institute Director: Wim A.L. Stokhof

The International Institute for Asian Studies (IIAS) is a postdoctoral research centre based in Leiden and Amsterdam, The Netherlands. Its main objective is to encourage Asian Studies in the Humanities and the Social Sciences and to promote national and international co-operation in these fields. The Institute was established in 1993 on the initiative of the Royal Netherlands Academy of Arts and Sciences, Leiden University, Universiteit van Amsterdam and Vrije Universiteit Amsterdam. It is mainly financed by The Netherlands Ministry of Education, Culture, and Sciences. IIAS has played an active role in co-ordinating and disseminating information on Asian Studies throughout the world. The Institute acts as an international mediator, bringing together various entities for the enhancement of Asian Studies both within and outside The Netherlands. The RoutledgeCurzon-IIAS Asian Studies series reflects the scope of the Institute. The Editorial Board consists of Erik Zurcher, Wang Gungwu, Om Prakash, Dru Gladney, Amiya K. Bagchi, James C. Scott, Jean-Luc Domenach and Frits Staal.

Images of the 'Modern Woman' in Asia
Edited by Shoma Munshi

Nomads in the Sedentary World
Edited by Anatoly M. Khazanov & Andre Wink

Reading Asia
Edited by Frans Husken & Dick van der Meij

Tourism, Heritage and National Culture in Java
Heidi Dahles

Asian-European Perspectives
Edited by Wim Stokhof & Paul van der Velde

Law and Development in East and Southeast Asia
Edited by Christoph Antons

The Indian Ocean Rim
Edited by Gwyn Campbell

Rethinking Chinese Transnational Enterprises
Edited by Leo Douw, Cen Huang & David Ip

'Hinduism' in Modern Indonesia
Edited by Martin Ramstedt

Indonesian Sea Nomads
Cynthia Chou

Diasporas and Interculturalism in Asian Performing Arts
Edited by Hae-Kyung Um

Reading East Asian Writing
Edited by Michel Hockx & Ivo Smits

LAW AND DEVELOPMENT IN EAST AND SOUTHEAST ASIA

EDITED BY
Christoph Antons

International Institute for Asian Studies

RoutledgeCurzon
Taylor & Francis Group
LONDON AND NEW YORK

First published 2003
by RoutledgeCurzon
11 New Fetter Lane, London EC4P 4EE

Simultaneously published in the USA and Canada
by RoutledgeCurzon
29 West 35th Street, New York, NY 10001

RoutledgeCurzon is an imprint of the Taylor & Francis Group

Typeset in Times New Roman by Dick van der Meij
Printed and bound in Great Britain by MPG Books Ltd, Bodmin

British Library Cataloguing in Publication Data
A catalogue record for this book is available from the British Library

Library of Congress Cataloging in Publication Data
A catalogue record for this book has been requested

ISBN 0-700-71321-2

TABLE OF CONTENTS

CONTRIBUTORS

CHRISTOPH ANTONS is a Senior Lecturer in the School of Law and Director of the Centre for Southeast Asian Law, Northern Territory University, Darwin, Australia.

HARALD BAUM is a Senior Research Fellow at the Max Planck Institute for Foreign and International Private Law, Hamburg, Germany.

BERNARD G. BISHOP is a Senior Lecturer in the Faculty of International Business and Politics, Griffith University, Brisbane, Australia.

MICHAEL BLAKENEY is Professor and Director of the Queen Mary Intellectual Property Institute, Queen Mary and Westfield College, University of London, United Kingdom.

RICHARD BOYD is Reader in law and society with respect to Japan in the Department of Languages and Cultures of Japan and Korea, Faculty of Arts, Leiden University, the Netherlands.

CONNIE CARTER is a Barrister and a Visiting Lecturer at the School of African and Oriental Studies, University of London, United Kingdom.

JIANFU CHEN is Associate Professor and Reader in the School of Law and Legal Studies, La Trobe University, Melbourne, Australia.

CHRISTOPHER HEATH is a Senior Research Fellow and Head of the East and Southeast Asia Department at the Max Planck Institute for Foreign and International Patent, Copyright and Competition Law in Munich, Germany.

ROBERT E. LUTZ is Professor in the School of Law, Southwestern University, Los Angeles, USA.

JOHN K.M. OHNESORGE is Assistant Professor in the School of Law, University of Wisconsin, Madison, USA.

ROMAN TOMASIC is Professor and Dean, Faculty of Law and Business, Victoria University, Melbourne, Australia.

Contributors

JESSE WU MIN AUN is Professor in the School of Law, Northern Territory University, Darwin, Australia.

NOBUYUKI YASUDA is Professor in the Graduate School of International Development, Nagoya University, Japan.

PREFACE

This books results from a workshop held at the International Institute for Asian Studies (IIAS) in Leiden, the Netherlands, in January 1998. Ten of the fourteen papers in this book were originally presented at the workshop, but due to the rapidly changing legal environment in the countries covered, most of the papers had to be revised during 1999 and 2000. The workshop was funded by a generous grant of the International Institute for Asian Studies and supported by smaller grants of the Van Vollenhoven Institute for Law and Administration in Non-Western Countries of Leiden University, and Kluwer Law International. At the IIAS, I would like to thank in particular its Director Professor W.A.L. Stokhof, for his continuing encouragement and support for this project and Dr Dick van der Meij for the excellent final editing of the papers for publication. Thanks also to Ms Marianne Langehenkel for organizing the workshop and making it such a pleasant event. I would further like to thank the director of the Van Vollenhoven Institute, Professor Jan-Michiel Otto, for supporting the workshop and suggesting some of the speakers. Many thanks are further due to Professor Martin Chanock, who was head of the school of law and legal studies at La Trobe University in Melbourne at the time, for allowing me to prolong my research stay in Europe for the workshop.

The concept of the workshop was based on my project 'Japan as a Model? - Law and Development in Japan, Singapore, and Indonesia', which was funded by a large grant of the Australian Research Council from 1994 to 1996. My stay in the Netherlands in 1997 and early 1998 was made possible by an outside study grant of La Trobe University and an exchange fellowship of the Research School of Pacific Studies at the Australian National University in Canberra. I would like to thank all these institutions for their support of my work. I would further like to thank Professor Masaji Chiba in Tokyo and Professor Bill Cornish in Cambridge for crucial support at the initial stages of my ARC project. Last but not least, many thanks to my research assistants Ms. Megan Lennie and Ms. Deborah Cooper at the Centre for Southeast Asian Law at Northern Territory University in Darwin and to Ms. Gillian Jenik for many hours of help in proof reading and formatting the chapters.

Darwin, October 2000
Christoph Antons

Part One

Paradigms of Law and Development in Asia

CHAPTER 1

INTRODUCTION

CHRISTOPH ANTONS

This is not simply another book on the Asian crisis. A lot has been written over the last few two years on the economic and political causes of the crisis. Nevertheless, the Asian crisis will provide an important background for the arguments in this book. At the core of the book are papers from a workshop at the International Institute for Asian Studies at Leiden in the Netherlands in January 1998. The workshop thus took place only a few months after the first shock waves of the crisis reached Asia in May 1997.[1] The crisis had an important impact on the workshop discussions as it brought the long neglected question of the role of law in what had become termed as Asian capitalism back into play. The idea for the workshop came from my earlier research on law and development in Japan, Singapore, and Indonesia which had been funded by the Australian Research Council (ARC) from 1994 to 1996. Participants thus consisted of many people that I had spoken to during my research and there was consequently a concentration of papers on the Japanese, Singaporean, and Indonesian developments, four of which (by Baum, Boyd, Carter, and Antons) are published in this volume. Other papers discussed the theoretical and cultural framework of Asian legal development (Yasuda, Ohnesorge) or analysed legal developments in China (Chen) or particular areas of business law in the region (Heath, Blakeney, and Lutz). During 1999 and 2000, for the publication of this book, the conference papers were updated and three further chapters (Wu on labour law in Malaysia, Bishop on APEC, industry policy and the role of law, and Tomasic on the Asian economic crisis and legal institutions in Singapore and Hong Kong) were added to them.

My earlier ARC funded project was entitled 'Japan as a Model? – Law and Development in Japan, Singapore and Indonesia.' It examined the question in how far the Japanese experience of development had provided a role model for Southeast Asian countries such as Singapore and Indonesia and in how far this was reflected in the approaches to legal development. During the course of the project it appeared that Singapore as one of the initial followers of Japan in the flying geese picture painted by political scientists at the time, was beginning to present itself to developing countries as a role model in its own right and was making attempts to export its approach to countries such as China and India. The structure of the workshop represented the debate surrounding these role models for Asian economic development and their influence on commercial law. While some chapters have been rearranged, this structure has basically been maintained for the present volume.

Part 1 provides a theoretical and historical background to the question of Asian legal development. It begins with a chapter by Nobuyuki Yasuda on Southeast Asian perceptions of the role of law in economic development. The first notable feature of this chapter is Yasuda's redefinition of the boundaries of Southeast Asia. He contrasts the accepted definition of Southeast Asia with what he calls Monsoon Asia. Apart from those countries commonly grouped under the label 'Southeast Asia,' Monsoon Asia includes also parts of India, China, Japan, and Korea. Yasuda returns to Wittfogel's (1977) argument of the importance of rice farming in these areas and the common characteristics created by this mode of production and the climatic circumstances of it. The scope of his paper is thus different from other politically and culturally defined notions of Southeast Asia, but it is also different from the ASEAN plus three group of countries that is currently harmonizing its policies to a certain extent. This is perhaps a timely reminder that the roots of the term Southeast Asia go back no further than fifty years and that the term was increasingly used during and after World War II to refer to what was previously called 'Further India,' predominantly former colonies between India and China (on the origins and the future of the term 'Southeast Asia' see Fifield, 1983). In the era of globalization and stronger rights to self-determination of various ethnic groups in border regions, the colonial distinction between South, Southeast, and East Asia might be increasingly questioned.

Yasuda's chapter is an appeal for inclusion of cultural aspects into the study of law and development. He proposes to analyse Asian legal developments by contrasting three types of law (indigenous law, imported law, and development law) and their operational concepts 'community,' 'market,' and 'command.' By applying these concepts to the historical development of Southeast Asian legal systems, to political, economic, and social development in 'Asian developmental states' and in post-crisis Southeast Asia, he comes to some interesting findings. While 'indigenous law' has been superseded by 'imported law' with origins mostly in Western jurisdictions it continues to play an important role in the daily life of Asian people, in particular in legal areas related to family or religious matters. There is even a revival of originally Asian laws as with Islamic law in much of South and Southeast Asia. Yasuda explains the relative lack of success in completely transplanting Western derived systems with the fact that they were mostly introduced during colonialism and, as a consequence, displayed an oppressive nature during much of their history. From the community principle, Asian states have inherited their tendency towards authoritarian forms of government and patron-client relationships, to which development law and the developmental state has added a large discretionary power.

In the epical struggle between the market and the community principle, globalization and the information technology revolution have led to a victory of the former over the latter and nationalism, nation states, and socialist regimes are losing their power. Business laws have been liberalized since the 1980s following demands of the IMF and the World Bank to combat inefficiencies in national economies. Yasuda sees this hasty liberalization as one of the main reasons for the Asian crisis, which was made worse by structural deficiencies such as lack of transparency, crony capitalism, and nepotism in the countries concerned. Yasuda believes that as a result of the developments of the last few years, the paradigm of the 'Asian developmental state' has come to an end. Southeast Asian countries have democratized their political systems considerably and crucial commercial laws have been amended. Nevertheless, the community principle still plays a role in dispute resolution, at the level of the family and in rural areas, but also in informal mutual assistance schemes, which in many parts of Asia are a substitute for a social security system. With the disastrous social consequences of the Asian crisis, these informal support systems have in fact seen a revival. While globalization means that the state becomes less important as a tool for identification, the community principle and local interests will in future be represented increasingly at a regional instead of at a national level.

The paradigm change in the law and development debate in Asia is also the topic of Bernard Bishop's Chapter 3. He presents an excellent overview of what he calls the 'old' idea of industry policy. Bureaucratic and political capacities were decisive for the success of this policy. By bureaucratic capacity, he means generally the competence of the bureaucracy, but also the degree of cohesion within and between government agencies. Political capacity refers to the degree that decision-makers are insulated from social pressures, but still 'embedded' enough within society to formulate policies that reflect market conditions. In this regard, Bishop sees factors at work in Northeast Asia that were not, or not to the same extent, present in Southeast Asia. In Northeast Asia, bureaucrats held prestigious social positions that made them less prone to rent seeking activities than their counterparts in Southeast Asia. The considerable ethnic and social divisions in Southeast Asia also made policies there less cohesive. Southeast Asian industrial policies were, therefore less insulated from politics and also more difficult to supervise, because of the important role of Overseas Chinese business networks for their economies.

Since the mid-1980s, the pressures resulting from democratization processes have reduced the effectiveness of developmental policies in Asia. Economic deregulation has required the separation of business-government links and the WTO agreement has restricted the possibilities for governments to intervene in key areas of the economy. What has also to be kept in mind is the increasing complexity of Asian economies, which makes them much more difficult to supervise than the relatively small economies of the 1960s and 1970s. Bishop perceives a growing consensus within APEC to replace the old industry policy with a new policy that favours a healthy degree of competition. The new policy requires the prevention of industry dominance, cartels, and unfair trade practices. Paradoxically, however, the implementation of this policy relies on the same bureaucratic and political capacities that are now under pressure. To decide about dominant market position and to define what this means, for example, requires a high degree of bureaucratic competence. Again, policy makers must be sufficiently independent to prevent a use of the new approach for particular interests. On both of these issues, Bishop is rather pessimistic. On the one hand, the intensive networks built between business and government in Asia will not disappear quickly. On the other hand, democratic institution building in Asia might ultimately take more time than the quickly changing international environment will allow. In the absence of strong bureaucratic and political capacity, the rule of law needs to fill this gap immediately. The competition policies will, therefore, lead to a renewed emphasis on the rule of law and away from the traditional Asian understanding of law as an instrument of state power, that suited the needs of the old industry policy.

John Ohnesorge questions in Chapter 4 precisely this renewed importance attached to the rule of law for economic development. If the rule of law was really such an important prerequisite for economic growth, then how was the East Asian success of the last few decades to be explained? Ohnesorge differentiates between an approach to the rule of law as an ideal of jurisprudence that is reached in different societies to a differing degree, but that is hardly ever fully established, and a vision of the rule of law as a complete and seamless legal infrastructure. The latter perception is often to be found in the writings of social scientists and economists rather than lawyers. The 'Rule of Law-Economic Development' literature focuses on two themes: the definition and enforcement of private property rights and the reduction of bureaucratic discretion in economic government. The first theme relates to the avoidance of 'transaction costs' in the economy, whereas the second theme relates to transparency and avoidance of corruption to attract foreign investment. It must be noted, however, that contrary to a common assumption by institutions such as the World Bank, the rising complexity of commercial transactions in Asia was not accompanied by a rising importance of contracts and courts. The small litigation rates actually suggest a relatively well functioning system, which is supported by socio-cultural values favourable to contractual market behaviour. This in turn either suggests that legal norms are well integrated into society or that they are simply not of primary importance. Similarly, the reasons for private property protection are often political rather than socio-legal and have to do with the attraction of foreign investment. However, portfolio investors in Asia seem generally little interested in questions of ownership rights and corporate control. The Asian crisis has demonstrated how little foreign banks cared for transparency in their lending to Asia. Furthermore, the lack of enforcement of intellectual property rights and of competition law in Asia belies the claim that these laws are necessary for development. Currently, the rule of law is on the rise in the national screening of foreign investment, yet its strict application may actually be disadvantageous to foreign investors, because the decision making in this area will lose its former flexibility. John Ohnesorge concludes that the rule of law needs a more concrete definition to defend itself against claims of 'Western' vs. 'Asian' versions. Finally, the assumption that the current Rule of Law approach with its focus on trade issues will have spillover benefits in other areas of law is questionable.

The book then proceeds in Part 2 to examine the impact of what has been called the 'Japanese model' on Asian legal developments. The alleged superiority of Japanese capitalism and its features was a topic for hefty debates during the 1970s and 1980s. The many titles of popular books on the topic from this period range from enthusiastic appraisals of the 'Japanese economic miracle' (e.g. Kahn, 1970; Morishima, 1982) to often gloomy pictures of a 'Nipponized' world painted at a time of heightened US–Japanese trade tensions (e.g. Burstein, 1988, and Prestowitz, 1988).[2] The picture changed again after the burst of the Japanese 'bubble economy' in the early 1990s, when 'the end of Japan Inc.' was promulgated (Wood, 1994), only to make way for publications asking how to restore the Japanese economy as an economic locomotive for Asia after the onset of the Asian crisis (Posen, 1998).

Perhaps the most famous and most influential appraisal of the particular features of Japanese economic development was made by Professor Chalmers Johnson in his book on 'MITI and the Japanese Miracle' (1982). Chalmers Johnson proposed a move away from an overemphasis on cultural explanations of Japan's economic development. In his view, the famous Japanese consensus was due to a large extent to the various economic and social emergencies the Japanese had been facing throughout their history (Johnson, 1982:8-9, 307). To explain Japan's economic performance, the view should rather be directed towards its nature as what he termed a plan-rational, developmental state. In a summary of his thoughts in the 1992 Panglaykim Memorial lecture on 'Capitalism: East Asian Style,' he cited former MITI official Koji Matsumoto for some of the key features of Japanese postwar development: de facto total separation of management from the wishes of the owners, a shift of the burden of corporate risk to the side of labour and the autonomy of management. A further interesting Japanese source for the features of the Japanese 'developmental state' is a chapter entitled 'Developmentalism as a System' in Yasusuke Murakami's book *An Anticlassical Political-Economic Analysis: A Vision for the Next Century.*[3] Here, Murakami finds the following policies fundamentally necessary for developmentalism: designation of priority industries, industry-specific indicative planning, policies to promote technological progress, and regulation of excessive price competition. Protectionist policies and a policy of subsidies may further supplement these policies.[4]

The state-centered view of Japanese development has not remained unchallenged. Kent Calder (1993:8-13) basically accepted most of Chalmers Johnson's analysis but has pointed to gaps in the existing theories and sees the power of the state institutions constrained by the political world and by the private sector.[5] In a matrix capturing state intervention and strategic resource allocation, Calder distinguishes between the developmental state (state intervention and strategic resource allocation), corporate-led strategic capitalism (strategic resource allocation without state intervention), the clientelized state (state intervention without strategic resource allocation) and what he calls 'Silicon Valley capitalism' (neither state intervention nor strategic resource allocation).[6] As the title of his book suggests, he prefers to see Japan in the second category as a state practicing corporate-led strategic capitalism. Apart from the more differentiated views of scholars such as Calder, there is also a type of analysis that rejects approaches based on state-intervention completely and explains Japan's economic development as a result of the famous invisible hands of Adam Smith (Miwa, 1996).

The state-centered view of the Japanese economy has important implications for the field of law. Chalmers Johnson has pointed out, how administrative guidance has prevailed over detailed legislation:

> Perhaps the most important market-conforming method of intervention is administrative guidance. This power, which amounts to an allocation of discretionary and unsupervised authority to the bureaucracy, is obviously open to abuse, and may, if used improperly, result in damage to the market. But it is an essential power of the capitalist developmental state for one critical reason: it is necessary to avoid overly detailed laws that, by their very nature, are never detailed enough to cover all contingencies and yet, because of their detail, put

> a strait jacket on creative administration. One of the great strengths of Japanese industrial policy is its ability to deal with discrete complex situations without first having to enact a law that covers the situation. Highly detailed statutes serve the interests primarily of lawyers, not of development. The Japanese political economy is strikingly free of lawyers; many of the functions performed by lawyers in other societies are performed in Japan by bureaucrats using administrative guidance. The Japanese of course rely on law, but on short and highly generalized laws. They then give concrete meaning to these laws through bureaucratically originated cabinet orders, ordinances, rules, and administrative guidance. (Johnson, 1982:318-19)

In his description of developmentalism and referring to Max Weber's 'Economy and Society,' Murakami also pays attention to this administrative discretion, which he regards in line with Weber as a phenomenon that is not exclusively Japanese (or Asian):

> There is therefore room for discretion in the enforcement of the law, and decisions by bureaucrats, who are supposed to be nothing more than executors of the law, will play a substantial role. Thus the law-dependent and the discretionary character of the bureaucracy make each other necessary, and at the same time they dispute each other's domain. At one extreme is the image of the bureaucracy as automatic executor of the law, and at the other one can imagine a *Kadi*-esque, precedent-based bureaucracy. '*Kadi*-justice' refers to making decisions not on the basis of a formal legal rationality but on the basis of 'informal judgments rendered in terms of concrete ethical or other practical valuations.' This tendency can be seen in the former 'administration by notables' in England and in the Japanese bureaucracy.

The influence of this administrative decision-making on Japanese and on East and Southeast Asian commercial laws is a recurring theme in the remaining chapters of this book. Because of its historical role as a pioneer of industrialization in Asia, Part 2 pays particular attention to Japan. In his appropriately entitled Chapter 5 'Globalization vs. Paternalistic Regulation: Some Thoughts About Economic Success, the Role of Law and the Regulation of Japan's Financial Markets' Harald Baum shares the view of Yasuda in Chapter 2 that the Japanese economic model has run out of steam. Different from Yasuda, however, Baum focuses on structural deficiencies rather than on culture. As a consequence, he sees similarities between Japan and non-Asian countries with stronger non-economic social objectives such as Germany. While he basically agrees with views of Japan as a 'planned market' and a country subscribing to 'developmental-state capitalism,' he sees important forces of change at work. Former nationalist economic policies of maximized production for exports and suppressed domestic consumption have become less acceptable for foreign trading partners and local consumers alike. With the end of Japan's catch up position, the development of new technologies has become much more difficult and bureaucratic interference has come to be regarded as an impediment to research and development activities.

Baum then turns to the example of the Japanese financial industry. This tightly controlled and protected sector of the economy proved little prepared for the deregulation and international competition that started in the 1980s. The fraud and corruption scandals of the 1990s pointed to severe regulatory problems. Baum sees the reasons for this in general in 'collusive regulation,' in particular in public law and economic regulation. The 'regulatory cartel' that governs Japanese financial markets consists of powerful elite bureaucrats in the Ministry of Finance that draft financial laws and ordinances with little or no parliamentary control, their retired former colleagues who under the *amakudari* system have come to head financial institutions, the carrot-and-stick mechanisms of administrative guidance (*gyosei shido)*, a discretionary 'licensing system' for all kinds of business activities, and a system of '*ex ante monitoring*' rather than '*ex post monitoring*' by the courts. With globalization, this 'regulatory cartel' has come under pressure and belatedly Japan has to follow the example of other international financial centres to find a balance between deregulation and re-regulation. The result is the Japanese version of the 'Big Bang' which will result in an increasingly important role of courts and lawyers in '*ex post monitoring*.' However, the reforms will not lead to a convergence with the Anglo-American model because of the staying power of what Baum calls 'path-dependent' institutional settings.

Richard Boyd returns in Chapter 6 to the examination of the common equation of the rule of law and economic development that Ohnesorge discussed in the introductory part of this book. However, Boyd puts his discussion into the specific context of Japan. As Ohnesorge in Chapter 3, he contrasts the neo-liberal view of the rule of law and secure property rights with the by now fairly large 'developmental state' literature that sees law rather as a tool of economic policies than as an essential pre-condition for a market economy. Interestingly, however, rather than simply contrasting these two ideal types, Boyd perceives a convergence of the 'rule of law' and the 'developmental state' literature. He cites as an example the 1997 World Bank report *The State in a Changing World* which at times interprets a wide ranging government discretion as the privileged means of successful government intervention. As Bishop in Chapter 2, Boyd points to the long historical tradition in Japan that regarded law as an instrument of state control. Law reform in Meiji Japan was then also driven by a desire to expand the instruments that the state had at its disposal. Boyd cites Meiji officials and their view of European-type legislation such as the Dutch civil code as 'an excellent instrument for regulating the people.' Accordingly, the Meiji constitution allowed for orders of the Emperor and of administrative agencies without a statutory authority. Judicial scrutiny was limited to 'administrative litigation enumerated by statutes.' The great freedom for administrative decision-making was further aided by a pre-war understanding of 'the national order,' in which law was a weapon of control of a strict hierarchy with the Emperor on the top.

Things improved somewhat after World War II. The independent administrative orders were abolished and administrative acts were subjected to reviews by the regular courts. However, when it came to enforcing crucial parts of the postwar legislation such as the Public Prosecutors Office Law, exceptions were made for political reasons. While Boyd regards the 'developmental state' literature as a useful starting point for a debate on law and development, he nevertheless finds a caveat appropriate, because the notion of the 'developmental state' has been rarely tested empirically and the few empirical studies that have been carried out have found little positive impact of industrial policies on economic development. In three areas, however, law did have an impact. First, in the area of trade restrictions to nurture new industries, but this area is of little importance today. Secondly, in the generation, collection, and transmission of information, which has little to do with law. Thirdly and finally, in the successful management of industries in decline. Boyd uses legislation from the last mentioned area to show that officials from MITI and other departments charged with industrial policy actually do make intensive use of the relevant laws, but these are so broadly worded that they only define policy goals. Actual bureaucratic action is then discretionary and informal and it cannot be scrutinized by the courts.

Turning to the specifics of legal informality in Japan, Boyd at first points out that 'administrative guidance' is not so much enforcement of law but of policy positions, which are the result of protracted negotiations between the bureaucracy and the industry. He then examines the concrete example of the declining Japanese shipbuilding industry in the 1970s and the various pieces of legislation that were enacted to make this process not too painful. As in other examples for administrative guidance, the responsible Ministry of Transport used its licensing powers to force the industry to accept the recommendations of the bureaucracy. An important prerequisite to achieve this without any legal challenge was a pledge by surviving businesses to bear the losses of the 'losers' collectively. The manner in which the Depressed Industries Law was discussed in Parliament and substantially amended contradicts the Western stereotype of a rubber-stamp parliament, which is often regarded as a pre-condition for the 'developmental state.' The bureaucracy's policy goals often put in it on collision course with the Fair Trade Commission (FTC). However, the FTC's position has been strengthened by a 1977 revision of the Anti-Monopoly Law and by a landmark decision of 1983 that requires the agreement of the FTC for measures restricting competition.

The specific Japanese bureaucratic culture is maintained through an emphasis on harmony within a Ministry, a protection of the interests of the industry rather than those of the public, continuity and seniority, and the practice of *amakudari* that Baum discussed in the previous chapter. Ultimately, Ministries tend to be competitive in bureaucratic politics, but anti-competitive within the industrial sectors for which they are responsible.

The following two chapters by Christopher Heath and Christoph Antons provide a bridge from Japanese approaches to law and development to the experiences in East and Southeast Asia. The preceding chapters repeatedly referred to intellectual property matters as a core topic of the law and development literature. Christopher Heath's Chapter 7 is the first of two chapters in this volume that look specifically at intellectual property issues. He examines the relationship between industrial property legislation and industrial policies in Japan and in other Asia-Pacific countries. The Japanese developed an interest in industrial property legislation only after the Meiji restoration. The former *Tokugawa* government had in fact prohibited technical innovations. A first Patent Act with initially little practical relevance was introduced in 1871 and the patent system was consolidated in the first few decades of the twentieth century. A particular success was the introduction of a utility model system that satisfied domestic needs for a short-term, low-level protection for minor improvements.

Significantly, industrial property legislation is nowadays the responsibility of the Ministry of Industry and Trade (MITI), but Guidelines on International Licensing are also issued by the Japanese Fair Trade Commission (FTC). Until the liberalization of these guidelines in 1997, the FTC rejected approximately one-fifth of the proposed licensing contracts, mostly because they contained 'grant-back clauses' providing for a transfer of improvement inventions from the licensee to the licensor. Both the FTC and the Japanese courts have continuously encouraged the parallel importation of intellectual property protected material. Patent infringement suits are rare, because *ex ante* monitoring by the Japanese administration largely prevents the *ex post* monitoring by the courts. In addition, there is a shortage of attorneys and judges and a lack of courts that are specialized in intellectual property matters.

In the international arena, the Japanese had used the accession to the Paris Convention for the protection of industrial property as a bargaining tool to achieve the revision of the 'unequal treaties' that were forced upon her by the Western imperialist nations of the nineteenth century to exempt their nationals from an 'inferior' Japanese jurisdiction. During the 1930s, Japan reluctantly complied with her international obligation to enact unfair competition legislation. Until 1950, however, there was only one reported case under this legislation.

Outside of Japan, Korea had largely modeled its intellectual property legislation after the Japanese example. Different from the Japanese jurisdiction, however, the Supreme Court of Korea took an active interest in intellectual property matters. A separate Patent Court was established in 1994 and the court took up its tasks in 1998. China and Taiwan, on the other hand, demonstrated, similar to Japan, a preference for bureaucratic institutions over independent courts. Intellectual property systems were used for domestic industrial development while enforcement has been weak. Singapore followed the Japanese example in as far as it promoted parallel importation of intellectual property material. In many other developing countries of Asia, in particular in India and Indonesia, opposition against a strengthening of the intellectual property system has been strong. Here, the remnants from the colonial period still have some impact, for example design protection in Malaysia is still based on the British legislation of 1949. In Heath's view, Asian developing countries would be well advised to see in the WTO Agreement on Trade-related intellectual property rights (TRIPS) an opportunity to enact intellectual property systems that are truly advantageous to the domestic industry, for example by introducing a utility model system and a narrow interpretation of patent claims, by permitting parallel importation and by tightly controlling clauses detrimental to technical progress. He believes that seen in this light, the introduction of intellectual property rights might even spearhead the introduction of subjective human rights on a more general level.

In my own Chapter 8, I have attempted to contrast the approaches of the often-cited development models of Japan and Singapore with those used in Indonesia. The chapter focuses on a few key strategies used during the industrialization process and on the laws to implement these strategies. As all three countries relied during the initial phase of their development on abundant cheap labour, the chapter begins with an examination of the regulation of industrial relations. During the first few decades of this century, the attitude of the Japanese government towards organized labour changed slowly from suppression to the encouragement of 'factory councils' as rivals of independent unions. These councils re-emerged after World War II in the form of 'enterprise unions,' which have largely marginalized the national unions. In Singapore, the union movement was streamlined by a system which allowed for the deregistration of unions. For a long time, wages were adjusted by the National Wages Council, a tripartite body comprising unionists, employers, and government representatives. From 1979 onwards, these wage guidelines were used to force employers to upgrade technologically and to create skill development funds for strategically important industries. Since the early 1980s, Japanese-style enterprise unions are encouraged and management is allowed greater flexibility in employment policies. In Indonesia, the Suharto government emphasized 'harmonious' industrial relations through its concept of '*Pancasila* industrial relations.' The Indonesian trade union movement became centralized with the formation of the All Indonesian Workers' Union. As a reaction to international scrutiny of Indonesia's labour conditions during the 1990s, the government encouraged the setting up of enterprise unions. Towards the end of the Suharto rule, the Law on Manpower finally gave a legal basis to the concept of *Pancasila* industrial relations.

Differences begin to appear when the strategies of the three countries to mobilize capital are examined. Japan has traditionally been hostile to foreign investment and relied instead for a long time on its tax system, a high rate of savings and the peculiarities of the Japanese banking system. While the Japanese banking system is currently being reformed, foreign investment is still carefully scrutinized and foreign investors still need to consult MITI and the Ministry of Finance for administrative guidance. In contrast to Japan, foreign investment has been an essential feature of Singapore's industrialization policy. The main regulatory instrument was the discretionary granting of tax incentives by the Minister of Finance. Besides foreign investment, the government encouraged domestic savings via the Central Provident Fund (CPF). Contributions to the CPF are currently at around 40 per cent of the monthly wage. Indonesia's policies alternated between a strict scrutiny of foreign investment and liberalization and deregulation. These shifts in policy depended largely on the price of oil as the main government revenue. The Indonesian banking system was for a long time under tight state control and state banks were responsible for allocating loans to priority sectors. However, regulatory mechanisms to oversee the system and the administrative capacity of the central bank were weak and as a consequence, corruption was rampant. The deregulation from 1988 on took place without prior improvement of the supervisory framework. This resulted in an unusually large number of undercapitalized banks. Many of those banks were part of Indonesia's conglomerates and they lent excessively to affiliated companies. When the value of the rupiah crashed in 1997, the Indonesian government prevented a total collapse of the system by closing many of the new private banks and by bringing other troubled banks under the supervision of the newly established Indonesian bank Restructuring Agency (IBRA). Recent amendments to the 1992 Banking Law provide for a tighter scrutiny of the system and a centralization of the Bank of Indonesia's supervisory powers.

In all three countries surveyed, the formation of powerful national enterprises was facilitated by the absence or lack of enforcement of anti-monopoly legislation and cross-shareholdings in strategic companies. However, the Japanese Anti-Monopoly law has been strengthened since the late 1970s, Indonesia has introduced anti-monopoly legislation in 1999 and Singapore is undertaking a review of the share of government-linked companies in the Singaporean economy. In summary, the commercial laws of the three countries were largely instrumentalized for development purposes. Developmental ideology became incorporated into legislation and the bureaucracy was given a large discretion in implementing it. With a similar emphasis on such administrative guidance, success depended largely on the quality of the administration and the absence of corruption.

In Part 3, Chapter 9 of this book, Jianfu Chen takes a close look at the role of law in the 'socialist market economy' of China. He points to the impressive law making efforts of the National People's Congress (NPC) since 1979. In the first part of his paper, he shows that China in fact experienced similar periods of active legal reform from 1949 to 1957 and then again from 1961 to 1963. However, under Mao Zedong's leadership, periods of legal reform alternated with periods of political re-education and disregard for law such as the 'Great Leap Forward' and the 'Cultural Revolution.' While a period of uninterrupted legal modernization began under Deng Xiaoping, Chen points out that Deng's understanding of law as a tool for party policies was hardly different from that of Mao. As a consequence, Chinese laws show the same features that are discussed in other chapters in this book with regards to capitalist states with a developmental outlook such as Japan or Indonesia. The actual laws embody only vague and general principles, which are then supplemented by various 'implementing rules' at a later stage according to prevailing policy considerations. Since these policy considerations are often the result of *ad hoc* developments, there is little consistency, clarity, or legal certainty and legal reform appears to proceed in a piecemeal fashion. After the adoption of the concept of a 'socialist market economy,' the Chinese government developed its notion of 'ruling the country by law.' Chen points out that Chinese legal scholars are mistaken, if they confuse the concept with the 'Rule of Law' in a Western sense. The Chinese notion of 'Rule by Law' contains little of the guarantees for judicial independence and supremacy of the law that is at the centre of the Western concept. It is still the Communist party whose final approval is required for important principles in legislation. Nevertheless, Chen believes that the increase in legal discourse and the involvement of legal experts in lawmaking are important steps in the right direction.

Connie Carter examines in Chapter 10 the emergence of Singapore as a development model in its own right. The chapter examines the export of the Singapore model to the China–Singapore Industrial Park in Suzhou. It provides, therefore, a useful bridge to the next part of this book that deals exclusively with Southeast Asia. The 1990s have seen a comeback of the 'law and development' paradigm. This time, however, it is used as an instrument by supra-national institutions, regional aid agencies, NGOs, and powerful individual countries. One of these countries with an assertive role and influence in developing countries is Singapore. The appearance of Singapore among the development models is significant in that it signals a departure from the old definition of a North-South dialogue.

Singapore's model of law and development diverges from currently dominant Western models. Carter describes the Singapore system as 'Westernistic' because of its emphasis on a Western form and as 'syncretistic' because of its borrowing from many different legal traditions. English law transplanted to Singapore was of a colonial variety aiming at running the colonial economy as profitable as possible. From 1965 onwards, Singapore's policies became clearly subordinated to the purposes of nation-building and economic development. With its export-oriented development approach, the fostering of social discipline and a strong work ethic became paramount. Carter characterizes Singapore as an enterprise association whose rules are different from a civic society in that they gain their credibility from the association's goals and purposes. The particular policy mix of Singapore includes selected free market access, an efficient infrastructure, investment in key export-led sectors, the maintaining of discipline and the education of the workforce and, last but not least, the delivery of tangible benefits to ensure the acquiescence of the population. The achievements of this policy mix include the abolition of corruption, an efficient health care and educational system, and social and political stability. Law was an important facilitator in this context and its nature was administrative with an abundance of subsidiary rules. The government regulated not only classical fields of development policies such as labour and education, but also many areas that are regarded as private in a Western context such as child-bearing or the failure to look after one's parents.

In the second part of her paper, Carter analyses the assistance of Singapore in building and administering the China–Singapore Industrial Park in Suzhou. Singapore's communitarian, corporatist ideology appeared attractive to Deng Xiaoping and in 1994, a bilateral economic development agreement was concluded between the city-state and China. Suzhou was planned as a modern industrial town and modeled after Jurong, the industrial estate of Singapore. At the centre of the administrative structure is the holding company China–Singapore Suzhou Development (CSSD). Both countries represented by the China Suzhou Industrial Park Corporation (CSIPC) and the Singapore Suzhou Trade and Development (SSTD) have shareholdings in the CSSD. There is a governing body headed by the mayor of Suzhou, which includes representatives of Singapore's Economic Development Board. There is also a joint working committee and a joint steering committee. The Singapore Software Project Office (SSPO) oversees the transfer of Singapore's administrative and management experiences. This transfer includes the training of Suzhou officials in Singapore and the borrowing of statutory law, procedures, and regulations. Carter described this borrowing as taking place within the context of China's incremental law reform that began in the late 1970s and that shows civil law as well as common law influences. Singapore's involvement in this regard was also meant to remedy weaknesses of the legal system such as a lack of transparency, ambiguities, and inconsistencies between different levels of legislation. The rules and regulations of the Suzhou Park are delegated administrative law within the Chinese national system. They are more precisely drafted and clearer than most Chinese laws, but they nevertheless embody an understanding of 'rule by law' rather than 'rule of law.' Foreign investors apparently appreciated successful reforms in Suzhou such as the setting up of a one-stop shop for business licenses and the reduction and publication of administrative fees. Yet, for a variety of reasons that might include a recent tendency towards a stronger central administrative control, Singapore announced a substantial reduction of its shareholding in Suzhou in 1999.

Part 4 of the book deals with 'Southeast Asian approaches.' The chapters presented here discuss two issues that have been central to the economic development debate in Southeast Asia: industrial relations and technology transfer. Jesse Wu returns in Chapter 11 to the issue of the regulation of organized labour. His discussion focuses on Malaysia, which after the financial crisis has become one of the cheapest places for foreign direct investment in the world. A restrictive regulation of trade unions has played a key role in keeping the production costs low. Prior to the independence of Malaysia, the British originally saw no necessity to introduce trade union legislation in the colony. They finally changed their mind only after a Colonial Development and Welfare Act of 1940 made certain financial assistance to the colony subject to the existence of such legislation. The Trade Union Enactment of 1940 introduced the same compulsory registration system for trade unions that became also a prominent feature of the industrial relations system of Singapore. Emergency provisions under the Internal Security Act that allowed for detention without trial were introduced during the period of violent Communist upheaval during the late 1940s and the 1950s. These provisions are still occasionally used by the Government to end a strike.

Malaysian trade unions are federally regulated by the Trade Unions Act of 1959 and the Industrial Relations Act of 1967. Freedom of association is guaranteed, but restricted to registered trade unions. Registration of unions will only be approved, if they are operating in 'similar trades, occupations or industry' and the decision whether this is the case is within the discretion of the Director General of Trade Unions. Malaysian courts have disallowed legal challenges to the Director-General's decision, which leaves an appeal to the Minister of Human Resources as the only remaining option for a union that is barred from registration. Trade unions may not engage in political activities and union funds may not be used to further 'any political object.' The definition of what constitutes a 'political object' is a matter of discretion for the Minister. According to regulations drafted during another emergency following race riots in 1969, office bearers and employees of political parties are disallowed from holding an office in a trade union. In exceptional cases, the King may exempt public officers from this prohibition. Employees of statutory authorities are basically confined to 'in-house' unions, unless the Minister of Human Resources makes an exception and allows employees of smaller statutory authorities to join other trade unions. The minister also has an extraordinary wide discretion to suspend trade unions which 'in his opinion' are used for purposes prejudicial to or incompatible with the interests of the security or public order of Malaysia or any part thereof.

The right to strike may be inferred from several provisions of the legislation, but strikes for political, economic or social purposes not immediately connected to a trade dispute with the employer are prohibited. Significantly, in case of unlawful industrial action the burden of proof is reversed, so that the union has to show that the quite burdensome requirements for a strike are complied with. Furthermore, the legislation gives considerable discretionary powers to the Director General to decide whether a proposed strike is lawful. Strikes are in general prohibited in 'essential industries' and they are prohibited in the public service and in statutory authorities if the King has refused to refer the industrial dispute to an Industrial Court for settlement. Penalties for unlawful strikes are harsh and may include the exclusion of participants in such strikes from the union and a prohibition to join other trade unions in the future. Restrictions on collective bargaining are particularly strong in so-called pioneer companies.

These companies often involve foreign direct investment and they are thereby guaranteed extremely low labour costs.

Michael Blakeney presents in Chapter 12 a survey of technology transfer regulations of ASEAN countries. There is a common assumption of a link between technology and economic development. As a consequence, international organizations such as WIPO and UNCTAD have been committed to advise developing countries on how to achieve suitable intellectual property systems and technology transfer arrangements. Increasingly, concepts are also developed within regional organizations such as APEC, NAFTA, the Anden Pact, Mercosur, and ASEAN. The most significant development in the regional harmonization of intellectual property laws has been the ASEAN Framework Agreement on Intellectual Property Cooperation of December 1995. A driving force behind the agreement has been Thailand, which has also concluded bilateral agreements with Cambodia, Laos, Myanmar, Vietnam, and China. The Framework Agreement envisages the creation of an ASEAN patents and trade marks system and an ASEAN Patents and Trade Marks Office. One of the most important aims of the agreement is the prevention of abuses of intellectual property rights that might adversely affect trade and technology transfer.

The approaches to technology transfer regulation in ASEAN have been as diverse as the members of this regional group. They range from a *laissez faire* attitude in Singapore over partial regulation of technology transfer agreements in Indonesia and Malaysia to a comprehensive transfer of technology code in Vietnam. Blakeney contrasts the very elaborate provisions of Vietnam with the approach in the Philippines, where the compulsory registration of technology transfer arrangements was abolished following a merger of the Technology Transfer Board and the Patent Office. In Vietnam, intellectual property and technology transfer is now regulated in the Vietnamese Civil Code. The provisions contain detailed prescriptions as to the nature and the price of technology, length of technology transfer contracts and warranties as to quality and title. In contrast to this, the Philippines has increasingly liberalized screening procedures for technology transfer since 1992. The previous cap on royalties to be earned has been removed. Cambodia, Laos, and Myanmar have so far only rudimentary systems of intellectual property protection, but new legislation is currently being drafted. Blakeney concludes that an increase in legislation was in the past often accompanied by an increase in corruption. Overlapping legislation has also often led to conflicts of authority and to fractional fighting over approaches to technology transfer between different ministries.

The final part of the book presents two chapters that traverse different countries of 'the region.' As a result of globalization, commercial arbitration and alternative means of dispute resolution have become increasingly important. Robert Lutz examines the different means of resolving trade disputes in Asia in Chapter 13. Lutz perceives a cultural fusion between East and West in litigation culture so that the traditional assumption of an Asian tendency to dispute avoidance is no longer entirely correct. Asians who are involved in international trade are increasingly willing to accept arbitration or even litigation to solve their disputes. The current shift towards privatization will inevitably lead to an increase in private trade disputes. Since arbitration rules become increasingly harmonized, the advances in communication and transportation technology shift the emphasis away from the place of arbitration. Besides international dispute settlement facilities such as the International Center for the Settlement of Investment Disputes (ICSID) of the World Bank, and WIPO and WTO mechanisms, regional economic groups such as the ASEAN Free Trade Area (AFTA) of ASEAN and the Asia Pacific Economic Cooperation (APEC) have also created their own mechanisms for dispute settlement. In particular the AFTA mechanism is designed to shield disagreements within AFTA from the public and to resolve disputes between member states within the circle of the Economic Ministers. Asian countries have also frequently used the dispute settlement mechanism of the WTO, but only a few of these cases have concerned disputes between Asian nations. Lutz assumes that Asian countries will increasingly resort to the regional mechanisms provided by ASEAN and APEC rather than using the more legalistic procedures of the WTO. These regional decisions may be able to pay greater attention to Asian cultural values of dispute solving and to emphasis harmony over strict interpretation of the law.

Enforcement of arbitral awards remains difficult in some countries. While most Asian nations have acceded to the New York Convention of 1958 on the Recognition and Enforcement of Foreign Arbitral Awards, the enforcement of foreign arbitral decisions remains unclear in Indonesia and subject to public policy considerations in China. Thai courts have to consider a broad number of defenses with the result that disputes frequently end up in the Thai legal system.

The fusion between Asian and Western culture in this area appears perhaps most clearly in the preference that businesses in Asia show for hybrid forms of consultation and arbitration. Consultation and arbitration may be blended, so that the parties shift back and forth between the two, or conjoined, so that the failure of consultation triggers arbitration. The fused process helps to come to a final decision without endangering the business relationship.

The number of foreigners acting as arbitrators is increasing in most Asian countries and even Singapore has given up its former hostile attitude towards foreign arbitrators. There is a further trend in Asia towards harmonization of arbitration law in accordance with the UNCITRAL Model Law and Arbitration Rules. Lutz ends his chapter with an optimistic outlook on the emerging international dispute resolution culture, although he adds a cautious note regarding the remaining enforcement problems in some countries.

As a nice conclusion to a book dealing with the issues of developmentalism and the rule of law, Roman Tomasic contrasts in Chapter 14 the views of former Singapore Prime Minister Lee Kuan Yew and those of former Hong Kong governor Chris Patten. Tomasic finds many examples in Lee Kuan Yew's memoirs for the instrumentalist view of law that Lee embraced. In this view, the role of law in guaranteeing individual rights is clearly subordinated to its primary function of maintaining order. Interesting is also the frequent use by Lee (and other members of the ruling PAP) of defamation and libel actions to restrain political opponents. In contrast to Lee's instrumentalist view of law, Chris Patten presents very much the idealist notion of the rule of law discussed by Ohnesorge in Chapter 4 of this book. While his views of law as a defence 'against anyone however powerful' will appear rather naïve to sociologists of law, Patten makes an interesting distinction between 'quality growth' and 'quantity-based' growth. He notes that 'quality growth' will be achieved by using the creativity and inventiveness of citizens and that these talents can be more easily nurtured in a pluralist political environment. In spite of their otherwise opposing views, Patten and Lee agree on the importance of the fight against corruption for a well-functioning economy. As to Asian values, Lee's memoirs show how he used a particular brand of Neo-Confucianism to rally the Chinese population of Singapore behind him. Patten rightly criticizes the overemphasis on hierarchy and authority in this interpretation of Confucianism, while the humanistic side of Confucius' teachings tends to be neglected. Again, however, Patten's assumption of emerging universalist values based on 'the same respect for human decency' and 'the same regard for an economic philosophy that maximizes the opportunity for the individual to excel' is simplistic. If anything, the economic globalization and cultural Americanization mentioned by Tomasic will be the driving forces behind such a process and their effects will not be the same in all parts of the legal system.

In the second part of his chapter, Tomasic's discusses some of the more recent examples of socio-legal scholarship on Asian commercial laws. The first of these is Anthony Woodiwiss's study of 'Globalization, Human Rights and Labour Law in Pacific Asia.' Woodiwiss analyses the labour laws of the Philippines, Hong Kong, Malaysia, and Singapore by using the concept of patriarchalism, by which he means a form of traditional authority with a strong familialist focus. Tomasic interest lies again with the labour laws of Hong Kong and Singapore, which are described as 'enforceable benevolence.' Under the Hong Kong legislation, labour disputes need to be transferred to the Labour Tribunal by the Labour Department, which will only do so after attempts at conciliation have failed. Short term or temporary employees also receive little protection under the Employment Ordinance which require some continuity in employment. Tomasic correctly questions Woodiwiss's assumption that the Japanese rather than the American style of capitalism will become archetypal in the Asia-Pacific region. As has been noted by several commentators in this book, the parameters of the 'Japanese model' are under pressure in Japan and elsewhere in Asia since quite some time and the Asian crisis has intensified this pressure.

Roman Tomasic's and Peter Little's project on 'Insolvency Law and Practice in Asia' included the findings from 115 interviews in the jurisdictions of the People's Republic of China (PRC), Hong Kong, Taiwan, Singapore, Malaysia, and Indonesia. The study found that traditional ideas of 'losing face' still played a role in the way Chinese businesses handled insolvency matters. This led to the seeking of alternative remedies, even in such 'modernized' jurisdictions as Singapore and Hong Kong. Interestingly, the social stigma associated with bankruptcy was less strongly perceived in Mainland China than in more traditionally oriented Taiwan. Nevertheless, in both jurisdictions, the study found significant non-cultural considerations for avoiding bankruptcy courts such as employment policies and debts of state enterprises in the PRC and an inefficient court system and archaic laws in Taiwan.

Tomasic finally takes a brief look at the study by Katharina Pistor and Philip Wellons of Harvard University on 'The Role of Law and Legal Institutions in Asian Economic Development 1960-1995.' The study finds that economic laws in Asia had at first little influence on the economy and developed only much later in line with the acceleration in economic development. While the current market-oriented economic policies have made Asian systems more market-allocative and more rule-based, differences in legal processes and institutions remain. This leads to a situation where the systems under study are partly converging and partly diverging. The study finds cultural factors not completely unimportant in that they influenced the nuances of a population's response to economic change but they are clearly subordinated to economic strategies. Tomasic concludes his survey of these recent studies by encouraging further studies into the 'big picture questions' of law and development that should provide for a balance of theory and data. The obstacles to carrying out such projects in the high stress environment that modern universities have become are formidable, but they can be overcome by heeding Tomasic's advice to engage in research collaboration.

NOTES

1 On the chronological development of the crisis see Henderson (1998), Garnaut (1998), Gough (1998), Delhaise (1998), Arndt & Hill (1999), and Department of Foreign Affairs and Trade-East Asia Analytical Unit (1999).
2 For a survey of the earlier literature on Japanese economic development see also Johnson, 1982:6-17.
3 Stanford University Press 1996.
4 Murakami, 1996:185-7; cf. also Boyd, in this volume.
5 Calder (1993:8-13).
6 Calder (1993:6) and Pistor and Wellons (1998:55) have used a similar matrix to capture allocative and procedural dimensions of law. Their distinction between 'market/rule-based,' 'state/rule based,' 'market/discretionary' and 'state/discretionary' are the legal equivalents of Calder's political and economic dimensions.

REFERENCES

Arndt, H.W. and Hal Hill (1999) *Southeast Asia's Economic Crisis: Origins, Lessons and the Way Forward.* Singapore: Institute of Southeast Asian Studies.

Burstein, Daniel (1988) *Yen! – Japan's New Financial Empire and its Threat to America.* New York: Simon & Schuster.

Calder, Kent E. (1993) *Strategic Capitalism: Private Business and Public Purpose in Japanese Industrial Finance.* Princeton: Princeton *University* Press.

Delhaise, Philippe F. (1998) *Asia in Crisis: The Implosion of the Banking and Finance Systems.* Singapore: John Wiley & Sons (Asia) Pte Ltd.

Department of Foreign Affairs and Trade – East Asia Analytical Unit (1998) *Asia's Financial Markets: Capitalising on Reform.* Canberra: Department of Foreign Affairs and Trade.

Fifield, Russell H. (1983) 'Southeast Asia as a Regional Concept,' *Southeast Asian Journal of Social Science* 11/2, pp 1-14.

Garnaut, Ross (1998) 'The East Asian Crisis,' in: Ross H. McLeod and Ross Garnaut (eds) *East Asia in Crisis: From being a miracle to needing one?* London–New York: Routledge.

Gough, Leo (1998) *Asia Meltdown: The End of the Miracle?* Oxford: Capstone.

Henderson, Callum (1998) *Asia Falling? – Making sense of the Asian currency crisis and its aftermath.* Singapore: McGraw-Hill Book Co.

Johnson, Chalmers (1982) *MITI and the Japanese Miracle: The Growth of Industrial Policy, 1925-1975*. Stanford: Stanford University Press.

– (1992) *Capitalism: East Asian Style*, The 1992 Panglaykim Memorial Lecture, Jakarta, 15 December 1992. Jakarta: Centre for Strategic and International Studies.

Kahn, Herman (1970) *The Emerging Japanese Superstate: Challenge and Response*. Harmondsworth: Penguin Books.

Miwa, Yoshiro (1996) *Firms and Industrial Organization in Japan*. New York: New York University Press.

Morishima, Michio (1985) *Warum Japan so erfolgreich ist: Westliche Technologie und japanisches Ethos* (Why has Japan 'succeeded'? – Western technology and the Japanese ethos). München: Verlag C.H. Beck.

Murakami, Yasusuke (1996) *An Anticlassical Political-Economic Analysis: A Vision for the Next Century*. Stanford: Stanford University Press.

Pistor, Katharina and Philip A. Wellons (1999) *The Role of Law and Legal Institutions in Asian Economic Development 1960-1995*. Oxford: Oxford University Press.

Posen, Adam S. (1996) *Restoring Japan's Economic Growth*. Washington: Institute for International Economics.

Prestowitz, Clyde V. (1988) *Trading Places: How We are Giving our Future to Japan and how to Reclaim it*. New York: Basic Books Inc., Publishers.

Wittfogel, Karl A. (1977) *Die Orientalische Despotie: Eine vergleichende Untersuchung totaler Macht*. Frankfurt–Berlin–Wien: Ullstein Materialien.

Wood, Christopher (1994) *The End of Japan Inc. – And How the New Japan Will Look*. New York: Simon & Schuster.

CHAPTER 2

LAW AND DEVELOPMENT FROM THE SOUTHEAST ASIAN PERSPECTIVE: METHODOLOGY, HISTORY, AND PARADIGM CHANGE

NOBUYUKI YASUDA

Since World War II, Southeast Asian countries have achieved the most successful development among all developing countries in the world.[1] This is an undeniable fact in spite of the fact that these countries were suddenly trapped by a serious financial crisis in mid-1997. At present, they are still striving to recover from the disastrous aftershock of this crisis in the economic, political, and social fields.[2]

There may be various economic and cultural reasons both for past praiseworthy performances of these economies and also their sudden collapse in the mid-1990s. In my understanding both their glittering success and their miserable failure have a common cause, which can be conceptualized by using the term 'Asiatic.' It is virtually impossible to define it in the articulate words of social science, but in this vague word I find the key not only for a reconsideration of the reality of the present crisis, but also to re-establish the framework of Law and Development Studies (LDS) from an Asian perspective.

It is well known that for various reasons, Law and Development Studies disappeared as a paradigm from tertiary establishments in the United States in the early 1970s. The main reason for this disappearance was that the conceptualization of law in Law and Development Studies was based substantially on Liberal Legalism, which was at the time a dominant paradigm of legal study. What was regarded as 'proper law' for developing countries was nothing more nor less than the laws and legal institutions of Western countries in general and of the United States in particular. The customs and mores surviving in non-Western societies were disregarded, or otherwise understood as obstacles which should be removed in the interests of national development. Needless to say that this paradigm was built wholly on Western ethnocentrism.[3] It was symbolic that the two leading scholars in this academic movement expressed their serious and sincere self-criticism in 1974, at a time when the United States, as the most hegemonic Western state, was defeated by Vietnam, a presumably small, traditional, and pre-modern Asian state.[4]

During the 1970s and 1980s, Asian countries continuously achieved remarkable economic and social development in contrast to other regions of the world that suffered serious economic stagnation. What is remarkable is that their development process was substantially different from the Western model of development that formed the basis of the above-mentioned LDS paradigm. This indicates effectively an 'Asiatic' nature of their development process, questioning the predominance of Western values.[5] As a result of this, 'Asian values' were claimed strongly in the early 1990s in opposition to modern Western values which had become universally accepted.[6] According to the proponents of Asian values, the secret of the successful development of Asian countries was a combination of the harmonious collectivist spirit of the people and a strong authoritative government. This was in clear contrast to the values of modern Western societies focusing on individualism and democratic government.

The sudden collapse of the Asian economies in 1997, however, disclosed the fatal defects in these Asian values. Many Western financial experts from institutions such as the IMF and the World Bank locate the main cause of the crisis in a lack of transparency and accountability, nepotism in business and various other political practices including corrupt crony capitalism, and authoritarian forms of government (Fisher, 1998). These defects have a strong affinity with the discourses regarding Asian values. What we currently need is to create a new framework for LDS, one which is able to answer the two contradicting questions of why Asia was prosperous and developing successfully from the late 1980s to the early 1990s, and of why it has been trapped by such a critical economic and social crisis since 1997. The term 'Asiatic' is presumably a key word to be infused into the LDS paradigm, although it is essential to refine it into a more effective and operational concept for social science. In other words, we must design LDS by including cultural elements in order to understand Asian legal systems in depth.[7]

For this purpose, the work will be divided into four parts. First, I set up a methodological framework by proposing several sets of concepts consisting of three types of law ('indigenous law,' 'imported law,' and 'development law'), three types of legal principles ('community,' 'market,' and 'command') as more operational concepts and 'community force' and 'market force' to refer to their dynamics. Second, in applying these concepts, I illustrate the historical development of Southeast Asian legal systems under the three different state concepts, the 'proto-state,' 'colonial state,' and 'developmental state.' The effectiveness of these concepts will be tested during this process. Third, I outline law and development problems with regards to the aspects of political, economic and social development under the regime of the 'developmental state,' which functioned most effectively during the 1970s and early 1980s and led to rapid development in the region. Finally, I inquire why the developmental legal systems of East and Southeast Asia have been facing such a serious crisis in the closing years of the twentieth century, and I will look for an answer which will state what lessons can be learned for global development in the next century.

THREE TYPES OF LAW AND LEGAL PRINCIPLES

Three Types of Law

Observing the legal systems in Asian and other non-Western countries, we can categorize them with regards to their origin into three groups. One group is 'indigenous law' originating in the proto-state, which is defined as the indigenous or traditional state before colonization by a Western power or modernization by the strong influence of such a power.[8] It is true that substantial parts of this law were degraded to mere customary mores or non-state law by the newly introduced modern Western law in the process of modernization under colonial rule. However, indigenous law still effectively regulates various aspects of the daily life of the people, and some of it is still recognized as state law in such fields as family and religious matters.[9] In many Southeast Asian countries, for example, Islamic personal law is state law for the Muslim people. Cogently, it is perceptible that this law is gaining new force and is expanding in comparison to some fields of secular law, which are based on imported Western law.[10] Even in China, still an anti-religious socialist country, there are indications of a revival of Confucianism and Taoism. It does not need to be stressed that these religions are deeply connected with family and community systems.

The second group is 'imported law' introduced or imposed by Western countries during their colonial rule.[11] At the initial stage of colonization, Western law was applied and adapted only to disputes between Western people. Only when colonial rule had been stabilized and had become a normal state of affairs was the jurisdiction of this law gradually expanded to indigenous peoples by state courts and local administrations which were created as institutions of colonial states. Naturally, this law displays typical characteristics of modern Western law such as individualism, although the transplantation to Asia of many such core values was, seemingly, unsuccessful, because of the oppressive nature of colonial rule and the vast cultural differences between the two distant regions. Nevertheless, what is most important is that this law forms an essential part of the present state legal systems of all countries.

The third group comprises what I have called 'development law.' This type of law is a series of products of the development policies implemented after the independence of these countries following World War II. The transfer of power from the former colonial rulers to the new governments within the region was peaceful with the exception of Indonesia and the countries of Indochina. Southeast Asian countries basically inherited the colonial legal systems for their new nations.[12] However, their political and economic systems were very fragile because of the disastrous result of World War II and they were destabilized even more by the post-war international order of the Cold War period. In order to overcome political instability and to achieve rapid political, economic, and social development, a different type of law emerged, which delegated to the state or government wide discretionary powers. These laws cover a huge area of both political and economic fields, as we will discuss later.

Three Legal Principles

We can deduce more functional and operational 'principles' from these three types of laws, which will help us not only to understand the contemporary Asian legal systems more systematically, but also to design more effective legal systems for their development. The origins of indigenous law, either in Western or in non-Western countries, is the customary law of village or tribal communities which can be traced back many generations into the mist of time. These communities were and still are the most primordial organizations of human beings and they represent the primal nature of human society. In comparison to a modern society, there is no specific 'individual' in these communities. Their members are unified and solidified as part of the community with others as cells of an organ. In the process of the development of the society, this unity is gradually loosened and independent and autonomous individuals will emerge. However, the feeling of togetherness and identification with the group has remained strong at least within families and to some extent in local or religious communities.

This is especially true in monsoon Southeast Asia, because wet rice farming as the basic mode of production requires collective and co-operative labour among peasants. This is the reason why until today 'harmony' is emphasized as a common cultural value in this region. We may call this the 'community principle.' This principle represents the most basic human feelings in which human beings seek to identify themselves with others or with a group like a family or a specific community. It may perhaps be compared to fraternity or brotherhood, which was one of three principles of the French Revolution. This value is also expressed as a communist ideal in 'one for all and all for one.' The community principle is the core concept for analysing a 'communal society' in the sense of an 'expanded family.'[13] Disputes between members within such a community shall be solved amicably through the mediation or conciliation of all members, but not in a legalistic or judicial (litigious) way in a court or a similar institution. From the viewpoint of Western legal tradition, this is of a non- or para-legal nature and does not strictly belong to the field of law.[14] Nevertheless, this principle plays an important role in Asian (and non-Western) legal systems. It is also another term for concepts such as 'dyadic relation of patrons and clients' and 'dependency,' used by the eminent political scientist Lucian Pye (1985:90-132) to express the common nature of Asian political powers. Roberto Unger (1976:50-1) correctly defines it as 'customary-interaction law' because of its unarticulated nature in his trichotomy.

'Imported law' is law transplanted from modern Western countries and supplies a basic legal infrastructure not only for the commercial and economic area but also for the state system as a whole in almost all non-Western countries. As expressed in the famous finding of a movement 'from status to contract,' modern society is based on the contractual network of the citizens. The most important element of this society is the contractual relation between autonomous individuals. I call this the 'market principle' because it reflects common human behaviour during transactions in a market place. It represents the exchange of goods and services for equivalent values between equal independent parties out of free will. Needless to say this is the essence of commercial and contract laws which typically regulate economic activities of human beings in a market system. In modern Western societies, the impact of this principle has expanded from the economic field to the political level. This expansion finds its expression in the discourse about a 'social contract' of modern political philosophy according to which the state is theoretically created by a social contract between free people. But it goes further than this. The principle has also penetrated into the arena of the community which we presume to be a simple gathering of free and independent 'individuals.' It seems to me that the democratic polity directly reflects this principle because it stands for 'free competition for power'.[15] We may express another aspect of it with the word 'liberty' which presupposes horizontal relations between human beings. The dispute settlement model in this field is 'adjudication' by legal experts (judges) as umpires, because obtaining a judgment from an independent and socially recognized authority can solve the disputes between equal and independent persons. It is quite understandable that Unger (1976: 52-8) expresses a similar principle simply as 'legal order and legal system' because it expresses the essential values of modern legal systems in his typology.

The purpose of 'development law' is to authorize a state or government to command people to commit or not to commit certain acts for the purpose of development, a key object of which is to achieve 'equality' or redistribution of common wealth among the people. From this aspect of development law we may abstract the 'command principle' which represents a vertical relation such as 'order and obedience' between human beings, in contrast to the horizontal relation of the market principle.[16] It is a dominant principle of public or political law, where a superior (the 'state' in a modern concept) enjoys a 'discretionary power' in the name of public interest in exercising its power. This principle is an essential part of any kind of 'state' or 'political society' because people are compelled by it conclusively whether in a legal or non-legal manner. Nevertheless, a dictatorial state as typically exemplified by the former socialist states is the most suitable model to represent this principle. Unger (1976:50) defines this type of law as 'bureaucratic law enforced ... by an identifiable government.'

Table I shows a comparative list of the three principles in certain fields of law and society. Needless to say the real world is much more complex and shows a mixture of these three principles.

TABLE I THREE TYPES OF LEGAL PRINCIPLES

Principles	*Community Principle*	*Market Principle*	*Command Principle*
Basic relation	Unifying and solidifying	Horizontal, and equivalent	Vertical order and obedience
Basic value	Fraternity	Liberty	Equality
Model social action	One for all, all for one	Voluntary exchange of goods	Compulsion by the superior
Core sphere or dimension	Communal society (community)	Economic society (economy)	Political society (state)
State model	(Commune state) Proto-states	Modern capitalist state Colonial states	(Former) Socialist state developmental states
General pattern of norms	Not clear, depending on community feeling	Supplying clear interpretation rules	Giving discre-tionary power to the authority
Typical branch of law	Family law	Civil and commercial law	Public (political) law
Nature of disputes settlement	Amicable settlement (mediation or reconciliation)	Adjudication by third party (like courts)	Reconsideration by authority
Basic value for the settlement	Identification (solidarity)	Legality (justice)	Reasonable-ness (fairness)
Typical settlement Agent	Community mediation or conciliation center	Judicial Courts	Administrative tribunal

SIMILAR TRICHOTOMY

Name	*Community Principle*	*Market Principle*	*Command Principle*
Unger, R, (1986)	Customary-inter action law	Legal order and legal system	Bureaucratic law
Nonnet & Selznick (1977)	Responsive law	Autonomy law	Strict law
Kamenka & Tay (1980)	Gemeinschaft type of law	Gesellschaft type of law	Bureaucratic -adminstrative type of law
Ghai Yash (1986)	Custom	Market	State and its law
Miller (1976)	Primitive	Market	Hierarchy
Pollani, P. (1977)	Reciprocity	Exchange	Market
Paul Tillich (1954)	Love	Justice	Power

Sources: R.M. Unger, *Law in Modern Society; Toward a Criticism of Social Theory*, New York, The State Press, 1976. P. Nonnet and P. Selznnik, *Law and Society in Transition, Towards Responsive Law*, New York, Happer Colphan Books, 1978. Kamenka Augen and A.E. Tay, 'Social Traditions, Legal Traditions' in Kamenka &Tay (eds), *Law and Social Control*, London, Edward Arnold, 1980. Ghai Yash, 'Land Reform and Paradigm of Development: Reflections in Melanesian Constitutions,' in: P. Sack (ed.) *Legal Pluralism*, Proceeding of Canberra Law Workshop VII, Research School of Social Science, ANU, 1986). Miller, D., *Social Justice*, Oxford, Clarendon, Press, 1976. K. Polanyi, *The Livelihood of Man*, ed. by H.W. Peason, New York, Academic Press, 1977. Paul Tillich, *Love, Power and Justice*, Oxford University Press, 1954.

MARKET FORCE AND COMMUNITY FORCE: TWO DYNAMIC ELEMENTS OF DEVELOPMENT

The word 'development' has various meanings, but in our context it definitely expresses a kind of progressive process of history. Therefore, it is essential to determine what are the driving forces motivating the development of society. Many historians and social scientists have been gripped by this question.[17] It is not my intention here to enter into this debate, but I do feel that it is unavoidable that this field should be drawn upon for concepts which, together with our three types of legal principles, can help explain such dynamic processes. The market principle and community principle clearly contrast with one another, and it seems to me that we can postulate a similarly opposing set of dynamic concepts which helps to explain the process of development. These corresponding concepts can be termed the 'market force' and the 'community force.'[18]

'Market force' is the dynamic counterpart of the market principle. The essence of the market principle is a horizontal relation based on free and autonomous individuals. If we look at history, we can easily understand that the dynamic expression of this relation is 'individualization,' which enables members of society to be liberated from various fetters of traditional communities. This forms the basis of the vitality of 'modern capitalist society.' Although numerous explanations might be offered as to how this force developed within Western feudal society, this process undoubtedly involved the merchandisation of all existences, especially of land and human labour, as has been explained by Marxist historians. In this process, all things have become merchandise, interchangeable for money. As the basic laws regulating this exchange process, contract and property law lie at the core of the whole legal system based on the market principle.

This force is characterized by three attributes. The first is the strong tendency to dissolve social or communal bonds as suggested by the words 'individualization' and 'atomization' often associated with modern capitalist society. This can be characterized as 'centrifugal power.' This power has functioned to dissolve and divide the primordial human relationships of traditional society which had been based on the community principle, and to reconstruct the society into a uniform and less humanistic gathering of individuals through contractual relations. As we saw, when this process occurs not only the economic but also the political society is rebuilt on the basis of the market principle. The second is the characteristic of calculable rationality. This rationality is realized in the process of individualization and atomization induced by the market force. This process has subjected human beings, and indeed all things in the world, to an evaluation in calculable (typically money) terms. Individuality and calculability are the basis for modern science. Max Weber refers to the concepts of 'rationality,' 'calculability,' and 'predictability' in this regard. The concept of bureaucratization that he foresaw as the final stage of the market society suggests that the rationality he posits is essentially of the mechanical and de-humanized sort.[19] The last nature is universality. By the nature of rationality, this force can obtain the universality expressed in the contractual relation of the individuals, which can apply equally to all social phenomena in the world. It is the universal nature of the market force which allows it to break through and even dissolve the traditional community, and produce modern Western society.

In contrast to the operation of the market force, the nature of the community force is and was conservative and defensive, because it usually impugns the expanding and break-through effect of the market force. Its conservative character might be due to the fact that this force is shaped in the daily life of a community through shared experience and tradition over a long period of time and, furthermore, because it was scattered and closed up among small communities – villages, churches, guilds, and so forth. As already mentioned, the community principle is postulated to have originated from the most primitive human feelings which unify people into a group or body. It is, however, observable even in modern society as a principle unifying and solidifying people into any group or organization to which they choose to adhere. We can see the dynamic dimension of this principle in contrast with the market force from the following:

First, it is clear that the nature of this force is a 'centripetal power' in contrast to the 'centrifugal power' of the market force. Any society in which there is a need for certain feelings or values with which its members are able to identify, is based on this power. The concrete expression of these values is innumerable in each community, and it is nearly impossible to specify what the bounds of these values might be. [20] Second, and related to this centripetality, it is impossible to expect this force to be rational in the same sense as the market force, because there is no room for calculability based on individuality. In this sense, it may be characterized by its 'irrationality' from the view of modern science. By the word 'irrationality,' however, we mean only something similar to 'incalculability' in contrast with the rationality of the market force.[21] There must be another type of rationality from the mere calculable one, which is not based on individuality, but on the totality or wholeness of the society. We can define it as 'holistic rationality.' Third, by the nature of centripetality, the community force is characterized to some extent by exclusiveness. It is natural that any community maintains its own culture and tradition which shows some level of exclusivity and there may be many variations of specific values across different communities. As a consequence, it is characterized by its 'particularity' in contrast to the universality of the market force (See Table II).

TABLE II CONTRAST BETWEEN MARKET FORCE AND COMMUNITY FORCE

	Market force	*Community force*
Basic nature	Individualization/atomization	Solidification
Nature of power	Centrifugal	Centripetal
Kind of rationality	Calculable rationality	Holistic rationality
Scope of effectiveness	Universal	Particular

While a dynamic counterpart can be given for both the market and the community principles, the command principle, the last of the above mentioned three principles, cannot be conceptualized in the same way. This is because of the hierarchical nature of this principle. I believe that hierarchies can evolve, be maintained, transformed, or destroyed as a result of the confrontation or contradiction between the market and the community forces in society. The command principle as a concept defines only a static relation for the operational function,[22] and cannot have its own force motivating the development of society. As noted, the community principle and force, which substantially influenced the operations of the command principle in proto-states, is still recognizable in the present political (command) structure of Asia. In contrast to this, we find in modern capitalist society a command principle in operation which is rationalized by the market principle and force.

Social history is often summarized in the way that the market force evolved among the primitive tribal societies in which human beings sustained their lives in an organic group unified by the primordial community force, and gradually created individuals within it. The market force steadily expanded and disbanded the group, while the community force resisted against it and reorganized itself into a larger size of society, a proto-state, by reunifying the dissolved communities. This type of state continued to exist for a long time in history with numerous variations, from small tribal or village states to feudal states and even to absolutist states, which appeared at the dawn of modern states in Europe. During this lengthy time span, the individual increasingly gained his or her independent autonomy.

It should be noted, however, that the absolute autonomy of the individual was only recognized from the birth of the modern capitalist state in which the market force has been unfolded to its full extent. The market force dissolved the various feudal communities based on personal (status) relations and reshaped them into an integrated nation-state. All citizens are presumed not only to enter into contracts among themselves as free, independent, and autonomous individuals in the sphere of economic and social relations, but also to create their state as exemplified in the social contract theory. The perception of the community was diversified from various local or kinship communities to the national and even international level although it remains most effective within the confines of a nuclear family. The larger the size of a community, the more it will be able to obtain an individual and universal nature because the influence of the market force will be more effective in larger communities.

The nation state became the fierce battlefield where the market force tried to expel the community force and to dissolve it in order to create a larger community beyond the state in which capitalism evolved. However, until recently, the market force could not succeed in this attempt because it simply did not have the power to do so. On the contrary, we were subjected to a wave of strong state nationalism at the turn of the twentieth century as exemplified in the various socialist ideologies from communism to state socialism. In addition, we may find similar examples even in the post-war era in the idea of welfare states in the advanced countries as well as in the concept of 'developmental states' in the developing countries.

Now it seems that the market force has regenerated its power with the help of the information technology revolution that started in the late 1970s. This reinvigorated market force has developed not only in the advanced countries but all over the world since the 1980s. The socialist regimes in East Europe and in the Soviet Union collapsed totally by the early 1990s. This fact is nothing short of a declaration of triumph of the market force against the nation state based community force, because these socialist regimes represented the very antithesis to any liberal ideology and market principle-based institutions. This force has been continuously breaking through the national borders of all nation states and disbanding or nullifying any kind of state regulatory systems not only in the economic sphere but also in the political and social dimensions.

We may presume that to resist the inroads of this expanding market force, the community force is now forced to reconstruct itself on a wider and more universal basis. Needless to say, this relates to the ideas of 'regionalism' or 'global community' which are very often on the agenda at the turn from the twentieth to the twenty-first century. It is a difficult task, however, to define this 'global community' theoretically because the community principle in my definition is particularly effective in more particular face-to-face community relationships than in the universal phase of human societies.[23]

HISTORICAL DEVELOPMENT OF SOUTHEAST ASIAN LAW

The development of Southeast Asian law is understood more constructively when we set up three state models; that is, the proto-state, the colonial state and the development state[24] (see Table III).

TABLE III VARIOUS TYPES OF LAWS IN ASEAN COUNTRIES

	Philippines	*Indonesia*	*Brunei*	*Malaysia*	*Singapore*
Primitive	Indigenous (Malay)	Malay (Adat)	Malay (Adat)	Malay (Adat)	Malay (Adat)
Proto-state 1	Hindu?	Hindu/ Buddhism	Hindu/ Buddhism	Hindu/ Buddhism	Hindu/ Buddhism

Proto-state 2	Islam in south	Islam	Islam	Islam	Islam
Colonial State	Spain US	Dutch	UK	UK	UK
Imported law from;	Spain US	Dutch	UK	UK	UK
Develop-mental State	Republic Presidency System	Republic Presidency System	Constitu-tional Monarchy	Constitu-tional /Federal Monarchy Parliament System	Republic Presidency System
Constitution (enacted in)	1987	1945	1959 (1984)	1963 (1958)	1963 (1965)
	Myanmar	*Thailand*	*Laos*	*Cambodia*	*Vietnam*
Primitive	Indigenous	Indigenous	Indigenous	Indigenous	Indigenous
Proto-state 1	Hindu/ Buddhism	Hindu/ Buddhism	Hindu/ Buddhism	Hindu/ Buddhism	Chinese
Proto-state 2	Buddhism	Buddhism	Buddhism	Buddhism	Chinese
Colonial State	UK	Non	France	France	France
Imported law from;	UK	France, Germany, Japan	Socialist	Socialist	France, Socialist
Develop-mental State	Republic Military Rule	Constitu-tional Monarchy Parliament System	Socialist Republic	Constitu-tional Monarchy Parliament System	Socialist Republic
Constitution (enacted in)	(1974)	1997	1991	1993	1992

Proto-State Legal Systems

In pre-historic Southeast Asia, there were scattered tribal communities based on local customs united in following animist religions. Gradually, these communities became integrated into small states through federation or conquest by a stronger community. At the initial stage of state building, Hinduism[25] (and Confucianism in the area of present North Vietnam[26]) was borrowed as state ideology. Funan, for example, probably the oldest 'state' in Southeast Asia, emerged in the first century and had a foundation strongly coloured by Hindu mythology. Various states evolved and disappeared and some of them grew to large empires such as Khmer and Srivijaya.

In the due course of development by the expansion of the market force within the region, the new universal religions were introduced from outside to supply fresh ideologies for the newly expanded proto-state. Among them was Theravada Buddhism which was introduced into the mainland of Southeast Asia in the eleventh century. It not only became the state religion of the Thai and Burmese proto-states, but it also penetrated into the spiritual or mental structure of the common people within this region. In the fourteenth century another religion, Islam, was brought to the Southeast Asian islands. The conversion of families of kings to Islam resulted subsequently in the formation of many sultanate states.

There were innumerable proto-states in the history of this region. It is, therefore, impossible to discuss their specific state or legal systems, but we can identify two common natures of these systems.[27] The first concerns the nature of kingship and state structure. The kings and their families were connected to the god, and sometimes they claimed to be of divine descent themselves (Deva-Raja – Divine-Kingship in Hindu ideology).[28] The state was constructed in a hierarchical and organic order, from a king on the top to slaves at the bottom, although each social group or class enjoyed wider autonomy within its community.

The second characteristic relates to the state territory. There was no clear state border as in modern Western states, partly because of scattered populations at that time. In the capital or centre, autocratic kings reigned, their power endorsed by the direct influence of a major religion such as Hinduism, Buddhism, or Islam, although royal effulgence was naturally diminished and eventually faded away the further one moved from the centre. The territorial limit of the 'sovereignty' of these states was the place where it was exhausted. Therefore, at the centre there was a fairly sophisticated state system influenced by borrowings from major civilizations, based on the command principle, but in scattered villages, daily lives were regulated by local customs related closely to the community principle. This was a common feature of Asian proto-states. It must be emphasized, however, that indigenous elements based on the community principle survived strongly even at the state level, because statecraft and ideology for proto-state building were borrowed from the outside world and therefore were not really equipped to root out the indigenous structures.[29]

Colonial State Legal Systems

Following the advent of Islam in Southeast Asia, Western colonialism reached this region in the early sixteenth century. The initial ventures led by the Spaniards and Portuguese were motivated by Christianity (Roman

Catholicism) as well as by mercantilism. But these were superseded by newly emerging powers generated by incipient industrial capitalism such as Britain, Holland, and a while later France and the United States. Almost all areas of Asia except Thailand (Siam), China, Korea, and Japan were colonized by Western powers until about the middle of the twentieth century.[30] As a result, the state systems were reshaped more or less on the Western model, although the autocratic nature either remained or was somewhat reconstructed, because of the essential nature of colonial rule which necessarily oppressed other nations. The laws and legal systems ineluctably assumed a more important part of this transformation. Western laws were imported as far as required by colonialism in order to rule the colonies, not only in the area of commerce and trade, but also in the sphere of political institutions such as judiciaries and central or local administrations.

Spanish law dominated by Roman Catholicism was imposed on the Philippines in 1565 when Legaspi conquered the islands. In the late nineteenth century, French Napoleonic Civil and Commercial Codes were introduced into this colony following the reception of these Codes in Spain. More important was, however, the introduction of American law after 1898 when sovereignty over the Philippines was transferred from Spain to the United States. As a result, the mixture of the two major Western legal families, Continental civil law and Anglo-American common law, constitutes a special feature of the official Philippine legal system.

In Indonesia, the Dutch had steadily expanded their colonial rule since the early seventeenth century and their territorial sovereignty was confirmed by a treaty with Britain in 1824. From then, Dutch law, which was influenced by French codes, was introduced into Indonesia (the Netherlands East Indies) on a large scale. However, Dutch colonial legal policy in Indonesia was characterized by what we may call a 'dual legal policy.' Dutch based Western law was applied only to Western people (and to a limited extent to so-called 'Foreign Orientals,' mainly Chinese and Arabs), but not to 'natives' who were governed by various indigenous *adat* laws. As a result of this policy, 'legal pluralism' has become a distinguishing feature of the present Indonesian legal system, in spite of various government attempts since independence to integrate the various systems into a *Hukum Nasional* (National Law) (Yusuf, 1998).

There were wide variations in the way common law was introduced into the Strait Settlements, British Malaya, and North Borneo, all of which were British colonies. Generally speaking, British law was introduced directly into the Strait Settlements, because of their position as the advanced commercial centre of the region. In contrast, its influence was only superficial in North Borneo (present-day Brunei, and Sabah and Sarawak in Malaysia) which was a distant outpost of British Colonialism. After three invasions by the British in the late nineteenth century, the entire territory of present-day Myanmar (Burma) was attached to the territory of British India as provinces of this Empire until 1937 when it became a separate colony. For this reason, this country was strongly influenced by Anglo-Indian law.[31]

In Indochina, France invaded the Mekong Delta ruled by the Nguyen Dynasty in the late nineteenth century and colonized almost all the areas of the Indochina Peninsula (present-day Vietnam, Laos, and Cambodia) until the early twentieth century. While French law was introduced into the entire region, there were wide variations about what law was introduced into each of the various types of colonies and protectorates. (Hooker, 1978:154-75). Thailand, the only country not colonized by a Western power in Southeast Asia, was also forced to Westernize its state and legal systems in order to repeal the unequal treaties that granted 'extra-territorial jurisdiction' to citizens of Western countries.[32] Thanks to its independence and sovereignty, however, Western laws were introduced into Thailand from various countries on a selective basis. The Royal Siam Government employed foreign legal consultants in the process of 'codification' from the early twentieth century. There were many countries whose laws were referred to and whose legal codes were examined as models. This is an important difference from the colonized states, which were forced to introduce law exclusively from their colonial ruling country.

Western power reached the East Asian region comparatively late, in the middle of nineteenth century. After several interventions following the Opium War (1840-2), the coastal points of China (the *Qing* Empire) were conceded to Western Powers. Japan was an exception in Asia because it was able to modernize its state system on its own initiatives, although its major aim was to amend the unequal treaties with the Western powers. After searching for models in the UK and France, Japan chose Germany as its main model for legal development, and had codified its major laws basically following the German law model by the end of the nineteenth century. These codified laws were introduced into Korea and Taiwan, then the colonies of Japan. They also exerted substantial influence on the codification in the new China after the Revolution of 1911 and to some extent on the legal development in Thailand.

As a result, Western imported laws became dominant and formed a substantial part of the 'state legal system' of these countries. But they were not able to replace indigenous laws completely. Numerous indigenous laws were left largely untouched in many areas of the daily lives of people such as family,[33] religion, and land, although many of them were degraded to non-state or customary law. This dual structure between imported state law and indigenous non-state law forms a remarkable feature, not only of Asian laws but also of non-Western Third World legal systems. It is also very often referred to as legal pluralism. Needless to say, this dualism reflected a serious problem in the colonial state system characterized by dual structures at economic, political, and socio-cultural levels.

Developmental State Legal Systems

After World War II, almost all of the Asian countries became independent, but they faced serious political instability both in domestic and in international spheres. The whole region was left in a political vacuum and in the concomitant confusion after the surrender of the occupying Japanese military and subsequently because of the post-war world order which became known as the Cold War. But by the mid-1960s, these countries, with the exception of the Indochina region, were to some extent successfully controlling these instabilities and they had started a state building process in the true sense of the word. This process is nothing more or less than development, and this is why I call these states 'developmental states.'[34]

Although this development has many aspects, one of its main concerns has undoubtedly been solving the problem of the dual political, economic, and social structure that had evolved during colonial rule. In order to achieve this aim, various types of development laws have emerged, which generally confer discretionary power on the government under the command principle. I will discuss the situation with regard to law and development in Southeast Asian developmental states in the 1970s and 1980s in greater detail in the next section.

LAW AND DEVELOPMENT UNDER THE DEVELOPMENTAL STATE REGIME IN SOUTHEAST ASIA

It is convenient to examine LD problems in three different dimensions of society; the political society (state), the economic society (economy), and the communal society (society), each of which is based mainly on the principles of 'command,' 'market,' and 'community' respectively.

Law and Political Development

Political development can be defined as an achievement of a democratic system in the government structure that necessarily reflects the relation between a rule and the people ruled by it, that is the command principle. A constitution is the most important document in the political regime of a nation.[35] With a few exceptions, Southeast Asian states have adopted more or less Western-style constitutions, which deal with two major subjects: the structure of government and the protection of human rights (Bill of Rights).[36]

In the structure of government, all of those countries except Brunei[37] have opted for a 'democratically' elected government, either through a parliamentary system (Singapore, Malaysia, and Thailand) or through a Presidency system (the Philippines and Indonesia).[38] However, this does not necessarily mean that these countries have copied the Western model of the state. Strong nationalist and cultural values can be observed even in the constitutional systems. National religion (Buddhism in Thailand and Islam in Muslim majority states) and nationalist ideology (*Pancasila* in Indonesia) play an important role in tying a diverse population to a new nation. The kings of Thailand and Malaysia are not only to some extent a symbol of their nation, but they are also expected to act as the fathers of their nations who will take care of their subjects as if they were their children.[39]

The governments in operation are characterized more or less by authoritarianism, which was justified during the Cold War when it was considered necessary to oppress the political rights of the people in order to control communist movements and to promote the rapid development of the nation. The Philippines came under martial rule under President Marcos from 1972 to 1981, and even after martial law was lifted, continued to experience his dictatorial rule until 1989 when it was finally ended by the Aquino revolution. In Thailand, there were regular cycles of military coups and constitutional amendments until the early 1990s.[40] Indonesia presented a typical model of 'developmental dictatorship' under President Suharto for thirty years until 1998, when public pressure forced him to resign in the thick of an economic and political crisis. Malaysia and Singapore were categorized as comparatively democratic parliamentary states as far as their formal system was concerned, but it is well known that these elected government systems were maintained by similarly oppressive internal security legislation.[41] The socialist regimes in Vietnam, Laos, Cambodia, and Burma (Myanmar) were dictatorial in their nature.

It should be noted that Asian authoritarianism is deeply rooted in cultural tradition and is characterized by 'patron and client relationships' and 'dependency' (Pye, 1985:127-32), both of which are closely linked to our community principle. There is abundant evidence for this. Most remarkable in this context is the tendency to build family dynasties, as has been the case with the Marcos government in the Philippines and with the Suharto government in Indonesia.

Almost all constitutions in Southeast Asian countries contain provisions for the protection of human rights (fundamental rights),[42] but it is true that, because of the nature of the authoritarian governments, in practice these rights were not sufficiently guaranteed. However, political developments during the late 1980s showed that human rights became an increasingly important political agenda. The development of a human rights movement in the region undoubtedly reflects an emerging urban middle class in the wake of a successful economic development. In addition, drastically changing international political circumstances after the collapse of the Soviet and East European socialist regimes contributed to an explosion of the human rights discourse as an expression of the universal value of humans.

It should be noted in this context that a new concept of human rights called 'rights to development' (Rich, 1988; Baxi, 1988) has evolved and is advocated in these countries. Although it is difficult to conceptualize it in strict legal terms, it seems to refer to a set of rights to achieve justice for common people in the development process, which includes the right to protect the environment, and to the preservation of cultural identities of various ethnic groups. These rights are meaningful only when they are constructed on the basis of a group of people; a kind of 'community' to be distinguished either from a 'state' or an 'individual.' Needless to say that society is a sphere where the 'community principle' works most effectively, and we can learn a lot from existing rural and ethnic communities. The concept of rights to development has a certain affinity to the idea of 'Asian values,' although the latter concept is thrown into the arena in the context of national culture and tradition by Asian authoritarian governments in order to justify their oppression of human rights.[43] But, it also undeniably represents values of common people such as harmonious collectivism based on our community principle.

In sum, during the 1980s Southeast Asian countries gradually started to democratize their political systems, but they maintained basically authoritarian systems, which were not only based on the command principle, but also deeply rooted in their own cultural traditions based on the community principle. In the early 1990s, we can witness the same development if we look at the process and result of the election in the Philippines, Thailand, and Indonesia. As we will discuss later, this process was suddenly accelerated by the Asian economic crisis that erupted in 1997.

Law and Economic Development

Economic development aims to achieve the material prosperity of the people. It has been the most important agenda for Asian developmental states and often justified the authoritarian nature of their political regimes during the 1970s and 1980s. In order to achieve this objective, innumerable laws were drafted to promote rapid industrialization and to solve the dual economic structure, which was regarded as a major cause of underdevelopment. These legal measures are influenced by the theories and practices of 'development economics,' and vary in accordance to changing theoretical frameworks. It is virtually impossible to examine all aspects of law and economic development, but a short discussion of foreign investment laws, company laws and transfer of technology regulations will give some indication of the importance of this area.

Foreign investment laws are the most important instruments to motivate foreign capital to assist domestic economic development. Forced with the inadequacy of domestic capital, by the 1960s almost all ASEAN countries started to enact laws to promote foreign investment.[44] The common feature of these laws was to set up regulatory boards with wide discretionary power to approve and regulate foreign investments and to provide for various incentives to raise investment in desired areas of national development. Foreign investment policies have varied in time and space, but a glance is enough to show that the emphasis has shifted from import substitute industries to an export oriented approach from the early 1970s onwards.

There were no significant reforms of company laws before 1965, when Malaysia introduced the new Companies Act, in part because there were not yet many large-scale business corporations. As time passed, as a result of industrialization and with the help of foreign capital, the number of big businesses of either a domestic character (mainly Chinese-dominated) or operated as joint ventures with Transnational Corporations (TNCs) increased rapidly during the 1960s. Under the influence of economic nationalism in the early 1970s, some countries started revising their company laws in order to control such big corporations. This philosophy expressed itself in three elements: nationalization or 'fading out' (which means transfer of foreign shares to local shareholders), dispersal of shareholdings or private (family) companies going public, and the securing of professional management. The first mentioned aspect is also a subject of foreign investment laws, whereas the second is closely connected with capital market regulation.[45] In addition, the equal distribution of national wealth between ethnic groups has been an important area of corporate policies in a multi-racial society such as Malaysia (Yasuda, 1991:331-49).

Transfer of technology (ToT) was also an important measure in the promotion of 'industrialization.' Some ASEAN countries began introducing ToT regulations as a part of foreign investment regulations, influenced by the UN and UNCTAD discussions on TNCs, restrictive trade practices and ToT, which took place during the 1970s.[46]

Changes were in the air and the policies behind many of the above-mentioned laws changed during the 1980s because of the transformation of the world economies. The world recession in the early 1980s revealed critical problems of economic management of Third World developmental governments. The strict regulatory systems caused not only inefficiency through delays in policy making and implementation, but also induced serious problems of corruption based on nepotism, which still remained a strong feature of Third World societies. Foreign debt accumulation loured as a crucial problem in many countries. The IMF and the World Bank thought it appropriate to compel these countries to take a step towards 'structural adjustment,' which generally means deregulation or liberalization of economic systems.

Although ASEAN economies with the exception of the Philippines showed rather good performances during the recession in the 1980s, the governments implemented various policies towards deregulation and liberalization. Foreign investment laws were amended in order to simplify the regulatory process and the types of incentives.[47] The ToT policies of these countries changed radically in nature and have emphasized the legal protection of intellectual property since the late 1980s.[48] Besides this, it should also be recalled that socio-economic legislation such as environment laws and consumer protection laws have been developed rapidly in the ASEAN region, although legislation in these areas does go back to the 1970s.

As discussed earlier, economic activities are generally based on the market principle. It is, therefore, natural to think that the more development the countries achieve, the wider liberalization required. This means their economic systems will shift from state centred command systems to market-oriented ones. Pertinently Southeast Asian economic systems are not based completely on the market principle which requires economic rationality, but are also still substantially influenced by the community principle which emphasizes personal relationship. This defect became apparent in the Asian financial crisis as discussed in the next section.

Law and Social Development

Social development, from local communities to the global human community, aims to maximize people's moral and spiritual satisfaction through the sense of identity or feeling of unity within a society. Society is based on what we refer to as the community principle, and is distinguished clearly from the state (political society) which concerns our command principle, as well as from the economy (economic society) dominated mainly by the market principle. The basic unit of society is the 'family' where members enjoy maximum autonomy under different personal laws.[49] Family law tends to be modernized more slowly than other branches of law, because family systems are profoundly intertwined with the traditional feelings of people as a group. It is true, however, that the modern nuclear family based on individualism, has also become common in urban areas and has expanded rapidly in the process of economic development during the 1970s and 1980s.

Local communities are the most important areas for social development, where members feel happy to identify themselves with such development and participate in the decision-making and in the implementation of its management. The governmental structure of many Asian countries is still centralized under the inexorable influence of developmentalism and authoritarianism, with the local government adequately recognized at the official level.[50] Although this is so, villages have maintained a rich tradition of autonomy at the informal level, a continuation from the proto-state stage. These communities have been playing an important role as social security systems in providing mutual assistance for their members. Such informal mutual assistance systems protect the poor from the violent upheavals necessarily resulting from the course of economic development. There are clear signs that such community systems have been expanded to urban areas in general, especially to the slums of metropolitan cities. During the 1970s and 1980s, so many migrants poured in from rural areas and having done so, introduced their systems in order to sustain their lives in the cities. These informal systems are characterized by methods of solving social problems through mutual or collective approaches based on the community principle.

As far as legal systems are concerned, there have been strong indications of a revival of traditional informal justice systems, which endeavour to solve disputes through conciliation or compromise between the disputing parties. Any such attempts ineluctably modify the Western imported legal system model, which is characterized more or less as an 'adversary system.' The informal justice systems are more effective and efficient in the solution of disputes at the community level. Not only do they save the formal courts from becoming overburdened and very costly, but they also satisfy community members by allowing them participation in the settlement process and thus securing harmony within the community.[51]

The social systems of Southeast Asian developmental states remain strongly anchored to their cultural traditions based on our community principle, although they have been affected by both the market and the command principle that evolved rapidly during the process of development. In sum, we can observe two contrasting or even contradictory directions in law and development problems of Asian developmental states in the 1970s and 1980s. One direction, motivated by the market force, was to modernize and liberalize (democratize) their economic and political systems. The other direction was a kind of revivalism, clearly apparent in the political and social field, to reunite people through traditional values based on the community force.

THE END OF DEVELOPMENTAL STATES OR THE BEGINNING OF POST DEVELOPMENTAL STATES?

A newly emerging powerful wave of the market force, created by the electronics and information revolution and starting from the late 1970s, has been nullifying existing state and economic systems all over the world. Initially, this wave made its impact on Western developed countries and forced them to deregulate and privatize their economic system, as in the United States under the presidency of Reagan and in the United Kingdom under the Thatcher Government in the early 1980s. during the rest of the 1980s this new force gradually penetrated all countries of the world and forced them to transform not only their economies drastically but also to overhaul their political regimes. The fiercest impact is exemplified by the collapse of the socialist states of Eastern Europe and the Soviet Union from the end of the 1980s to the early 1990s. The globalizing market force eroded the socialist command systems through the leaking of information in various sectors that had previously been strictly monopolized by these states. It was symbolic that the various electronic media, the main products of the continuing information technology revolution, disseminated the epoch making news of the collapse of the socialist regimes.

The wave of globalization then swept up Asian developing countries in the mid-1980s. At an initial stage, East and Southeast Asian countries adapted themselves successfully to this wave, and continued to achieve the highest economic growth in the world, while economies elsewhere were suffering from serious recession in their attempts to cope with globalization. During the 1980s, all Asian, including socialist, countries substantially liberated and deregulated their economic systems and they took various steps to induce foreign investment which in turn accelerated their economic growth. China has been developing successfully since the early 1980s after the gradual liberation of its economic system under the new label of 'market socialism.' This may be contrasted with the drastic dissolution of the European and Soviet socialist systems.

What was unforeseen was that in this process the states themselves gradually started to erode the controlling power of national economies. One typical instance is the amendment of intellectual property laws in almost all countries, a move which was strongly urged by government and businesses of the United States. It means that technology transfer policy shifted drastically from industrial policies in which the state had a powerful regulatory role to the protection of property as the core concept of the market system (Uphoff, 1991). In this context, it should be noted that since the early 1990s trade liberalization in the Asia Pacific region has been promoted by Asia Pacific Economic Co-operation (APEC) and on a more global level by the establishment of the World Trade Organization (WTO) in 1995. Inexorably in this global wave of trade liberalization, nation states would naturally lose the effective regulatory power over their national economies. This is the reason why in the Southeast Asian region during the 1990s ASEAN has strengthened its solidarity through implementing various measures of co-operation and co-ordination among its members.[52] These phenomena show that the community force, which was about to be dissolved at the national level, was now reconstructing itself at a wider regional level within ASEAN.

The financial crisis suddenly exploded first in Thailand in mid-1997 and subsequently expanded to almost all East and Southeast Asian countries. A major cause of this crisis was a hasty liberalization of the financial systems of these countries, compelled not only by international organizations such as the IMF and WTO but also by governments of developed countries in general and of the United States in particular. There is also evidence that a regenerated and globalizing market force shows its supremacy over the rather outdated financial systems of Asian countries through its sophisticated financial techniques, as demonstrated by the activities of hedge funds. The IMF pointed out that the crisis 'was exacerbated by governance issues, notably government involvement in the private sector and lack of transparency in corporate and fiscal accounting and provision of financial and economic data...'[53] This shows that this crisis is not only to be blamed on the failure of economic management, but is also deeply rooted in the cultural structure of these countries.

What implication does this crisis have for the future of legal systems of Asian countries? It is not easy to answer this question, but it is foreseeable that the paradigm of the developmental state will lose its effectiveness for an analysis of Southeast Asian legal systems. The reason is that globalization has been corroding the efficacy of state power in various fields as is demonstrated by the present crisis. Nevertheless, I will try to search for a tentative answer to this question. I will now briefly discuss what law reforms, divided over political, economic, and social fields, are required to overcome this crisis.

The Political Field

Although the present crisis occurred because of the financial sector and its disastrous shock waves mainly concerns the economic and social fields of the society, political systems have also been forced to change radically. The actual direction that this change is taking differs widely among the nations, but we may generally identify a greater democratization of the political system. In Southeast Asian countries, democratization itself proceeded gradually from the late 1980s and stepped up its speed in the early 1990s because of the effect of globalization and the rapidly expanding market force as seen in the Philippines, Thailand, and even in Indonesia. However, the accelerated liberalization of the financial system as the main cause of the present crisis confirms that Southeast Asian states are losing effective control over international financial activities. The failure of governments seriously discredited the political justification of authoritarian developmental state regimes, as the crisis expanded from the economic to the social field.

Although the situation of each country is different, Thailand, Indonesia, and Malaysia have been facing a serious political crisis in the wake of the economic and social effect of this financial turmoil. In Thailand, where the crisis began, the government was forced to accelerate the democratization of its polity; partly to ease the anti-government mood caused by the economic collapse but also because of the pressure exerted by the IMF and other international organizations coming to the rescue. As a result, the Constitution was totally amended and taken in a radically democratic direction in September 1997.[54] The new Constitution consists of twelve Chapters and 336 Articles and is intended to promote the democratization of the Thai political systems through the introduction of an elected Senate and the limitation of its power and through widening local autonomy.[55] It also strengthens the protection of human rights not only through the expansion of the catalogue of rights, but also by establishing a National Human Rights Commission in order to guarantee implementation.[56] It also incorporates various measures to end a lengthy tradition of patronage and corrupt 'money' politics. Among these are the compulsory disclosure of assets of Parliamentarians and other political officials and the establishment of the powerful National Counter Corruption Commission. It is important to note that 50,000 voters have the right to request the Senate to remove corrupt high officials including the prime minister. It is too early to evaluate how this Constitution will impact on Thai politics, but no one can deny that it supplies a firm base for the future development of democracy in Thailand.

In Indonesia, the situation is more complicated. Indonesia has been most seriously affected by the present financial crisis within the region, partly because of its authoritarian political system for more than three decades. As the economic crisis expanded to the social and political fields, President Suharto, previously dubbed 'father of development,' was forced to terminate his authoritarian regime in the midst of miserable political and social turmoil in May 1998. Vice-President Habibie succeeded him as the third president in Indonesian history.[57] Habibie and his government have struggled to stabilize the Indonesian polity through gradual democratization of the political system. In early 1999, bills for a reform of the election system as well as for a more democratic reorganization of the Peoples Consultative Council and the House of Representative were passed and, in June 1999, a general election was held under the new regulations.[58] It was the first democratic election in Indonesian history. However, because of an after effect of the long authoritarian regime, the future of the Indonesian polity is not looking very bright. This assumption is based on several reasons. First, the armed forces still have a strong influence on politics. Secondly, the economic crisis has led to violent ethnic conflicts between the majority poor *pribumi* and the rich Chinese minority. This antagonism had deepened during the developmental era of the 1980s, but it had been suppressed by the authoritarian political regime.[59] Thirdly and perhaps most seriously, partly because of the liberalization of the political system, Indonesia has been facing a potential dissolution of its state system. There have been the outbreaks of separatist movements not only in East Timor, but also in Aceh, Sumatra, and in many other places.[60] It will be a difficult job to democratize and liberalize Indonesia's political system while at the same time trying to control these unstable tendencies in various parts of the country.[61]

In observing these two cases of democratization of political systems in Thailand and Indonesia, we can come to the conclusion that the introduction of liberal democracy into Southeast Asia is inevitable. However, at the same time it will be essential to maintain or recreate a feeling of national unity based on the community principle, if the countries want to avoid the tragedies of state dissolution that have been experienced by the former Yugoslavia.

The Economic Field

The crisis occurred in the financial sector and, as mentioned above, its main cause was the weak monitoring and controlling mechanisms within both government and corporations. Many analysts have pointed out that the origins of the crisis are rooted in the Asian-style of management itself. For instance, Rajan and Zingales contrast the nature of Asian and Western financial transactions by using the term 'relationship v. arm's length.' According to them,

> relationship-based system[s] ensure a return to [the] financier by granting some form of power over the firm being financed. ... the financier attempts to secure her return on investment by retaining some kind of monopoly over the firm she finances. As with every monopoly, this requires some barriers to entry. These barriers may be due to regulation or to lack of transparency – or 'opacity' of the system, which subsequently raises the cost of entry to potential competitors. Contrast this with the arm's length, Anglo-Saxon system, where the financier is protected by explicit contracts. In such systems, contract and associated prices determine the transactions that are undertaken.[62]

This contrast can be related to the contrast between community and market principles in our analysis. Having said this it is undeniable that the collectivist style in business management was one of the important factors of rapid economic development within the region (Hefner (ed.), 1998). This method mobilized limited resources for economic growth through organizing and sometimes manipulating group identity within the family, corporate sector, and nation, based on the community principle. It is correct that group solidarity or unity can operate effectively at the production stage within a factory or in personal management, because the co-operation of workers is indispensable to the work place. But when a great deal of weight is exerted on this group feeling it pushes the organization in the direction of a lack of calculable rationality and transparency because of the rejection of 'otherness' or individualism. As a necessary result of this collectivist system and collectivist feeling, crony capitalism and nepotism cause a fatal flaw especially in financial management, in which transparency and accountability are essential.

The main cause of the Asian financial crisis has been, therefore, that Asian collectivist capitalism based on harmony in family and work place was defeated by Western individualist capitalism which attained much more sophisticated financial techniques while globalizing their approaches to management. This means that economic law reform is indispensable in areas related to financial management, in both the banking and corporate sectors of these countries. Needless to say, financial and banking law reforms are essential to the reconstruction of these sectors. Almost all governments affected by the ongoing crisis within the region have been forced to create more transparent and accountable financial systems as a condition for rescue exacted under the severe pressure by the IMF and the World Bank.[63] Under the influence of these institutions, the law has been amended to secure strict financial stability, transparent accounting systems and, more importantly, to induce foreign investment (World Bank, 1998b:62-70).

In this operation, laws dealing with corporate bankruptcy and reconstruction have been the most urgent topic for reform, because many financial and corporate firms were facing insolvency, floored by the outstanding heavy debt burden after the bubble burst. This reform is also essential to enable foreign enterprises to buy these firms.[64] It is intimately related to judicial reforms because these laws are generally operated and enforced by the civil courts. This is also the reason why the reform of the judicial system and the establishment of the rule of law has been emphasized so strongly.[65]

Competition law and policy have also been strengthened in the process of recovery from the crisis. From the Anglo Saxon viewpoint mentioned above, a relationship-based system of 'opacity,' monopoly must be transformed to a more competitive market-oriented system.[66] As a result, competition laws were enacted in Indonesia and Thailand in early 1999.[67] In this area, international co-operation has been promoted, not only within the region, but also more widely in APEC and universally in the WTO (Lloyd, 1998:157-77). The reform in the economic field, especially in the financial and corporate sectors will lead to the introduction of more transparency and accountability in order to adjust the economy to the rapidly globalizing business environment based on the market principle. The downside is that marketization will necessarily also cause society to disorganize and to lose its solidarity. How to prevent this is an urgent concern, because such disorganization is resulting in serious poverty problems among common people as well as in the deterioration of the natural environment.

The Social Field

The result of the crisis has been disastrous to Asian countries. For instance, Indonesia's currency was devalued six months after the onset of the crisis to less than one-fifth to the US Dollar. It means that the per capita GNP of these countries suddenly dropped from a little more than US$1000 to less than US$200, the same level as LLDC countries. The serious economic recession resulting from the crisis has caused grave unemployment and poverty problems.[68]

This region made great strides in various fields of social development as a result of rapid economic development from the 1970s to the early 1990s. Life expectancy, infant mortality rates, and the primary/secondary education rate were remarkably improved and poverty was alleviated substantially during this period.[69] After such remarkable success, the people suddenly lost their achievements. In 1998, the number of poor was expected to increase from 5 to 10 percentage points in Indonesia, from 2 to 12 per cent in Korea, and from 3 to 12 per cent in Thailand.[70]

The abrupt degradation of the social life of the common people has been more serious than expected, especially in Southeast Asian countries. Paradoxically the crisis produced more disastrous results precisely because these countries had succeeded in rapid economic development. There are several reasons for this. First, the traditional community-based social safety net systems were eroded during the period of rapid urbanization and evolution of middle class people as a necessary result of development. Before the industrialization, there were traditional systems of mutual assistance and co-operation at the village and family level. These were informal, but so resilient and autonomous within such communities that people did not need to rely heavily on state social security schemes.[71] These informal systems protected poor and vulnerable people against harsh and negative effects of development during the 1970s and 1980s, but they withered away when the people started to gain from development. The crisis attacked just at a time when those systems had disappeared.

Secondly, formal or state social security systems were underdeveloped, even after successful economic development, because the traditional safety nets had been functioning so well.[72] The developmental state could concentrate on mobilizing resources to achieve economic growth by placing the social costs on those informal social institutions. It should be noted that income disparity widened during the process of economic growth (World

Bank, 1998b:77-8) while traditional safety nets were eroded and the state neglected the duty incumbent on it to take measures to protect the poor. The poor, therefore, became increasingly vulnerable as a result of development. They are now left without the protection of either traditional/informal safety nets or of modern/formal social security systems.

Therefore, law reforms in the social field will take two directions. One direction is to create or strengthen official security systems such as unemployment insurance, medical or health care schemes, and pension funds. These measures can be planned and implemented at the national level. In this context, the state or government is expected to play an increasingly important role through its regulatory measures and its financial resources. This may be contrasted with the state being forced to retreat substantially from the economic sphere and to some extent from the political field. The state should enforce vigorous legislation for the protection of vulnerable people such as workers, peasants, and the urban poor. This can only be implemented by a state that has sufficient financial and personal capacities to set up and implement nation-wide social security systems.

Another direction is either to revive traditional community systems which have nearly vanished or to construct new community systems based on the community principle. There has been a strong tendency during this period to favour mutual assistance and co-operation, not only within traditional villages but also in urban areas through the migration of rural people. This is why 'community development' has become an important agenda in the newly advocated paradigm of 'alternative development' since 1980, and of 'social development' as asserted by International Development Organizations such as UNDP and World Bank in the 1990s.[73]

As the crisis deepened within the region, solutions to various social problems became more urgent. A recent World Bank paper dealt with this topic, under (1) employment generation and income maintenance; (2) monitoring poverty impact and income distribution; (3) maintaining basic social services; (4) small and medium enterprise development and micro-finance; (5) protecting the social fabric; (6) social consequence at city and community level (World Bank, 1999a, 1999b). This agenda not only requests that international aid organizations and governments take various policy measures, but also that local communities and local and international NGOs play a progressive role in co-operation with those national and international official organizations. In this context, the community principle is expected to maintain or even expand to wider perspectives its effectiveness in the social field.

CONCLUSION

I have proposed the concepts of three legal principles; community, market, and command, and two dynamic forces for development; market and community. These concepts have proved their effectiveness for a systematic understanding of the historical development of legal systems of Southeast Asian countries, divided into three state concepts; the proto-state, colonial state, and developmental state. But their usefulness is not confined to this. As part of the analysis of developmental states, they are competent operational concepts for setting up a framework of legal policies, by dividing society into political society (state), economic society (market), and societal society (community), each of which is in turn based on the command, market, or community principle.

Needless to say, LDS will not be a branch of orthodox dogmatic law research, but rather a kind of policy study mobilizing the knowledge of various branches of social sciences to design more suitable legal systems and law for developing countries. In this context, I strongly advocate the need to infuse cultural aspects into LDS. The problem is that because of the universal nature of law influenced by modern Western legal science, legal scholars are accustomed to deal with hierarchical (command) and vertical (market) relationships, but tend to disregard the cultural elements of society which show affinity with our community principle. This is one of the reasons why the old LDS paradigm of the 1960s and 1970s lost its influence.

Legal pluralism or comparative legal culture (Varga, 1992) has emerged as a post-LDS paradigm during the 1980s and 1990s, but it has not yet been successful in exploring any effective methodological concepts which can apply to both academic and practical (policy making) fields. I have presented the concept of community principle in order to throw light on this dark area of culture from the perspective of legal study. Of course this concept is still primitive and in need of improvement not only in specific fields but also for general theory.

Finally, I would like to add a little more to make a sketch of the international aspects of globalization from the perspectives of the three legal principles and two development forces. The accelerated wave of the market force has been rampaging all over the world, collapsing the nearly one century-old socialist regimes and causing serious political, economic and social crises to Southeast Asian countries. As a result, developmental states are facing a grave crisis both from an international and from a domestic perspective. In the international arena, states start losing their 'sovereignty.' In the political dimension we witness the evolution of regionalism as typified by the establishment of the European Union and the assertion of international human rights. But beyond this, states have lost their regulatory power to the

IMF, World Bank, WTO, and other international institutions in various economic fields. In the domestic arena, the developmental state has lost its wide power substantially because of the ongoing democratization and decentralization of the political system. It shall be noted that democratization closely relates not only to the political movements in the narrow sense, but also to various social (community) reform movements initiated by domestic NGOs in co-operation with international counterparts. Needless to say, these NGOs base their ideas and values substantially on the community principle.

In sum, the state will lose its effective power and retreat to the position of an arbitrator of conflicts between groups representing the market and community forces. The market force is represented by international businesses together with international economic organizations such as the IMF, World Bank, and WTO, which aim to produce economic surplus using individualist rational methods such as securing transparency and accountability. The serious fault of these approaches is a tendency to disregard the value of the community which is often characterized as being incompatible with the market value. In contrast, the community force is represented by various communities in co-operation with domestic and international NGOs. They strongly oppose the anarchical profit-seeking behaviour of international businesses, which often damages the natural environment and traditional human life based on holistic community values. Therefore, uncompromising disputes between business/economic interest groups based on the individualistic market principle, and social/community groups based on the holistic community principle in various fields of development policies especially with regard to environmental problems, are inevitable. As political systems in Southeast Asian countries are democratized, the state will fade out its authoritarian nature and assume increasingly the nature of an arbitrator whose legitimacy is secured through elections.

NOTES

1 The Southeast Asian region (and to some extent East Asia) is part of Monsoon Asia, which may be defined geographically as an area stretching from the Indian Sub-continent through continental and island Southeast Asia via South or Coastal China and the Korean Peninsula to the Japanese islands. This region is characterized by either a tropical or a temperate wet zone with agriculture based on rice farming. These characteristics are clearly different not only from the West European region but also from other dry regions of Asia such as Central and West Asia and parts of North India and China where agriculture is based on grazing land, and wheat and cereal production.

2 Before the crisis, they were applauded by the World Bank for their economic success in *The East Asian Miracle* (World Bank, 1993). Only five years later, after the onset of the crisis, the World Bank denounced the same countries in a further publication (World Bank, 1998b).

3 For a critical survey of the Law and Development paradigm in the United States see also John Henry Merryman (1977) and Elliot M. Burg (1977). For a further collection of important works on the topic see Anthony Carty (1992).

4 David M. Trubek and Mark Galanter (1974). In my view this is the most important work in understanding the LDS paradigm in the 1960-70s and from which to learn lessons for a future reconstruction of LDS.

5 The *East Asian Miracle* report of the World Bank admitted this. The universal applicability of this 'Asiatic development' seems limited.

6 One of the most controversial issues concerned the question of universal human rights versus Asian values. There are many articles on this topic in journals such as *Foreign Affairs*. It was also a major topic of 'Law in a Changing World; Asian Alternatives; Proceedings of the Fourth Kobe Lecture' *ARSP*, Beiheft Nr. 72, though the focus was not specifically on this issue. See also Joanne R. Bauer and Daniel A. Bell (1999).

7 See Amy L. Chua (1998). She argues for a reconstruction of LDS by infusing the fairly cultural concept of 'ethnicity' into the dualism between Market and Democracy. The latter has been a classic paradigm of LDS since it was formulated by David M. Trubek in his article 'Toward a Social Theory of Law: An essay on the Study of Law and Development,' (Trubek, 1972). This chapter aims to achieve the same purpose from a different point of view.

8 There are only three countries in East and Southeast Asia which were officially never colonized: China, Japan, and Thailand. These countries were forced to modernize their legal systems in a Western mode, however, to achieve amendments to unequal treaties concluded with Western hegemonic powers.

9 I define state law in a wider sense here as including law authorized or recognized by state authorities. Islamic legislation in many countries stipulates procedural matters as well as substantive laws which Islamic courts apply. In this case, these substantive laws, if recognized by a state are a kind of 'state law' and they show affinity with 'official law' as defined by Masaji Chiba (1989:107-18).

10 The most remarkable example is the 'Islamization' of the state systems in Pakistan, Bangladesh, and Malaysia. In these countries, not only are legislative measures such as the establishment of Islamic banks remarkable, but also the expansion of power and jurisdiction of Islamic courts noteworthy. For Malaysia, see 'In God's Name: Kelantan

continues push to implement Islamic law,' *Far Eastern Economic Review*, 2 September 1992, p. 13.

11 In Southeast Asia, there is yet another type of 'imported' laws, such as Islamic, Hindu, and traditional Chinese laws. However, these laws were integrated with native laws, in contrast to the imported Western laws, which is what brought about the present 'legal pluralism' in these countries. This is why M.B. Hooker (1978) divides his book into two parts under the headings of 'status' and 'contract.'

12 Former French Indochina countries (Vietnam, Laos, and Cambodia) adopted socialist legal regimes, although they have been transforming their systems to legal systems based on market economy principles since the mid-1980s.

13 This concept has strong affinity with the 'community' as defined by Tönnies in his *Community and Society* (1957).

14 When Van Hoecke and Warrington emphasize the rational and individual nature of Western legal systems, the law is understood as an independent and autonomous system from other social norms like morality or religion (Van Hoecke and Warrington, 1998).

15 Schumpeter defines democracy as an 'institutional arrangement for arriving at political decision in which individuals acquire the power to decide by means of competitive struggle for the people's vote' in his *Capitalism, Socialism and Democracy* (1950). See Chua (1998:9 fn. 27).

16 Initially, I used the term 'direction' in my article, 'Law and Development in ASEAN Countries' (1993). I changed this to 'imperative' in 'The Evolution of the Easy Asian Law region' (1995) and finally adopted the term 'command' in this paper. Needless to say, the contrast between market and command is very popular, not only for the comparative analysis of capitalist and socialist economies, but also for the LDS approach. See Trubek (1972:24-34); Robert B. Seidman (1978).

17 The most effective and comprehensive theory is Karl Marx's historical materialism which explains the historical development of society as the process of the conflict between two different elements; that is, increasing production capacity and social relations regarding production.

18 This idea is tentative and not yet well refined. Although it is essential to make it more sophisticated in the light of such grand theories of social development as Marx's 'historical materialism,' I believe that it is useful and effective as an explanation of the development of the legal system within the framework of this paper.

19 Although it is necessary to study what Weber said as a whole, I think this continuity between market rationality and bureaucracy is one of the key elements of his thinking.

20 Theoretically, the community principle and force are not necessarily presupposed to have a centre. Unitary or solidarity feeling between members in the network without a centre is effective and sufficient. It is true that the centre strengthens such feelings among people, but it seems the centre has more affinity to the command principle defined earlier.

21 Here, I can only pose the question of whether there might be different types of rationality in industrial societies, where everything is calculable over a relatively short time span, and non-industrial societies (e.g. purely agrarian societies) where the measuring time interval is much longer, because of the different nature of their production cycle. This idea of 'social time' is hinted by Barbara Adam (1990:148-69).

22 This does not mean that the command principle is not effective for an analysis of social relations or phenomenon, or that it is only an operational concept without any value. A feeling of order and obedience certainly must have some value. Rather, what I mean here is that it cannot be a dynamic concept which serves as a decisive force in the development process of society.

23 I am rather sceptical about the idea of the 'Internet community' as an alternative to the future community. But it is undeniable that NGOs would be important components of such a global community, because they represent a countervailing power against a fierce market force pushed by multinational enterprises.

24 In this section, I refer mainly for general history to D.G.E. Hall (1981); for legal history to M.B. Hooker (1978, 1986-7) and for legal systems to Poh-Ling Tan (1997). See also Nobuyuki Yasuda (1993).

25 See G. Coedes (1968) on the introduction of Hinduism in the Southeast Asian region.

26 Japan borrowed the Chinese state system and ideology when it started creating its own state in the seventh century, although Confucian influence came much later, after the fifteenth century, and this influence is limited. See Yasuda (1995) on the legal development in peripheral East Asia (Japan and Korea).

27 Mabbet (1985:3-5) summarizes nine common natures of Asian kingship.

28 To some extent, this concept is applicable to the Chinese idea of the emperor, a Chinese term which literally means the 'son of heaven.' The Japanese concept of the emperor shows more affinity with Southeast Asian thought, because the emperor was defined officially as a 'living god' up to the end of World War II.

29 See Hooker (1978:17-94) and Hooker (ed.) (1986), on law texts of proto-states in the region, which were imported or 'borrowed' from major oriental legal systems. The introduction of Chinese systems into the

proto-states of Vietnam, Korea, and Japan can basically be explained in the same way.

30 Japan colonized Korea in 1910. This was a very rare case of colonization of a modern Asian State by its neighbouring state.

31 In India, British laws had been introduced substantially through 'codification' since the late nineteenth century. The products such as Contract Act, Penal Code, Criminal Procedure Code, etc. were spread not only to Asian but also to all other British colonies.

32 The first of these treaties was concluded in 1855 with Britain. Treaties with other European countries followed. Japan entered into similar treaties with the United States, the Netherlands, Britain, France, and Russia in 1858.

33 It is notable that there is a substantial inheritance of indigenous norms in the codification of family law in almost all countries. In Japan as well as in Thailand, the indigenous family system was incorporated into the Civil Codes after fierce debates about whether or not to introduce modern Western family law.

34 'Developmentalism' is the main cause for the authoritarian regimes of these nations, although there is also some close relationship with the cultural structure of the 'proto-states.' For a more detailed definition of the 'developmental state' in the context of Japan, see Chalmers Johnson (1982:17-19). I believe that socialist systems, especially in Asia, may be categorized as extreme types of developmental states, although Chalmers Johnson contrasts his concept with both the American market system and the Soviet command system.

35 See Lawrence W. Beer (1992), on a general view of the present constitutional problems of each country. See also Sison (1990) with complete texts of the constitution of each country. See Poh-Ling Tan (1997) about the contemporary legal systems of some East Asian countries more generally.

36 Vietnam, Laos, and Cambodia adopted a socialist system after fierce independence and national liberation wars.

37 The Brunei Constitution provides for a partly elected 'Legislative Council,' but it has not been operating since 1984 when the country became independent.

38 In 1987, the Philippines returned to the American presidency model originally introduced in the Commonwealth Constitution of 1935, after previously changing its political regime from a parliamentary system in the 1973 Constitution (which was not operative because of martial law) to a Presidency Cabinet system (a Gaullist style presidency) in a 1981 amendment under Marcos. The present Indonesian Constitution enacted in 1945 (and re-introduced in 1959 to replace a provisional Constitution

of 1950) provides that the president shall be elected by the People's Consultative Council (MPR) composed of elected parliament members and other members appointed by the president.

39 It is interesting that the stress on these traditional values grew stronger during the 1980s when these countries successfully achieved economic development, as we can see from the emphasis on *Pancasila* in Indonesia and on Islamic values in Malaysia and from the increasing political role of the king in Thailand.

40 It was only in 1995 that the Constitution was amended for the first time democratically and constitutionally without a military coup. In 1997 there was a further democratic amendment.

41 The Internal Security Acts of Malaysia and Singapore both have the same colonial origin, although they were slightly differentiated after the separation of these two countries in 1965.

42 The Brunei constitution is an exception. All constitutions other than that of Indonesia have comprehensive catalogues of human rights under the head of an independent chapter. By human rights I mean fundamental or basic rights as in a Bill of Rights, although there is a widening gap between these two conceptions of rights.

43 It is well known that arguments between mainly Western advocates of the universal nature of human rights and their Asian counterparts propagating Asian values were a critical agenda during the International Human Rights Conferences in Bangkok and Vienna in 1993. See Daniel A. Bell, 'The East Asian Challenge to Human Rights: Reflection on an East West Dialogue,' *Human Rights Quarterly* 18 (Aug. 1996), Joseph Chan (1998), Yash Ghai (1994) and Onuma Yasuaki (1996).

44 The earliest legislation is the 'Industries Promotion Act' in Thailand (1957), the 'Pioneer Investment Ordinance' in Malaysia (1958), the 'Investment Promotion Act' in the Philippines (1967), and the 'Foreign Investment Law' in Indonesia (1967), all of which were repeatedly amended in part or in total.

45 See the 'Public Companies Act' in Thailand (1979) and the 'Philippines Corporation Code' (1980). See also Nobuyuki Yasuda (1986) on the development of company laws with brief reference to securities regulation within the region. It should be noted that the city state of Singapore has kept a 'liberal approach to both domestic and foreign capitals, although her company law has been amended repeatedly with the intention to build a financial centre of the region since its enactment in 1968.'

46 Pedro Roff (1985). 'Rules & Regulations to implement the Intent & Provisions of S.5 creating the Technology Transfer Board within the Ministry of Industry (PD.52, 10 October 1978)' of the Philippines

provide for comprehensive guidelines on ToT by foreign investors. In other countries, foreign investment bodies exercise a regulatory power under similar guidelines.

47 Typical examples are the 'Promotion of Investment Act' (1986) in Malaysia and the 'New Omnibus Investment Code' (1987) both of which have been substituted for former investment laws.

48 See Elisabeth Uphoff (1991) on how the US Government influenced the amendment of the relevant legislation in Southeast Asian countries.

49 Only Thailand and the Philippines have a general family law applicable to all citizens, although they also have special laws applicable to Muslims in the Southern parts of their nations.

50 It seems that the Philippines is the only country which has a comprehensive 'Local Government Code' (1991) providing for all kinds of local governments elected by the local people.

51 It is true, however, that there will be serious problems if these systems are manipulated and abused by rural bosses, as can be seen in some cases of the *Barangai* Justice System in the Philippines.

52 ASEAN (Association of Southeast Asian Nations) was established in 1967, but it was only from the late 1980s that it started to produce documents such as agreements and protocols, which focused on economic issues. These activities have been accelerated since the early 1990s. Member states agreed to set up the 'ASEAN Free Trade Area (AFTA)' by the Agreement on the Common Effective Preferential Tariff Scheme (CEPT) for the ASEAN Free Trade Area in 1992. For intellectual property laws, they agreed on a 'Framework Agreement on Intellectual Property Cooperation' in 1995, and at a more general level in the same year on a 'Framework Agreement on Enhancing Economic Cooperation.' It is interesting that there is a general Agreement on the Protocol on the ASEAN Disputes Settlement Mechanism which was concluded in 1996. Its aim is to establish the different mechanisms drawn from the universal WTO system. See Nobuyuki Yasuda (1997). On co-operation in the field of the intellectual property law, see Michael Blakeney, 'The Legal Regulation of Technology Transfer Arrangements within ASEAN,' in this book.

53 http://www.imf.org/External/np/exr/facts/asia.HTM, 'The IMF's Response to the Asian Crisis' (1999). This document also proposes six lessons from this crisis, (1) more effective surveillance of countries' economic policies and practice; (2) financial sector reform, including better prudential regulation and supervision; (3) ensuring that the integration of international financial markets is orderly and properly sequenced; (4) promoting regional surveillance; (5) a world wide effort to promote good governance and fight against corruption; and (6) more

effective structures for orderly debt workout, including better bankruptcy law.

54 The Amendment of the Constitution started with a first meeting on 9 January 1997 (*Bangkok Post*, 12 Jan. 1997), and the Constitutional Drafting Committee completed its first draft on 20 April 1997 (*Bangkok Post*, 20 and 22 April, 1997). This was presented to the Constitution Drafting Assembly (CDA) for first reading on 7 May 1997 (*Bangkok Post*, 8 May 1997) and faced strong resistance from politicians and bureaucrats (*Bangkok Post* 23, 25 May, 25 June 1997). The Draft also received a strongly negative response from parliament (*Bangkok Post*, 3 Aug. 1997). Nevertheless, bowing to public pressure, parliament finally adopted the Draft with an overwhelming majority of 578 of its 651 Members. A *Bangkok Post* article of 11 October 1997 expressed the linkage between economic crisis and democratization. '... with the promulgation of the new constitution, the country will quickly be rid of this government which is perceived to have failed in all respects so that the process of economic recovery can begin in earnest.' This Constitution received the Royal Assent on 11 October 1997.

55 http://www.krisdika.go.th/law/text/lawpub/e11102540/

56 It should be noted that the Philippine Constitution of 1987 set up the Philippine Commission of Human Rights and Indonesia established such a commission by a Presidential Decree of 1994.

57 See 'Indonesia's May Revolution' *Far Eastern Economic Review*, 28 May 1998, pp. 12-23.

58 Parliament passed three laws concerning political reforms ón 28 January 1999, *Asahi Shimbun*, 29 January 1999. See also 'No Fear or favor' *Far Eastern Economic Review*, 11 February 1999, pp. 22-3.

59 See 'Indonesian Chinese, Fight or Flee,' *Far East Economic Review*, 30 July 1998, pp. 12-16. These conflicts are also interwoven with religious antagonism between the predominantly Muslim *Pribumi* and the predominantly Christian Chinese.

60 The Habibie government has softened its attitude on the East Timor problem and it has hinted at wide autonomy for this province and even the possibility of its independence. 'Sudden Impact,' *Far Eastern Economic Review*, 11 February 1999, pp. 18-20.

61 President Wahid, elected by the first democratic process in the Indonesian political history in 1999, has shown comparatively remarkable results of democratization, although he is still facing too many problems to see a bright future of Indonesian polity (10 April 2000).

62 Raghuram G. Rajan and Luigi Zingales (1998). They define the relationship by emphasizing the aspect of power relation (which relates to command principle), but the core of this relation seems to rest on the

family like community feeling among parties. See Wendy Dobson (1998:24-47). She identified four patterns; Japanese *Keiretsu*, Korean *Chaebol*, Chinese family firms, and Southeast Asian conglomerates.

63 Only Malaysia took a different approach, when it introduced foreign exchange controls on 1 September 1998, *South China Morning Star*, 2 September 1998. See IMF, 'The IMF's Response to the Asian Crisis,' 17 January 1999. (http://www.imf.org/external/np/exr/facts/asia.htm) for the general stance of the IMF on the Asian Crisis and its response to it.

64 The IMF clearly mentioned that among the aims of the reform is to 'increase(d) potential for foreign participation in domestic financial systems.' See IMF, *op. cit.* See also World Bank (1998a:105-9). Bankruptcy laws were enacted or substantially amended in Korea (February 1998), Indonesia (April 1998), and Thailand (October 1998), see Timothy Lane, Atish R. Ghosh, Javier Hamann, Steven Phillips, Marianne Schulze-Ghattas, and Tsidi Tsikata (1999:98).

65 In Indonesia, a special court for bankruptcy was established in 1998, *South China Morning Star*, 1 September 1998.

66 The IMF paper above under footnote 63 mentions that 'reform to promote governance and competition in the program countries included dismantling state-sponsored monopolies and cartels; privatizing state enterprise that had served as vehicles of 'crony capitalism'; strengthening competition law; improving corporate disclosure requirements...; and restructuring or dismantling corporate network...' Timothy Lane *et al.* (1999:112).

67 The Business Competition Act (BE 2542) in Thailand and the Law Concerning Prohibition of Monopolistic Practices and Unfair Business Competition (Law No. 5, 1999) in Indonesia, both of which passed Parliament in February 1999. Malaysia drafted the Trade Practices Bill in 1996, but the draft has not yet received consent of the cabinet.

68 From 1996 to 1998 the unemployment rate jumped from 7.5 to 15.5 per cent in Indonesia, 2.0 to 9.0 per cent in Korea, 2.6 to 6.4 per cent in Malaysia, 8.3 to 14.0 per cent in the Philippines and 2.0 to 9.0 per cent in Thailand, ILO (1998a). See also 'Will Government Help?' (Cover Story) *Far Eastern Economic Review*, 8 October 1998, pp. 10-16.

69 Throughout the whole of East Asia, life expectancy at birth increased from 59.6 to 68.8 years between 1970 and 1995, while the infant mortality rate (per 1,000 births) decreased from 76 to 34 cases during same period. The head-count index of poverty (percentage) decreased from 57.6 to 21.2 during 1975 and 1990. World Bank (1998b).

70 Lane, *et al.,* ibid, p. 115, note 104. See also ILO (1998a) for more statistical data on the affected countries.

71 See Roger Goodman, Gordon White, and Huck-ju Kwon (1998). This book deals with Japan, Korea, China, Taiwan, Hong Kong, and Singapore and thus with countries that have come under the influence of Confucianism. However, we may discuss Southeast Asian countries in the same way, when we look at their emphasis on a 'harmonious community' based on collectivist wet rice farming agriculture.

72 No East or Southeast Asian country with the exception of Korea had an unemployment insurance scheme, World Bank (1998b:89). Thailand enacted the Labor Protection Act in January 1998, but the ILO pointed out its inadequacy to protect labourers, ILO (1998b).

73 See ESCAP (1998) on Asian perspectives of social development.

REFERENCES

Adam, Barbara (1990) *Time and Social Theory*. Cambridge: Polity Press.

ASEAN Economic Bulletin 'Law and Development in ASEAN Countries,' (1993) November, p. 144.

Asahi Shimbun, 29 January 1999.

Bangkok Post, 12 Jan.; 20, 22 April; 8, 23, 25 May; 25 June; 3 August; 11 October 1997.

Bauer, Joanne R. and Daniel A. Bell (eds) (1999) *The East Asian Challenge for Human Rights*. Cambridge University Press.

Baxi, Upendra (1988) 'The Development of the Right to Development,' in: E.S. Venkataramiah (ed.) *Human Rights in the Changing World*. New Delhi: International Law Association, Regional Branch (India).

Beer, Lawrence W. (1992) *Constitutional Systems in Late Twentieth Century Asia*. University of Washington Press.

Bell, Daniel A. (1996) 'The East Asian Challenge to Human Rights: Reflection on an East West Dialogue,' *Human Rights Quarterly* 18 (August 1996).

Blakeney, Michael 'The Legal Regulation of Technology Transfer Arrangements within ASEA [in this book].

Burg, Elliot M. (1977) 'Law and Development: A Review of the Literature & a Critique of Scholars in Self-Estrangement,' *AJCL* 25, pp. 492-530.

Carty, A. (ed.) (1992) *Law and Development*. Aldershot: Dartmouth.

Chan, Joseph (1998) 'Asian Values and Human Rights: An Alternative View,' in: L. Diamond and M.F. Plattner (eds) *Democracy in East Asia*. Baltimore and London: The Johns Hopkins University Press.

Chiba, Masaji (1989) *Legal Pluralism: Toward a General Theory through Japanese Legal Culture*. Tokyo: Tokai University Press.

Chua, Amy L. (1998) 'Markets, Democracy, and Ethnicity: Toward a New Paradigm for Law and Development,' *The Yale Law Journal* 106, pp. 1-107.

Coedes, G. (1968) *The Indianized States of Southeast Asia*. East-West Center Press, University of Hawaii.

Dobson, Wendy (1998) 'Business Networks in East Asia Diversity and Evolution,' in: Rong-I Wu and Yun-Peng Chu (eds) *Business, Market and Government in the Asia Pacific*. London: Routledge, pp. 24-47.

ESCAP (1998) *Asian and the Pacific into the 21st Century : Prospects for Social Development* (Theme Study of the 54th Session of ESCAP), 20-28 April 1998, (http://unescap.org/theme/part2).

Far Eastern Economic Review, 'In God's Name: Kelantan continues push to implement Islamic law,' 2 September 1992, p. 13.

Far Eastern Economic Review 'Indonesia's May Revolution,' 28 May 1998, pp. 12-23.

Far East Economic Review 'Indonesian Chinese, Fight or Flee' 30 July 1998, pp. 12-16.

Far Eastern Economic Review 'Will Government Help?' (Cover Story), 8 Oct. 1998, pp. 10-16.

Far Eastern Economic Review 'No Fear or favor,' 11 Feb. 1999, pp. 22-3.

Far Eastern Economic Review, 'Sudden Impact,' 11 Feb. 1999, pp. 18-20.

Fisher, Stanley (1998) *The IMF and Asian Crisis* (1998), (http://www.imf.-org/External/np/speeches/1998/032098.HTM.6).

Ghai, Yash (1994)'Human Rights and Governance: the Asian Debates,' *Asian Foundation's Center for Asian Pacific Affairs Occasional Paper Series No.1*.

Goodman, Roger, Gordon White and Huck-Ju Kwon (eds) (1998) *The East Asian Welfare Model, Welfare Orientalism and the State*. London: Routledge.

Hall, D.G.E. (1981) *A History of South-East Asia, Fourth Ed.* London: Macmillan.

Hefner, Robert W. (ed.) (1998) *Market Cultures; Society and Morality in the New Asian Capitalisms*. St. Leonards, NSW: Allen & Unwin.

Hooker, M.B. (1978) *A Concise History of South-East Asia.* Oxford: Clarendon Press.

– (1986-7) (ed.) *The Laws of South East Asia, Vol. 1: The Pre-Modern Texts* (1986) and *Vol. II: European Laws in South East Asia*. Singapore: Butterworths Asia.

ILO (1998a) Report of the Director-General *First Supplementary Report: ILO Activities to the Financial Crisis in East and South-East Asia*, (GB.273/14/1, 273rd Session, Geneva, Nov. 1998) (http://www.ilo.org/public/english/20gb/docs/gb273/gb-14-1.htm).

– (1998b) Cross-Departmental Analysis and Reports Team, *The social impact of the Asian financial crisis, Technical report for discussion at the High-Level Tripartite Meeting on Social Responses to the Financial Crisis in East and South-East Asian Countries*, (Bangkok, 22-24 April 1998, AFC/Bangkok/1998 ILO Regional Office for Asia and the Pacific Bangkok) Chapter 3. http.//ww.ilo/public/english/60empfor/cdart/bangkok/chapter3.htm.

– (1999) 'The IMF's Response to the Asian Crisis,' 17 January 1999. (http://www.imf.org/external/np/exr/facts/asia.htm).

Johnson, Chalmers (1982) *MITI and the Japanese Miracle, the Growth of Industrial Policy, 1925-1975*, Tokyo: Turtle.

Lane, Timothy *et al.* (1999) *IMF-Supported Programs in Indonesia, Korea, and Thailand: A Preliminary Assessment.* Jan. http://www.imf.org/external/pubs/ft/op/opasia.

Lloyd, P.J. (1998) 'Competition Policy in APEC[:] Principles of harmonisation,' in: Rong-I Wu *et al.* (eds) *Business, Market and governemnt in the Asia Pacific,* London [etc.]: Routledge, p. 157.

Mabbet, Ian W. (ed.) (1985) *Patterns of Kingship and Authority in Traditional Asian Political Institution.* London: Croom Helm.

Masaji, Chiba (1989) *Legal Pluralism: Toward a General Theory through Japanese Legal Culture.* Tokai University Press, pp. 107-18.

Merryman, John Henry (1977) 'Comparative Law and Social Change: On Origins, Style, Decline & Revival of the Law and Development Movement,' *AJCL* 25, pp. 457-91.

Onuma, Yasuaki (1996) 'In Quest of Intercivilizational Human Rights: "Universal" vs. "Relative" Human Rights Viewed from Asian Perspective,' *Asian Foundation's Centre for Asian Pacific Affairs Occasional Paper No.2.*

Pye, Lucian W. (1985) *Asian Power and Politics: The Cultural Dimensions of Authority.* Cambridge, Massachusetts: The Belknap Press of Harvard University.

Rajan, Raghuram G. and Luigi Zingales (1998) *Which Capitalism? Lessons from the East Asian Crisis*, http://www.stern.nyu.edu/globalmacro/ (9/1998).

Rich, Roland (1988) 'The Rights to Development: A Right of Peoples,' in: James Crawford (ed.) *The Rights of People*. Oxford: Clarendon Press.

Roff, Pedro (1985) 'Transfer of Technology UNCTAD Draft International Code of Conduct,' *International Lawyer* 19/2.

Schumpeter, Joseph A. (1950) *Capitalism, Socialism and Democracy*. New York: Harper & Brothers.

Seidman, Robert B. (1978) *The State, Law and Development.* London: Croom Helm.

Sison, Carmelo V. (1990) *Constitutional and Legal Systems of ASEAN Countries*. The Academy of ASEAN Law and Jurisprudence, Univ. of the Philippines Law Complex, Quezon City.
South China Morning Star, 1st and 2nd Sept. 1998.
Tan, Poh-Ling (ed.) (1997) *Asian Legal Systems, Law, Society and Pluralism in East Asia*. Sydney: Butterworths.
Thonnies, Ferdinand (translated by J. Suginohara) (1957) *Gemainshaghuto to Gezerushahuto (Gemeinschaft und Gesellschaft: Grundbegriffe der reinen Soziologie)*. Tokyo: Iwamami Bunko
Trubek David M. (1972) 'Toward a Social Theory of Law: An essay on the Study of Law and Development,' *The Yale Law Journal* 82/1, pp. 1-50.
Trubek, David M. and Mark Galanter (1974) 'Scholars in Self-estrangement: Some Reflections on the Crisis in Law and Development Studies in the United States,' *Wisconsin Law Review* 4, pp. 1062-102.
Unger, Roberto (1976) *Law and Modern Society: Towards a Criticism of Social Theory*. New York: The Free Press.
Uphoff, Elisabeth (1991) *Intellectual Property and US Relations with Indonesia, Malaysia, Singapore and Thailand.* SEAP, Cornell University.
Van Hoecke, Mark and Mark Warrington (1998) 'Legal Cultures, Legal Paradigms and legal Doctrine; Towards a New model for Comparative Law,' *International and Comparative Law Quarterly* 47.
Varga, Csaba (ed.) (1992) *Comparative Legal Cultures.* Aldershot: Dartmouth.
World Bank (1993) *The East Asian Miracle.* Oxford University Press.
– (1998a) *Global Economic Prospects and the Developing Countries 1998/99: Beyond Financial Crisis*. New York: World Bank.
– (1998b) *East Asia: The Road to Recovery*. New York: World Bank.
– (1999a) *Social Issues Arising from the East Asia Economic Crisis and Policy Implication for the Future* (21-22 January 1999) Bangkok, Thailand. *Summary Discussions of Working Group*, (http://www/worldbank.org/eacrisis/meeting/group1/htm).
– (1999b) *Social Issues Arising from the East Asia Economic Crisis, A Work-in-Progress,* Draft to be updated February 1999, following consultations (21-22 January,1999) Bangkok, Thailand.
Yasuda, Nobuyuki (1997) *Disputes Settlement Mechanism in Asia Pacific Region-APEC DMS and ASEAN DSM*, APEC Discussion Paper Series, APEC Center, GSID, Nagoya University.
– (1986) 'Corporation and Law in ASEAN Countries,' in: Teuku Mohammad Radhie *et al.* (eds) *Corporation and Law in ASEAN Countries*. IDE, JRP Series 58, pp. 155-242.
– (1991) 'Malaysia's New Economic policy and the Industrial Co-ordination Act,' *The Developing Economies* XXIX/4, pp. 331-49.

– (1993) 'Law and Development in ASEAN Countries,' *ASEAN Economic Bulletin* 10/2, pp. 144-54.
– (1995) 'The Evolution of the East Asian Law region,' in: Karl Kroeschell and Albrecht Cordes (eds) *Vom nationalen zum transnationalen Recht*, *C.F. Muller*, pp. 279-95.
Yusuf, Adijaya (1998) 'Integrating the Country through Legal Reform: The Indonesian Experience,' ARSP Beiheft Nr. 72 *Law in a Changing World: Asian Alternatives, Proceedings of the Fourth Kobe Lecture being The First Asia Symposium in Jurisprudence.* 10 and 12 October, Tokyo and Kyoto, pp. 110-20.

CHAPTER 3

APEC, INDUSTRY POLICY, AND THE ROLE OF LAW

BERNARD G. BISHOP

A sea change may be underway in industry policy in many of the East Asian states within APEC. The old idea of industry policy where states sought to alter their industrial structure through the deliberate guidance and supervision of industry is giving way to newer ideas of maintaining international competitiveness through competition policy. The ability to implement old style industry policy was dependent upon the state's bureaucratic capacity and political capacity. Bureaucratic capacity refers to the competence and cohesiveness of the bureaucracy. Political capacity refers to the extent to which the state was insulated from rent seeking demands yet embedded enough within society to carry society along with its goals. The twin forces of democratization and deregulation have resulted in diminished bureaucratic and political capacity to undertake the detailed supervision of industries required by the industry policy of the past.

However a close examination of the details of competition policy reveals that its effective implementation also relies on policy makers being insulated from rent seeking pressures and consistency and cohesiveness within the bureaucracy. The difficulty for the new industry policy rests with achieving bureaucratic and political capacity in an environment where democratization and deregulation have tended to reduce the capacity of the state in policy implementation. This chapter suggests that adherence to a rule of law may provide sufficient capacity to successfully devise and implement competition policies. The competition principles recently adopted by APEC appear to rely to a considerable extent on greater adherence to the rule of law by politicians, bureaucrats, and business alike. There are both optimistic and pessimistic assessments of this occurring in the near future. It may be the case that the Asian crisis has provided the necessary impetus for the institutional change needed to bring about a greater prominence of the rule of law in the more developed capitalist societies in East Asia.

The chapter commences with an explanation of old style industry policy and its institutional underpinnings – bureaucratic and political capacity. It then proceeds to show how the twin forces of democratization and deregulation have undermined the capacity of the state to implement old style industry policy. Following this is an analysis of competition policy and

APEC's role in seeking to establish it as the new industry policy for member economies. Finally, an argument is made that greater adherence to a rule of law will be necessary in order to restore sufficient bureaucratic and political capacity to make the new style industry policy workable.

THE 'OLD' IDEA OF INDUSTRY POLICY

In the East Asian context, the term industry policy is most often identified with what Johnson (1992) describes as the tired old cliché of governments targeting particular industries for growth or 'picking winners.' The Japanese government's targeting of consumer electronics industries in the late 1960s and early 1970s, the Korean government's targeting of heavy and chemical industries also during the 1970s, the Malaysian government's national car project in the 1980s and multimedia super-corridor in the late 1990s, and Indonesia's aircraft industry are all often cited examples of the practice. Picking winners, however, is not confined to East Asian countries. Weiss (1992) uses examples from the United States and Europe to highlight the pervasiveness of this form of government intervention. He includes the US space programme and high technology defence industries, the European airbus project, and the various attempts to develop industrial clusters and high technology hubs as evidence of the tendency of all governments to engage in targeting practices.

This narrow view of industry policy fails to explain whether industry policy has been different in East Asia and if so in what ways. There is now considerable agreement that East Asian countries have gone much further than utilizing industry policy to occasionally select particular industries for promotion. Rather in the developmental states of Japan, Korea, and Taiwan governments liaised closely with business not only to determine which industries should be promoted and which wound down but also to plan on a broader level the future industrial structure of the economy. The reason was simple. Key policy makers in those countries were of the view that without change in industrial structure they may not have been able to catch up with the more advanced nations and would forever have been locked into production of agricultural products and light manufactured goods (Amsden, 1994). The resulting failure to raise living standards would have drastically limited their tenuous holds on power. Accordingly, the developmental states clearly aimed to shift comparative advantage by deliberate intervention to change the industrial structure via an industry policy that entailed, in Johnson's words, the 'development, guidance, and supervision of industry' (Johnson, 1992:20).

Korea provides a useful example here. In the early 1960s, Korea was an impoverished nation recovering from the devastation of the Korean War. The Park Chung Hee government in conjunction with advice from international development agencies (Haggard, 1994:274) and in close co-operation with business embarked upon a strategy of export promotion to first of all develop light manufacturing industries. The foreign exchange obtained was used to finance the development of heavy industries such as steel, chemicals, and metals with both the sources and uses of finance closely controlled by the state. These provided the basis for industries such as shipbuilding and automobiles that in turn were encouraged to become exporters. Once these became successful in the international market place, the government turned its attention to broadening high technology capabilities particularly among small and medium firms in an attempt to create an industrial structure on par with other advanced industrialized countries such as Japan and the USA.

In this respect Korea, and also Taiwan, followed a similar strategy to that pursued earlier by Japan. The larger Southeast Asian countries of Indonesia, Malaysia, and Thailand have also sought to deliberately intervene to move their industrial base away from primary products and towards manufactures for export. In addition, they have intervened in the market place to develop heavy industries such as automobiles and petrochemicals. In Malaysia's case, there has been a recent move towards developing a high technology base.

While there is considerable agreement that the East Asian countries have extensively utilized an industrial policy of this genre, there is much disagreement about its effectiveness (Smith, 1995). The issue is whether successful internationally competitive industries developed as a result of industry policy or in spite of it. The in-depth studies by Johnson (1982, 1995) on Japan, Amsden (1989) on Korea, and Wade (1991) on Korea and Taiwan suggest that those countries had an active industry policy and further that it was an integral part of their success in achieving high rates of growth over several decades. Others attribute East Asia's economic 'miracle' to sound underlying macroeconomic policies and careful attention by governments to the underlying factors necessary for growth including the provision of infrastructure, education, a healthy environment for technological development, and an equitable distribution of income (World Bank, 1993). They favour the view that if industry policy was used it only succeeded if it was in conformity with what the market would have produced in any event (Ostry, 1994).

To review the many arguments and counter arguments that have been advanced in this debate is beyond the scope of this work. The issue of most significance here concerns the underlying institutional factors that allowed industry policy to be practised in the manner that it was. To the extent that industry policy has been successful, it may well be due to particular institutional features of the Northeast Asian developmental states that were only present in part in Southeast Asia. These features warrant some discussion because, as will be seen, they also have considerable bearing on the effectiveness of the 'new' industry policy.

To successfully devise and implement an industry policy in the East Asian style requires a high degree of both bureaucratic capacity and political capacity. During their period as developmental states, Japan, Korea, and Taiwan can all be argued to have possessed high levels of bureaucratic and political capacity. Bureaucratic capacity includes not only the competence of the bureaucracy in being able to plan the details of industrial development but also a high degree of cohesion within and between government agencies to implement the necessary supporting policies. Political capacity refers to the extent to which those who formulate and implement policies are insulated from internal and external social pressures yet are 'embedded' enough within society to ensure that those policies reflect market conditions.

The structure and stability of the political and bureaucratic arms of the state are critical to bureaucratic capacity. Without a well-structured state in which different agencies have clearly defined responsibilities, coherent policies will not be able to be formulated. Without continuity in political leadership, it is difficult to ensure a sufficient time frame for policies to be implemented consistently. In terms of stability, Japan had a single political party in power from the 1950s until the 1990s, Taiwan's KMT has continuously held power since the late 1940s, and in Korea Park Chung Hee ruled from 1961 until 1979 and was followed by another army general, Chun Doo Hwan from 1980 until 1987.

But as Johnson (1982) notes, while the politicians may have reigned, it is the bureaucrats who ruled in the developmental states. The bureaucracy was carefully structured with a lead agency in a co-ordinating role. Many attribute this role to MITI in Japan and the EPB in Korea. In Taiwan, while a lead agency did not exist to the same extent, the KMT itself played a major role in resolving disputes between Ministries. In all three countries, the best talent was recruited into the bureaucracy with this being facilitated by a pre-existing culture of respect for the bureaucrat's role in the social order. The prestigious social positions that bureaucrats held also promoted loyalty although this was reinforced with careful screening and training to ensure that civil servants remained 'politically correct.'

Political capacity also depends very much on the features of the political system. In Japan, Korea, and Taiwan government agencies were insulated to a significant extent from social pressure and rent seeking activities partly due to the social position that bureaucrats held but more significantly because of the widespread acceptance within the bureaucracy, and society generally, of an ideology of developmentalism whereby personal goals and aspiration were subordinated to the greater welfare of society. In addition, Japan, Korea, and Taiwan were insulated from external economic and political pressures due in large part to the geopolitical circumstances at the time of the cold war. This allowed them considerable latitude to do as they pleased in internal policy matters as long as those policies reinforced their positions as strong and vibrant 'frontline' states (Wade, 1992). Geopolitical circumstances also contributed significantly to the stability of the political order.

As Evans (1995) argues, insulation from societal pressures is a necessary but insufficient condition to bring forth sound economic policy and outcomes. Policy makers must also be 'embedded' within society to ensure that policy goals align with market capabilities. In Japan, Korea, and Taiwan, the bureaucracy was firmly connected to industry through both formal and informal mechanisms. In these three countries, key economic agencies had formal links with industry through industry associations thereby enabling them to monitor individual firms' compliance with policy initiatives (Weiss, 1994). All firms were required to belong to an industry association in order to obtain an operating licence and were subject to the discipline of the industry association (Singh and Weisse, 1999). The leaders of industry associations were often directly or indirectly appointed by the relevant ministry thereby guaranteeing co-operation in industry development plans. Formal consultations also occurred between industry and the bureaucracy as to future industry development such as the Japanese and Korean deliberation councils where key business leaders and bureaucrats thrashed out future plans for the development of industry and the economy generally (Weiss, 1994). Informal ties existed in all three countries. In Korea the old school tie network meant that key bureaucrats and industry leaders often shared an educational history. In Japan, ex-bureaucrats were often appointed to the boards of major corporations while in Taiwan the pervasiveness of the KMT ensured that key industries and key bureaucrats were linked together through the party.

It is arguable that the degree of bureaucratic capacity and political capacity was less in Southeast Asia than in Northeast Asia. While Indonesia, Malaysia, and Thailand all have had industry policy devised and implemented by a core of technocrats, the bureaucracies were never as insulated as those in Northeast Asia (Macintyre, 1994). Patrimonial ties in Suharto's Indonesia, Mahathir's Malaysia, and in the era of military government, in Thailand led to extensive rent seeking (Haggard, 1994). In addition the bureaucracies may not have been as co-ordinated as in Northeast Asia as Smith (1995) and Macintyre (1994) have pointed out in the case of

Indonesia. Further, the control of finance as an important instrument of industrial policy may not have been as strong and the links between industry associations and the bureaucracy were also less developed than in Japan, Korea, and Taiwan.

A further explanation for the variance in bureaucratic and political capacity between Northeast and Southeast Asian countries is the degree to which the political leadership, the bureaucracy, and society at large were united by an ideology of developmentalism. In Northeast Asia the economic policies of authoritarian regimes were accepted by the population at large who were prepared for a time to defer narrow self-interest in the interests of national wealth (Krugman, 1994). It is arguable that in the Southeast Asian nations where significant ethnic and social divisions existed between the business class and the rest of the population, an overriding ideology of developmentalism was unable to be firmly implanted thus leading to a greater willingness of the business, bureaucratic, and political elite to engage in rent seeking and predatory behaviour. This may provide one explanation for the relatively less effective implementation of industry policy in those countries than in the Northeast Asian developmental states. However, as Booth (1999:310) notes, while there are differences between Northeast and Southeast Asia, the relative ability of the various states to implement growth related policies was much greater in these two regions than in other parts of the developing world.

THE DEMISE OF THE OLD INDUSTRY POLICY

The institutional foundations of the old industry policy have been described above as high levels of bureaucratic and political capacity particularly in Northeast Asia. However, since the mid-1980s serious cracks have begun to appear in these foundations. Perhaps the most significant of these is the weakening of the East Asian states' political capacity as a result of the pressures flowing from the trend towards democratization in the region since the mid-1980s.

In 1986 and 1987, both Korea and Taiwan made significant moves towards democracy with the transition to democratically elected governments complete in the early 1990s. At this same time, the monolithic political power of the LDP came to an end when a coalition of opposition parties formed the government in Japan. In Thailand, the end of the reign of the army generals came in the late 1980s and, despite a brief interlude of a non-elected government in the early 1990s, the country has utilized the electoral process for political change since that time. In Indonesia, the fall of the Suharto regime brought about the first democratic elections in more than three decades. Within the more developed group of Southeast Asian countries, Malaysia and perhaps Singapore remain the only ones where quasi-authoritarian regimes remain in power.

The impact of democratization on the capacity to implement the broad ranging style of industry policy practiced in East Asia is significant. It is now much more necessary for political leaders and parties to take into account the demands of a wide range of interest groups. With differing demands for support from big business, small business, labour, environmental, and regional groups, governments are faced with making policy compromises. The detailed press scrutiny that accompanies democratization imposes further on the state's ability to single-mindedly pursue policies that favour one sector of industry over another, or over other interest groups, without significant political consequences. With democracy also comes a greater awareness by the population at large of their civil rights and liberties. The coercive agencies of the authoritarian state and supporting propaganda in the form of a developmental ideology may have kept political unrest at bay during this phase of development but a greater awareness of the ability to assert rights and freedoms makes it more difficult to carry the population along with government policies that overtly favour capital over, for example, the interests of consumers. In Japan, for instance, consumers are becoming much less sympathetic to a system that has delivered national wealth but not quality of life (Ohmae, 1995). Thus, democratization reduces the state's insulation from interest group demands and accordingly reduces political capacity.

A further key element of the state's political capacity to implement industry policy was the close relationship between business and government described earlier. While the old structures remain in place for the most part, there are increasing pressures on the governments of most East Asian states to separate the functions of the state from those of the private sector. Foremost among these is a general international trend towards deregulation led by the US government, international organizations including the World Trade Organisation and the IMF, as well as regional groupings such as APEC and NAFTA.

The end of the cold war, together with spiralling trade deficits with many Northeast Asian countries, led the US to become more strident in demanding access to Asian markets for its goods and services. The enactment of Section 301 of the US Trade Law was designed specifically to allow the US government to place countries on notice that if they did not sufficiently open their markets to US products they would face retaliatory actions against their exports. Thus Asian countries were placed in a position of reviewing their regulatory measures with regard to trade matters. In addition US concerns regarding the restrictiveness of the Japanese and Korean distribution systems has resulted in those countries reviewing various regulations regarding access to their markets although not without some bitter international feuding as demonstrated by the US–Japan dispute over auto parts (Mollins, 1994).

While the successful conclusion of the GATT Uruguay round and its establishment of a more powerful World Trade Organisation has tended to result in a more ordered format for the resolution of bilateral disputes, it has also resulted in increased pressure on member states to deregulate many areas of their economy. The new agreement has significantly narrowed the ability of governments to intervene in economic activity by expanding the potential coverage of the WTO to such areas as agriculture, textiles, services, intellectual property rights, and trade related investment measures. The effect of the WTO agreement is to aim to achieve an ordered reduction in the barriers to entry in these sectors through deregulation. This in turn makes it more difficult for states to maintain the instruments previously utilized for industry policy. In the past these included import controls in the form of quantitative restrictions and non-tariff barriers, controls over technology development, export promotion measures, and controls over foreign investment particularly in the services sector. These are the very areas where adherence to the WTO agreement will require deregulation.

A further key instrument of industrial policy was the state's control over credit and the practice of directing it to sectors of the economy which were priorities in terms of industry policy. While moves have been underway in Japan, Korea, and Taiwan to deregulate the finance sector since the early 1990s, the Asian crisis has given significant impetus to this. Many observers attribute the underlying causes of the Asian crisis to the lending policies of banks and more particularly to the practice of governments interfering with bank lending policies in their pursuit of industry policy and other more political objectives. One of the main conditions that the IMF has imposed on Thailand, Indonesia, and Korea is to restructure the banking sector including the removal of the power of politicians and bureaucrats to directly interfere with lending policies. Thus the Asian crisis has produced further pressure for deregulation not only on IMF recipient countries but also in Japan and Malaysia where there are also major structural problems in the finance sector.

Regional organizations including APEC are adding to the deregulatory pressures confronting member states. Formed in 1989, APEC's major goals are the liberalization and facilitation of trade and investment in the region and economic co-operation. In particular, it has the aim of free trade and investment for developed countries in the region by 2010 and for developing countries by 2020. While APEC is often criticized for its slow progress towards these goals due to its consensus based decision making process, there are many co-operative initiatives being implemented by the working groups established under the auspices of its Committee on Trade and Investment (APEC, 1998). The output from these groups and other advisory bodies including the APEC business advisory council (ABAC) and the Pacific Economic Cooperation Council (PECC) feeds into regular senior officials and ministerial meetings and the annual leaders meeting. There is therefore significant contact at governmental level among APEC's member economies to advance the goal of a liberalized trade and investment environment. Although there are major domestic constraints (such as industry policy) on the pace of liberalization and deregulation, the pressure for deregulation that a consensus based process imposes should not be underestimated.

The combined forces of deregulation and democratization have meant that the state now has reduced political capacity to implement a coherent industry policy. This does not mean that the state will desist altogether from promoting various industries at various times if there is an advantage in doing so. However, to successfully implement an industry policy that covers many sectors including the politically difficult task of winding down some industries while promoting others may well be beyond the political capacity of the more democratic societies emerging in East Asia.

The bureaucratic capacity of the state to implement a coherent industry policy has also declined. The developmental states of Korea and Taiwan in the 1960s and 1970s were economies of relatively small size and complexity. It was not beyond the competence of a highly trained team of technocrats to closely monitor changes in the international competitiveness of various industry subgroups and put in place policies that either promoted or wound down particular industries. However as the economy matured and became more internationalized, it became much more difficult for bureaucrats to monitor the business activities of individual firms that were increasingly locating parts of their operations in overseas countries beyond the reach of the bureaucratic agencies of their home states.

Bureaucratic capacity also requires a high degree of cohesiveness within the bureaucratic agencies of the state. As was seen earlier this was achieved by key co-ordinating agencies. In Japan and Korea, these co-ordinating agencies have themselves been downgraded in the 1990s with Korea abolishing the Economic Planning Board and Japan's MITI suffering setbacks as some of its 'mistakes' in industry policy were more widely publicized (Callon, 1995). In addition the general international deregulatory climate has seen increasing criticism of the role of bureaucrats interfering in the private sector (Tanzi, 1998). For bureaucrats this leads to a tendency to protect one's turf thereby reducing the potential for co-operation across government agencies. Increasing democratization also leads to greater scrutiny of bureaucratic activities leading perhaps to less enthusiasm for old style industry policy in the bureaucracy because of the more severe consequences of policy error.

It may be argued that the bureaucracy in Southeast Asian countries has always been less co-ordinated than in the developmental states of East Asia where a long tradition of an elite bureaucracy was entrenched. Co-ordination may therefore have been more a matter for the political leadership rather than government agencies. For example, while there has been significant growth of an indigenous entrepreneurial class in Malaysia and Indonesia, both they and the traditional Chinese business class continue to look to the political leadership rather than the bureaucracy for industry support (Jesudason, 1997). In addition, the highly developed international networks of the overseas Chinese, the dominant business class in Southeast Asia, has always made co-ordination difficult in any event thereby resulting in a less comprehensive industry policy. Further, the Southeast Asian states as later developers than the states in Northeast Asia, faced a more open and more rapidly changing international economic environment making it more difficult to implement an industry policy that relied upon the protection of selected industries from international competition until those industries themselves became internationally competitive.

While both the political capacity and the bureaucratic capacity necessary for devising and implementing industry policy across a broad range of industries has declined sharply in many of the East Asian states, this does not mean that the practice is likely to disappear altogether as the examples from the developed countries mentioned above demonstrate. Regardless of the economic merits of any particular case, it seems that it is just too tempting for governments to stay away completely from some form of industry promotion if there is political mileage to be gained by pump priming a certain industry interest group. Nonetheless, in both Northeast and Southeast Asia the institutional underpinnings of the old style of industry policy have been severely shaken. The question that naturally follows is what, if anything, is taking its place.

APEC AND THE NEW INDUSTRY POLICY

The old idea of industry policy relied upon detailed development, supervision, and guidance of industry in order to effect changes in the state's industrial structure to maintain the international competitiveness of its industrial base. Mody (1999) has argued that a new idea of industry policy is emerging that seeks to maintain competitiveness not through industry development and guidance but rather through ensuring that firms and the industries to which they belong are exposed to healthy competition. If firms are constantly faced with competitive pressures from internal and external sources, they will be placed in the position of keeping up with the competition or going out of business. Thus, Mody argues, competition policy is rapidly gaining international acceptance as the new form of industry policy.

Competition policy seeks to maintain competitiveness in a number of ways. The first of these is to prevent any firm abusing a position of dominance in an industry. Dominance can arise from the state granting enterprise monopoly rights through a firm gradually increasing its market share or through merger and acquisition. Examples of abuse of a dominant position include preventing new firms from entering the industry or eliminating existing competition through pricing or other policies. If a firm is able to use its dominant position in this fashion in a domestic market, then the overall efficiency and international competitiveness of that industry will decline making consumers within that market relatively worse off.

There are difficult issues involved in determining whether a firm is abusing a position of dominance. Initially it is necessary to establish that a position of dominance exists. Different countries have different guidelines to resolve this (Wood, 1995). Further, abuse of dominance rather than dominance itself is the objective of competition policy. To seek to prevent firms obtaining a position of dominance at all would provide a major disincentive to firms to grow and hence to overall growth and competitiveness. In addition, a political issue arises as to whether free competition should be allowed in industries that are considered to be of strategic importance to the state. For example, many countries maintain a less than competitive environment in industries considered to be of national importance such as transport, telecommunications, energy, media, and agriculture. Preventing the abuse of dominance therefore involves fairly sophisticated analysis of industrial structure while keeping an eye on political priorities. The aim however is clear. It is to maximize the number of industries where free competition is allowed and in those industries prevent any firm from abusing a position of dominance.

The second element of competition policy is to prevent firms from entering into restrictive agreements including agreements to fix prices, quantities, or market share. This also includes agreements to eliminate some sellers or buyers from the market and arrangements that involve a refusal to deal. The objective here is to prevent firms from entering into cartel type arrangements because they are seen as limiting competition and hence reducing the industry's overall international competitiveness. Again there are difficult issues to be resolved. For example, the protection of intellectual property rights is often accompanied by the right to grant exclusive licences.

This appears to amount to a restrictive business practice. There are therefore difficult choices to be made between providing continuing incentives for innovation and ensuring that consumers receive quality products on the one hand, and the availability of goods and services at the best possible prices for consumers, on the other.

The third feature of competition policy is to prevent firms from engaging in unfair practices such as providing misleading information damaging to other firms or making false claims with respect to goods or services. If firms are able to gain unfair advantage through the dissemination of misleading information about competitors, this provides them with an artificial advantage in the market place, which in turn affects the true competitiveness of the industry.

There is a growing consensus in the APEC region towards the adoption of competition policies in member economies. Perhaps the first tentative steps towards this goal were taken by the Group of Eminent persons appointed by member economies to advise on the future direction that APEC should take. The 1993 report of this group recommended that a necessary accompaniment to trade and investment liberalization was a strengthening of competition policies in the region. This view was accepted and in 1994, APEC's Committee on Trade and Investment was mandated to establish a working party on competition policy with a view to developing an understanding in relation to competition policies among member economies. The working party has held several workshops on competition policy and has developed a database of the competition policies and laws of all those member economies that have them. In 1996, in recognition of the fact that deregulation and competition policies were complementary policy measures, APEC merged the deregulation and competition working groups. The Asian crisis gave added impetus to the work of this committee and in 1999, the Pacific Economic Co-operation Council used its official status in APEC processes to put forward a set of competition principles for the consideration of member economies. These principles were subsequently endorsed at the formal APEC meetings that took place in Auckland in September 1999.

The PECC competition principles (PECC, 1999) are an important milestone in building understanding on competition policy in the region. They endorse the notion that competition policy is central in enhancing economic efficiency and is a necessary accompaniment to trade and investment liberalization. Rather than stating the details of what competition policy should be, the PECC competition principles set out broad underlying principles upon which more detailed laws regarding such matters as abuse of market dominance, restrictive business practices, and unfair competition can be based. One reason for adopting general principles rather than the specifics of competition lies in the fact that different members of APEC have different views about what amounts to abuse of dominance or restrictive business practices (Rosenthal and Matsushita, 1995). For example, many of the bilateral disputes between Japan and the US such as the automotive parts dispute referred to earlier, rest upon very different views as to the extent to which restrictive business practices should be permitted in the interests of industry efficiency.

The four core principles set out in the PECC report are comprehensiveness, transparency, accountability, and non-discrimination. Comprehensiveness refers to the need for competition policies to apply to all goods and services. Transparency means that the policies and laws based upon them should be clear in substance and consistent in the way in which they are implemented. In addition, those devising and implementing the laws should be accountable for their operation and should apply them in a non-discriminatory manner between domestic and internationally sourced goods and services.

It is immediately apparent that the principles of this new industry policy are diametrically opposed to those upon which the old idea of industry policy was based. Frequently, the old industry policy was selective rather than comprehensive and its operation lacked transparency for those outside the narrow confines of the network of business government relationship in any particular industry. Further, those implementing the old industry policies had significant discretion and frequently lacked accountability either to an elected government or to any form of administrative review. The old industry policies were often deliberately designed to be discriminatory in order to protect local industries from foreign competition until those industries could compete in the international market place.

Somewhat curiously however, it can be argued that many of the institutional features necessary to implement the old industry policy are equally as important to implement an effective competition policy. The institutional underpinnings of the old industry policy were described earlier as bureaucratic capacity and political capacity. The extent to which these are present in the APEC member economies may well determine the effectiveness or otherwise of the new industry policy.

High levels of both bureaucratic competence and cohesiveness are needed to devise and implement competition policy. The old industry policy required bureaucrats working with business to select sectors of industry for promotion or for winding down as they lost competitiveness. While this is a complicated task subject to many errors of judgment, so too is the task of determining if, for example, an industry has a particular firm or group of firms that hold a dominant position in the market. Even if arbitrary levels of market share (such as 30 per cent) are set as indicating that a firm holds a dominant position, considerable skill is needed to determine the relevant market and what percentage any firm holds in such a market. The market dominance question remains a major difficulty in countries that have had active competition policies for many years and is exacerbated by the fact that firms that may be dominant may be controlled from outside of the territorial jurisdiction of the state.

In addition, the old industry policy involved the development of industries as well as supervision and guidance. The new competition policy has shifted the role of the bureaucrats away from development and guidance and much more towards supervision. A bureaucracy trained in the old ways cannot be reasonably expected to change its mindset and approach overnight. Competition policies require bureaucrats to detect and weed out uncompetitive practices rather than work closely with industry to select areas for growth and then support industry in achieving that growth. Bureaucrats must therefore be more independent of their constituent industries than may have been the case under the old industry policy. The networks that have been built up over generations and the expectations that bureaucracy and business has of each other will make the new roles assumed by competition policy difficult to accept.

Cohesiveness in the bureaucracy is also needed to implement a sound competition policy. As pointed out in some detail in the US submission to the Competition and Deregulation Workshop in Christchurch (APEC, 1999), it is necessary for significant inter-agency co-operation to occur in antitrust matters. In the light of this, suggestions have been made that the agency responsible for competition policy should assume a high status within the overall structure of the bureaucracy in order to ensure that the overriding goals of competition policy are built into all other policy initiatives (Cooke and Elliott, 1999). Some have suggested that the competition agency should also play a major role as an advocate of competition policy within the bureaucracy offsetting the inevitable arguments that will come from other parts of the bureaucracy for protection of their industry constituents (Hoekman and Holmes, 1999).

While some of APEC's member economies have had a tradition of 'key' agencies playing leadership roles in industry policy, few have given a competition authority such status. In countries such as Japan and Korea where there have been competition authorities for several decades, those agencies were often overridden by the more important agencies associated with the old industry policy. It should theoretically be feasible for countries to change the role of these lead agencies from implementing the old industry policy to implementing a competition policy. As indicated earlier however, the skills and different roles required may make this quite difficult to achieve in practice.

As was the case for the old style industry policy, competition policy also requires a high level of political capacity in order to be effective. If those formulating and implementing competition policy are insufficiently insulated from societal groups with an interest in the outcomes of those policies, then it is likely that rent seeking will occur with competition policy being tailored to suit particular interests rather than achieving the broader societal goals referred to earlier. There are clearly winners and losers from competition policy (Jenny, 1995) and this therefore requires policy makers to have the ability to make choices between competing groups. For example, the large industrial combines in Japan and Korea are likely to oppose laws that attack either their market dominance or their vertical distribution arrangements. Likewise, business interests closely allied to the former Suharto regime in Indonesia are likely to lobby against attempts to break up the lucrative monopolies created for them by that regime. Although there is now significant pressure from powerful external sources including the IMF for Korea and Indonesia to reform past business practices this is proving difficult in practice in the more democratic settings that exist in these two countries.

It was noted earlier that increasing democratization in East Asian countries has resulted in a reduction of the political capacity to implement difficult policies. This may have serious implications for competition policy unless sufficiently strong democratic institutions can be constructed to provide the necessary degree of insulation for policy makers. In this respect it has to be noted that democratic institutions took many years to develop in the older democracies in the region with refinements occurring on a continuing basis. It may be difficult for the newer democracies to change their institutions quickly enough to keep pace with the rapidly developing international policy environment in which competition policy is emerging as an important force in dealing with the effects of globalization.

Bureaucratic capacity and political capacity can therefore be argued to be as necessary for the implementation of an effective competition policy as they were for the implementation of old style industry policy. However, the twin forces of democratization and deregulation have significantly eroded both of these elements of state capacity. The question is whether a degree of competence and cohesiveness in the bureaucracy and political insulation from rent seeking can be obtained in other ways. It is suggested here that an argument can be made that greater reliance upon a rule of law may fill this gap. However, a rule of law tradition is relatively new to many states in the APEC grouping. The following section sets out the basis for divergent views as to the role of law and the prospects for its enhanced role in maintaining the bureaucratic and political capacity necessary to implement competition policies as a new form of industry policy.

ROLE OF LAW

The role that law plays in the relationship between citizens and the state differs and can be argued to depend largely on the tradition of political culture in the country concerned. In the APEC region two major traditions stand out in any analysis of the role of law in determining state-citizen relations. These are traditions that have been loosely derived from Chinese political culture and traditions derived from European and more particularly Anglo Saxon traditions. The Chinese tradition has historically seen law used as an instrument of state power. A major influence here has been Confucian principles whereby rulers were encouraged to lead by example rather than by reliance upon the law itself. Certainly law had its uses but these tended to be confined to prescribing standards of behaviour for different classes, setting out broad principles of state organization and governance and imposing obligations on citizens in relation to revenue and other matters directly relevant to the maintenance of state power.

Citizens were therefore conditioned to see law as a tool that an all-powerful state might use against them if they failed to follow the standards of behaviour appropriate to their station in life. Political culture in traditional China thus revolved around the power of the state. Rulers were only accountable to the population for the maintenance of stability in the broadest sense. There was no independent body to monitor the exercise of state power although an extra-legal and elaborate system of checking the behaviour of others evolved to minimize challenges to the state and ensure that state officials performed their duty in accordance with the standards set for them. Any direct challenge to officials in their exercise of state power was impossible, as citizens would inevitably end up worse off. In their day-to-day business and social affairs citizens had little use for the law. Business relationships developed on the basis of trust rather than contract and the settlement of disputes was actively encouraged to occur through mediation presided over by those in a superior social position.

Japanese and Korean political culture was derived from China. In the seventh and eighth centuries Japan adopted many of the principles of the Tang dynasty codes and principles of governance while the Yi dynasty in Korea adopted their successor, the Ming codes, in the fourteenth century. If anything, the Yi dynasty in Korea and the Tokugawa shogunate in Japan, allowed far less freedom to the citizenry and had their own elaborate systems in place to preserve state power. The five hundred years of the Yi dynasty and the two hundred and sixty years of Tokugawa rule in Japan entrenched an authoritarian political culture that has been difficult to change even with the advent of more democratic institutions in the past fifty years in Japan and even more recently in Korea.

During the time of the Qing, Tokugawa, and Yi dynasties in Northeast Asia, Southeast Asian societies were being actively colonized by Europeans – the Dutch in Indonesia, the Spanish in the Philippines, and later the British in Malaysia. At the time of colonization these countries consisted of a series of kingdoms and among them only Thailand bore any resemblance to the all-powerful dynasties to the North. Yet the detailed *adat* laws existing in Indonesia and Malaysia and the major legal codes in Thailand tended to have had the effect of preserving the power of local rulers. While the British in Malaysia and the Dutch in Indonesia displaced the power that these rulers enjoyed, they did little to change an authoritarian political culture. The colonizers were far from accountable to local populations and their administrations were as unchallengeable as those of the dynasties of Northeast Asia.

The old idea of industry policy fits in neatly with the traditional role of law and political culture in East Asia. State direction and power was seen as the established order of things and it was only natural for this power to be extended to the regulation and ordering of economic activity in the aim of economic development. As tradition might have predicted, law was used as a back-up device. The intricate web of regulations that accompanied industry policy in Northeast Asia was there to force business to comply if persuasion failed. Bureaucrats were provided with wide discretion in the administration of the law (Pistor and Wellons, 1999:106). There were frequently layers of laws, regulations, enforcement decrees, and internal procedures which, while giving the bureaucracy discretion in a general sense, maintained some consistency. However, to those outside the bureaucracy, internal procedures and the interpretation of regulations remained a mystery thereby leading to them being characterized as lacking 'transparency' and predictability. In addition in accordance with tradition there was little redress for those aggrieved by the decisions of the bureaucracy.

As noted earlier, political culture in East Asia is changing rapidly towards increased accountability of governments, bureaucrats, and business to the law. Politicians are becoming more accountable through the development of democratic institutions such as electoral systems and constitutions. Bureaucrats are becoming more accountable through the gradual evolution of greater power to elected politicians, a system of review of administrative decisions by the courts (Pistor and Wellons, 1999:248-61) and the scrutiny of a free press. The breakdown of old patterns of business government relations means that business itself is being held more directly accountable to the law rather than to its bureaucratic masters. In addition, there has been a slow but steady trend towards the development of the courts as independent monitors of accountability of politicians to the constitution and bureaucrats and business to the law.

The new industry policy is consistent with this evolution towards a rule of law approach.

The underlying values of the PECC competition principles highlight this. The first of these is comprehensiveness. This implies that competition policy should apply equally to all sectors of the economy. Equality of application is also a fundamental principle underlying a rule of law approach and democratic values. The second of the principles is transparency. This suggests a much larger role for clear rules and a rule of law rather than obscure layers of regulation designed to give the bureaucracy maximum power and discretion. The third of the competition principles is accountability. One of the fundamental values of a rule of law approach is accountability of lawmakers, bureaucrats, and business. Finally competition policy should also be non-discriminatory. Again this suggests that the same rules should apply to both domestic and international suppliers which is a departure from the different-rules-for-different-players approach that prevailed under the old industry policy.

It can be argued that the future success of the new industry policy is intricately bound up with the acceptance of a rule of law approach. It was suggested earlier that both bureaucratic and political capacity is necessary to successfully implement the new style of industry policy. A rule of law enhances bureaucratic capacity by promoting consistency in bureaucratic actions. It also ensures that all parts of the bureaucracy are accountable to the same standards and in that respect may promote cohesiveness. However adherence to a rule of law may be a necessary but insufficient condition for the cohesive implementation of the new industry policy. As was the case for the old style industry policy, the structuring of the agencies of the state is crucial. If competition authorities have little status among the agencies of the state, competition policy issues may be overridden by those agencies whose policy measures are aimed at more short-term political gain. Political capacity will also be enhanced by adherence to a rule of law. If competition law is transparent, and politicians, bureaucrats, and business are accountable to the law, then a measure of protection against rent seeking and predation is provided. However, this requires not only acceptance of a rule of law approach but also an independent judiciary with the ability to monitor the business–bureaucracy relationship to ensure that actions taken are in accordance with the law (Cooke and Elliott, 1999). What then are the prospects in the APEC region for the evolution of the institutions, attitudes and political culture necessary for a rule of law?

Carothers (1998) argues there is more to a rule of law than the enactment of pertinent legislation. Rather he suggests that bureaucrats must accept that the law applies to their conduct and that the judiciary acts as an independent monitor to ensure that this is the case. Further, governments themselves must seek to be law abiding and that it is more through enlightened leadership rather than technical measures that a rule of law approach will become entrenched. Carothers's prognosis is pessimistic. His view is that the breaking down of entrenched political interests, the transformation of values, and the evolution of sufficiently enlightened leadership to bring about a change to wide acceptance of the rule of law will take generations.

On the other hand, Pistor and Wellons (1999) find in their study of the role of law in Japan, China, Taiwan, India, Malaysia, and Korea that there has been a shift to what has been described here as a rule of law approach. In their study they examine the role of law in economic development from two dimensions. The first of these is to regard economic activity as either state based or market based. In a state-based system, the role of law will be to support the state's control over the economic activity of firms. In a market-based system law will play the major role of preserving order in the market place. The second dimension of the role of law concerns the legal process itself. They see economic law making and enforcement as either discretionary or rule based. In discretionary based legal systems, those administering the law have wide discretion and are largely immune from any form of judicial review. In rule-based systems, politicians, bureaucrats, and business are all subject to the law with an independent judiciary ensuring that this occurs. Pistor and Wellons conclude that there has been a shift in the six Asian countries from state-based to market-based law. More significantly they also find that in all countries studied other than Malaysia, there has been a trend away from a discretionary based role of law to a rule-based role of law.

Their findings can also be interpreted as evidence of a change in political culture away from authoritarianism and state guidance of economic activity towards democracies and a market led economy. Democracy implies that governments and bureaucrats are accountable to citizens and it follows that institutions will develop to enforce this. A rule of law and its associated values are one such institution. A market-based system also relies for its proper working on a rule of law. Under a state based economic system, bureaucrats are able to closely guide business activity to ensure that there is order, predictability, and certainty in the market place. However, under a market based system the state is precluded from playing such a close supervisory role. Some other mechanism must therefore be found to maintain order and certainty. Again a rule of law approach allows the state to withdraw but at the same time do so without affecting order in the marketplace provided that governments, bureaucrats, and business all accept this approach.

Both Pistor and Wellons, and Carothers agree however that the transition process to a rule of law is a slow one. On the issue of institutional change generally, Akyuz, Chang, and Wright (1998) note that changes in the role of institutions will occur slowly and in a piecemeal fashion. They argue that fundamental changes to the economic system involve not only a change in substantive law but changes in traditional values and modes of behaviour. However, what may have been overlooked is the increased rapidity with which social and political change now seems to be able to occur. Davis (1998:322) refers to Krasner's view of institutional change as 'punctuated equilibrium.' Krasner argues that institutions tend to remain relatively stable and only change radically at times of significant social disruption. It may yet be the case that the Asian crisis will provide the impetus that brings about a rule of law approach and establishes competition policy as the new industry policy in the APEC region.

CONCLUSION

The East Asian states used old style industry policy in an attempt to bring about changes in their industrial structure. To this end, the state played a key role in the development, guidance, and supervision of industry and its constituent firms. The degree to which industry policy succeeded may well have been determined by the bureaucratic and political capacity of each individual state.

The decline of the institutional underpinnings of old style industry policy in East Asia has left the door open for competition policy to emerge as a new approach in the maintenance of international competitiveness. However, just as bureaucratic capacity and political capacity were necessary to implement the close supervision and guidance of industry under the old industry policy, they are also essential institutional foundations for the successful implementation of competition policy.

This chapter has advanced an argument that bureaucratic and political capacity may be strengthened if a rule of law and its associated institutions develop in the East Asian states. However, the traditional role of law has been much better suited to old style industry policy being grounded in a political culture that entailed authoritarian regimes and state directed economic activity. Nothing short of a change in this political culture can bring about a change in the traditional role of law.

While democracy and deregulation have tended to weaken bureaucratic and political capacity, they may also yet produce a new political culture that develops the institutions associated with a rule of law. It is these institutions that may provide the necessary bureaucratic and political capacity to implement competition policy as the new industry policy in the APEC region. The speed at which these institutions develop, or whether they develop at all, may provide the most effective indicator of potential success in achieving the objectives of competition policy.

REFERENCES

Akyuz, Y., H.J. Chang and R. Wright (1998) 'New Perspectives on East Asian Development,' *Journal of Development Studies* 34/6, pp. 4-37.

Amsden, A.H. (1989) *Asia's Next Giant: South Korea and Late Industrialization*. New York: Oxford University Press.

– (1994) 'Why isn't the whole world experimenting with the East Asian model to develop?: A review of the East Asian Miracle,' *World Development* 22/4, pp. 627-33.

Anon. (1999) 'Regulatory Practices and their effect on market access in a globalizing economy,' a paper presented by the United States representative at the APEC Competition and Deregulation Workshop, Christchurch.

APEC Committee on Trade and Investment (1998) *1998 Annual Report to Ministers*. Singapore: APEC Secretariat

Booth, A. (1999) 'Initial Conditions and Miraculous Growth: Why is South East Asia Different From Taiwan and South Korea,' *World Development* 27/2, pp. 301-22.

Callon, S. (1995) *Divided Sun: MITI and the Breakdown of Japanese High-Tech Policy 1975-1993*. Stanford: Stanford University Press.

Carothers, T. (1998) 'The rule of law revival,' *Foreign Affairs*, March/April, pp. 95-106.

Cooke, S. and D. Elliott (1999) *Study on Competition Laws for Developing Countries*. Singapore: APEC Secretariat.

Davis, M.C. (1998) 'The Price of Rights: Constitutionalism and East Asian Economic Development,' *Human Rights Quarterly* 20/2, pp. 303-37.

Evans, P.B. (1995) *Embedded Autonomy: States and Industrial Transformation*. New Jersey: Princeton University Press.

Haggard, S. (1994) 'Business, politics and policy in Northeast and Southeast Asia,' in: A. MacIntyre (ed.) *Business and Government in Industrializing Asia.* Sydney: Allen & Unwin.

Hoekman, B. and P. Holmes (1999) *Competition Policy, Developing Countries and the WTO*. World Bank Policy Research Working Paper, No. 2211, Washington: World Bank.

Jenny, F. (1995) 'Domestic Competition, International Trade and Economic Development,' *International Business Lawyer*, Nov., pp. 474-6.

Jesudason, J.V. (1997) 'Chinese Business and Ethnic Equilibrium in Malaysia,' *Development and Change* 28, pp. 119-41.

Johnson, C. (1982) *MITI and the Japanese Miracle: the growth of industrial policy 1925-1975*. Stanford: Stanford University Press.

– (1992) *Capitalism: East Asian Style*, Paper prepared for the Panglaykim Memorial Lecture, Jakarta, 15 December.

– (1995) *Japan: Who Governs?: The rise of the developmental state*. New York: Norton.

Krugman, P.R. (1994) 'The Myth of Asia's Miracle,' *Foreign Affairs*, Nov/Dec, pp. 62-79.

MacIntyre, A.J. (1994) *Business and Government in Industrializing Asia*. Sydney: Allen & Unwin.

Mody, A. (1999) *Industry Policy after the East Asian Crisis: from Outward Orientation to New Internal Capabilities*. World Bank Policy Research working paper No. 2112, Washington: World Bank.

Mollins, C. (1994) Unfavorable trade winds: a chronic trade surplus adds tensions between Japan and the United States,' *Macleans* 107/9, p. 36.

Ohmae, K. (1995) 'Letter from Japan,' *Harvard Business Review*, May-June, pp. 154-63.

Ostry, J.D. (1994) 'Are Growth Strategies of East Asia relevant for New Zealand?' *Finance and Development* 31/1, pp. 13-16.

Pacific Economic Cooperation Council. (1999) *PECC Competition Policies for Guiding the Development of a Competition-Driven Policy Framework for APEC Economies*. Singapore: PECC International Secretariat.

Pistor, K. and P.A. Wellons. (1998) *The Role of Law and Legal Institutions in Asian Economic Development*. Hong Kong: Oxford University Press.

Rosenthal D.E. and M. Matsushita. (1996) 'Competition in Japan and the West: Can the Approaches be Reconciled?' *World Competition* 19, pp. 5-27.

Singh, A. and B.A. Weiss. (1999) 'The Asian model: a crisis foretold?' *International Social Science Journal*, June, pp. 203ff.

Smith, H. (1995) 'Industry Policy in East Asia,' *Asian Pacific Economic Literature* 9/1, pp. 17-39.

Tanzi, V. (1998) *The Demise of the Nation State*. IMF Staff Policy Paper 98/120, Washington: International Monetary Fund.

Wade, R. (1991) *Governing the Market: Economic Theory and the Role of Government*. New Jersey: Princeton University Press.

– (1992) 'East Asia's economic success: conflicting perspectives, partial insights, shaky evidence,' *World Politics* 44, pp. 270-320.

Weiss, J.M. (1992) 'Who's Afraid of Industrial Policy?' *Europe*, June, pp. 28-32.

Weiss, L. (1994) 'Government–business relations in East Asia: the changing basis of state capacity,' *Asian Perspective* 18/2, pp. 85-188.
Wood, D.P. (1995) 'Competition and the Single Firm,' *International Business Lawyer*, November, pp. 456-7.
World Bank. (1993) *The East Asian Miracle: Economic Growth and Public Policy*. New York: Oxford University Press.

CHAPTER 4

THE RULE OF LAW, ECONOMIC DEVELOPMENT, AND THE DEVELOPMENTAL STATES OF NORTHEAST ASIA

JOHN K.M. OHNESORGE

Rule of Law rhetoric is all around us – in the business press, in the programs and publications of the World Bank, International Monetary Fund (IMF) and Asian Development Bank (ADB), in bilateral development assistance projects, and even in US–China diplomatic dialogue. Notably, however, the Rule of Law is not being touted in these primarily for its traditional political role as a protector of human rights and individual dignity. Rather, the new rhetoric makes the claim that the Rule of Law is a crucial element in economic development, not only in formerly socialist countries ('transition economies') (World Bank, 1996), but in developing capitalist countries as well.[1]

More recently, a separate torrent of Rule of Law language has been unleashed, this time in reaction to the Asian financial crisis. Some of this is serious and well intentioned,[2] while some of it has a distinctly gloating tone.[3] It should be clear, however, that these two claims cannot both be true. If the claim that East and Southeast Asian societies lack the Rule of Law is true, this presents a serious challenge to the first claim, given that these parts of Asia have been the economic development success story of the twentieth century. A compromise position might be to posit that the Rule of Law becomes necessary once a certain level of economic development and complexity has been reached, now the case in a country like South Korea. This position would fit well with the idea being put forth elsewhere that an 'Asian model' was effective for catching-up, but that the model suffers from inherent flaws that make it ineffective for an advanced economy. But even this more nuanced approach, to the extent that it admits a lack of the Rule of Law in, for example, Taiwan of the 1960s and 1970s, presents a clear challenge to claims for the necessity of the Rule of Law for economic development.

This chapter will attempt to evaluate some of these economic claims for the Rule of Law in the context of post-World War II Northeast Asia, defined as Japan, South Korea, and Taiwan. The focus will be on economic governance in these countries during the decades of high economic growth, the 1960s and 1970s, the era that spawned the moniker 'developmental state.'[4] A necessary starting point for such an exercise is a working understanding of the Rule of Law as a concept, found in the second part of the chapter. The third part moves from a discussion of the Rule of Law to an examination of how the concept is being used in the Rule of Law-economic development literature. The nature of that literature requires that this effort be somewhat impressionistic, but two interrelated concerns are apparent: the Rule of Law as the protection of private property rights, and the Rule of Law as a limit on government discretion.

The fourth part of the chapter explores to what extent the Rule of Law in these two senses functioned in the 'developmental states' of Northeast Asia. The conclusion is that the Rule of Law as a system of fairly stable property rights and contractual relations functioned well, but that this was not necessarily a result of the Rule of Law in any full sense. Other functions of the Rule of Law, for example as a curb on government discretion in economic governance, were just as clearly not met, however. Out of the empirical investigation of the fourth part, the fifth part argues that there are serious problems with the present Rule of Law-economic development rhetoric, problems that are related to the fact that the rhetoric doesn't reconcile easily with the Northeast Asian experience. The chapter concludes with a call for further use of empirical knowledge of Northeast Asia to test universalist theories in the social sciences generally, not only in the relationship between law and economic development.

AN INITIAL PROBLEM: WHAT IS THE RULE OF LAW?

The first task in this exercise must be a definition of the Rule of Law. Below I discuss two related, but somewhat distinct, ways of thinking about the Rule of Law, the first more traditionally jurisprudential, the second more in the socio-economic tradition.

To many jurists and philosophers of law, the term 'Rule of Law' brings to mind an array of particular yet related concerns about how a just legal system should operate.[5] These concerns with the administration of justice mark this approach as more procedural than substantive, and most would agree that these are aspirations, and that failures to meet the aspirations are found in all legal systems.[6] In this tradition, therefore, to say that a society is characterized by the Rule of Law could only mean a high number of these goals being met a high percentage of the time, and it is rare to find jurists using the term as a benchmark for comparing different legal systems.[7]

An alternative way of thinking about the Rule of Law is as describing the condition of a society governed by a complete and functioning legal infrastructure, governing relations both among private actors, and between private actors and public authorities. The independent judge as enforcer of the rules and of privately bargained out contracts is important in this way of thinking about the Rule of Law, but the phenomenon of judging itself, and the challenges that the act of judging pose for the Rule of Law, is not the focus. It is in this sense, which could be described as heavily positivist formalism,[8] that the term is being used in the economic development literature.[9]

The relationship between these two paradigms is complex. Legal scholars tend to approach the Rule of Law in the first mode, testing the extent to which the various aspirations of the model are met by examining judicial decisions, often focusing on difficult cases. This approach highlights judicial discretion, judicial law making, and weaknesses in the system of rules, even if many who write in this tradition would accept that rules are often relatively clear, and often do shape social action in predictable, understandable ways. The jurisprudential approach tends not to address the broad issues of economic performance that are the focus of the Rule of Law-economic development literature.

Thinking about the Rule of Law in the second mode, as shorthand for a functioning legal infrastructure, requires one to proceed as if the aspirations of the first model were met without serious qualification in certain 'Rule of Law' societies. The goal is to reduce the Rule of Law to a fact about an economy, similar to its literacy rate, or the level of union membership in its workforce, thus facilitating a certain kind theorizing about the relationship between the system of courts and rules, and socio-economic behaviour (Knack and Keefer, 1995).

In spite of obvious conflict between the two approaches, the second approach appears able to exist alongside, but also in isolation from, the first for at least two reasons. First, its practitioners tend to be economists, political scientists, or historians, not jurists.[10] Thus they tend to lack formal training in law, at least not the experience of actually reading lots of cases deciding economic disputes in which the applicable rules, defining the rights of the parties, were surprisingly unclear or debatable. Not being jurists, they also have not had the additional education of working as a judicial clerk or as an attorney, situations which teach that the administration of a legal system is much more than the application of rules to facts, and that contracts are not always clear, written memorials documenting the results of market bargaining over property rights. Second, if those who approach the Rule of Law as legal infrastructure took the issues raised by the jurisprudential approach too seriously, it could undermine their effort to understand the relationship between the framework of rules and social life, just as ideas of bounded rationality tend to undermine simplistic rational actor models of politics and economics.[11]

SUBSTANTIVE CONCERNS OF THE RULE OF LAW-ECONOMIC DEVELOPMENT RHETORIC[12]

As an alternative to focusing on definitions, which might reflect an unrealistic concern with conceptual clarity, a more productive approach may be to identify the substantive concerns underlying the Rule of Law–economic development literature. The rhetoric generally revolves around two core themes: defining and enforcing private property rights, and reducing bureaucratic discretion in economic governance.[13] The 'property rights–Rule of Law' branch can be again divided into at least two separate strands. A more theoretical and abstract strand focuses on property rights for their role in the functioning of a market economy (World Bank, 1996:44-65), while a second strand focuses on the effective enforcement of statutory law creating and protecting more particular economic rights, such as statutes on intellectual property or competition law. The second main branch of the Rule of Law-economic development rhetoric addresses itself to limiting bureaucratic discretion, to binding official action within the strictures of the law and the machinery of justice. In this sense it tends to overlap with contemporaneous discussions of transparency, anti-corruption, and 'good governance.'

Private Property Rights and Economic Development

Rule of Law rhetoric focusing on the creation and protection of property rights can be seen as guided by two different clusters of themes and concerns. The first addresses itself to property rights as the basic object of market activity. This literature is grounded on the truism that market exchange implies at least some basic right of control over the object to be exchanged. The literature then addresses itself to the 'security' of these property rights as a precursor to economic success or failure. The second area where Rule of Law rhetoric arises in connection with property rights focuses on the effective enforcement of statutory regimes creating particular rights, or enforcing certain market conditions.

The Rule of Law as the Creator of Property Rights, Building Block of Markets

The primary focus of this branch is on positive law enshrining private property rights, courts to enforce those rights according to the pre-established law, and state organs ready to enforce the rulings of the courts.[14] Enforcement *vis-à-vis* other private actors, which includes both the enforcement of contracts and the enforcement of criminal law,[15] is seen as necessary for the free contractual exchange of property rights, the basic activity in a market economy.[16] Enforcement *vis-à-vis* the state is seen as necessary to prevent arbitrary state interference with private property.[17] In the words of the World Bank, 'markets cannot develop very far without effective property rights. Those rights can only work with three preconditions: first, protection from theft, violence, and other predatory acts; second, protection from arbitrary actions, ranging from ad-hoc regulation and taxes to outright corruption that disrupts business activity; and third, a fair and predictable judicial system (World Bank, News Rel: No 97/1380/S).'

Writings in this more abstract branch of the property rights-Rule of Law rhetoric, in their emphasis on legally created and enforced property rights as part of the structure of a market economy, reflect the influence of 'new institutionalism' in economics and political economy, and more specifically, the claims of Douglass North (1990:139), Mancur Olson (1993:567, 574) and others concerning the importance of property rights in the economic development of the West.[18] Although North's extremely broad definition of an 'institution' seems clearly drawn from Weber's sociological approach, or perhaps from Karl Popper (1976:103-4) (institutions include 'any form of constraint that human beings devise to shape human interaction,' (North, 1990:4) including formal legal rules as well as social norms), North still sees the institutional structure in essentially positivist-formalist terms, demonstrating his affiliation with the 'legal infrastructure' approach to the Rule of Law. For North, institutions are 'the framework within which human interaction takes place. ... perfectly analogous to the rules of the game in a competitive team sport' (North, 1990:4). These rules determine the cost and incentive structures of societies, and can be more or less congenial toward productive behaviour.[19]

Of particular interest to those with East Asian expertise is how easily government with any degree of autonomy from the private sphere, a hallmark of the 'developmental state,' becomes the villain in this story in terms of economic development. Government unresponsiveness to private interests (the 'transaction costs of the political marketplace') explains for North, in large part, the inability of a society to move to a more efficient property rights regime.[20] Taking seriously the prescriptive implications of this view would encourage even well-intentioned international bureaucrats to suppress reservations about intervening in domestic political affairs, as inefficient property rights are now seen as the result of unjustified transaction costs in the local political system, ripe for progressive reform. The shape and content of a country's entire domestic legal regime can thus be reduced from sovereign political to purely technocratic economic matters.[21] It seems clear from reading the literature that the speculations of North, Olson, and others have provided important theoretical justification for the drastic expansion of the IMF's involvement in domestic legal and political affairs that is finally being brought to mainstream attention by the crisis in East Asia.[22]

The Rule of Law as Effective Enforcement of Statutory Regimes

The second strand of the 'property rights' branch of the Rule of Law-economic development literature attempts to connect economic development to the aggressive enforcement of legal regimes that protect rights and interests beyond those normally seen as necessary to constitute a market economy.[23] These claims are probably most prevalent in the areas of intellectual property rights (IPR) and trade, but are heard often now in connection with competition law.

Enforcement of a statutory regime in Rule of Law terms is enforcement on non-political, purely formal legal grounds, uninfluenced by substantive political concerns and without instrumental aims. For example, a Rule of Law IPR regime would mean, in these terms, not only positive law creating rights, but also a court system that is practically available to private litigants, that reaches its decisions on the basis of the law alone, uninfluenced by non-legal objectives, and that has effective enforcement powers.[24] Legal assistance programs thus often emphasize the training of the legal functionaries, the examiners, judges, and prosecutors, of developing countries,[25] presumably in the hope that they will begin to aggressively enforce existing IPR regimes in a Rule of Law manner, i.e., without reference to extraneous substantive considerations such as whether the law is being invoked by a foreign entity against a domestic manufacturer trying to localize an expensive, or perhaps unavailable, technology.

A good example from the area of international trade is the way in which the US State Department invokes the Rule of Law to suggest why joining the WTO will benefit China:

> To meet WTO requirements, China must make laws public, require judicial review of all trade actions, apply all trade laws uniformly, and submit to WTO dispute settlement to ensure compliance with WTO rules. *All of these measures will enhance the rule of law* and the application of international norms in China's trade regime, to the benefit of China and the United States. *The rule of law in trade has spillover benefits to the rule of law elsewhere.*[26]

In the area of competition law we find a similar set of concerns: effective enforcement means not only an appropriate statutory framework, but also an enforcement authority that is adequately staffed, adequately insulated from political and private pressures, and that seeks to actively enforce a non-cartelized, non-monopolized market economy (World Bank, 1996:92-3).

The Rule of Law as invoked here tends to mean, in historical terms, the active enforcement, primarily for the benefit of foreigners, of positive law that countries have adopted in order to comply with international norms, or to benefit from participation in the international economic system, but which has been implemented in ways which are not seen by the international community as appropriate.

Limiting Discretion in Economic Governance

The second main branch of the Rule of Law-economic development rhetoric focuses on using law and the courts to legalize government processes and strictly limit official discretion, often put in terms of increasing the transparency or accountability of governance.[27] A good example of this vision of the Rule of Law can be found in the World Bank's *World Development Report 1997: The State in a Changing World*. In the Report, the Bank puts forth a two-prong strategy for defining the proper role of the state in a developing economy: i) matching the state's role to its capabilities, and ii) increasing state capability by reinvigorating public institutions (World Bank, 1997:3). Not surprisingly, however, 'reinvigorating public institutions' involves a heavy dose of 'new institutionalist' Rule of Law thinking, which itself draws heavily on 'public/rational choice' analyses of politics.[28] The report emphasizes first and foremost the need to bind state actors within a system of 'effective rules and restraints,' before moving on to list other approaches to improving the performance of state institutions (World Bank, 1997:3, 7-11).

Limiting official discretion is not always put forth as a goal in itself; rather, what is usually put forth is one of the assumed benefits of limiting official discretion, such as reducing opportunities for official corruption,[29] or increasing the predictability of the regulatory environment by preventing arbitrary state action, thus encouraging private investment activity. In this way, limiting official discretion tends to become synonymous with 'good governance,' and it is here that the IMF in particular seems to have found justification for the 'mission creep' that has brought it into the Rule of Law business. Although there is no necessary connection between the desire to bring bureaucratic discretion within the Rule of Law and a deregulatory substantive agenda, cynicism about the ability of an activist government to refrain from rent-seeking seems to result in a blending of the two, so that subjecting government discretion to the Rule of Law is presented as requiring substantive deregulation.[30]

Arguments for the importance of transparency in governance are most persuasive in discussions of foreign investment climates,[31] while they appear less persuasive than the 'property rights-Rule of Law' rhetoric with regard to the purely domestic functioning of an economy. After all, what is opaque to outsiders may be perfectly transparent to national economic actors, particularly large ones.[32] Perhaps reflecting this issue of perspective, transparency from the outsider's perspective is raised to an economic necessity by the claim that it is a key to a country's attractiveness to foreign investors, who, in turn, are presented as being necessary for economic development.

WHAT THE NORTHEAST ASIAN 'DEVELOPMENTAL STATES' SUGGEST ABOUT THE RULE OF LAW AND ECONOMIC DEVELOPMENT

Following this rough outline of the major themes of the Rule of Law-economic development literature, we now turn to an evaluation of these claims in light of Northeast Asia's experience in economic development post-1945.

Private Property Rights and Effective Enforcement of Statutory Regimes

In the third part above, the concerns addressed by the Rule of Law-economic development literature were first divided into two branches, one concerned with property rights, the other concerned with limiting government discretion in economic governance. The property rights branch was then divided into two strands, one focusing on property rights as the basis for market behaviour, the other on the effective enforcement of particular statutory regimes.

Creation and Protection of Private Property Rights

This strand of the 'property rights-Rule of Law' rhetoric emphasizes the role of law in creating and protecting the private property rights owned and traded by private actors in the market. Independent courts are a key component of this vision of the Rule of Law, as protectors of the sanctity of contract, and as a check on arbitrary interference by the state with private property.

At first glance, Northeast Asian economic development seems to support the connection between economic development and this 'property rights' version of the Rule of Law, given that Japan, South Korea, and Taiwan were all market economies based largely on private ownership, though with some important qualifications, such as state ownership of banks in both South Korea and Taiwan, and a very large state enterprise sector in Taiwan. The importance of the particular rights created by the positive law, and the necessity of active, independent courts for the protection and functioning of these rights, is less well supported, however.

First, at least some forms of private property were long present in Northeast Asian societies prior to the importation of Western law, as were sophisticated trading systems (Scogin, 1990:1325; Henderson, 1968:203), yet traditional Northeast Asian formal law did not concern itself primarily with the creation and enforcement of private property rights. When Western rights-oriented law was adopted in Northeast Asia, it accompanied other modern economic institutions such as modern banking and accounting practices, modern corporate forms, modern manufacturing technology, etc., which might have functioned in Northeast Asia even without the same legal infrastructure with which they grew up in the West. The existence of traditional socio-cultural norms and practices favourable to private property and market behaviour at least raises the possibility that the more complex legal relationships of a modern economy were effectively instituted and have functioned in Northeast Asia without being as dependent upon the legal system as the Rule of Law-economic development literature would posit as necessary, in particular, with comparatively less enforcement by the judicial system. While some clearly understate the role law has played in the economic systems of Northeast Asia,[33] the experience there does at least suggest that the creation of clear positive law as well as highly user-friendly and powerful courts may not be strictly necessary in societies with an existing social/cultural consensus favouring private property and trade.

Second, it is no coincidence that Northeast Asian societies have been the inspiration for much speculation about socio-cultural factors as supplements to, or functional equivalents to, judicial enforcement of contracts.[34] Although the literature on 'relational contracting,' 'social capital,' and Chinese business networks tends to praise the pervasiveness of these extra-legal sources of stability in exchange relations, suggesting a gain from legal informality (Winn, 1994:193; Upham, 1994:233), it is interesting to remember here Franz Neumann's argument that the formal Rule of Law may have been demanded by economic actors in the 'competitive capitalism' of the nineteenth century West, as Weber argued, but that 'monopoly' capitalists did not need formal legality to protect their rights in the market, and actually benefited from greater informality.[35] Thus, against all the potentially positive aspects of relational contracting and legal informality in Northeast Asia we should counterpoise the potentially negative aspects of private ordering unconstrained by law. We should also take this into account when trying to understand to what extent demand for the Rule of Law at even this basic level existed in the 'developmental states.'[36] This is not simply an interesting academic question, however. As the international economic institutions try to compel both mass privatization/deregulation and the Rule of Law in countries like Russia and the People's Republic of China (China), we should keep in mind that the first objective, especially if it takes place too quickly, may result in societies dominated by private economic actors not only indifferent, but hostile to, the Rule of Law (Liu and Link, 1998:19-23).

Northeast Asian societies are also cited for their low rates of civil litigation, and even if these claims are overstated, they suggest caution in making strong claims for the necessity of easily accessible and effective judicial dispute settlement for a functioning market economy.[37] Low litigation rates in Northeast Asia arguably have more to do with material disincentives such as legal fee structures and inconvenient court procedures and fees than with cultural aversions to judicial conflict resolution, though arguably these material disincentives are themselves the result of political/cultural factors shaping the implementation of the imported legal institutions. In any case, however, low levels of litigation suggest either that the formal legal norms are so clear and well integrated into these societies that they are law-governed without much resort to the courts, ironic considering the usual thinking that the assimilation of Western law has been difficult in Northeast Asia, or that the particular form of the positive law and the threat of court enforcement has not been of primary importance in market behaviour there. The relatively low incidence of civil litigation in Northeast Asia should at least caution against simplistic approaches to understanding the complex relationship between courts, rules, and market behaviour.

Turning to the clarity and judicial enforcement of contracts, a theme often emphasized in the economic development literature that deals with the Rule of Law, one would expect the greatest clarity of rights in fairly simple transactions, where it is plausible that the language of the contract and the relevant law would be sufficiently clear so that a judge could simply enforce bargained-for rights. This, however, is precisely the level at which so much is made of the importance of relationships in Northeast Asia, and the reluctance to litigate contract disputes. As the level of complexity of exchange increases, a paradox arises. According to North's evolutionary model, which seems to be accepted by the World Bank, social norms or other non-legal institutions can be relied upon to enforce simple exchange contracts, but increasing complexity of exchange will not be possible without reliable, authoritative judicial enforcement.[38] This certainly seems right, but on the other hand, as the complexity of the contract to be enforced increases, it seems to become increasingly difficult for a judge to perform his/her Rule of Law role of simply sorting out bargained-for rights based on the existing infrastructure of rules.

At least according to the perceived wisdom, Northeast Asian economic actors have not dealt with increasing transactional complexity by attempting to draft contracts that cover all possible contingencies, as we tend to do in the US, and which would thus assist a court in parsing out rights in a complex transaction. The amount of even relatively complex, long-term contracting done on the basis of fairly simple written contracts suggests that the demand for full clarity of rights, especially through judicial enforcement, has been lower in Northeast Asia than would seem necessary from reading the Rule of Law-economic development literature.

In the context of present-day East Asia, the rhetoric of clear property rights is often employed with regard to the transformation of Chinese State-owned enterprises (SOEs), and the necessity of creating stable private property interests in these entities so that the dysfunctional incentives of current managers can be replaced by the appropriate incentives of private shareholders (World Bank, News Rel: No 98/1425). However, this emphasis on the necessity of creating clear private property rights in Chinese SOEs, based as it seems to be on prevailing US corporate governance theory, is also called into question by the Northeast Asian experience in corporate governance. Few would argue that Japanese, South Korean, or Taiwanese corporate managers have been effectively disciplined by shareholders in the way that liberal corporate governance theory calls for. They were not disciplined by market forces created by widely dispersed shareholders buying and selling shares in highly liquid markets, nor by 'markets for corporate control,' nor by shareholder derivative suits, despite the existence of provisions for such suits in the corporate laws.[39] This has long been discussed in the comparative corporate governance literature, where the focus has been on the comparative effectiveness of Japanese corporate governance, particularly the *keiretsu* structure of stable cross-shareholding arrangements and 'main bank' monitoring of management. To the extent, therefore, that the property rights-Rule of Law rhetoric makes strong claims for the necessity of corporate governance arrangements based on current US thinking, the history of corporate governance in East Asia suggests that such claims are overdrawn.[40] This call for caution is supported by the candid admission of one writer for the OECD that, 'the interrelation of corporate governance and corporate performance ... is a subject which is in its infancy and it is unquestionably premature to base policy decisions on the evidence which is available to date' (Mayer, OECD Working Paper: No 164).

One also encounters property rights-Rule of Law language in discussions of foreign investment climates, claiming that foreign investment is conditional upon the Rule of Law.[41] But the Northeast Asian experience shows that what passes for the Rule of Law in this context should be understood as essentially a political commitment to keep order and to not expropriate foreign investments, and should not be confused with a Rule of Law in any deeper sense.[42] This simple commitment probably is necessary for economic development that depends to any degree on private initiative, but should not be confused even with a Rule of Law limited to strict judicial protection of private property rights.[43] In China, for example, one finds enormous foreign and domestic investment in the shadow of a political and quasi-legal commitment to protect private property in the constitution and various statements in specific laws and regulations, but no sense that at this point this commitment is met through a domestic Rule of Law in the sense that foreign (or domestic) investors could count on effective judicial protection of their property interests. There are grave difficulties with the enforcement of purely domestic civil judgments against private parties in China,[44] to say nothing of judgments against the government. Whether or not China would have more foreign investment if it had a more developed legal system cannot be proven, but at least over the last fifteen years foreign investment and domestic economic activity have proceeded in the presence of a political commitment in favour of development and to protect foreign-invested property, but in the absence of even a 'property rights' Rule of Law.[45]

Portfolio investment by foreign investors is also often said to depend upon clear, enforceable shareholder rights, although this claim too seems problematic in light of the Northeast Asian experience. Foreign portfolio investors have invested in Northeast Asian stock markets with little interest in exercising their rights as shareholders, primarily to gain exposure to fast growing economies and to diversify their portfolios. The 'developmental state' model forced this approach by limiting foreign portfolio investment, so it is impossible to say how investors would have behaved in the absence of such limits. Clearly the 'developmental states' developed rapidly with limited foreign portfolio investment, which served political objectives of industrial and technological autonomy and self-sufficiency, and relative insulation from international market forces.

Finally, the current financial crisis has demonstrated how willing banks have been to lend to private borrowers around Asia, a form of foreign investment, despite the absence of legal regimes requiring a great deal of transparency, or providing effective creditor protection in cases of bankruptcy.[46] The Asian Development Bank would have us believe that, '[C]ommercial lenders ...will not come to a country unless it can offer an attractive ... lending climate, an important component of which is an effective and protective legal and regulatory framework (Asian Development Bank, 1997), but such a broad claim risks over-emphasizing legality at the expense of a realistic assessment of business interests. The current crisis shows that we would all have been better off had lending banks insisted on transparency and clearly enforceable rights in their Asian lending operations, but the crisis itself puts lie to the claim that lenders' own interests lead them to demand these elements of the Rule of Law.[47]

Effective Enforcement of Statutory Regimes

Rule of Law rhetoric is also commonly invoked in connection with attempts to encourage developing countries to enforce certain statutory regimes more aggressively, particularly IPR and competition law regimes. For example, the US Government's trade strategy now includes a drastically increased emphasis on effective enforcement, and often puts this emphasis in Rule of Law terms. The aggressiveness of this new emphasis on enforcement in developing countries suggests that important actors now recognize that such legal regimes were systematically and intentionally 'under enforced' in developing Northeast Asia. For example, the agenda of the United States Trade Representative (USTR) in China seems to be an implicit acknowledgment that IPR enforcement in other Northeast Asian countries was intentionally weak, as well as a commitment to preventing China from following the same path.[48]

Given this tacit acknowledgment, and the fact that the other Northeast Asian countries are now technologically very advanced, it seems absurd to argue that effective IPR protection is intrinsically necessary to economic development, though of course it can be made necessary by threat of technology boycotts, or by linking IPR protection with other trade issues. It is often argued that the incentive structure for local intellectual property (IP) creators also depends upon effective IPR enforcement, but at what point the benefits of protecting locally-produced IP outweigh the costs of protecting foreign IP obviously varies from country to country, and with technological change, and would seem impossible to calculate absent drastic simplifying assumptions.

A relatively new agenda for international Rule of Law advocacy is in competition law. Here again, the notorious under-enforcement of competition law and monopoly regulation in Japan, South Korea, and Taiwan provides reason for scepticism about claims that active competition law enforcement is in some way necessary for economic development. Part of the 'developmental state' model has included the creation of business groups large enough to compete internationally in industries where economies of scale are crucial, as well as the *de facto* and at times *de jure* cartelization of many industries. Both of these features of the 'developmental state' would be undermined by fully independent, enforcement-oriented competition law authorities, which perhaps best explains why competition law has played such a minor role in shaping the economies of Japan, South Korea, and Taiwan. In the words of Japan scholar Christopher Heath, '[w]ithin the framework of an economic policy that clearly puts Japanese interests first, an independent antitrust agency that upholds the rule of law and thereby prohibits cartels simply does not fit in.' (Heath, 1997:433).

LIMITING GOVERNMENT DISCRETION IN ECONOMIC GOVERNANCE

The other main branch of Rule of Law-economic development rhetoric speaks in terms of making the government as well as the citizen subject to the law, though it tends to focus on the activities of lower level state functionaries, rather than insisting on democratic participation in the law making process. This section of the chapter will examine some areas of bureaucratic governance integral to industrial policy in the 'developmental states' to see whether, or to what extent, a Rule of Law functioned.[49]

Credit Allocation

One of the central elements of the 'developmental state' model has been government involvement in the allocation of credit, beyond simply providing the framework for financial market activities. This has been accomplished through direct government ownership of the banks, as in South Korea (Jung-En, 1991) or Taiwan (Jia-Don and Yang, 1994:193), or through less direct means in Japan.[50] Governments have sometimes 'replaced' markets, as where all lending for a particular project or industry has come from the government or at government direction, and sometimes governments have 'guided' markets by providing some funding, and thus signalling that private lending to that company or industry was favoured and would be relatively secure.

Although government involvement in credit allocation raises interesting questions for political science[51] and economics,[52] for purposes of an inquiry into the Rule of Law the important questions concern neither the existence nor the effectiveness of policy lending, but rather the means by which it was and is carried out. Once government involves itself directly in the allocation of credit its actions can be analysed in Rule of Law terms. Assuming that the government is pursuing substantive objectives in allocating credit, some way to decide between different applicants for credit is necessary. Inquiry into the Rule of Law would then centre on how allocation decisions are made, and how the discretion retained by the relevant government actors is contained and structured. Assuming that the government actors act under some general statutory authority, do they themselves act to cabin their authority by publishing binding rules or even non-binding policy statements governing how lending decisions will be made? Are criteria publicly available which, if met, would entitle an applicant to receive policy loans, in some sense as a matter of right? Is judicial review available to enforce transparency in policy loan administration or to try to ensure that decisions are made based on legitimate rather than on irrelevant or corrupt grounds?

These questions are crucial to any exploration of the Rule of Law in this crucial facet of the 'developmental state.' Like any similar regulatory program, policy lending will involve a good deal of discretion on the part of the implementing officials. But this discretion can be limited and shaped by various means to meet some of the objectives of the Rule of Law, or this discretion can be exercised within a 'black box,' so that only insiders can guess at the exact constellation of considerations, legitimate or otherwise, that lead to a particular decision. The freeze that South Korea's Kim Young-sam government imposed on lending by formally private banks to the Hyundai Group, sadly reminiscent of the destruction of the *Kukje* Group by the Chun Doo Hwan government, suggests that at least in the South Korean context executive branch influence over lending policy is little constrained by Rule of Law considerations.[53] There was reportedly concern that current President Kim Dae-Jung would attempt similar reprisals against the Samsung group because of personal antagonism against Chairman Lee Kun-hee (Lee, 1998), and while international observers generally praise the South Korean government's 'Big Deal' policy, under which *chaebol* are exchanging and merging subsidiaries in order to rationalize the Korean industrial structure, serious concerns are being raised as to the legality of the methods the government is employing to obtain *chaebol* co-operation. In Japan, as well, the ability of the Ministry of Finance to influence the Bank of Japan, which in turn was able to influence private bank lending decisions, has been described as a particularly lawless phenomenon (Mabuchi, 1993; 1997).

Screening of Foreign Investment

The Rule of Law has traditionally been seen as an attribute of national governance, between a government and its citizens, or it is invoked in the international arena, to describe a situation where relations between states are governed by international law, rather than simply by force. What is not found in these two traditional contexts, but what seems to be implicit in the Rule of Law-economic development conception, is that a sort of administrative, or procedural, Rule of Law should govern relations between sovereign governments and foreign economic actors.

But should a government be criticized for not upholding the Rule of Law because it retains discretion to screen foreign investment based on non-Rule of Law concerns, such as foreign dominance of its domestic industry, or the amount or appropriateness of technology being transferred by foreign investors? Although Northeast Asia generally escapes attacks on the 'New International Economic Order' (NIEO) movement of the 1970s, which sought to legitimate screening of foreign investment,[54] such discretion was rampant in the heyday of the 'developmental states,' which did not recognize 'rights of establishment,' 'national treatment' or MFN obligations with regard to foreign investment applications, and where foreign investors generally went to the governments, rather than to the courts, to try to influence exercises of bureaucratic discretion in the foreign investment approval process.[55]

This raises again the conflict between Rule of Law-economic development rhetoric, and the complex reality of foreign investment decisions.[56] It is often stressed that foreign investors demand certain Rule of Law attributes from the legal systems of the countries in which they invest, yet foreign investors might fare worse under a Rule of Law system that forced respect for lawful exercises of bureaucratic discretion, unless at the same time they can have the scope within which such discretion can operate permanently narrowed. This is in fact the tack that is being taken internationally, in the various initiatives to create a multilateral regime to discipline national foreign investment regimes[57]

Tax Administration

A third area of economic governance that raises Rule of Law concerns is tax administration. Given the impossibility of auditing all taxpayers, tax officials in perhaps any system will be left with discretion to decide which taxpayers will be audited, a discretion similar to prosecutorial discretion. Rule of Law concerns could be met by a purely random selection system, by a system where all taxpayers meeting certain pre-established criteria would be audited, or by some sort of 'probable cause' requirement to preclude audits based solely on criteria unrelated to the likelihood of improper underpayment. What the Rule of Law would seem to exclude would be a decision to audit based upon considerations unrelated to revenue collection, such as whether the taxpayer had followed 'administrative guidance' in some formally unrelated matter.

Although evidence is difficult to find, it is often alleged that tax audits have been used as a disciplinary tool by the 'developmental state' to enforce administrative guidance that was unenforceable through legal means.[58] This flies in the face of the Rule of Law, but it is not entirely clear that such behaviour by the government would undermine the predictability objective of the Rule of Law, considered necessary for economic activity.

This raises again the issue of administrative guidance and the Rule of Law, and highlights the fact that the problem with administrative guidance from a Rule of Law perspective is not its existence, but its enforcement. If, as is often alleged, ministries are able to coerce compliance with administrative guidance in one field by threatening retaliatory measures in other regulatory fields, such as taxation, policy lending, access to foreign exchange, or business licensing,[59] such retaliatory measures would be motivated by considerations unrelated to that other field, and thus arbitrary from a Rule of Law perspective.[60] Aggressive judicial review would seem to be the only way to stamp out such cross-jurisdiction, or cross-issue, enforcement, even if appealing for relief through political channels is effective in individual cases.

To conclude this part, it seems that from the role of courts, to the enforcement of statutory regimes, to government discretion in economic governance, the experiences of Japan, South Korea, and Taiwan in the 'developmental state' era at least raise questions about easy connections between the Rule of Law and successful economic development.

ENGAGING THE RULE OF LAW-ECONOMIC DEVELOPMENT RHETORIC

If it is so difficult to reconcile the Rule of Law-economic development rhetoric with the actual development experience of Northeast Asia, it makes sense to examine the usefulness of that rhetoric with regard to today's developing economies. The following passages will examine first what it means to try to reduce the Rule of Law to a social science variable. The question will then be raised whether the Rule of Law-economic development approach is likely to help, or hinder, development of a normatively attractive Rule of Law in any society.

Problems with the Rule of Law as a Social Science Variable

Whether one takes a jurisprudential or a legal infrastructure approach to the Rule of Law, caution is called for when trying to reduce the concept to a variable for social science theorizing. Looking first at the jurisprudential approach, while most in the Anglo-American tradition could, if pressed, agree on a core set of concepts required in any definition of the Rule of Law, there is ample room for disagreement over the inclusion of additional concepts within the core, and over the interpretation and carrying out in practice of the principles in the core.[61] Second, the specific principles that are included within the definition, whatever they are, are in the nature of goals toward which it is thought a legal system should aspire. Thus, even if one proceeds on the assumption that the goals are in fact desired, the utility of an over-arching concept such as the Rule of Law can have only relative significance when all the elements of the umbrella concept are in fact aspirations rather than concrete achievements of any existing system. A final problem arises once one treats the elements as aspirational, however, because even if one favours the Rule of Law, few who think seriously about the relationship between formal rules and substantive justice, however defined, are likely to favour complete fulfilment of all of its elements all of the time.[62] Perhaps reflecting this seemingly perpetual problem, actual legal systems since Aristotle have arguably violated a strict Rule of Law by allowing judges discretion to pursue substantive justice when strict rule application would result in injustice (Vinogradoff, 1914:208-33).

Use of the Rule of Law in the second sense, as describing a comprehensive functioning infrastructure of rules, rights, and courts to enforce them, runs into problems of its own, however. As a factual matter, modern legal systems have moved from a reliance on rules to a reliance on more indeterminate principles and standards in many fields of law. Nearly sixty years ago, Roscoe Pound wrote:

> If we look only at the precept element [of law], that element includes principles and conceptions and standards as well as rules, and the technique of developing and applying rules, principles, conceptions, and standards, and the received ideals in the light of which they are developed and applied, are as much authoritative and as much part of the law, using law to mean the body of authoritative grounds of and guides to determination, as the rules themselves.[63]

Even Justice Scalia (1989), in a recent article entitled, 'The Rule of Law as a Law of Rules', concedes that 'legal determinations that do not reflect a general rule can [not] be entirely avoided. We will have totality of the circumstances tests and balancing modes of analysis with us forever... All I urge is that those modes of analysis be avoided where possible; that the *Rule* of Law, the law of *rules*, be extended as far as the nature of the question allows (Scalia, 1989:1186-7).' Furthermore, an independent judiciary, seen as necessary in this approach to prevent arbitrary state interference with private property rights, ensures a certain level of unpredictability in judicial decision-making. Judges insulated from political and economic pressures are arguably constrained by the positive law, by their professional training and culture, and perhaps in other ways, but they are not automatons.[64] Thus the idea that one could accurately model the combined economic effects of statutory change and a truly independent judiciary contradicts itself. Some Rule of Law-economic development literature seeks to minimize this obvious problem by suggesting that these 'independent' judges be trained to apply the law in a market-friendly manner, echoing a tactic employed by property rights advocates in the US.[65] In their admission of judicial discretion and open call for instrumental, results-oriented judging, however, these calls reflect a fundamental scepticism about the Rule of Law, as well as a willingness to sacrifice Rule of Law ideals to substantive economic aims.

Is the Rhetoric Likely to Contribute to the Rule of Law?

Two claims about this rhetoric that have been raised above are i) that the 'property rights-Rule of Law' strand tends to limit itself to an economistic emphasis on the creation of secure private property rights which individuals can trade in market transactions and can be enforced in court, and ii) that the strand concerned with limiting government discretion tends toward an opposite extreme of being so vague that the Rule of Law becomes somehow synonymous with good governance. Both of these facts are unfortunate for those concerned with the Rule of Law as an end in itself.

The vision behind the 'property rights-Rule of Law' rhetoric seems to see the ideal society as one governed by two forces, the market and a framework of legal rules and rule-like norms, that provide clear, objective guidance around which, or within which, private market actors can orient their behaviour. In this sense the rhetoric has moved beyond simplistic visions of a self-regulating market, but still leaves little or no room for legitimate judicial or bureaucratic discretion. This is unfortunate because it is so obviously inaccurate as a description of any advanced economy (Davis, 1969) that it can be easily dismissed by political leaders in countries that one might hope would be moving toward a Rule of Law.

Another major problem with this approach is that it does little to prevent authoritarian governments ruling over market economies from claiming that they are Rule of Law societies, when in fact these are simply societies ruled by leadership committed to private property for political/economic reasons, but with no commitment to being governed by law themselves. This tends to reproduce Cold War-era attempts to distinguish Left from Right dictatorships, since many of the latter would enforce a Rule of Law at this level. But what Locke wrote of law in the absolute monarchies is instructive here:

> [T]he Subjects have an Appeal to the Law, and Judges to decide any Controversies, and restrain any Violence that may happen betwixt the Subjects themselves, one amongst another. [But] 'this is no more, than what every Man who loves his own Power, Profit, or Greatness, may, and naturally must do, [to] keep those Animals from hurting or destroying one another who labour and drudge only for his Pleasure and Advantage, and so are taken care of, not out of any Love the Master has for them, but Love of himself, and the Profit they bring him. For if it be asked, what Security, *what Fence* is there in such a State, *against the Violence of Oppression of this Absolute Ruler*? The very Question can scarce be born (Locke, 1960:371).

Seeing the Rule of Law in terms of the enforcement of particular statutory regimes raises additional issues, as the experience of Northeast Asia shows.

The region provides an important early example of globalization in areas like competition and intellectual property law, whereby countries were pressured to adopt formal law inconsistent with their strategic economic policies. When this occurs the Rule of Law is bound to suffer, as subversion of the formal law becomes a necessary, if unstated, component of government economic policy. That this is at least part of the story of legality in Northeast Asia seems clear, and suggests that the best strategy for fostering the Rule of Law might include a good deal of tolerance of divergent substantive policies among legal regimes, so that governments are not forced by the internal logic of their own policies to undermine enforcement of the formal law.

The prevailing vagueness in the Rule of Law rhetoric presents different sorts of problems. Vagueness invites objections based on critiques of the claimed universality of 'Western' values, one of which is the Rule of Law. Just as has occurred in the field of human rights, if grandiose terms are not broken down into specific issues, the way is left open for claims that there are one or more equally valid 'styles' of human rights, or of the Rule of Law. If, however, one raises a concrete issue, such as whether people should be subject to arrest or other legal harassment for peacefully criticizing their government, then culture-based arguments tend to lose their rhetorical effectiveness. If people and institutions are serious about advancing particular elements of the Rule of Law around the world, they should enunciate clearly what those elements are, so that they can be evaluated individually on their merits. This will have the added benefit of encouraging consistency in the positions of those advocating the Rule of Law, so that they do not undercut the credibility of the entire effort by advocating inconsistent positions.[66]

Finally, it is legitimate to question some of the more extravagant claims about the Rule of Law in economic development, even if one believes that the Rule of Law is a worthy aspiration. One could take the position that the more extravagant claims do no harm, and may actually do some good, so why bother contesting them? There are problems with this approach, however. China's leadership, for example, knows perfectly well the growth trajectories of countries like South Korea and Taiwan, which grew dramatically in decades when any comprehensive Rule of Law was lacking.[67] They may well be convinced that a certain level of legalization or legal infrastructure is crucial for continued economic development, but as people raised on Marxism they are fully cognizant of arguments that such a legalized society, as it develops economically, will eventually evolve into a liberal, rights-based society. This is what the hopes for, and fears of, 'peaceful evolution' are all about. Exaggerated claims for the economic necessity of the Rule of Law could thus be seized upon by Chinese conservatives as evidence that international organizations such as the World Bank are being used as Trojan Horses by Western opponents of China's political system.

If no particular form of the Rule of Law is necessary for economic development, some Rule of Law is certainly a necessary condition for representative democracy, as aspirations of the Rule of Law seek to ensure that the rules and policies enacted by the legislative branch are enforced as intended, and that the government cannot act against a citizen except pursuant to authority granted to it through democratic means. But the argument that a Rule of Law in the limited sense of a legalized system of property rights will evolve into liberal, representative democracy, though attractive, is basically speculative, and clearly open to manipulation.[68] We certainly want to believe the State Department when it promises that 'the rule of law in trade has spill-over benefits elsewhere,' but we should ask ourselves whether we can name a nation in which a just and democratic Rule of Law has evolved smoothly out of a system in which the Rule of Law meant only that private property rights were protected by a system of courts and rules. South Korea and Taiwan have made great strides toward democracy, but it is only possible to see this as an inevitable evolution based on a growing middle class, etc., if one adopts an extremely wide-angle and deterministic view of history, one in which the contingencies and human agency involved in, for example, the 1987 democracy movement in Korea, are ignored. And it may be that in the rush to create the private interests to propel this evolution we will create private concentrations of wealth that have no interest in a general Rule of Law, but find they are better served by non-legalized relations with other private parties and with the State. If the Rule of Law is what we care about, it might be preferable to demand less in the way of deregulation and privatization, but to pay more attention to the legalization of the relationships and procedures that tie governments to private actors. A functioning Rule of Law requires a civil society that is willing to resort to legality, and is used to doing so, in its relations with the State. Mass privatization and deregulation may not be the best way to foster such a civil society, and may in fact work against it. Again Northeast Asia provides a valuable example: an administrative procedure law was debated in Japan for decades, but it was apparently not until the 1980s or 1990s that Japanese business interests put their political muscle behind such a basic element of the Rule of Law in the modern administrative state.

CONCLUSION

US Federal Reserve Board Chairman Alan Greenspan (1998) seized the opportunity provided by the Asian financial crisis to proclaim that '[t]he current turmoil in East Asia ... appears to be an important milestone in what evidently has been a significant and seemingly inexorable trend toward market capitalism and political systems that stress the rule of law (Greenspan, 1998).' Chairman Greenspan may be right about the trend, but in the light of three decades of high-speed economic growth and social progress in much of East Asia, how do we reconcile Greenspan's view with claims that the Rule of Law is necessary for economic development? This chapter has sought to approach this seeming contradiction by bringing up examples from the Northeast Asian experience that call into question the necessity, and in some cases the appropriateness, of a strong version of the Rule of Law in all areas of the economy. The point of this is not to disparage the Rule of Law as a political ideal, but rather to encourage intellectual inquiry, and to suggest why some in developed and developing East Asia might find the Rule of Law-economic development rhetoric unpersuasive. Perhaps the Rule of Law as understood by the development community doesn't include all aspects of the Rule of Law that are familiar to lawyers, but in that case perhaps institutions such as the World Bank should use more care when choosing their rhetoric. This suggests a corresponding responsibility on lawyers not to abstain from this debate, however, unless we are willing to see a central normative concept of our tradition trivialized. Weber (1968:1465, fn. 14) long ago called the idea that Roman law promoted capitalism 'nursery school lore.' Perhaps he would be amused that statements of his on the relationship between capitalism and legal formality have achieved the same status in the Rule of Law-economic development literature, as it relies on Weber, North, Olson, *et al.* to tell the world what form of legal system is 'demanded' by a market economy.[69]

In a broader sense, those who study law in Northeast Asia must be aggressive in using their empirical knowledge to test universalist claims in the social sciences generally, not simply in law, or in the relationship between law and economic development. Given its economic success, any global theory addressing economic issues must be fully compatible with the actual history of modern Northeast Asia. The most important task for those interested in the Rule of Law and economic development is to develop an understanding of the Rule of Law that can be effectively distinguished from the simple legalization of society, or from the suppression of government discretion in economic governance. A legal infrastructure is certainly a necessary precondition of any worthwhile Rule of Law, but the latter will not necessarily evolve out of the former.

NOTES

1 '[I]t is an accepted fact that the weakness of the [Peruvian] judicial system has been an obstacle to that growth, discouraging investors and innovative economic activities while contributing to a general sense of insecurity' (World Bank, News Rel: No 98/1555/LAC).

2 'The first lesson from the Asian crisis is that a government that is not answerable to its people will not be likely to have open markets or the institutions required to impose discipline to overcome a financial crisis. A second lesson is that *guanxi*, or connections, are never a substitute for the rule of law' (Lee, 1998:8).

3 'Rules are there for a reason. In the United States, we do business under a lot of annoying regulations that require company managements to report profits and losses accurately, that prevent banks and those they lend to from getting too friendly, and so on. And we also made it hard for government officials and businessmen to strike deals without a lot of lawyers present. In Asia, they scoffed. They did business on the basis of personal relationships, not narrow legalisms. And now we know the results' (Krugman, 1998:6A).

4 'Developmental state' is used broadly here, to refer to the approach to state-society relations in post-World War II Japan, South Korea, and Taiwan pioneered by Chalmers Johnson, then enhanced and qualified by Alice Amsden, Richard Samuels, Robert Wade, Peter Evans and others. (Johnson, 1982; Amsden, 1989; Samuels, 1987; Wade, 1990; Evans, 1995).

5 '[T]he rule of law may not be a single concept at all; rather, it may be more accurate to understand the ideal of the rule of law as a set of ideals connected more by family resemblance than by a unifying conceptual structure' (Solum, 1994).

6 The following is a list of some of these concerns according to the aspect of the legal process in which they arise:
Positive Law: The positive law should be clear and knowable in advance, so that citizens are not held liable, civilly or criminally, based on legal rules of which they could not, through normal means, have been aware. The legal norms must be of general applicability, rather than being directed toward individuals.
Judiciary: In deciding cases, the judge should have no personal interest in the matter, should not prejudge the matter, and should decide a case by applying the pre-existing law to the facts as developed during the proceeding. Like cases should be decided alike, and the judge should not be influenced by non-legal substantive or instrumental considerations.

Basic procedural rights, such as a right to be heard and to contest adverse evidence, are also presumed.

Executive Branch: Officials of the executive branch should have pre-existing legal authority for any action they take that affects private rights. This means both that officers should have been granted a general statutory authority to act in a particular field, and that such action, when taken, should not exceed the scope of any discretion that has been granted to the officer.

7 Dicey's famous mischaracterization of the French *droit administratif* in comparison to the English Rule of Law is instructive (Dicey, 1982; Hayek, 1960).

8 Formalist in its assumption that the materials and methods of the law are sufficient to provide single correct answers to particular legal issues; positivist in the assumption that the materials of the law consist primarily of rules and rule-like social norms not subject to significant indeterminacy, and that these are sufficient to provide single correct solutions without resorting to principles, policies or purposes.

9 This admittedly impressionistic view was gleaned from a reading of the Rule of Law-economic development literature cited herein, which makes regrettably few efforts to define the Rule of Law. One definition that did appear was from Hayek, 1944. '... this means that government in all its actions is bound by rules fixed and announced beforehand – rules which make it possible to foresee with fair certainty how the authority will use its coercive powers in given circumstances and to plan one's individual affairs on the basis of this knowledge' (Dhonte and Kapur, 1996). Another work defines the Rule of Law as reflecting 'the degree to which the citizens of a country are willing to accept the established institutions to make and implement laws and adjudicate disputes.' (Knack and Keefer, 1995). Knack and Keefer take their definition from the International Country Risk Guide, a privately produced political risk guide marketed toward multinational investors, which had originally used the pithy 'law and order tradition' to describe this variable (Knack and Keefer, 1995:225).

10 Important current examples are Douglass North (economist), Mancur Olson (economist), Jeffrey Sachs (economist), and Barry Weingast (political scientist). Two pioneers in this tradition, Max Weber and Friedrich Hayek, were exceptions.

11 (North, 1990). On bounded rationality generally, see Conlisk (1996).

12 As noted above, this chapter was prompted by the seeming general explosion of Rule of Law language in publications dealing with economic development, not simply its use by the World Bank or another particular institution. It seemed appropriate, therefore, to look at many

sources, rather than simply analysing one particular document. The danger of this approach is that one could easily select only those sources that support one's argument. I can only say that I have tried to avoid doing so.

13 Many of the sources consulted for this chapter discuss two or more of these concerns, but I have tried to separate them for purposes of analysis.

14 Perhaps not surprisingly, these concerns track exactly Locke's explanation of how property was inadequately protected in the State of Nature: want of '*establish'd*, settled, known Law,' want of a '*known and indifferent Judge*, with Authority to determine all differences according to established Law,' and want of 'a *Power* to back and support the Sentence when right, and to *give* it due *Execution*' (Locke, 1960).

15 A truly disturbing over-emphasis on such criminal law aspects is found in Posner (1998).

16 'Property rights are at the heart of the incentive structure of market economies. They determine who bears risk and who gains or loses from transactions. In so doing they spur worthwhile investment, encourage careful monitoring and supervision, promote work effort, and create a constituency for enforceable contracts' (World Bank, 1996:48-9).

17 '[W]ell functioning markets also need a clear sense of where the state's role ends. The government must itself be ruled by law and trusted by private entities not to intervene arbitrarily in their affairs, to follow its announced policy statements, and to deliver on its obligations' (World Bank, 1996:93-4).

18 North (1990:139) writes, 'The security of property rights and the development of the public and private capital market were instrumental factors not only in England's subsequent rapid economic development, but in its political hegemony and ultimate dominance of the world.' Olson is no less adamant: 'With a carefully constrained monarchy, an independent judiciary, and a bill of Rights, people in England in due course came to have a relatively high degree of confidence that any contracts they entered into would be impartially enforced and that private property rights, even for critics of the government, were relatively secure. Individual rights to property and contract enforcement were probably more secure in Britain after 1689 than anywhere else, and it was in Britain, not long after the Glorious Revolution, that the Industrial Revolution began' (Olson, 1993:574).

19 'If organizations – firms, trade unions, farm groups, political parties, and congressional committees to name a few – devote their efforts to unproductive activity, the institutional constraints have provided the incentive structure for such activity. Third World countries are poor

because the institutional constraints define a set of payoffs to political/economic activity that do not encourage productive activity' (North, 1990:110).

20 'If political transaction costs are low and the political actors have accurate models to guide them, then efficient property rights will result. But the high transaction costs of political markets and subjective perceptions of the actors more often have resulted in property rights that do not induce economic growth, and the consequent organizations may have no incentive to create more productive economic rules' (North, 1990:52).

21 It will only be noted here that this depoliticization of the very core of politics – private rights, the separation of powers, and checks and balances – is also necessary if international financial organizations are to comply with prohibitions typically found in their charters against interfering in the domestic political affairs of their member states.

22 'Although many of the structural reforms that the IMF included in its early-December [1997] program for Korea would probably improve the long-term performance of the Korean economy, they are not needed for Korea to gain access to capital markets. They are also among the most politically sensitive issues: labor market rules, regulations of corporate structure and governance, government-business relations, and international trade. The specific policies that the IMF insists must be changed are not so different from those in the major countries of Europe' (Feldstein, 1998:27-8).

23 These rights do not differ fundamentally from those discussed in the previous section, and are also often justified on economic grounds. They are treated separately here because they tend to be advocated by different Rule of Law publicists, for example, the United States Trade Representative (USTR) rather than the World Bank, and they are often supported more directly by international obligations.

24 Former USTR Mickey Kantor made this connection between IPR enforcement and the Rule of Law when describing the 1995 US–China agreement on IPR enforcement: 'The essence of that agreement, and all our trade agreements, is respect for the rule of law. The IPR agreement promotes citizen access to the judicial process, by requiring China to publish relevant laws, and standards, and by requiring the creation of guidebooks to the enforcement system. The IPR agreement applies these principles in a commercial sphere, but its ramifications for China go far beyond patents and trademarks.' Statement of Ambassador Michael Kantor, Prepared for Delivery to US–China Business Council, 31 January 1996 (transcript on file with the author).

25 'The US Customs service, the FBI, Department of Justice, Patent and Trademark Office, the Department of Commerce and the US Information Agency have all offered training – and will continue to do so. Chinese prosecutors and Chinese Customs officials are receiving training right now in facilities in the United States and China. US industries have been equally generous.' Statement of Ambassador Michael Kantor before the Senate Foreign Relations Subcommittee on East Asian and Pacific Affairs and the House International Relations Subcommittees on Asia and the Pacific and International Economic Policy and Trade, 7 March 1996.

26 Perhaps the Rule of Law in China will then 'spillover' into the State Department's exercise of its authority to issue tourist visas, which a Federal District Court found to be illegal (Bureau of Public Affairs, 1997). See *Olsen v. Albright*, 990 F. Supp. 31 (D.D.C. 1997) and Shenon (1998:1).

27 'Formal constraints on arbitrary state power in established market economies derive partly from constitutional and administrative law. These bodies of law ensure that all legislation is consistent with the national constitution and that regulations, in turn, are consistent with the law. They delineate the rulemaking authority of various state bodies, lay out the procedures for enacting laws and promulgating regulations, and provide individuals recourse against unlawful or capricious state action' (World Bank 1996:94).

28 A useful introduction is Faber and Frickey (1991).

29 'Uncertain rules, heavy regulation, and pervasive controls give officials exceptional power, many opportunities to seek bribes, and wide scope for appropriating public wealth' (World Bank, 1996:95).

30 '[G]overnments are particularly susceptible to corruption during the phase when the state retains both vast assets and extensive powers to intervene in a growing private economy. Liberalization, demonopolization, and – if transparent – rapid privatization are key steps to reducing these two sources of huge economic rents and to strengthen demand for the rule of law' (World Bank, 1996:144).

31 Corrupt practices could also occur in other government activities, including the regulation of private sector activities that do not have a direct impact on the budget or public finances, such as ad hoc decisions made in relation to the regulation of foreign direct investment. Such practices would be counter to the IMF's general policy advice aimed at providing a level playing field to foster private sector activity' (IMF, 1997:par 10).

32 An exception to this general pattern is, World Bank (News Rel: No. 98/1515) 'Noting that corruption and financial crises flourish in the

dark, Wolfensohn said that, irrespective of political systems, public decisions must be brought into the light of public scrutiny. This is not a luxury: this is a fundamental prerequisite for maximizing growth and poverty reduction.'

33 '[T]he East Asian example would seem to suggest that high levels of economic performance bear little or no relation to the development of a credible legal system' (Jayasuriya, 1999).

34 See, Greif (1996) and Greenhalgh (1988). In an example of economic dogmatism, one of the IMF's prolific writers on governance and economic performance defines corruption as 'noncompliance with [the] principle of the arm's length relationship, which states that *personal or family relationships ought not to play a role in economic decisions by private economic agents* ... This principle is essential for the efficient functioning of markets.' Summary of Vito Tanzi, Governmental Activities, and Markets (IMF Working Paper WP/94/99-EA) (visited Nov. 24, 1998) (emphasis added). Given the importance of family businesses in pre-World War II Japan, and in post-World War II South Korea and Taiwan, Tanzi's statement can only be taken to mean that 'the efficient functioning of markets' is not necessary for economic development.

35 'The monopolist cannot only do without calculable law, formal rationality is even a fetter to the full development of his power. The rational law has ... not only the function of rendering exchange processes calculable, it has an equalizing function also. It protects the weak. The monopolist can dispense with the aid of the courts; he does not go to the courts. His power of command is a sufficient substitute for the coercive power of the state' (Neumann, 1986:282).

36 South Korean president Kim Dae-Jung has 'called for an improvement in the relationship between *chaebol*s and small companies by which large enterprises can no longer rule or dictate over small ones.' Hyoung-min Kim, 'Pres.-Elect, Chaebol Owners Agree on Reform', *Korea Times* 13 January 1998.

37 The World Bank makes strong claims in this regard. 'Most day-to-day contracts in market economies do not require formal enforcement. ... But an economy still needs credible, low-cost formal enforcement mechanisms to which aggrieved parties can turn when all else fails' (World Bank, 1996:90).

38 'The inevitable conclusion that one arrives at in a wealth-maximizing world is that complex contracting that would allow one to capture the gains from trade in a world of impersonal exchange must be accompanied by some kind of third-party enforcement' (North, 1990:57) 'The shortage of institutions to enforce contracts limits the scope of

transactions, makes contracting more costly, and prohibits some contracts altogether' (World Bank, 1996:90).

39 This is changing in Japan and South Korea, where the legal regimes have been amended to make shareholder derivative actions more attractive to litigants. This is clearly an important change; how it will effect the Japanese and South Korean economies remains to be seen.

40 Anyone trying to predict the future path of corporate governance in China should note that government's interest in the South Korean *chaebol* model. 'Hu Xiongfei, deputy director of the Shanghai Economic Commission, voices an opinion held by many Chinese officials: 'These *chaebol*s contributed a lot in transforming Korea from an agricultural country into an emerging industrial one, with GNP increasing from US$2.1 billion in 1961 to US$480 billion in 1996' (Yatsko, 1998).

41 The OECD explains the need for its proposed Multilateral Agreement on Investment (MAI) as follows: 'While markets are, of course, the main reason for investment decisions, the investment climate is also a major factor in decision-making. Investors need long-term stability of rules and procedures. They need open markets and equal competitive opportunities with domestic investors' (OECD Policy Brief No. 2-1997).

42 The International Country Risk Guide's original variable, 'law and order tradition,' thus seems to more accurately describe the state of affairs their clients value (Knack and Keefer, 1995:225).

43 Mancur Olson, perhaps in a nod toward South Korea and Taiwan, acknowledges that some dictatorships have presided over periods of exceptional economic growth by providing secure property and contract rights absent democracy or the Rule of Law. He argues, however, that such growth cannot last because the rights provided by a dictator are not sufficiently secure in the long run (Olson, 1997:572-2).

44 China's Hunan Province reportedly has a back-log of 100,000 unenforced commercial verdicts, dating back to 1992. 'Court Delays Force Chinese Litigants to Turn to Gangsters' *Agence France-Presse*, 2 December 1997 (quoting the Worker's Daily).

45 The tale of foreign investment in the Chinese telecoms industry provides a fascinating example. The world's top telecom companies invested US$1,400,000,000 in China's telecoms service industry via complicated contractual arrangements designed to circumvent a ban on foreign investment in that sector. The existence of the ban was known, but investors relied on the 'repeated blessings of top Chinese officials.' James Kynge, 'Blow for telecoms investors in China', *Financial Times*, 22 September 1998, at 8.

46 'Many European, Asian and some American lenders overlooked the inadequacies of the Indonesian legal system and decided to put their trust in their debtors' connections ...' (Paal, 1998:6).

47 Indeed, IMF, World Bank, and International Finance Corporation interest in Indonesia's bankruptcy law appears driven by a desire of foreign investors to limit losses on investments they have already made. Thoenes, Sander, 'Indonesian Bankruptcy Law Dealt Fresh Blow', *Financial Times*, 25 November 1998, at 4.

48 The same point could be made with regard to negotiations over China's accession to the WTO.

49 Government exercises of discretion here might be analysed through the lens of 'administrative guidance,' but discussions of administrative guidance in the abstract can be more confusing than enlightening. The propensity to regulate through informal rather than formal means is probably inherent in modern bureaucratic governance. For an inquiry into the Rule of Law in Northeast Asia the interesting questions include, i) whether government actors possessed means to enforce their informal 'guidance' that are contrary to the Rule of Law, and ii) whether they exercised guidance over the economy that was central to the 'developmental state.'

50 A good discussion of the 'traditional' Japanese system, and how and why that system is becoming more legalized, is Masaru Mabuchi (1993:130).

51 The fundamental debate concerns whether policy lending was conducted by relatively insulated technocrats in such a way as to exert effective guidance over the path of economic development, or whether such loans should be better understood as part of a corrupt government-business cycle in which loans were obtained in exchange for political contributions, which were obtained in exchange for loans, and so on.

52 Economists have been more concerned with the effects of policy lending, and whether growth would have been even faster in Northeast Asia if credit allocation had been left more to market forces.

53 In 1993, Korea's Constitutional Court held that the destruction of the *Kukje* Group was unconstitutional, invoking the Rule of Law as a check on government action necessary for legal security and predictability in the economic realm. The Kukje case and its possible implications are discussed in James M. West, *Kukje and Beyond: Constitutionalism and the Market* (June, 1998) (unpublished manuscript, on file with the author).

54 A typically cynical 'new institutionalist' discussion of foreign investment screening is Thomas W. Waelde, *A Requiem for the 'New*

International Economic Order', 1 CEPMLP On-Line Journal 2 (June, 1995) <http://www.dundee.ac.uk/petroleumlaw/html/article1-2.htm>.

55 '[T]hose charged with the application and enforcement of the Foreign Investment Law and the regulations thereunder possess virtually unreviewable power to control inward capital investments. Much of the law and regulations have left to government administrators the discretion to fashion the details and working policies by which validation applications are screened. For the most part, such applications are judged by current economic and political considerations rather than by precise standards and rules formulated in statutes, cabinet orders and court decisions' (Hartman, 1972:376). The OECD's proposed MAI would make it very difficult for any developing country to follow the 'developmental state' model for screening foreign investment by i) concerning itself with the making of investments, not just the treatment of investments once made, ii) requiring 'national treatment' for foreign investors, iii) requiring 'most-favored-nation' treatment for foreign investors, iv) requiring that laws, regulations and procedures of general application be publicly available, and v) prohibiting performance requirements. In return, parties to the MAI 'will enjoy the benefits of a better investment environment' OECD (1997).

56 Some investors are more candid than others about investing in Asia and the Rule of Law. Founder of the failed Peregrine investment bank, Philip Tose, reportedly 'went out of his way to emphasize an "Asian way" of doing business. This included contempt for democratic countries that he viewed as unlikely to make economic progress. He publicly preferred to deal with authoritarian governments, holding in contempt India, Australia and the Philippines, where democracy and the rule of law operated, however inadequately.' Philip Bowring, 'Wake-Up Call from Peregrine to Bankers Everywhere', *International Herald Tribune*, Wednesday, 14 January 1998, at 8.

57 As one commentator notes, 'national treatment,' which like the Rule of Law goes to the administration rather than the scope of regulatory authority, 'means little to a foreign investor if the treatment meted out to national companies is below *reasonable standards of state regulation* ('international minimum standards') in developed countries. The criterium of national treatment, in our view, is therefore only a stopover...' (Waelde, 1995: par 44) (emphasis added).

58 Typical is the report that Taiwan's tax authorities, as part of a government effort to defend Taiwan's currency, have threatened to 'look into those [financial institutions] that might have profited from "speculation".' Chad Rademan, 'Taipei Banker Gets Tough to Uphold Currency,' *International Herald Tribune*, 18-19 April 1998, p. 17. The

Rule of Law ideal would seem to demand that trading activities be subject to a system of rules defining what is allowed and what is not allowed, and that the government not be able to discourage allowed activities by threatening tax audits or similar measures.

59 Discussions of administrative guidance in Japan often mention almost as an afterthought that those giving the 'guidance' have this tool to coerce compliance, as if it is less important than, for example, the identity of interests between regulators and regulated that is presumed to arise out of Japan's corporatist regulatory system (Akira, 1985:279).

60 One standard American analysis of Japanese administrative guidance calls this 'collateral enforcement,' and wastes little ink on Rule of Law concerns (Young, 1984). This non-judgmental relativism seems to be the norm in academic writing on administrative guidance, at least in the US.

61 Fallon (1997) identifying four Rule of Law 'ideal types' within US Constitutional law discourse alone.

62 This also ignores the related problems of whether the aspirations that make up the Rule of Law in this approach have much to do with how actual cases are decided, or whether such higher level aspirations, if they are important in judicial decision making, are in fact neutral and just, or simply reflect existing social relations.

63 (Pound, 1942). Much important twentieth century legal scholarship has in fact been driven by the difficulty of reconciling Rule of Law ideals with the modern governance. See, Neumann (1986), Davis (1969), Lowi (1969), and Sunstein (1990).

64 The view of the judge implied in the Rule of Law-economic development literature seems inspired by Weber's implausible claim that 'the judge ... in the bureaucratic state with its rational laws, is more or less an automaton of paragraphs: the legal documents, together with the costs and fees, are dropped in at the top with the expectation that the judgement will emerge at the bottom together with more or less sound arguments – an apparatus, that is, whose functioning is by and large calculable or predictable' (Weber, 1968).

65 Marcus (1998:A01) describing property rights education seminars for US federal judges sponsored by the Foundation for Research on Economics and the Environment (FREE), a foundation funded by conservative groups that also fund legal challenges to regulatory limitations on absolute property rights.

66 A notorious example of this was the US government's support for arguably authoritarian measures by the government of China to reduce IPR infringement, including the registration of all printing facilities.

67 The effectiveness of China's foreign investment screening system, which shares much with the systems employed by South Korea and Taiwan, is testified to by the fact that it has become a matter of political concern in Washington (Office of Strategic Industries and Economic Security, 1999).
68 In these aspects, the argument resembles the '*deux-commerce*' thesis of the eighteenth century, which held that 'the market and capitalism were going to create a moral environment in which a good society as well as the market itself were bound to flourish' (Hirschman, 1992). Like the *deux-commerce* thesis, current evolutionary arguments are an important part of a complex reality (Hirschman, 1992:139).
69 The core 'Weberian' claim appears Weber (1968:1393-5) (Appendix II, ii: Bureaucracy and Political Leadership).

REFERENCES

Agence France-Presse 'Court Delays Force Chinese Litigants to Turn to Gangsters,' 2 December 1997 (quoting the *Worker's Daily*).

Akira Negishi (1985) 'Administrative Guidance and the Japanese Antimonopoly Law,' *Rabels Zeitschrift für ausländisches und internationales Privatrecht* 49, pp. 276 and 279.

Amsden, Alice (1989) *Asia's Next Giant*. New York: Oxford University Press.

Asian Development Bank (1997) Office of the General Counsel, *Law and Development at the Asian Development Bank* 1. Manila.

Bowring, Philip (1998) 'Wake-Up Call from Peregrine to Bankers Everywhere,' *International Herald Tribune* 14, January 1998, p. 8.

Bureau of Public Affairs, U.S. Department of State, 'China and the World Trade Organization (WTO),' *Fact Sheet* released 3 June 1997.

Conlisk, John (1996) 'Why Bounded Rationality?' *Journal of Economic Literature* 34, p. 669.

Davis, Kenneth C. (1969) *Discretionary Justice: A Preliminary Inquiry*. Baton Rouge: Louisiana State University Press.

Dhonte, Pierre and Ishan Kapur (1996) *Towards a Market Economy: Structures of Governance* 6 (IMF Working Paper WP/97/11, 1996).

Dicey, A.V. (1982) *Introduction to the Study of the Law of the Constitution*. Liberty Fund (8th ed. 1915).

Evans, Peter (1995) *Embedded Autonomy*. Princeton: Princeton University Press.

Fallon, Richard H. Jr. (1997) 'The "Rule of Law" as a Concept in Constitutional Discourse,' *Columbia Law Review* 97, p. 1.

Farber, Daniel A. and Philip P. Frickey (1991) *Law and public choice: a critical introduction.* Chicago: University of Chicago Press

Feldstein, Martin (1998) 'Refocusing the IMF,' *Foreign Affairs* 77/2, March/April, p. 20.

Greenhalgh, Susan (1988) 'Families and Networks in Taiwan's Economic Development,' in: Edwin A. Winckler and Susan Greenhalgh (eds) *Contending Approaches to the Political Economy of Taiwan.* Armonk: M.E. Sharpe, p. 224.

Greenspan, Alan (1998) 'Asian Model: Asian crisis acclerates (sic) the triumph of market capitalism,' *Capital Trends* 3(5) Nikko Research Center, Washington DC, 17 April <http://www.gwjapan.com/ftp/pub/-nrca/ctv3n05c.html>.

Greif, Avner (1996) 'Contracting, Enforcement, and Efficiency: Economics beyond the Law,' in: *World Bank, Annual World Bank Conference on Development Economics.* (World Bank). With comments by R. Ellickson and S. Falk Moore.

Hartman, F.L. (1972) 'Japanese Foreign Investment Regulation: Semantics and Reality,' *New York Law Forum* XVIII, pp. 355 and 376.

Hayek, Friedrich A. (1960) *The Constitution of Liberty.* Chicago: University of Chicago Press.

Hayek, Friedrich (1944) *The Road to Serfdom.* Chicago: University of Chicago Press.

Heath, Christopher (1997) 'Book Review of Menkhaus, Heinrich (ed.) *Das Japanische im japanischen Recht* (1994),' *International Review of Industrial Property and Copyright Law* 28, p. 431.

Henderson, Dan Fenno 'The Evolution of Tokugawa Law,' in: John W. Hall and Marius B. Jansen (eds) *Studies in the Institutional History of Early Modern Japan.* Princeton: Princeton University Press.

Hirschman, Albert O. (1992) *Rival Views of Market Society.* Cambridge: Harvard University Press.

IMF, *The Role of the IMF in Governance Issues: Guidance Note* (Approved by IMF Executive Board, July 25, 1997)

Jayasuriya, Kanishka (1999) 'Introduction,' in: *Law, Capitalism and Power in Asia.* London: Routledge, p. 7.

Jia-Dong Shea and Ya-Hwei Yang (1994) 'Taiwan's Financial System and the Allocation of Investment Funds,' in: Joel D. Aberbach *et al.* (eds) *The Role of the State in Taiwan's Development.* M.E. Sharpe, p. 193.

Johnson, Chalmers (1982) *MITI and the Japanese Miracle.* Stanford: Stanford University Press.

Jung-En Woo (1991) *Race to the Swift.* New York: Columbia University Press.

Kantor, Michael (Ambassador) *Statement before the Senate Foreign Relations Subcommittee on East Asian and Pacific Affairs and the House International Relations Subcommittees on Asia and the Pacific and International Economic Policy and Trade*, 7 March 1996.

Kantor, Michael (Ambassador) *Statement prepared for Delivery to U.S.-China Business Council* 31 January 1996 (transcript on file with author).

Kaufman Winn, Jane (1994) 'Relational Practices and the Marginalization of Law: Informal Financial Practices of Small Businesses in Taiwan,' *Law and Society Review* 28, p. 193.

Kim, Hyoung-min (1998) 'Pres.-Elect, Chaebol Owners Agree on Reform,' *Korea Times*, 13 January 1998.

Knack, Stephen and Philip Keefer (1995) 'Institutions and Economic Performance: Cross-Country Tests Using Alternative Institutional Measures,' *Economics and Politics* 7, p. 207.

Krugman, Paul (1998) 'Asia's Economic Pain for Real,' *USA Today*, 2 January 1998 p. 6A

Kynge, James (1998) 'Blow for telecoms investors in China,' *Financial Times*, 22 September 1998, p. 8.

Lee Chang-sup (1998) 'Public Anxiety over Political Retaliation by Kim DJ Subsiding,' *Korea Times*, 14 Jan 1998.

Lee, Martin (1998) 'Economic Crisis is Proof the Asians Need Democracy,' *International Herald Tribune*, 21 January 1998, p. 8

Liu Binyan and Link, Perry (1998) 'A Great Leap Backward?' *New York Review of Books*, 8 October 1998, pp. 19-23 (reviewing He Qinglian, Zhongguo de xianjing [China's Pitfall](1998)).

Locke, John and Peter Laslett (eds) (1960) *Two Treatises of Government*. Cambridge: Cambridge University Press.

Lowi, Theodore J. (1969) *The End of Liberalism*. New York : Norton.

Mancur, Olson (1993) 'Dictatorship, Democracy, and Development,' *American Political Science Review* 87, pp. 567 and 574.

Marcus, Ruth (1998) 'Issues Groups Fund Seminars for Judges: Classes at Resorts Cover Property Rights,' *Washington Post*, 9 April 1998, p. A01.

Masaru Mabuchi (1993) 'Deregulation and Legalization of Financial Policy,' in: Gary D. Allinson and Yasunori Sone (eds) *Political Dynamics in Contemporary Japan*. Ithaca: Cornell University Press, p. 130.

– (1997) 'Financing the Japanese Industries,' in: Michio Muramatsu and Frieder Naschold (eds) *State and Administration in Japan and Germany*. Berlin: W. de Gruyter.

Mayer, Colin P. 'Corporate Governance, Competition and Performance' *OECD Economics Department Working Paper* No. 164 (OCED/GD (96)99).

Neumann, Franz (1986) *The Rule of Law*. Leamington Spa: Berg.

North, Douglass C. (1990) *Institutions, Institutional Change and Economic Performance*. Cambridge: Cambridge University Press.

OECD, MAI: *The Multilateral Agreement on Investment* (OECD Policy Brief No. 2-1997).

Office of Strategic Industries and Economic Security, US Department of Commerce and DFI International, *US Commercial Technology Transfers to the People's Republic of China* (1999).

Olsen v. Albright, 990 F. Supp. 31 (D.D.C. 1997).

Paal, Douglas H. (1998) 'IMF Ignores the Bigger Problems,' in: *Indonesia, International Herald Tribune*, 24-25 January 1998, p. 6.

Popper, Karl R. (1976) 'The Logic of the Social Sciences,' in: Theodor W. Adorno *et al. The Positivist Dispute in German Sociology*. New York: Harper and Row, p. 87.

Posner, Richard A. (1998) 'Creating a Legal Framework for Economic Development,' *World Bank Research Observer* 13, pp. 1 and 8-9.

Pound, Roscoe (1942) *Administrative Law*. Pittsburgh: Fred B. Rothman and Co.

Rademan, Chad (1998) 'Taipei Banker Gets Tough to Uphold Currency,' *International Herald Tribune*, 18-19 April 1998, p. 17.

Samuels, Richard (1987) *The Business of the Japanese State*. Ithaca: Cornell University Press.

Scalia, Antonin (1989) 'The Rule of Law as a Law of Rules,' 56 *U.Chi.L.Rev*. 1175

Scogin, Hugh (1990) 'Between Heaven and Man: Contract and the State in Han Dynasty China,' *Southern California Law Review* 63, p. 1325.

Shenon, Philip (1998) 'Huddled Masses Welcome, But Not if They Look Poor: Tourists Illegally Kept Out of US, Judge Rules,' *International Herald Tribune*, 24-25 Jan 1998, p. 1.

Solum, Lawrence (1994) 'Equity and the Rule of Law,' in: Ian Shapiro (ed.) *The Rule of Law: NOMOS XXXVI*. New York: New York University Press.

Sunstein, Cass (1990) *After the Rights Revolution*. Harvard University Press.

Tanzi, Vito (1998) 'Summary of, Governmental Activities, and Markets' *IMF Working Paper* (WP/94/99-EA) (visited Nov. 24 1998) http://-www.imf.org/external/pubs/cat/doctext.cfm?docno=WP/94/99-EA. The full text of Tanzi's paper appears as 'Corruption: arm's-length relationships and markets' in Fiorentini, Gianluca and Peltzman, Sam (eds) *The Economics of Organised Crime* (1995), p. 161.

Thoenes, Sander (1998) 'Indonesian Bankruptcy Law Dealt Fresh Blow,' *Financial Times*, 25 November 1998, p. 4.

Upham, Frank K. (1994) 'Speculations on Legal Informality: On Winn's "Relational Practices and the Marginalization of Law",' 28 *Law and Society* 193, p. 233.

Vinogradoff, Paul (1914) *Common Sense in Law*. New York: Henry Holt and Co.

Wade, Robert (1990) *Governing the Market*. Princeton: Princeton University Press.

Waelde, Thomas W. (1995) 'A Requiem for the "New International Economic Order",' 1 *CEPMLP On-Line Journal* 2 (June). <http://www.dundee.ac.uk/petroleumlaw/html/article1-2.htm>

Weber, Max in: Roth, Guenther and Claus Wittich (eds) (1968) *Economy and Society* (edited by Guenther Roth and Claus Wittich). New York.

West, James M. (1998) 'Kukje and Beyond: Constitutionalism and the Market,' (June, 1998) (unpub).

World Bank, *Reforming China's State Enterprises* (News Release No. 98/1425).

World Bank, *Rethinking the State: World Bank Says an 'Effective State' Helps People and Markets Flourish* (News Release No. 97/1380/S).

World Bank, *World Bank Development Report 1996: From Plan to Market* (1996).

World Bank, *World Bank Helps Pioneer Judicial Reform in Peru* (News Release No. 98/1555/LAC).

World Bank, *World Bank President Urges Business, Governments to take Bolder Steps Against Corruption* (News Release No. 98/1515).

Yatsko, Pamela (1998) 'The Bigger, The Better,' *Far Eastern Economic Review*, 21 May 1998.

Young, Michael K. (1984) 'Judicial Review of Administrative Guidance: Governmentally Encouraged Consensual Dispute Resolution in Japan,' *Columbia Law Review* 84, p. 923.

Part Two

Japan as a Model for Law and Development in Asia

CHAPTER 5

GLOBALIZATION VS. PATERNALISTIC REGULATION: SOME THOUGHTS ABOUT ECONOMIC SUCCESS, THE ROLE OF LAW, AND THE REGULATION OF JAPAN'S FINANCIAL MARKETS

HARALD BAUM[1]

ASIAN MODEL OR ASIAN CRISIS?

In 1997, Japan held net external assets of more than one trillion dollars; the United States had about the same amount of net external debt. As is well known, Japan is the second largest economy, its citizens have the highest per capita income world-wide and Japanese households hold more than 30 per cent of the world's savings.

We clearly see a story of a tremendous economic success in the decades after World War II, which has raised the interest in many developing economies which wish to examine the situation to discover whether Japan could be a model for them. In the West, the Japanese success also caused a mild panic in the 1980s when we saw a seemingly endless flood of articles concerned with a perceived threat of Japan turning the Western societies into technological colonies and thereby attaining its allegedly imminent world supremacy.

However, the prolonged structural recession lasting for more than a decade after the bursting of the so-called *baberu keizai*, the 'bubble economy' in 1990 has cast growing doubt on that role. Although it took some time for the Western public to realize this, at least the worsening financial crisis in the mid-1990s worked as an eye-opener for many. Suddenly it has become clear that the Japanese system has not only given rise to world leaders like *Toyota*, *Sony*, or *Kyocera* – as was common knowledge in the heydays of the 1980s – but has also created a financial industry with firms like *Daiwa, Yamaichi,* and many others which were collectively responsible for one of the biggest peacetime economic losses in history. It became clear that Japan had a surprisingly divided dual economy: internationally successful exporters on the one hand and countless inefficient domestic firms serving the sheltered national market only on the other. This has changed the tune: now Japan is regarded as the country of the 'miracle economy' which had lost its aura.

Quite surprising for some, but not at all surprising for others, in a significant change of fortune the US has returned to the stage. The American economy keeps growing, unemployment is at a record low, stock prices on Wall Street are on a constant rise and US companies have successfully seized back various markets long thought lost, like those for semiconductors or computer technology, and in the information revolution they are undisputed leaders.

So, according to common wisdom, we first had the Asian model supposedly based on 'Asian values,' and we now have the Asian crisis supposedly caused by the 'Asian malaise.' However, this seems to be an oversimplified and misleading perspective. It is rather doubtful whether there is any such thing as an 'Asian value' or an interconnected 'Asian crisis' – at least if that is meant to include Japan.

DIFFERENT MODELS OF CAPITALISM

The main reason for this is that Japan and its neighbours are at very different stages of economic development. Whereas the former is a matured economy, the Southeast Asian nations have not yet reached this point. The *financial* crisis that occurred there in the second half of the 1990s and the *structural* crisis from which Japan has been suffering for more than a decade have at best a very loose correlation or vague similarity.

More interesting for gaining an understanding of the Japanese situation seems to be a comparative look at Germany, another matured economy. Like Japan, Germany too – to name but one continental European country – is in the midst of a severe structural crisis and has problems in adapting to a changing international economic environment. The world-wide trend towards greater liberalization and globalization seems to favour more liberally structured, market-based economies like the US or the UK and has made it increasingly difficult for socially more constrained economies like Germany or Japan to compete successfully with their liberal counterparts.

This indicates that Japan's troubles are *not* a specific Asian phenomenon but rather one example among others of a clash between two different social and economic models that occurs in Asia as well as in Europe.

The market structures of the various successful countries differ, as they are *embedded* in social institutions and corresponding regulatory regimes. In practice, there is not just one most efficient market structure but, according to the institutional setting, different patterns at work combining varying strengths and weaknesses into a country-specific mould. These distinctive settings have developed over time, adapting to cultural and historical forces and they are in a constant state of flux, they are, in other words, 'path-dependent' (Roe, 1996; Gilson, 1996; Leipold, 1996). However global the world economy may become, these specific institutional arrangements will not easily shed their specific character and they may become a burden in a changed international environment.

At a fairly abstract level, one can say that the economies in post-war Germany and Japan are constrained more by non-economic objectives than, for example, the American economy which is to a greater extent liberated from collective obligations to serve others. Although for different reasons and in varying degrees and shapes, in comparison to the US investment in both countries is – or at least used to be – more patient and employment more long-term orientated. These long-term relationships result to a greater degree of co-operation and mutual trust, and they are shielded against short-term market pressures by political institutions like, for example, more intense and paternalistic regulatory regimes. Generally we can observe a greater distrust towards potentially disruptive market forces. In this respect, obviously some structural similarities do exist between the German and the Japanese economic system. However, to avoid a possible misunderstanding that might arise at this point: of course the two systems *as such* do differ significantly in many other aspects, for example, corporate governance and legal structures to name but two aspects (cf. Baum, 1998 and 1995a).

Although observers of the Japanese economy mostly take recourse to a broad description of a market-driven economy as a model, it is not a free market in the neo-classical sense they have in mind. It seems to be more what one analyst called a 'planned market' (Tabb, 1995) – regardless of the fact that this term is a contradiction in itself. What is meant is not 'big government' in the sense of the ubiquitous welfare state *à la* Europe, but a policy of constant interference in or meddling with the markets by a dominant bureaucracy to achieve previously stipulated goals. Chalmers Johnson put it clearly: 'The institutions of capitalism inherited from the occupation ... were modified by the government's industrial policy. Lying behind industrial policy is the strong Japanese State itself. It is the *sine qua non* of Japan's economic achievements' (Johnson, 1995).

Many highly influential Japanese scholars and writers – those with bureaucratic background as well as those who have not – still believe in a model of the Japanese economy as a 'non-capitalistic market economy' (Sakakibara 1993). In this view, the real choice facing the world nowadays is not between capitalism and socialism, but between a capitalistic market economy like, for example in the US, and the Japanese model which is described as an 'extremely humanitarian economic regime' in comparison to capitalistic societies (ibid). And, those who hold this opinion argue, this owes much to the guiding and supervising role of the state or the administrative sector. As one critical voice puts it: 'It is an unspoken doctrine in Japan that political decisions must always prevail over market forces' (Mikuni, 2000).

Actually, these features of the 'Japanese economic model' seem to a lesser degree to be an indicator for a *different* kind of capitalism than rather simply a sign of a holdover from an *earlier* stage of capitalism (Katz, 1998). Therefore the term 'developmental-state capitalism' (Johnson, 1995) may be more precise. Furthermore, the idea of an allegedly 'extremely humanitarian economic regime' is somewhat difficult to reconcile with the fact that Japan is probably the *only* OECD country where premature death from overwork (*karôshi*) is such a widespread phenomenon that a citizens' movement against it was set up some years ago and courts are forcing employers to pay damages to the relatives of the victims.

FORCES OF CHANGE

Whatever the right label for it may be, the Japanese economic system has come under increasing pressure. Three reasons for this stick out:

First, Japan's trading partners have stopped accepting that the Japanese developmentalism, used to catch up with the West, has now moved on to exploiting the international trading system to achieve nationalistic goals. In the first decades after World War II, the Japanese economy was a late-comer in a catch-up situation where foreign technology could be easily bought, where it was possible to shelter the home market at least partly against foreign competition while at the same time having a ready market for exports in the United States and Europe (Brown, 1993). All of this is well known – though often officially denied – and has recently been described with rare clarity by a former government advisor: '… paternalistic administrative guidance enabled [the leading industries] to strike a happy balance between competition at home and government support for sales abroad' (Tsuru, 1993). Since the days of the early post-war reconstruction, the governing Japanese bureaucracy has successfully implemented an economic policy of maximizing production far in excess of domestic demand. The resulting surplus together with suppressed household consumption – or put differently, maximized household savings – has allowed the financing of industrial development *independent* of foreign capital and influence which was regarded as a prerequisite of Japan's national safety and independence. Being part of this institutional setting, Japanese producers, and their financiers understood perfectly that the tight bureaucratic control of market forces was in their favour. Of course, such an economic system requires isolation from outside forces (Mikuni, 2000). One result was the dual economy mentioned before, where some super-strong exporters contrast with a large number of hopelessly inefficient domestic sectors (Katz, 1998).

However, over time there has been no alternative but to open up markets. This has resulted in increased competition at home, which in turn makes it difficult to sustain a costly social fabric that has been designed to guarantee stability, egalitarianism and rent seeking by favoured groups rather than achieving the highest allocative efficiency. Furthermore, the significant rise of the yen since the mid-1980s, the so-called *endaka*, has eroded most of the cost advantages Japanese industry had. Therefore, to stay competitive, Japanese firms are increasingly forced to produce abroad and that causes a further disruption to the social cohesion and trust in stable employment.

Second, not only foreign pressure (*gaiatsu*), but also its domestic counterpart (*naiatsu*) is contributing to the present need to reform (Kusano, 1999). The past goal of Japanese industrial policy, the strengthening of exports, has helped to shape a producer- instead of a consumer-oriented society. In some ways, the consumer existed for the benefit of the manufacturer, rather than the other way round as would be normal (Samuels, 1989). Naturally, it was the consumers who bore the high costs of the closed and cartelized market. On top of this, the public was made liable for the cost of an increasingly expensive socialization of risks when the individual players responsible for failures were bailed out directly or indirectly with the money of taxpayers and savers (Mikuni, 1998).

Dire as this might seem, Japanese citizens obviously participated in the country's economic success at least to a sufficient degree so that they did not object to the general policy at elections, although, without doubt specific features of the political system too had helped the conservatives to stay in power (Pempel, 1997). But during the course of the lasting recession it became increasingly difficult for the government to dole out favours. People started to feel the true price of a policy allowing for widespread rent seeking and discontent grew as was shown in a 1995 poll.

On the occasion of the fiftieth anniversary of the end of World War II, three leading newspapers from the US, Japan, and Germany – the *Wallstreet Journal,* the *Nihon Keizai Shinbun*, and the *Handelsblatt* – commissioned a comprehensive survey in each of the three countries (Handelsblatt/Infas, 1995). Among facts which were unearthed, significant differences could be seen in the degree of satisfaction with the living conditions in the three countries. The polled parameters included the personal financial situation, cost of living, health care, provisions for old age, and job security and the like. On average, half of the Germans were content with their present situation, and the figure for the Americans was marginally but not significantly lower. The big surprise was the Japanese. Despite Japan's tremendous economic success in the past, only 15 per cent of the Japanese were content with their situation. This meant that over three-quarters of those polled were dissatisfied with the conditions of life in Japan in early 1995. Perhaps they were no longer willing to pay the price for development in the form of high prices for consumer goods and deferred consumption as a non-efficient financial system forces them to save an ever bigger share of their income to provide for their old age.

However, recent studies show that in spite of growing discontent and a general preference for liberalization, consumers have in fact been less demanding in their calls for political and administrative reforms and less focused on their own interests than one might have expected. Thus reforms so far have been slow and have often come in the form of complex compromises with considerable compensation for those who are likely to lose from change (Vogel, 1999).

Third, crucial technological and institutional innovations are impeded by some kind of 'institutional fatigue' (Nakatani, 1997). Even if industrial policy – rather than the vigour of the Japanese private sector, especially in the new sectors like cars and consumer electronics – should have been instrumental or at least partially useful in Japan's economic success in the past, this must be seen in a historical context which will not repeat itself. The catch-up position has long since ended. New technology must be developed rather than simply acquired (Brown, 1993).

Consequently, the government has tried to foster technological development and innovations by encouraging and financing research cartels and the like. But, with little success: the so-called 'Fifth Generation Computer Project' has failed to deliver the expected results, and the collective effort to develop high-definition television has turned out to be a flop in the face of independent American producers' advanced technology (Brown, 1993). As mentioned before, US companies have successfully seized back various markets long thought lost, like those for semiconductors or computer technology. In telecommunications or multimedia, the hesitant bureaucratic attitude has been described by Japanese industry itself as a kind of 'negative industrial policy' (Wood, 1994). Japan still lacks a flourishing domestic industry in these areas thanks to overregulation and bureaucratic interference in the market. It looks as if – as elsewhere and not surprisingly – it is competition based on a risk-taking ethic combined with an active venture capital industry like that in the US, rather than state-induced co-operation which creates the optimal environment for innovation (Dunn, 1995).

Accordingly, the need to reform is now widely recognized by industry itself. Leading economists, major research institutions and important business associations are demanding far-reaching changes towards more liberalized and market-oriented economic and administrative structures (cf.

e.g. Carlile and Tilton, 1998; from a critical perspective Dore, 1999). A prominent example is the report 'Efficiency and Trust: Creating a Market-Oriented Economy in Japan' published by the influential *Keizai Dôyûki* (Japan Association of Corporate Executives) in 1997.[2] The report calls for an end to the traditional 'high-price, high-cost structure' and constant government interventions in the markets. Instead it promotes such features as enhanced transparency, reduced regulation, and the build up of a market structure consistent with international practices. This being so changes are likely, but how quickly they will come, how far-reaching they will be, and what the precise outcome will be is still open as reformist and conservative forces are still in the midst of the battle (cf. Vogel, 1999; Carlile and Tilton, 1998; Pempel, 1997; Yamamura, 1997).

To sum up, in spite of its past success, growing sections of the Japanese economic system now seem to work in a rather problematic way. In fact, it looks as if it was exactly those sections on which, in the past, Japan watchers heaped the most praise for their instrumental role in Japan's economic success (e.g. emphatically by Dore and Whitacker, 1994) which are causing problems today. The guiding hand of the state has been at least a partial substitute for the market forces and it is hampered by its preference for some kind of vague paternalism instead of clear-cut rules. As the prominent economist *Iwao Nakatani* has aptly put it: '[A]n important cause of Japan's poor economic performance is regulation' (Nakatani, 1997). This view has been confirmed by a recent study of the OECD on regulatory reform in Japan that argues that 'a sharp break with past regulatory practices is needed' (OECD, 1999).

JAPAN'S FINANCIAL CRISIS

A prime example of this is Japan's ongoing financial crisis. The financial sector has long been a pet industry of the Japanese bureaucracy. The Ministry of Finance (*Ôkura-shô*, hereafter MoF) with its far-reaching powers could easily be described as the most powerful public institution in Japan, regulating, guiding, and protecting almost every aspect of the financial industry over the last fifty years (cf. Brown, 1999; Hartcher, 1998; Milhaupt, 1994; Baum and Hayakawa, 1994). But was it a success for *all* actors involved?

With respect to the policy goal stated above, the answer is clearly affirmative. Tightly controlled banks gave so-called strategic industries cheap access to household savings and helped to finance the export-oriented excessive production. However, although the Japanese have accumulated the biggest savings world-wide, they get the lowest dividend of all countries

(Courtis, 1997). This means, Japan's graying population has not and still does not get the necessary returns on their huge savings they need to provide for old age. So at least some players in the market might not have received a fair share of the spoils.

But has the paternalistic regime at least been a *lasting* success for the industry of which it has been taking care? In their criticism of market forces some observers do indeed expressively quote Japan's financial system as an example of successful management of the markets and the positive outcome of bureaucratic paternalism. In this view, the financial industry in Japan is 'more strictly and prudently governed than most others' (Sheridan, 1993).

However, if one looks at the gigantic losses which have been accumulated by that industry, the idea that this has been a great success seems rather outlandish. In the mid-1990s these losses had amounted to more than *one trillion* of US dollars and were caused by a mountain of bad loans, misguided speculation, and derivative trading that dwarfed the 'savings & loan crisis' of the early 1980s in the US. The collapse of major brokers, life assurers, banks, various credit co-operatives, and nearly all housing loan companies (*jûsen*) was something unheard of during the first five decades after World War II when the so-called 'no failure system' was practiced, under which the stronger institutions were forced to take care of the weaker ones.

The tight control together with the feeling of being ultimately protected by the authorities bred complacency and gave little incentive to prepare for the deregulation of the 1980s and the confrontation with growing international competition. While during the post-war period the banks had mainly served as instruments for collecting and allocating scarce resources to the manufacturing industries based on fixed and low interest rates, by the 1980s when industry started to make use of liberalization and to look for cheaper direct financing at home and abroad, the banks had increasingly turned to other business for which they were not prepared. Finally, the moral hazard caused by the implicit guarantee of no failure had become too costly to be sustained (Horiuchi, 1999). With the refusal of *Fuji Bank* to come to aid to its *keiretsu*-member *Yamaichi Securities* this system finally collapsed in 1997.

The result of this specific paternalistic treatment is what Western observers have called the 'archaic' nature of Japanese finance (Wood, 1994). Saddled with the permanent guidance of MoF and its refusal to let clear winners and losers emerge – as has been the case in the Japanese electronic industry, for example, which is significantly less guided – Japanese banks and securities companies lag far behind their American or even European competitors. It is not coincidental that, though Japanese banks are among the biggest banks world-wide, among the list of the most *profitable* banks one cannot find a single Japanese name. Japanese financial institutions have so far not been able to catch up with the impressive international success of the Japanese manufacturing industry; *Sony*, *Toyota*, or *Kyocera* have no counterparts in the financial world, which reflects the dual pattern of the post-war Japanese economy in which competitive and protected sectors co-existed and were bound together by numerous economic relationships and political bargains (Vogel, 1999).

Especially worrying has been that the losses in the financial industry were for the most part inseparably intertwined with fraud, corruption, and other misdemeanours involving politicians and – though formerly considered sacrosanct – elite bureaucrats. Either directly or indirectly via subsidiaries, nearly all the big names in Japanese finance were involved in one way or another. In other words, in more or less all sectors of the financial system, severe regulatory problems surfaced in the 1990s to expose systemic defects (Milhaupt and Miller, 1997b). This has shaken the very roots of the post-war financial system in Japan. Seeing the state prosecutors raiding the Ministry of Finance on television did not help to pacify the dissatisfied Japanese public that had been forced to subsidize the country's ailing financial industry to a significant degree. The uncovering of an involvement of organized crime in various scandals did not help either. Even worse, the considerable welfare loss caused by the financial mess was unnecessarily enlarged because of the severely inept mishandling of the crisis by a bureaucracy that wasted precious time trying to cover up scandals and block reforms as a means to defend its own power bases.

Given all this it was not by chance that in the aforementioned survey of 1995, the Japanese stated *bureaucracy* and *state intervention* as their third biggest problem – far more serious than unemployment (Handelsblatt/Infas, 1995). The seemingly endless series of scandals that surfaced in the 1990s have thoroughly discredited politicians – even more importantly parts of the bureaucracy as well as. The positive aspect is that it has become difficult for die-hard apologists of the former system to fend off administrative and regulatory changes necessary to restore public confidence. This brings us to the question of what role law and economic regulation have played so far and how that role might change in the future.

PATERNALISTIC REGULATION

The financial crisis of the 1990s is correctly perceived as primarily one of governance and regulation. The paternalistic regulatory approach – some observers even talk of 'collusive regulation' (Schaede, 1996) – has bred disaster by setting wrong incentive structures and preserving a system that was incompatible with the forces of globalization sweeping the international financial markets.

Talking about the role of law and regulatory concerns in economic development, one has to distinguish between the private law aspects – civil law, business law, procedural laws, a functioning court system for private litigation, and the like – and the era of public law and economic regulation.

With respect to the first, without any doubt we can see a modern functioning legal system in Japan. Courts are working, rights can be enforced, and judgments are predictable. The foundations for this system were successfully laid in only three decades between 1868 and 1900 when European (mostly German) legal institutions were adopted and assimilated into an entirely different legal culture – a remarkable and lasting achievement. Although the legal frame is thus similar to that of other modern industrial nations, we do not see a litigious society in Japan. Litigation rates are only a fraction of those in comparable other jurisdictions (cf. Wollschläger, 1997). This may raise a couple of questions. How does Japan manage to function with a significantly lower number of judges and lawyers and correspondingly fewer court proceedings than for example, Germany or the United States? (Cf. Henderson, 1997). Are a non-litigious people cleverly *not* wasting scarce resources on lawyers and lawsuits and still providing for an adequate measure of intra-societal justice? (for a critical view cf. Miyazawa, 1997). If so, what alternative conflict-avoiding or conflict-solving mechanisms take the place of contentious disputes? Do we see some kind of bargaining in the shadow of the law, to use a common phrase?

These questions cannot be answered here but it seems fairly safe to state that these differences seem to be more of gradual and less of a principal nature when compared with Western legal systems. The best explanation may be seen in a mixture of reasons, including path-dependent institutional settings as well as legal mentality and conscious political steering (cf. Wollschläger, 1997; Baum, 1995a).

However, with respect to the area of public law and economic regulation there seem to be more fundamental differences. Therefore, this second body of law seems to be of particular interest when studying what is called 'the Japanese regulatory system' and its contribution to economic success – or failure. At a first level, the written – and unwritten – public law governs the relationships between state and industry. At a second level, it also shapes the relationship between the industry and its customers, albeit more indirectly and to a lesser extent. Regulation and governance of the Japanese financial markets are a prime example of the specific ways in which industrial policies as well as bureaucratic and political interests are taken care of in Japan.

What are the origins of this regulatory regime? American law has heavily influenced economic regulation in Japan and especially the regulation of its financial markets after World War II. The Japanese Securities and Exchange Law of 1948 (SEL)[3] was modeled after the US securities laws of the 1930s. The adoption of the law was part of the so-called 'democratization' of the Japanese economy by the Allied Powers after the end of the War. However, since then the *practice* under that law has been markedly different from the US experiences and expectations (cf. Henderson, 1991). A prominent example is the use respectively non-use of the antifraud provisions in both countries. In the US, Rule 10b-5 under the 1934 Act[4] had been the subject of countless decisions by courts and a key element for regulating the American capital market. The contrary is true for Japan. Although the Japanese Act of 1948 had an identical provision with the former Art. 58 for almost half a century, it has more or less never been evoked and therefore played no significant role at all – as has private litigation in general in Japanese capital markets regulation.

This observation raises the question of what kind of regulatory regime is actually governing the Japanese financial markets. We can see a regime that has been adequately described as 'regulatory cartel' (Milhaupt and Miller, 1997a and 1997b). It is characterized by a couple of specific features:[5]

The *first* characteristic is – or at least has been till very recently – a unique concentration of power in the hands of just one institution: the Ministry of Finance run by elite bureaucrats most of whom graduated from the University of Tokyo. Under the roof of the Ministry various functions were combined that are located with different agencies in other countries. The most important are the drafting of financial laws and ordinances with little or no actual parliamentary control, the supervision of almost all segments of the financial markets from securities trading to banking and insurance business, the drafting of the budget, the sole authority over the so called Fiscal Investment and Loan Program (*Zaito*), a giant public sector financing system equivalent to some 70 per cent of the Japanese economy and as important as the budget, and, finally, the responsibility for the country's tax collection (cf. e.g. Hartcher, 1998).

Second, we see a close relationship between the regulators and the regulated. Many former finance bureaucrats held responsible positions in most failed financial institutions, and some of the bankrupt *jûsen* were even headed by them (cf. Kliesow, 1996). This refers to the phenomenon of *amakudari*, the 'descent from heaven' (which, financially, might be more appropriately called 'ascent into heaven'), a common practice of retired bureaucrats in their mid-fifties taking well-paid positions in the industries they had formerly been supervising. Sometimes this occurs directly, sometimes indirectly via a stopover in a semi-public institution. The resulting

'Old Boy' network has far reaching effects on the government-business relations (cf. Schaede, 1997).

A *third* important aspect of the particular regulatory structure is informality or situational regulation by administrative guidance (*gyôsei shidô*), resulting in a non-transparent character with aspects of collusive regulation. The laws and ordinances grant the authorities wide discretionary powers which are used to persuade and guide the party concerned to act in a certain way, in order to realize an administrative goal through that party's co-operation. The enforcement of decisions and their translation into the industrial level work with the help of a pronounced carrot-and-stick mechanism. It is typically effective because relationships between the ministries and the industry are long-term and work through various channels. Firms know that following an 'advice' could reap rewards later. In case of non-compliance with administrative guidance, the ministries have a wide variety of options to obstruct the future business of the party concerned, either directly or via other governmental branches (cf. e.g. Baum, 1997b).

In the view of a prominent American observer 'administrative guidance not justifiable law is the predominant instrument of bureaucratic power [in Japanese governments]. But administrative guidance should not be regarded as law. It is at best a-legal, and at worst illegal' (Henderson, 1991). Another evaluation matches this pretty closely: 'In Japan informal enforcement is not a *process* of governing, but has become *the* process of governing' (Haley, 1991).

The *fourth* characteristic feature is limited competition bolstered by pervasive entry controls, exclusion of outsiders, and strict market segmentation between securities business, trust and retail banking, insurance, and the like. Japan's financial markets were governed till very recently by an important although unwritten rule: any kind of business activity that was not expressively allowed was forbidden. Therefore, all kinds of business activities, new financial products, and so forth needed to be licensed by the Ministry of Finance, the (in)famous 'licensing system.' The granting of a licence was in most cases discretionary. The pace of innovation used to be set by the weakest members of an industry, the so-called 'convoy system.'

This protected the industry in a cartel-like manner. Furthermore, in the securities market for a long time the MoF used the four big securities firms that dominated the market as 'foot soldiers' to regulate the industry. The MoF created some kind of 'public-private joint venture' for capital market regulation (Milhaupt, 1994), that helped the understaffed Ministry and secured an overwhelming market share for the Big Four. By using the licensing system the Ministry restrained the entry of potential competitors.

Foreign financial institutions had rather painful experiences when they tried to enter the Japanese market in larger numbers in the 1980s. Interested Japanese institutions needed more than a decade of discussion and pressure before they finally received the chance to do business in different segments of the market via subsidiaries in the 1990s. The result was anti-competitive pricing and cartel-like allocation of rents. Examples of these are the long time fixed interests rates that were only fully liberated in the early 1990s and the fixed commissions for brokers that were fully liberalized only in 1999.

In case of failure, there was an unwritten guarantee for help by stronger members of the industry or, as last resort, public money (cf. Kanda, 1997a). Among other things, this has led to dicing with morality and the reckless lending, leading to the bubble and ultimately the crash (cf. Milhaupt and Miller, 1997b; Schaede, 1996).

A *fifth* important characteristic is a process of pre-clearance or '*ex ante monitoring*' that has to large degree substituted the '*ex post monitoring*' by the courts seen in other financial markets like the US market (Kanda, 1991 and 1997a). Parties with multiple interests participate in the administrative rulemaking process via advisory councils (*shingi-kai*). In other words, bureaucrats and industry are involved in the rulemaking procedure. Compromises reached informally with the parties concerned during that procedure help to promote acceptance.

However, there often seems to be less positive co-ordination – open negotiations within the ministerial bureaucracy – than there is some kind of negative co-ordination, meaning the endeavour of leading bureaucrats to restrict options *a priori* in such a way that there is potential consensus between all parties on any alternative. This constitutes the negative way of consensus finding by *a priori* exclusion of options that are deemed undesirable, and ensures that no one will lose face and the outcome of negotiations will not be totally unexpected. In any case, at least in the past, this mechanism has worked. There have been next to no judicial challenges to financial legislation or administrative rules. The process of *ex ante monitoring* promoting acceptance of specific regulatory outcome is reinforced by the fact that compliance with regulation in a given situation means in most cases compliance with administrative guidance. As that is considered legally 'voluntary,' there is little ground for a judicial review by the courts in such a case.

The central aim of this cartel-like regulatory regime has been – and to a somewhat lesser degree still is – to generate and allocate rents. As Milhaupt and Miller (1997a) have observed, 'votes, political patronage, and bribes are allocated among the political elite; regulatory property rights and concomitant distributions of power, prestige and budgetary appropriations are allocated among separate ministries; similar rights are allocated among intra-ministry bureaux; licenses to engage in lucrative activities are allocated among industries; and profits are allocated among large and small firms.' As always with all cartels, the consumers paid the price and the system did run into difficulties when outsiders started to enter the field and losses had to be allocated.

This regulatory structure obviously differs – in parts to a significant degree – from the regulatory approaches to be observed in other international financial markets. As in more or less all sectors of the Japanese financial system severe regulatory problems have surfaced which have exposed systemic defects, taking the part for the whole we may be able to see some limitations of the overall Japanese regulatory model based on the idea of a strong state and paternalistic governance (Nakatani, 1997; Milhaupt and Miller, 1997b) that is still heralded by some as the future blueprint for regulation in advanced economies (cf. e.g. Dore, 1999).

REGULATORY CHALLENGES OF GLOBALIZATION

To the extent it did work, the paternalistic and cartel-like regulatory system could only function as long as financial markets were closed. For the reasons described above (pp. 136-9) that is no longer feasible. The same profound impact globalization has on other financial markets and their regulation can now be felt in Japan, too. The result is a double challenge to the Japanese policy makers. They have to cope with substantial hangovers of the financial mess caused by the bursting of the 'bubble' and at the same time they have to prepare somewhat belatedly for the 'brave new world' of globalized finance.

The dynamics of the internationalization of investment and finance can be mainly traced back to (a) innovation in information and communication technologies; (b) government policies easing cross-border capital flows and market access by deregulation; (c) the institutionalization (and professionalization) of market participants; and (d) increasing importance of equity financing accompanied by disintermediation, securitization, and development of new financial products (cf. Baum, 2000).

Globalized financial markets confront national policy makers with a specific trilemma which can be labelled the 'impossible trinity' (Beddoes, 1999). A policy maker may very much want to achieve three goals when designing a financial system: (1) continuing national sovereignty; (2) financial markets that are regulated, supervised, and somehow protected; and (3) the advantages of a globalized capital market. Unfortunately these three objectives are incompatible.

Any coherent reform cannot avoid favoring two parts of the trinity at the expense of the third. If the regulation of the market as well as the maintaining of national sovereignty is the primary objective, capital market integration will have to be sacrificed. If, on the other hand, capital market integration and global regulation are the dominant aims of reform, this can only be achieved at the expense of national sovereignty. If, thirdly, the policy maker wishes to keep sovereignty and at the same time allow the integration of capital markets, he has to accept an entirely free market structure at the global level.

The dynamics described above have already led to significantly intensified competition worldwide, not only among market participants, but also among national markets and their regulatory systems as such. Globalization makes weaknesses in individual financial markets more transparent than before (Mailander, 1997/98). At the same time it provides open markets and advanced technology institutional investors with the chance of a regulatory arbitrage. Internet technology especially is increasingly providing an extremely efficient exit option.

A competitive market for regulatory regimes challenges not only the cross-border or international aspects of financial regulation, but to an even greater extent it confronts the *domestic* regulatory substance. Here lies the core of the 'regulatory challenge' in the financial markets for national legislators and administrators (Baum, 2000). To the extent that a national regulation only requires what the market would provide in any case, no difficulties will arise, but the rule seems rather pointless. If, however, something is required that the market would otherwise not provide because market participants are disinterested and not willing to pay for it, regulatory competition will undermine the specific market design.

Regulators can only enforce such a market structure if they have the means to suppress regulatory competition successfully. The 'classic way' to do so is to make an agreement with your competitors not to compete (Kitch, 1996). In a globalized market the only acceptable way to suppress regulatory competition is by legal harmonization. From this perspective, an international harmonization arrangement can be viewed as something similar to a 'cartel arrangement' that limits supranational competition among national regulatory regimes for the sake of keeping market forces at bay. However, as this is not a likely option at the moment, national policy makers are better advised to reform their regulatory regimes in a functional and attractive way that maintains the right balance between de-regulation and re-regulation. And indeed this is what we have seen happening over the last years in most international financial centres. Somewhat late, the Japanese policy makers too have joined the race.

CHANGE OF THE REGULATORY PARADIGM?

Attempts to reform Japan's financial system had cautiously got off to a start already in the 1980s. Those were focused mostly on a careful loosening of the strict market fragmentation. But in contrast to the British liberalization, the so called 'Big Bang' of 1986, that opened up the market and allowed foreign investment banks to take over weak domestic institutions, the Japanese reforms were structured in a way that secured the survival of domestic institutions and kept most foreigners out (Vogel, 1996). In the wake of a number of scandals including insider trading and large-scale loss compensating by securities firms to favored clients, the government tried to improve market surveillance and to create an independent supervisory agency. But these reform proposals met fierce resistance from the MoF (cf. Char, 1993). The ministry was able to defend its position and to water down the reforms (cf. Milhaupt, 1994). The result was the creation of a semi-independent body, the so-called Securities and Exchange Surveillance Commission (SESC) in 1992. This was in effect nothing more than renamed bureau of the MoF stacked with people from the ministry and with no powers of its own to impose sanctions in case of violations of the SEL (cf. Keehn, 1997).

The picture started to change somewhat in November 1996 when then Prime Minister Hashimoto announced a comprehensive reform package – dubbed 'Big Bang' after the British reform of 1986 – to be implemented over a five year period till 2001. The reform proposals were backed by important advisory councils that called for a complete overhaul of the regulatory structure and policies governing Japanese finance towards a more market-oriented system with the aim of reviving the Tokyo market into a financial market comparable to those of New York and London (cf. Royama, 1998). Implementation of the various interconnected individual reform steps started in late 1997 and is still ongoing. Whether the planned time schedule can be kept to remains to be seen. The complex structure of the Japanese Big Bang cannot be described here in detail.[6] However, the most important elements of the reform and the date of becoming effective are (cf. Kanda 2000):

- Lifting of the ban on holding companies (December 1997);
- Abolition of exchange controls (April 1998);
- Setting up of new and independent supervisory and regulatory agencies: the Financial Supervisory Agency, FSA (June 1998), and the Financial Reconstruction Commission, FRC (December 1998);
- Securing of loans, receivables, and real property (September 1998);

- Changing from the licensing to a registration system with respect to market entry (December 1998);
- Full liberalization of brokerage commissions (October 1999);
- Improvement in accounting (fiscal year 1999);
- Defragmentation among banking, securities business, and insurance industry (ongoing).

The reforms are praised as a breakthrough and a radical change from the 'ancient regime' (Oda, 1998) and regarded as a shift from industry to market protection as well as a shift from direct to indirect protection of markets (Kanda, 1997b). The probable impact on the Japanese economy will be a change from a bank-centred to a capital market-centred system in which the emphasis shifts from stability to adaptability resulting in a greater choice for investors and consumers (Kanda, 2000).

The long-term implication for the legal system may be substantial too. The aforementioned *ex ante* monitoring will probably lose some of its importance over time, and *ex post* monitoring by courts will accordingly increase. The judiciary has to respond to the change towards a rule-based system of finance by becoming larger and one likely and necessary outcome will be a drastic increase in the number of lawyers (Kanda, 2000).

Less clear is the future role of the financial bureaucracy. For sure, its powers have become diminished but to what extent remains to be seen. In the past, it has managed to keep its power and to stick basically to its way of regulating the markets in spite of obvious setbacks and strong public criticism by cleverly averting or, if need be, adapting reforms to its needs. This time it may be more difficult, but although the ministry has clearly lost its supervisory functions, it has retained the more important policy supervision and kept the exclusive right to draw up the national budget. More generally, it has maintained its capacity for 'steering Japanese funds to public ends' (Norville, 1998). Also its system of recruitment and retirement – 'the University of Tokyo club-type entry and the *amakudari* exit' (Hartcher, 1998) – has remained largely intact.

A full implementation of the reforms may take longer than five years given the fact that so much of the ruling LDP and the bureaucracy rest on the support of the inefficient sectors that have most to lose by the very reforms.[7] However, given the present state of affairs and the pressures of globalization, reforms will come and they will unlock Japan's enormous potential blocked at the moment by a straitjacket of obsolete institutions (Katz, 1998). At least one positive outcome is obvious: the improved access to the Japanese market for foreign financial institutions, which has been rather limited for a long time (cf. Baum, 1995b). Some such bodies were not only allowed but also even encouraged to take over (ailing) Japanese banks, securities companies, and insurers.

Another question is to what extent we can expect a convergence of Japan's political economy and regulation with the Anglo-American model. A far-reaching convergence can be ruled out with respect to the staying power of institutions and path-dependent development (cf. Baum, 1998; Yamamura, 1997). But freer and more strongly market-oriented structures will at least *partly* (and gradually) replace the paternalistic cartel-like regulatory regime. However, although the present reform has brought a liberalization of rules, it has just begun to make 'a dent in the traditional procedures for making and implementing financial regulation in Japan' (Norville, 1998).

NOTES

1 Parts of this article are based on Baum, 1997a.
2 See <http://www.doyukai.or.jp/database/teigen /970624e.htm>.
3 *Shôken torihiki-hô*, Law No. 25 of 1948 as amended.
4 17 C.F.R. § 240.10b-5.
5 See also Kanda 1997a, Baum 1997b, Schaede 1996, Milhaupt 1994, Baum/Hayakawa 1994, Kanda 1991, Henderson 1991, each emphasizing different aspects of the regulatory regime.
6 For a general overview and analysis see Kanda 2000 and 1997b, and Oda 1998. A discussion of special features of the reforms can be found with e.g. Hall 1999, 1998a, 1998b, 1998c, McAlinn 1999, Wiley 1999, Satusky 1999, Thorson and Siegfanz 1999, Sibbitt 1998, and Ruback 1998. Reports of the advisory councils as well as information about the goals of the reform, details of individual segments, and the current state of implementation are available in English at the website of the Ministry of Finance <http://www.mof.go.jp>.
7 An example is the forced resignation of the chairman of the FRC, *Michio Ochi*, in February 2000, after he publicly stated that the FSA might be 'unduly severe' with its inspections of the hundreds of small credit unions and credit associations that are also weighted down with bad loans. Together with the numerous agriculture co-operatives, these may be the worst bit of Japan's financial mess still waiting to be cleaned up; cf. *The Economist*, 4 March 2000, p. 89. Another example is the delay in ending the full protection of deposits by the government. This was scheduled for April 2001 but that date has been postponed for at least a year, as it would have exposed the weakest lenders to market forces.

REFERENCES

Baum, H. (1995a) 'Rechtsdenken, Rechtssystem und Rechtswirklichkeit in Japan: Rechtsvergleichung mit Japan' [Legal Thought, Legal System, and Legal Reality in Japan: Comparison of Law with Japan], *Rabels Zeitschrift für ausländisches und internationales Privatrecht* 59, pp. 258-92.

– (1995b) *Marktzugang und Unternehmenserwerb in Japan* [Market Access and Acquisitions of Companies in Japan]. Heidelberg: Verlag Recht und Wirtschaft.

– (1997a) 'Emulating Japan?' in: H. Baum (ed.) *Japan: Economic Success and Legal System*. Berlin–New York: Walter de Gruyter, pp. 1-24.

– (1997b) 'Börsen- und Kapitalmarktrecht in Japan' [Regulation of Exchanges and Capital Markets in Japan], in: K.J. Hopt, B. Rudolph and H. Baum (eds) *Börsenreform*. Stuttgart: Schäffer–Poeschel, pp. 1265-395.

– (1998) 'Zur Diskussion über vergleichende Corporate Governance mit Japan' [Comparative Corporate Governance with Japan], *Rabels Zeitschrift für ausländisches und internationales Privatrecht* 62, pp. 739-86.

– (2000) 'Globalizing Capital Markets and Possible Regulatory Responses,' in: J. Basedow and T. Kono (eds) *Legal Aspects of Globalisation – Conflict of Laws, Internet, Capital Markets and Insolvency in a Global Economy*. Den Haag: Kluwer Law International, pp. 77-132.

Baum, H. and M. Hayakawa (1994) 'Die rechtliche Gestaltung der japanischen Finanzmärkte' [The Regulation of Japan's Financial Markets], in: H. Baum and U. Drobnig (eds) *Japanisches Handels- und Wirtschaftsrecht* [Japanese Economic and Business Law]. Berlin/New York: Walter de Gruyter, pp. 516-639.

Beddoes, Z.M. (1999) 'Time for a Redesign?' *The Economist*, 30 January 1999, Special Supplement, *A Survey of Global Finance*.

Brown, J.R. (1993) 'Industrial Policy and the Dangers of Emulating Japan,' *The George Washington Journal of International Law and Economics* 27, pp. 1-68.

– (1999) *The Ministry of Finance: Bureaucratic Practices and the Transformation of the Japanese Economy*. Westport, Conn.: Quorum Books.

Carlile L.E. and M.C. Tilton (1998) 'Is Japan Really Changing,' in: L.E. Carlile and M.C. Tilton (eds) *Is Japan Really Changing Its Ways? Regulatory Reform and the Japanese Economy*. pp. 197-218.

Char, J.C. (1993) 'Reforming Japan's Securities Market: The Loss Compensation Scandal,' *International Tax & Business Lawyer*, pp. 173-227.

Courtis, K. (1997) *Japan – Big Bang or Wee Whimper*. Paper, on file with the author.

Dore, R. (1999) 'Japan's Reform Debate: Patriotic Concern or Class Interest? Or Both?' *Journal of Japanese Studies* 25, pp. 65-89.

Dore, R. and H. Whitacker (1994) 'Introduction,' in: K. Imai and R. Komiya (eds) *Business Enterprise in Japan: Views of Leading Japanese Economists*. Cambridge, Mass.: The MIT Press.

Dunn, M.H. (1995) 'Neue Industriepolitik oder Stärkung der Marktkräfte?' [New Industrial Policy or Strengthening of Market Forces?], *ORDO. Jahrbuch für die Ordnung von Wirtschaft und Gesellschaft* 46, pp. 165-83.

Gilson, R.J. (1996) 'Corporate Governance and Economic Efficiency: When Do Institutions Matter?' *Washington University Law Quarterly* 74, pp. 327-45.

Haley, J.O. (1991) *Authority without Power. Law and the Japanese Paradox*. Oxford: Oxford University Press.

Hall, M.J.B. (1998a) 'Financial Reform in Japan: Redefining the Role of the Ministry of Finance.' *Journal of International Banking Law* 5, pp. 171-6.

– (1998b) 'Financial Reform in Japan: "Big Bang",' *Journal of International Banking Law* 2, pp. 58-70.

– (1998c) 'Supervisory Reform in Japan,' *Journal of Financial Regulation and Compliance* 7/3, pp. 256-69.

– (1999) 'Japan's Big Bang: The Likely Winners and Losers,' *Journal of International Banking Law*, Issue 7, pp. 204-16.

Handelsblatt and infas (1995) *USA, Japan, Deutschland 1995. Wirtschaftsmächte im Spiegel der Nationen* [The US, Japan, Germany 1995: Economic Powers in the Mirror of the Nations]. Düsseldorf.

Hartcher, P. (1998) *The Ministry. How Japan's Most Powerful Institution Endangers World Markets*. Boston: Harvard Business School Press.

Henderson, D.F. (1991) 'Security Markets in the United States and Japan. Distinctive Aspects Molded Cultural, Social, Economic, and Political Differences,' *Hastings International and Comparative Law Review* 14, pp. 263-301.

– (1997) 'The Role of Lawyers in Japan,' in: H. Baum (ed.) *Japan: Economic Success and Legal System*. Berlin/New York: Walter de Gruyter, pp. 27-67.

Horiuchi, A. (1999) 'Financial Fragility and Recent Developments in the Japanese Safety Net,' *Social Science Japan Journal* 2, pp. 23-43.

Johnson, C. (1995) *Japan: Who Governs? The Rise of the Developmental State*. New York–London: W.W. Norton & Co.

Kanda, H. (1991) 'Politics, Formalism, and the Elusive Goal of Investor Protection: Regulation of Structured Investment Funds in Japan,' *University of Pennsylvania Journal of International Business Law* 12, pp. 569-88.

– (1997a) 'Finance Bureaucracy and the Regulation of Financial Markets in Japan,' in: H. Baum (ed.) *Japan: Economic Success and Legal System*. Berlin–New York: Walter de Gruyter, pp. 305-19.

– (1997b) 'Globalization of Financial Markets and Financial Regulation in Japan,' *Zeitschrift für Japanisches Recht* 2/4, pp. 9-17.

– (2000) 'Globalization of Capital Markets: A Perspective from Japan,' in: J. Basedow and T. Kono (eds) *Legal Aspects of Globalisation – Conflict of Laws, Internet, Capital Markets and Insolvency in a Global Economy*. Den Haag: Kluwer Law International, pp. 69-76.

Katz, R. (1998) *Japan: The System that Soured. The Rise and Fall of the Japanese Economic Miracle*. Armonk, N.Y.: M. E. Sharpe.

Keehn, E.B. (1997) 'Virtual Reality in Japan's Regulatory Agencies,' in: H. Baum (ed.) *Japan: Economic Success and Legal System*. Berlin–New York: Walter de Gruyter, pp. 321-30.

Kitch, E.W. (1996) 'Competition Between Securities Markets: Good or Bad?' in: F. Oditah (ed.) *The Future for the Global Securities Market: Legal and Regulatory Aspects*. Oxford: Clarendon Press, pp. 233-42.

Kliesow, O. (1996) 'Jûsen: Absurdes Theater in Japans Finanzwelt' [Jûsen: Theater of the Absurd in Japan's Financial World]. *Zeitschrift für Japanisches Recht* 1/2, pp. 59-71.

Kusano, A. (1999) 'Deregulation in Japan and the Role of Naiatsu (Domestic Pressure),' *Social Science Japan Journal* 2, pp. 65-84.

Leipold, H. (1996) 'Zur Pfadabhängigkeit der institutionellen Entwicklung' [Path Dependency and Institutional Development], in: Cassel (ed.) *Entstehung und Wettbewerb von Systemen* [Formation of and Competition between Systems]. Berlin: Duncker & Humblot.

Mailander, C.J. (1997-8) 'Financial Innovation, Domestic Regulation and the International Marketplace: Lessons to be Drawn from the International Bond Market,' *The George Washington Journal of International Law and Economics* 31, pp. 341-92.

McAlinn, G.P. (1999) 'The Financial Crisis in Japan – Reforming a System in Chaos,' *Asia Business Law Review* 23, pp. 3-11.

Miyazawa, S. (1997) 'For the Liberal Transformation of Japanese Legal Culture: A Review of the Recent Scholarship and Practice,' *Zeitschrift für Japanisches Recht* 2/4, pp. 101-15.

Mikuni, A. (1998) 'Why Japan Can't Reform Its Economy,' *Zeitschrift für Japanisches Recht* 3/6, pp. 157-65.

– (2000) *How Japan's Financial System is Administered and Protected by the Government*. Paper, on file with the author.

Milhaupt, C.J. (1994) 'Managing the Market: The Ministry of Finance and Securities Regulation in Japan,' *Stanford Journal of International Law* 30, pp. 423-81.

Milhaupt, C.J. and G.P. Miller (1997a) 'A Regulatory Cartel Model of Decisionmaking in Japanese Finance,' *Zeitschrift für Japanisches Recht* 2/4, pp. 18-29.

– (1997b) 'Cooperation, Conflict, and Convergence in Japanese Finance: Evidence from the "Jusen" Problem,' *Law and Policy in International Business* 29, pp. 1-78.

Nakatani, I. (1997) 'A Design for Transforming the Japanese Economy,' *Journal of Japanese Studies* 23, pp. 399-417.

Norville, E. (1998) 'The "Illiberal" Roots of Japanese Financial Regulatory Reform,' in: L.E. Carlile and M.C. Tilton (eds) *Is Japan Really Changing Its Ways? Regulatory Reform and the Japanese Economy.* Washington D.C.: Brookings Institution Press, pp. 111-41.

Oda, H. (1998) 'The Reform of Financial System in Japan,' *Zeitschrift für Japanisches Recht* 3/6, pp. 3-18.

Organisation For Economic Co-operation And Development (1999), *Regulatory Reform in Japan.* Paris: OECD.

Pempel, T.J. (1997) 'Regime Shift: Japanese Politics in a Changing World Economy,' *Journal of Japanese Studies* 23, pp. 333-61.

Roe, M.J. (1996) 'Chaos and Evolution in Law and Economics,' *Harvard Law Review* 109, pp. 641-68.

Royama, S. (1998) 'Big Bang in the Japanese Securities Market,' *Japan Review of International Affairs*, Winter 1998, pp. 300-20.

Ruback, G.D. (1998) 'Master of Puppets: How Japan's Ministry of Finance Orchestrates Its Own Reformation,' *Fordham International Law Journal* 22, pp. 185-228.

Sakakibara, E. (1993) *Beyond Capitalism: The Japanese Model of Market Economics.* Lanham [etc.]: University Press of America.

Samuels, R.J. (1989) 'Consuming for Production: National Security, the Domestic Economy, and Nuclear Fuel Procurement in Japan,' *International Organization* 43, pp. 625-46.

Satusky, E. (1999) 'Japanese Financial Market Reform from a Global Regulatory Perspective: A New Beginning for Market Oriented Regulation or the Status Quo?' *Banking & Finance Law Review* 14, pp. 275-328.

Schaede, U. (1996) *The Bad Loan Debacle: MOF and the Japanese Banking Crisis.* Paper, on file with the author.

– (1997) 'The "Old Boy" Network and Government-Business Relationships in Japan,' in: H. Baum (ed.) *Japan: Economic Success and Legal System.* Berlin–New York: Walter de Gruyter, pp. 345-69.

Sheridan, K. (1993) *Governing the Japanese Economy.* Cambridge: Polity Press.

Sibbitt, E.C. (1998) 'A Brave New World for M&A of Financial Institutions in Japan: Big Bang Financial Deregulation and the New Environment for Corporate Combinations of Financial Institutions,' *University of Pennsylvania Journal of International Business Law* 19, pp. 965-1027.

Tabb, W.K. (1995) *The Postwar Japanese System: Cultural Economy and Economic Transformation*. Oxford etc.: Oxford University Press.

Thorson, A.H. and F. Siegfanz (1999) 'The 1997 Deregulation of Japan's Holding Companies,' *Pacific Rim Law & Policy Journal* 8, pp. 261-349.

Tsuru, S. (1993) *Japan's Capitalism: Creative Defeat and Beyond*. Cambridge: Cambridge University Press.

Vogel, S.K. (1996) *Freer Markets, More Rules*. Ithaca–London: Cornell University Press.

– (1999) 'Can Japan Disengage? Winners and Losers in Japan's Political Economy, and the Ties that Bind Them,' *Social Science Japan Journal* 2, pp. 3-21.

Wiley, J.C. (1999) 'Will the "Bang" Mean "Big" Changes to Japanese Financial Laws?' *Hastings International and Comparative Law Review* 22, pp. 379-405.

Wollschläger, C. (1997) 'Historical Trends of Civil Litigation in Japan, Arizona, Sweden, and Germany: Japanese Legal Culture in the Light of Judicial Statistics,' in: H. Baum (ed.) *Japan: Economic Success and Legal System*. Berlin/New York: Walter de Gruyter, pp. 89-142.

Wood, C. (1994) *The End of Japan Inc. and How the New Japan Will Look*. New York etc.: Simon & Schuster.

Yamamura, K. (1997) 'The Japanese Political Economy after the "Bubble": Plus Ça Change?' *Journal of Japanese Studies* 23, pp. 291-331.

CHAPTER 6

THE RULE OF LAW OR LAW AS INSTRUMENT OF RULE? LAW AND THE ECONOMIC DEVELOPMENT OF JAPAN WITH PARTICULAR REGARD TO INDUSTRIAL POLICY[1]

RICHARD BOYD

'Rule of law rhetoric is all around us ... in the business press, in the publications of the World Bank, IMF and ADB' notes Ohnesorge elsewhere in this volume. He further notes that, 'the rule of law is not being touted in these primarily for its traditional political role as a protector of human rights and individual dignity. Rather the new rhetoric makes the claim that the rule of law is a crucial element in economic development, not only in former socialist countries but in poor capitalist countries as well' (Ohnesorge, 2000:2).

Undoubtedly the observation is sound.[2] It is, however, the merits of the claim itself that will be at issue in this chapter. Accordingly, it is worth saying at the outset, given that the erecting of straw men for subsequent demolition is not the most profitable use of the reader's time, that the linkage between the rule of law and economic development does not seem critical in the Japanese case at least. A first proximate reaction is that economic development was well under way in Japan and certainly predated the codification of law along Western lines at the end of the nineteenth century. A second reaction is that in so far as law figures – if at all – in the vast literatures concerning the economic development of Japan it is with respect to the possibilities it affords of administrative discretion in pursuit of developmental ends. That is almost the diametric opposite of the role for law envisioned by the institutions referred to above. As far as the 'rule of law' is concerned, particularly if this is to be understood in the strong sense as a set of formal, universal overarching constraints upon the actions of all players including government, there would seem, again at first sight, to be problems. Certainly there are those who would argue that the rule of law is something which might better be understood as a goal, than as a precondition of Japan's economic growth but even this could not be taken as read. An empirical exercise to establish whether or not and, if so, how far the 'rule of law' is goal or norm in Japan would be required. In short there would seem to be problems aplenty with the rhetoric of the rule of law in the case of Japan. To be blunt, the *prima facie* evidence suggests that the Japanese case does not confirm the rule of law hypothesis. Does this matter? It should but there are reasons to doubt that it does or will. At issue is the way in which the mainstream literatures (that is literatures that have as their first empirical point of reference the countries of the West) deal with East Asian cases. Johnson (1988) and Wade (1992) are only two of the serious minded scholars who have come close to irritation at the willingness to downplay, to marginalize, or to explain away the significance of uncomfortable Asian cases. There is a more sophisticated but no less dubious response to the case study that refutes the existence or the significance of what is said originally to be the cause. This is the search for the functional analogue – a 'something else' that does the job that (in this case) the rule of law would otherwise have done. Quite what conditions govern and produce the 'otherwise' is not usually clear but seems to be a matter of culture or time. To complete the puzzle, a curious logic has it that if the analogue is discovered the significance of the supposed original is thereby confirmed. The chapter proceeds from the assumption that there is little profit to be derived from the pursuit of the 'functional analogue,' (in Japan) to the presumed role of the rule of law in economic development. Not least of the reasons is that the underlying equation proceeds as if the latter (the rule of law) was the preferred means of history when history was fully awake or at least closer to 'home' but which might be substituted for when history was dozy and distant. The objection is simple; Japan is not a marginal case. It is one of the world's leading economies and remains so – notwithstanding apprehensions borne of the 'Asia Crisis.' Theory embraces Japan as a central empirical referent or is found wanting. More specifically, if theories regarding the rule of law and economic development are robust and persuasive they apply to Japan. If on close examination they prove not to, then the theory itself comes fundamentally into question.

Accordingly and broadly, the approach taken in this chapter will be to list the claims made for the rule of law, to check how far these have figured in the principal explanations of East Asian growth in general, and to move then to an assessment of how far law has figured in the analysis of the Japanese case. This will entail a brief historical sketch of the place of law in the economic development of Japan with particular regard to the hypotheses of the rule of law rhetoric (does Japan seem to confirm or refute them?) before an argument is developed along the lines that economic growth began in Japan long before the codification of property rights and that there is an entrenched legal tradition in Japan which understands law as the instrument of rule, as the tool rather than the limit of office. In the second part of the chapter the general and historical account of the first part will be set against a case study to anchor discussion, a case adumbrated to be sure, but nonetheless a means of moving from the abstract and hypothetical to the specific and empirical, from an economic context of growth to one of decline – a distinction of importance for the possibilities of political agency and equally a means of illustrating the extent to which legal and bureaucratic traditions persist. A particular concern will be the elucidation of the actual rather than the hypothesized significance of law in the management of economic change.

DEFINITIONAL PRELIMINARIES

Given the weight and importance of Japan in the world economy and even more so of the importance of Japan as a developmental success story, then the relative insignificance of law as a factor in the explanation of this case might prompt a degree of surprise at the attention which has been given to a hypothesis which falls at the first fence. The answer in part must be that for all its intellectual weaknesses, (problems of precision, conceptualization, verification, seeming incompatibility with significant cases) there are sound pragmatic reasons for the rhetoric. Bankers and bureaucrats in international organizations are practical men and they are accountable to publics for their management of large sums of other people's money. Fiascos such as that which attended the IMF's expensive and fruitless involvement with Russia are unwelcome and not to be repeated. They are likely to prompt a rethinking of the security of investments and to predispose such organizations to favour investments in countries where the 'rule of law' lessens the likelihood that public monies will be diverted for private ends. From such a perspective it may well seem axiomatic that the rule of law is the precondition for economic development. Doubtless security and predictability are a prerequisite of sustained economic performance and rare is the entrepreneur who does not perceive the converse as a threat to business. This sits easily as an intuition. It has also benefited from substantial empirical support. Thus the rule of law in terms of the existence of secure property rights is a determinant of the likelihood of the transfer of technology, incontestably an important element in economic development. Mansfield's study (Mansfield, 1994) concludes that the strength or weakness of a country's system of intellectual property protection has a substantial effect, particularly in high-technology industries, on the kinds of technology US firms will transfer to that country. Intellectual property rights also influence the extent of US foreign direct investment. This is true not only of property rights and not only in technology transfer. Brunetti and his colleagues set out to explore systematically the case studies and anecdotal evidence that have suggested that uncertainty about policies, laws, and regulations has hampered development of the private sector in many developing countries. The authors present results from a cross-country survey that provides comparable data on local investors' problems in dealing with the state. The survey was conducted in 69 countries and covers more than 3,600 entrepreneurs. It explores investors' perceptions of such issues as the predictability of laws and policies, the reliability of the judiciary, corruption in bureaucracies, and security of property rights. Perhaps not surprisingly the study found that in less developed countries the majority of entrepreneurs constantly fear policy surprises and unexpected changes in rules that can seriously affect their business. They note also that entrepreneurs world wide feel that the cost of doing business is substantially increased by theft and crime and in many developing countries the business community feels that authorities do not adequately guarantee their personal safety and do not reliably enforce their property rights. Unreliable judiciaries are perceived as major problems in many developing countries (particularly in the Commonwealth of Independent States and in Latin American countries). Entrepreneurs in Asia have the most trust in government announcements of policy changes and changes in rules; entrepreneurs in the Commonwealth of Independent States are the most cynical about new announcements; and half of businessmen surveyed in Latin America and Central and Eastern Europe do not believe government announcements (Brunetti, 1997).

At a practical level Brunetti's findings are striking but *they do not amount to a case for the rule of law rhetoric.* Quite simply because what is critical for the entrepreneur is predictability and while the rule of law may be one means of securing this it is not the only means. Trust is equally adept and in fact the study affords empirical support for the importance in economic affairs of trust in line with the claims of a rapidly expanding literature on this theme. The practical and pragmatic arguments for linking the rule of law and economic development are real enough but they fall short of an adequate theoretical account of the linkage. Scholarly legitimacy for this came in the wake of the writings of North and Thomas (1973), which championed the view that the right to property is a fundamental institutional condition for market based economic development – a view to which North remains committed 25 years later (North, 1998:553). The rule of law rhetoric has come to embrace rather more than property rights; at times attention shifts to the guarantee (so to both the law and to its effective enforcement) of economic rights, concretely intellectual property rights, and the right to compete, so to competition law and to competition policy. The former (intellectual property rights) will not figure in this discussion, the latter, competition law and practice will. The rhetoric also makes claims as to the status of law in respect of the state itself. Here the explicit normative concern is that the state and its agents should be subject to, constrained and limited by law – a concern that moves issues of bureaucratic discretion and of administrative accountability to centre stage. In this second sense the rhetoric would have it again that the rule of law is the essential precondition for market based economic development. Here too discussion slips quickly from the abstract to the concrete and so to the institutions and procedures which lock private and public actors into binding legal relations the nature, terms and limits of which are determined not by the public actors more than the private actors, not indeed by the actors themselves but by courts and judges. Issues of bureaucratic discretion and of the justiciability of administrative acts will become central. We will look now more closely at how far law figures in the standard explanations of economic growth in East Asia before turning to the particular case of Japan. In respect of Japan our survey will look at the economic development of Japan in general in the context of growth and offer a brief historical sketch of some relevant features of Japanese legal tradition before turning to the concrete and particular experience of law in the management of decline in heavy industry in the post-war period.

THE PLACE OF LAW IN THE DEBATE OVER EAST ASIAN DEVELOPMENT

When we turn from general considerations to the substance of East Asian development we find, inter alia, a body of neo-liberal writing on East Asian development within which it is axiomatic that a sound and reliable legal system which guarantees property rights is one of the essential 'public goods' to be provided by a government sensitive to its proper role.[3] Once law is enforced, the argument is competitive markets will emerge to permit efficient resource allocation which is the sufficient basis for long-term growth. This much is axiomatic. The axiom is, however, better regarded as a core presumption of the neo-liberal view – so obvious as to require neither evidence nor argument. Thus for Hughes 'Political stability and the rule of law are essential' (Hughes, 1988) while Riedel asserts that 'neo-classical principles are alive and well, and working particularly effectively in the East Asian countries. Once public goods are provided for ... markets seem to do the job of allocating resources reasonably well.[4] The adequacy of the neo-liberal explanation of East Asian development has been widely questioned[5] but it is not, in general at issue here where the concern is the rule of law. In so far as this has a place in the literatures on East Asian development it does so within the corpus of neo-liberal work where it figures as an untested (untestable?) unevidenced presumption of an approach that has been generalized to East Asia.

The thrust of the literature is elsewhere. Studies of the role of government in the provision of public goods and in the direct promotion of economic growth led to characterizations of East Asian growth in terms of the developmental state.[6] This was controversial once, precisely because of its challenge to neo-liberal views to which it has long been empirically richer and historically more sensitive. It is less controversial now at a time when the WDB itself has seen fit to commission studies on the role of government in East Asian development[7] we will return to these shortly. For the moment it is sufficient to note that law, much less the rule of law is not held to be a feature of the developmental state in its various guises. An early and influential account put it (effectively the key features of the developmental state) as follows:

> My contention is that the Japanese, Koreans and Taiwanese have put together the political economy of capitalism in ways unprecedented in the West ... [These are] (1) Financial control over the economy; (2) labour relations; (3) the degree of autonomy of the economic bureaucracy; (4) the degree to which the state has been captured by its main economic clients; (5) the balance between incentive and command in economic guidance; (6) special private sector organizations ... and (7) the role of foreign capital (Johnson, 1987:147).

Law is undoubtedly an aspect or an instrument of each of these but it is not an item on the list. Legislation for property rights barely merits a mention in the literature. The central bone of contention in the initial debate between those broadly supportive of the developmental state and market theorists was the evaluation of government intervention and of its significance for economic outcomes. There are signs a decade or two on that the boundaries between the camps are blurred and a role for government beyond the provision of 'pure' public goods is universally acknowledged (Aoki *et al.*, 1998). In so far as this is true then the implications for the rhetoric of the rule of law are substantial since there are moments in the literature at which a very wide ranging bureaucratic discretion (almost the inverse, we have noted, of norms envisaged by the rule of law rhetoric) is presented as the privileged means of successful government intervention.

The World Bank, arguably the principal institutional support of the rhetoric of the rule of law, made its own authoritative contribution to the East Asian Development debate with the publication of its report *The East Asian Miracle* in 1993 (World Bank, 1993). The report argued that the diversity of experience, the variety of institutions, and the variations in the policies of the High Performing East Asian Economies did not permit one to speak of a single model – tacit rejection of the developmental state thesis. However, there are lessons that might be learnt from Asia; first it is essential to get the fundamentals right, (and one such is the rule of law) thereafter high levels of domestic saving, broad based human capital, good macro-economic management, and limited price distortions provide the basis for growth. The report garnered little sympathy in East Asia either in the course of its preparation (Wade, 1996) or consequently upon its publication. The Institute of Developing Economies (IDE) in Tokyo prepared its own counterblast because it believed that the Bank was simply wrong. 'We questioned whether the World Bank had actually discovered the secret of growth in the East Asian area' (Yanagihara and Sambommatsu, 1997:v). The IDE implicitly rejects the 'rule of law' approach: in their study 'law' in the sense of the drafting of basic market rules is subsumed under one of five rubrics – government policies and institutions concerning the establishment of the market system. Under this heading are three groups of policies and systems; 'i) those having to do with the drafting of basic market rules, including civil and commercial law, ii) those having to do with the fostering of various markets including such economic agents as companies and iii) those which complement and support economic co-ordination of private investment' (ibid:xv). Of these three elements only ii) and iii), and so *not law*, are said to have played important roles. A possible reason for this view is offered in the keynote address of Masahiro Okuno-Fujiwara. He contrasts the situation in communities or kinship relations of the sort which obtained in pre-industrial Japan where economic transactions are agreed upon by trust and where 'individuals violating the agreements are expelled from the group or penalized in some other manner, so an incentive is given to honouring the agreement' with the circumstances of industrial society. In the latter differences of scale, complexity, and mobility are such that trust based systems can no longer cope. These require a framework so that all members know what the agreements are and who has offended them. There follows the requirement for a fixed membership and a fairly small membership at that so that the costs of managing the requisite information do not become excessive. In industrial society power displaces trust as the basis for the implementation of agreements. This entails legal institutions to enforce social agreements, contracts in law to guarantee private agreements, courts and other parties to decide whether an agreement has been broken or not and if so to enforce the punishment. The rule of law is ideally suited to the challenges of scale, complexity, and mobility since it permits even complete strangers to enter safely into economic agreements.

Ideally suited to the demands of industrial society this mode of enforcing economic agreements though the rule of law may be, it is no guarantee of economic growth since even if property rights systems are set up and courts, police, and other authorities are established, it does not mean that the market mechanism will start to function immediately. Indeed the fundamental problem often is that either there is no market 'or what market ever there is does not work sufficiently' (ibid:462) – a problem which the rule of law discourse does not address. Simply put the rule of law tells us nothing about the emergence of the market, of the transformation of peasant producers into industrial workers, about the processes which expanded the labour market, endowed the labour force with the necessary and changing mix of skills for growth, determined the pattern of wage negotiation and gave (Japanese) industry its distinctive employer-employee relations (Lapavitsas, 1990).

LAW AND ECONOMIC DEVELOPMENT IN JAPAN

The Japanese case is paradigmatic, the critical and indispensable empirical referent for the developmental state and equally for the thinking which underpins the market enhancing view endorsed by recent World Bank commissioned studies (see above).

It is to Japan that we now turn. A useful starting point is a thoughtful piece by Raphael and Rohlen with the challenging title, 'How many models of Japanese growth do we want or need?' (Raphael and Rohlen, 1998).

Property Rights and the Economic Development of Japan

Their informed and authoritative synthesis downplays the development state but makes of property rights no more than an item in a list: '(the Meiji leadership) – they tell us – created institutions to support modern business (universal commercial codes and property right laws, a national banking and financial system, etc.) (ibid:281). In their account not only are property rights an item in a list (so ingredient rather than precondition) but the absence of the rule of law (in the sense of constraints on bureaucratic discretion) is more important than its presence – thus we are reminded that 'strategic industries evolved ties between government and business that became the foundation of the post World War II system (involving frequent consultation, recourse to various instruments supporting entire sectors, industry compliance with "administrative guidance," and so forth)' (ibid:282). In fact it was not until the 1870s that property rights were legally protected by statute in Japan. First to be established was a property right to land. This entailed the identification by the government of owners of land, the issuance of certificates, setting land prices as the criterion of taxation, and the imposition of a land tax. The process of codification generalized property rights and transaction rules begun in 1879 on the basis of French (civil law) and German (commercial law) models. It was completed in 1900.

These facts are silent as to the relationship between property rights established by legal statute and economic development. Okazaki and Okuno-Fujiwara[8] two prominent scholars who have present a comprehensive listing of the institutional foundations of growth in Japan include property rights but posit no causal relation between the two and provide no empirical evidence of such a relationship. However the temptation to assume such a linkage is almost too much for another contributor to the World Bank volume. Feeney points out that property rights were the institutional predicate of the new taxation system and that this *perhaps* (it is Feeney's 'perhaps' not ours) provided greater incentives to increase productivity and *possibly* the new formal documentation of individual property rights provided security which enhanced the incentives to make long-term investments in land quality. From there it is a short step to the assertion that the Meiji oligarchs moved quickly to create institutional arrangements in the form of individual property rights in land that would underwrite investments in productivity growth as well as the transfer of agricultural surpluses to the financing of industrialization. Feeney provides no evidence to suggest that this was either the intention or the outcome (Feeney 1998). How could he? A moment's reflection confirms how unlikely all this is. If the evidence existed we could only stand back and wonder at the sagacity, far-sightedness, and public spiritedness of these Japanese leaders to conceive such a strategy, marvel at their genius in implementing their strategy, and warmly recommend them all (posthumously) for senior positions at the World Bank.

The fact of the matter is that *de facto* property rights existed prior to the legal codifications of the 1890s; that the imposition of control and regulation are of great urgency to a newly nascent state and that the establishment of a taxation system affords immediate benefits to the fledgling state which are first and foremost political. Haley is of the same opinion. He notes the existence in the Tokugawa period and prior to the interventions of Meiji law makers of *de facto* property rights. He cites with approval a contemporary observer who wrote that 'nearly all of the presumably new, Western derived institutions of the 1890 codes with respect to property rights and commercial practices were analogous to pre-existing institutions and practices (Haley, 1991:70). Japan had also long been familiar with registry systems, complex procedures for adjudication, and sophisticated commercial instruments. How long is long? Well, at least as far back as the seventeenth century (land registers and personal registration) and earlier still for sophisticated adjudication procedures. Interestingly, the expansion of adjudication procedures in the seventeenth and eighteenth centuries was stimulated by the growth of commercial activity at that time – rather than the converse. By the end of the eighteenth century a wide range of commercial instruments was in place: shares in commercial enterprises, certification, promissory notes and different types of bills of exchange.

In short *de facto* property rights developed during the Tokugawa era. This does not in itself constitute a challenge to the property rights – economic development equation[9] but it obliges one to recognize, in the Japanese case at least, the reciprocal nature of economic activity and the development of rights in property and techniques of adjudication and it causes one to doubt the catalytic and transformational nature of the legislation enacted by the Meiji state. Haley has no doubts, 'for the most part the new codes and statutes were responses as a means of regulation and control rather than catalysts to entrepreneurial activity. New legislation was prompted *less* by the desire to initiate or stimulate economic growth than a felt need to channel and control economic activity' (Haley, 1991:72). And we might add, that the development of the taxation system was motivated not least by the desire to secure the fiscal foundations of the new state. In short legal codification was an adjunct to rule. In this respect the Meiji leaders construed Western law in traditional East Asian terms: that is law as an instrument of the state, as a privileged means of rule. At this point 'property rights' and the 'rule of law' which have coexisted quite happily within the rhetoric of the rule of law come together in a highly paradoxical relationship; seemingly, (the claim is) the guarantee of the private realm and of private economic activity (the market) but simultaneously an endorsement of the privileges of the state over and above those of the law. The point is important enough to detain us a while.

The Relationship between 'Rule' and 'Law' in the Economic Development of Japan

The understanding and practice of law as the instrument of rule has been described as the essence of the Japanese legal tradition: 'a tradition in which law was no more nor less than an indispensable instrument of state control' (Haley, 1991:19). Self evidently traditions do not persist unchanged and unchanging across the centuries. In so far as they do persist it speaks more of their contemporary utility than of any historical inertia. Japan has known a long history of adaptation of its own institutions and of the importing of and accommodation to the (legal) institutions of China and of the West. But that there is a Japanese legal tradition is beyond doubt. That tradition in the late Tokugawa period neither recognized law as the source of authority nor as the determinant of the limits of rule. This is not to say that within the Japanese legal tradition there was no notion of law as a constraint upon the exercise of the power of the state. By the end of the Tokugawa period a complex and highly evolved set of legal institutions were in place but these had no more than a certain disciplinary status. Equally the understanding developed that the legitimacy of rule was related to questions of law but here law was the emblem not the source of authority – a distinction that is fundamental but refractory to presentation in the legal formulae of the West.

The conception of law as the instrument of rule governed the approach of Meiji leaders to the progress of legal reform in the late nineteenth century. Indeed the process was substantially driven by the desire to expand the instrumentality of the state. Haley perfectly communicates the excitement of Meiji leaders on discovery of the possibilities available to rulers that were inherent in Western legal codes. Thus, the Dutch civil code was 'an excellent instrument for regulating the people.' The French civil code was possibly even more functional for rule. 'Almost every order issued by Napoleon [III], the present emperor, is rooted in this code' (!) (Haley, 1991:74). In short even with regard to private law the dominant conception was not of an autonomous private realm but of enhanced possibilities of societal regulation by the state. With the promulgation of the Meiji constitution in 1889 (enacted in 1890) the principle of Japan's administrative law, that is an administration based on law and in compliance with law, was established. The arrangement was defective when viewed from the perspective of the rule of law (Ogawa, 1984:13). The chief limitation was the 'independent order of the executive' by virtue of which the Emperor and his administrative agencies could enact orders or regulations without statutory authority. The limitations were compounded by the weakness of the administrative court system. This was largely borrowed from German and Austrian models which separated judicial and administrative jurisdictions with the consequence that disputes concerning administrative laws were not to be dealt with by regular judicial courts. Moreover the actual jurisdiction of the Administrative Court was limited to 'administrative litigations enumerated by statute.' The net effect of these limitations was that the scope of administration that escaped judicial control was very large and became still larger with the growth of the modern economy and the associated expansion of bureaucratic activities. This net effect was not simply a consequence of, nor was it reducible to, imperfect constitutional design or the shortcomings of the Meiji legal and institutional architecture. It owed much to, and was designed to protect and to accommodate, the Tokugawa legacy of which we have spoken. The Emperor and not the people was sovereign. It was the emperor, and not the people and neither their agents and representative institutions, who was the legislator. It is difficult then to construe the administration as a public service bureaucracy fully subject to legal scrutiny. (A much remarked upon weakness of the constitutional machinery of Meiji was the rivalry of Diet and Cabinet.) The Meiji administration was coterminous with rule. The constitutional arrangements of Meiji recognized this and cemented the practice of bureaucratic independence and discretion.

The process of legal codification and the enactment of the constitution itself served neither to eradicate the Tokugawa legacy of law as an instrument of rule nor to transform the status of law to that of overarching constraint which would govern and limit the actions of the rulers. Maruyama is not only adamant that this did not happen but equally that it was never likely to given the highly informal nature of pre-war understandings of sovereignty or 'the national order.' The latter was a very powerful notion that reached its apogee in the ultra nationalist period. It alluded to the emperor and to the gods. It was simultaneously evocative of a quintessential Japan, the people and the place itself. Equally, it was a highly nebulous notion and one that did not lend itself to formalization and as a taboo even resisted formalization. Accordingly, what determined the behaviour of the bureaucrats and of the military was not primarily a sense of legality, but the consciousness of some force that was higher than they were, in other words that was nearer the 'ultimate entity.' Inasmuch as the formal quality of the national order was not recognized, it was inevitable that the concept of legality should be poorly developed. The law was not regarded as some general body of regulations that collectively circumscribed the ruler and the ruled, but simply as a concrete weapon of control operating in the hierarchy of authority of which the emperor was the head. In a society in which every element was judged according its respective connection in a direct vertical line with the ultimate entity the exercise of bureaucratic discretion was not only likely but also 'legitimate' (Maruyama, 1964).

This situation obtained for more than fifty years and was, at the very least, compatible with extremely fast rates of economic growth. If we date the beginnings of modern industry in Japan as somewhere around 1885 then we can say that Japan witnessed a century of uninterrupted economic growth which saw it transformed from a feudal agricultural economy to a fully fledged industrial power on a world scale without the benefit of the rule of law if the latter is understood in terms of a framework of overarching legal constraint upon the exercise of bureaucratic power.

Promulgation and enactment of the Showa constitution represented a considerable advance both in terms of the rule of law, 'The Rule of Law is a fundamental principle underlying the present Constitution' (Oda, 192:35) and the development of administrative and judicial remedies for administrative actions. This is also the period of economic reconstruction, of post-war recovery and, in the 1960s, of spectacularly high growth. How far was this attributable to the constitutional advances initiated by the occupation authorities in the establishment of the rule of law? Here caution is in order. Many factors other than law were present in a complex equation. So for all that the country knew the bitter taste of defeat and the prodigious damage of war, Japan in the post-war period enjoyed enormous advantages compared to newly developing countries in face of the challenge of economic development. Material losses were enormous but the collective riches of a century of industrial experience, the hard won knowledge of what it was to be industrial, to work, to profit, familiarity with the challenge of entrepreneurship and of innovation, of manufacture and distribution, of finance, commerce and trade remained in place imprinted on the minds of men and women. International circumstances were also propitious; post-war reconstruction in many lands meant booming markets; economic opportunities were presented by new wars which for all their horrors stimulated trade and production and in the case of the Korean war renewed confidence in the business class; world trade grew exponentially; and to some extent Japan had the field to itself, at least competition from the NICs was an anxiety yet to be borne.

Equally any constitutional innovation would have to prove its worth in overcoming indigenous resistance. Traditions change of course, but they do not surrender lightly particularly when institutionally entrenched and championed by powerful interests. And in this case there was reason to believe that constitutional arrangements were defective from the first. Advances undoubtedly there were. The new constitution requires that the Cabinet administer the law faithfully (Article 73 paragraph 1) and ends the 'independent administrative order.' Henceforth orders that emanate from the administration are confined to delegated orders authorized by laws or instructions for the execution of laws.

The Administrative court was abolished and substituted for a system of judicial review by the regular courts (see Article 73, paragraph 6 of the Constitution, Article 11 of the Cabinet Law and article 12 of the National Government Organisation Law and Article 3 of the Court Organisation law). A shortcoming of the new arrangements was the absence of legislation for general administrative procedures. In the absence of such legislation the possibility of effectively monitoring the bureaucratic exercise of power and discretion and its conformity to substantive law was decreased (Ogawa, 1984:13-19).

As in all other areas of legal and constitutional revision in Japan (much as elsewhere) the new arrangements had necessarily to accommodate themselves to earlier traditions, arrangements, and understandings. Quite what accommodation was to be effected in the post-war period between the recently constitutionally entrenched rule of law and the tradition that since law is the instrument of rule the 'ruler' is to enjoy a wide margin of discretion was suggested by the history of article 14 of the Public Prosecutors Office Law (1947). The article in question specified that 'The

Minister of Justice may control and supervise public prosecutors generally in regard to the functions provided for in articles 4 and 6. However in regard to the investigation and disposition of individual cases he may control only the Prosecutor General.' Of the functions listed under articles 4 and 6 of particular relevance to the current discussion is the prosecutor's function in requesting that the courts properly apply the law, in supervising the execution of court judgments, investigating cases, and charging crimes. Article 14 was widely understood to be a rock upon which the rule of law was built from its enactment in 1947. It seemed to guarantee public prosecutors from political interference and so helped ensure that all levels of rule would be subject to legal scrutiny. This was the understanding at least until the eruption of the Shipbuilding scandal in 1954. To be brief[10] more than thirty senior officials from the Ministry of Transportation and a number of senior politicians received bribes from shipping and ship building companies in return for favourable legislation and large government loans designed to bail them out of the business downturn at the end of the Korean War. Among those implicated was Sato Eisaku, then the Secretary General of the ruling Liberal Democratic Party. Had he been arrested, charged, and tried the balance between 'rule' and 'law' would have shifted so decisively in favour of the latter that it may well have proved possible to speak of the rule of law in Japan. It did not happen. Mr Yoshida, the Prime Minister, used his authority under article 14 (which is how it now came to be seen) to order the postponement of Sato's arrest. The result was a significant diminution of the power and political independence of the procuracy. The damage to the rule of law was commensurately great.

What are we to make of this open collision of the interests and privileges of rule with the exigencies of the rule of law? It would be wrong to pretend that it was a clear-cut matter. Yoshida's decision triggered a furore and prompted the resignation of the Minister of Justice. But the furore ultimately died down, Yoshida remained in place and the procuracy backed off. It is hard to escape the conclusion that even in the full flush of democratic reform, (the constitution was not yet ten years old) the norms and assumptions of Japanese society favoured a degree of flexibility when rulers and the law collide. This is certainly the understanding of a leading authority upon Japanese politics who, reflecting upon the axioms and procedural assumptions of Japan's political life and with the Shipbuilding scandal of 1954 very much in mind, echoed the traditional view:

> Political professionals (in Japan) are expected to base their behaviour and perform their functions in accordance with law. It is understood that the preservation of the Constitution and the legal structure are their professional responsibilities. However acting according to the

> law and performing one's job in accordance with law cannot be approved unconditionally ... Political authorities are expected to use their discretion in applying the law, taking into consideration common understandings as an unwritten law. On the one hand, legally unauthorized bureaucratic intervention in the form of administrative guidance is demanded, and when the political authorities go against these expectations they are criticized for being hard headed. On the other hand compassionate justice that ignores the legal codes, the kind that was shown by Ooka, a famous magistrate in the city of Edo during the Tokugawa period is sought, and when this is not displayed by the authorities, they are criticized for being inhuman and devoid of blood and tears (Kyogoku, 1987:139-40).

It is a long quote from a brilliant observer of the Japanese polity whose book, (the source of the quote) *Nihon no Seiji* (Kyogoku, 1983) was a best-seller in Japan. Suffice it to say that a) its predicate is an understanding of legitimacy which demands the exercise of discretion and which makes of the rule of law a *mikoshi*[11] to be borne by the political elite which confirms but does not derive its authority in the process and that b) Showa constitutionalism has not expunged the tradition of law as the instrument of rule and as the badge rather than the source of authority. In short we can say that Japan has known a legal tradition, seemingly to the present, in which law is understood as the necessary adjunct or legitimating seal of rule but in which law is understood neither to be the source of rule and authority nor the final determinant of the limits of rule. At its strongest law is seen as the instrument of rule, at its weakest (and again to the present) the understanding is that the rule of law must be flexible and may be even suspended if it conflicts with the exigencies of rule.

Before we turn to concrete cases let us summarize the argument so far.

i) A rhetoric in which the rule of law is central is close to establishing itself as a hegemonic discourse for the discussion and explanation of economic development;

ii) In so far as the discourse is sanctioned by bodies such as the World Bank, the IMF and the ADB it becomes the authoritative basis upon which policy is made, projects are approved, and funding is determined;

iii) Such is the significance of the development that the persuasiveness and coherence of the rhetoric merits careful examination and, it is to be hoped, empirical testing. The need for caution is the greater because a decade of official analyses of East Asian development have proved highly controversial. *The East Asian Miracle* report of the World Bank is a case in point;

iv) The developmental state literature is a useful vantage point for a preliminary consideration of the place of law in development – not least because this is arguably the empirically richest source of writing on East Asia. When the matter is considered from this perspective it is readily apparent that the rule of law has not usually been seen as a pivotal moment in the economic development of East Asia;

v) Japan furnished the empirical foundations for the original notion of the developmental state where the concept of property rights has not been central to underlying explanations of economic development. Indeed a highly developed system of *de facto* property rights significantly predated modern economic growth. Whether or not these are seen as the foundation or precondition for subsequent economic growth it is the case that *de facto* property rights were long compatible with vigorous but much lower levels of economic activity;

vi) The late nineteenth century writing of civil and commercial codes under Western influence established property rights on a new legal basis but did this in a manner not readily consistent with the rule of law if this is to be understood as an overarching constraint upon the state and its officials and rather more readily compatible with a traditional Japanese and East Asian understanding of law as the instrument of rule, as a tool of the state. We might more accurately speak of 'law as rule' than of the 'rule of law.' This legal tradition persisted until at least the end of the Second World War and (at a minimum) coexisted with a hundred years of sustained economic growth. There is moreover little good reason to believe that it was expunged by defeat in war and the promulgation of the Showa constitution. Indeed, defining moments in the shaping of the limits of law in respect of the privileges of office in the 1950s argue that the primacy of the political over the legal was conceded, albeit not without question well into the period of post-war recovery and through to the high growth of the 1960s.

From Rhetoric to Reality, the Role of Law in the Management of Economic Change in Japan: Some Reflections on Industrial Policy in the 1970s

Our discussion to this point affords very little comfort to the rule of law rhetoricians. Modern economic growth in Japan significantly predated the establishment and systematization of property rights along Western lines. Industrialization and growth knew extraordinary successes for a hundred years before the constitutional revisions of 1947 set in place institutions and procedures intended to secure the rule of law. The revisions were incomplete, their design, we have suggested, was defective. Moreover the accommodation of the new legal institutions to local practice as evidenced in the history of article 14 of the public prosecutors law suggested that Japanese society preferred a qualified approach to the rule of law. This should not finally be allowed to threaten the stability and integrity of a rule which should itself be allowed (or even required) to exercise a large degree of discretion to the extent of not applying the law. All this at precisely the moment Japan knew its greatest economic successes.

Thus far discussion has been concerned with what law *is not*. Plainly, we cannot leave matters here and it is time to move beyond rhetoric to consider what law *is* – that is to the actual rather than the claimed role of law in economic matters. The focus will be the role of law in the management of economic change and specifically in the conduct of industrial policy in Japan in the 1970s. Something will be said later about the choice of this case. But first we need to return to the notion of the developmental state since this for all its shortcomings is a more suitable vehicle for consideration of the place of law in the economic life of East Asian nations than the overgeneralized abstractions of the rule of law rhetoric. Indeed the hope is that examination of the place of law in the management of the post-war Japanese economy will contribute to a more detailed specification of the legal dimensions of the developmental state. The linking of law and the 'developmental state' is more than a convenience, since, as we argue, law is close to the heart of government endeavours to manage economic change in Japan. Even so there are problems in making and in justifying the linkage. It is useful to delineate the legal dimensions of the developmental state in so far as law is an important aspect of the developmental state. More fundamentally still it is useful in so far as the notion of the developmental state is itself powerful and persuasive – since the initial concern of the rule of law rhetoricians is the delineation of the legal conditions for economic development. The phrase 'developmental state' has proved to be useful and popular so much so that its use has broadened so as to denote any government with developmental policies, ambitions or minimally, developmental rhetoric – at which point the analytic utility of the phrase is lost. While there is little further that need be said in respect of this unfortunate slippage it is important to recognize that even where the phrase is used with caution it remains an analytic convenience, a concatenation of hypotheses about the developmental process. In short, for all its ubiquity the phrase should not be taken for the fact. The sources of economic growth are debated as hotly as ever even in Japan and a critical caveat attends the impact and efficacy of industrial policy itself. Given the looseness of the usage and the fact that the developmental state remains a contentious and contested notion it is all the more important to ground the discussion empirically. A related further aim is to note how law seems to have been understood and used in the industrial policy process by key players and above all by the economic bureaucrats in the difficult economic circumstances of the 1970s. But first the caveat.

The Impact and Effectiveness of Industrial Policy

The impact and effectiveness of industrial policy is not the first concern of a volume concerned with the place of law in the processes of development. It is, for all that, of no little significance if the link between law and development is effected through the concept of the developmental state. As was said at the outset the specification of the legal dimensions of the developmental state is of interest in so far as the concept is itself of use. This depends in turn upon estimates of the effectiveness of policies developed by the developmental state. In short, what is at issue is the developmental efficacy of government policy, specifically industrial policy. This might seem odd and inappropriate. Chalmers Johnson has written an excellent, popular, and influential work that is seen to have made the case for a third way to successful industrialization (Johnson, 1982). State-led economic development is all but an axiom. The Japan model is pored over by economic bureaucrats and their academic peers in Latin America and Southeast Asia. But there are reasons to wonder at all of this. Johnson's account is a lively institutional biography of the Ministry of International Trade and Industry (MITI). It details convincingly and entertainingly, the evolution of MITI's ambitions and pretensions. It charts accurately the legal developments that articulated those pretensions and ambitions. We can even live with a sometimes cavalier equation of law with policy. However, Johnson is all but silent on the questions of implementation and impact. It is as if all that is required is for MITI to formulate a position, that this then becomes law, the law is implemented exactly as MITI intends and produces all and nothing but the anticipated consequences. This is doubtful to say the least. David Friedman looked at one set of MITI's prescriptions, those for the machine tool industry, and subjected them to an empirical analysis and concluded that MITI's plans, policies, and laws had failed to achieve their goals.[12] An elite group of more than twenty leading Japanese economists broadened the scope of inquiry. They engaged in a wide-ranging review of industrial policy, of how far it was implemented, and of its impact. The report of their findings has become the standard text on industrial policy in Japan. The report was written after Johnson's publication and with full knowledge of his views. It makes no explicit criticism of Johnson's work. It is however, quietly but firmly dismissive of the commonplace 'Westerners misunderstandings and misinterpretations of Japanese industrial policy' (Komiya, 1984, 1988). Later works by Trezise, Hadley, and Patrick are welcomed as correctives to western ignorance. These authors, Trezise, Hadley and Patrick – all Japan specialists in their own right – do not regard industrial policy as a core element in the economic development of Japan. Their position is as follows: 'All participants in this project recognize that, excluding the brief period immediately after the end of the war, the foundation of growth was competition operating through the price mechanism and a flourishing entrepreneurial spirit ... It can even be said, (they continue), that the course of the history of industrial policy in the principal postwar periods (in particular the 1950s and 1960s) has often been that the initiative and vitality of the private sector undermined the plans of the government authorities to try to utilize direct intervention in the nature of controls.'[13] In short, they simply do not see state intervention as the defining characteristic of Japan's post-war economic experience and still less as the prime cause of successful economic development. They are not insensitive to the difficulties of measuring the impact of policy upon the economy and they are not entirely negative about government intervention in industry. Indeed they have good things to say about industrial policy but at their very best their evaluation is that industrial policy is at best marginal and even then subordinate to, and supportive of, the price mechanism and good only for a time, a limited time.[14] Two features of industrial policy are said to be effective, namely, the use of trade restrictions to protect and nurture new industries and the various mechanisms that functioned to effectively transmit information valuable for the activities of private enterprise. The first of these is a characteristic of the pre-1973 watershed and of rapidly diminishing importance since then. Law was often an important instrument in the development of such industrial promotion policies. The second successful feature alluded to, namely, the generation, collection, and transmission of information from firms and to firms has continued to be of significance across the watershed of the mid-1970s. Law is a significantly less important instrument in this respect.

As for the third dimension of industrial policy, the kind of direct interventionist policies which characterized attempts to manage the problems of industries in decline – the key policy challenge of the decade after the oil crisis – these our Japanese colleagues note, have been relatively successful. Law played a part in the management of decline – this will be taken up below.

What is the significance of the critique of industrial policy? We should not exaggerate. The position of Komiya and his associates is not universally conceded. There are Western commentators who refuse to accept their judgment. But let us be frank. Many of us in Europe, in North America, in Latin America, and in Southeast Asia are strenuously engaged in making general and generalizable sense of a particular experience – that of Japan –

where neither the facts nor their significance is conceded by the relevant academic authorities. The Jury is still out on this one while scholars search for models which more happily reconcile 'market' and 'state led' approaches. At a minimum caution is advisable in our use of the term developmental state.[15]

LAW AND INDUSTRIAL POLICY IN JAPAN OF THE 1970S

It is legitimate to ask at the outset, 'why the 1970s?' since this is neither the heyday of industrial policy nor a decade which justifies attention in respect of topical concerns. Arguably it is the period of post-war reconstruction and high growth until the end of the 1960s that is the high point of industrial policy. In contrast the focus of concern in the 1990s has been the efforts of the state to disengage from the economy, a decade in which 'liberalization' not intervention has been the watchword. However it can be argued that the likely success of industrial policy is the greater in times of world growth than at a time of recession. In that respect the 1970s, a time at which the world economy had to absorb the consequences of the oil crisis affords a more realistic perspective on both the possibilities and limits of government intervention. Particularly vulnerable at that time were the old manufacturing industries, iron and steel, shipbuilding and such like, labour intensive, energy guzzling industries which faced the double jeopardy of higher fuel prices and low cost competition from the newly industrializing countries of East and Southeast Asia. If market theorists were to be believed then the prospect which greeted these industries was lingering decline with all of the attendant social and economic costs. The Japanese experience held out the hope that the problems of industrial decline and of restructuring might be amenable to government policy. It was the message from the 1970s that 'Japan has demonstrated an ability to face major issues of industrial policy squarely' (Magaziner and Hout, 1980) and the associated hope that there was something that other governments could do to manage and ease the transition to the technological high ground which justifies our concern.

The principal rubric (one is reluctant to say 'instrument' for reasons which will become apparent) for the management of economic decline in Japan in the 1970s was a law, two laws in fact: the Depressed Industries Laws of 1978 and 1983. The first of these was a reaction to the oil shock of 1973 that increased energy prices made critical raw materials much more costly and reduced demand for Japanese manufactures. Industries in the middle of the production cycle were particularly hard hit, trapped as they were between rising input costs and declining demand. The belief was widespread in government and industrial circles that these industries could not survive without state help to promote their fundamental restructuring. Economic anxieties were critically underpinned by political concerns. Hard hit industries such as the shipbuilding industry were not only labour intensive but also geographically concentrated, characteristics which served to dramatize the political dimensions of industrial crisis and sharpen the governmental appetite for legislation. The result was the Law of Special Measures for the Stabilisation of Specific Depressed Industries (*Tokutei Fukyo Sangyo Antei Rinji Sochi ho*) (hereinafter the Depressed Industries Law). The law was designed to help 'designated' industries reduce excess capacity, to encourage diversification into more value added products, to the development of new technologies, and to the streamlining of distribution and marketing channels. The law was seen by it authors as a short to medium term response to crisis and so by its own terms required the Diet to reinvestigate industrial restructuring and the effectiveness of the law after five years. This was duly done. The problems had not passed and further legislation was deemed necessary. The Law of Special Measures for the Structural Improvement of Specific Industries (*Tokutei Sangyo Kozo Kaizen Rinji Sochi ho*) (in brief, the Structural Improvements Law) was a modified version of the earlier law which sought to extend the number of industries which might benefit from its provisions and to permit designated industries to organize cartels for capacity reduction and to promote a further rationalization of their marketing and distribution. The detailed story of the passage and use of these laws has been told elsewhere (Boyd, 1989; Boyd and Nagamori, 1991; Uriu, 1996; Yonezawa, 1988; Young, 1986, 1991). Here attention will focus upon the general significance of law in the industrial policy process as revealed in respect of the first of these two laws, the Depressed Industries Law of 1978.

A number of conclusions present themselves in the body of research on this exercise in economic management.

i) Formal written law is of great importance in the industrial policy process – notwithstanding the conventional wisdom concerning the relative unimportance of law in Japan and the competing explanations (cultural and procedural) of that unimportance. However, its importance is not readily evoked by the notion, 'rule of law' as used elsewhere in this study. Indeed, it is more accurate to think of law as an instrumentality or resource available to the policy maker than as a single and uniform, transparent, and overarching constraint. Something to be thought of in terms of usage rather than interpretation – since if it is not deemed useful it will not be applied;
ii) The Japanese legislature cannot be regarded as a 'rubber stamp.' In the case considered here it proves itself to be a significant and effective

forum for debate and the passage of laws with which the bureaucrats would have to work and which they did not always favour. In short one at least of the major institutions, the existence of which is implied by the rule of law rhetoric is alive and well in Japan;

iii) The body of formal law functions in close parallel to practices borne of legal informality which continues to be of great practical importance and which are justified by reference to particular legal statutes;

iv) The notorious weaknesses of Anti-Trust Law in Japan are a consequence of specific structural and procedural incompatibilities between the economic bureaucracies and the values enshrined in the Anti-Trust Laws. To exacerbate matters the bureaucratic culture is profoundly anticompetitive in economic matters;

v) Bureaucratic culture has changed relatively little despite the constitutional revisions of 1947 and is supportive of a legal philosophy that sees law as an instrument of rule.

THE IMPORTANCE OF LAW

Much has been made of the relatively small number of lawyers in Japan, of a culture which favours consensus and which has been described as non-litigious. Equally a Western excitement about legal informality – the reliance upon informal procedures and in the case of the business-government relation of administrative guidance has encouraged some observers to argue the relative unimportance of law in Japan.[16] In the case of the state bureaucracy and industrial policy, as evidenced by our work on legislation for declining industries, nothing could be further from the truth. The officials in question are overwhelmingly lawyers, graduates from the elite university law faculties. They have on their desks volumes of their industry laws, plastic bound in flexible covers so as to withstand constant use and reference, the laws are printed upon special tough paper for the same reason. This is not to suggest that the bureaucrat is constrained to proceed daily according to the letter of the law – even if this were either his wish or a normative requirement the characteristically general wording of the industry law would make it impossible. In much the same way that wording obviates the need for the niceties of legal interpretation. If the law has as its goal the 'best interests' or the 'smooth running' of the industry the challenge is not to understand the law but to understand the industry. This is particularly apparent at times of crisis. When 'something must be done,' when a solution must be found then particular laws are viewed as resources to be mobilized, to be combined, to be implemented selectively and with discretion so as to confect a solution. The operational code of the bureaucrat is to seek post hoc (legal) authorization for actions he may wish to make in the name of the community of policy makers, once those actions have been agreed.

In the particular case of the shipbuilding industry the responsible MITI official or Ministry of Transport (MOT) official (shipbuilding is in MOT's bailiwick), confronted by the problems of decline in his industry is surrounded by a forest of legislation. We can talk about the legislative framework but this implies too high a degree of coherence and stasis. We can pick our way through on one or more paths: one path, neatly mapped for us by Frank Upham (1987:166-204) departs from the statutory basis of the ministry's authority and the administrative law doctrines that define its limits. Thus in the case of MITI: at the foundation of MITI's authority is the MITI Establishment Act that defines MITI's jurisdiction, goals, and structure. On the next level are statutes like the Foreign Exchange and Foreign Trade Control Law (FECL) that give MITI responsibility for broad areas of economic policy. At a third level of specificity are statutes like the Petroleum Industry Law that give MITI general authority to promote particular industries, and statutes like the depressed industries law that give MITI specific authority to deal with economic conditions affecting a number of industries.

Two characteristics of these statutes are worth noting: firstly the wide scope of authority delegated to MITI and secondly the vagueness of the standards by which MITI is to exercise that authority. Upham is surely right when he says that economic statutes are better viewed as identifying an area or a problem (for example the decline in the competitiveness of industries after the oil crisis) and delegating legal authority to MITI to deal with it as it sees fit. So broad are the terms of the statutes that when it comes to how, when or to what end that legal entitlement should be used the statutes are so broad as to be all but meaningless. This is not unusual: the shipbuilding law by means of which the jurisdictional competence of MOT for the shipbuilding industry is constituted defines the goal of the legislation as 'the smooth functioning of the shipbuilding industry.' This is the sole criterion to guide the bureaucracy's exercise of many of the specific powers granted by the law.

We might here add an important rider to Upham's assessment: it is not only that MITI or MOT or any other agency responsible for industrial policy is empowered to handle problems as it sees fit but also to do this 'as best it can.' Why as 'best MITI can? Because typically MITI's broad jurisdictional competence is not matched by matching specific statutory authority. This can mean that to discharge its responsibilities MITI is obliged sometimes to stitch and mend and make do as best it can. As it does so it benefits from a set of circumstances that effectively insulate it and its actions from judicial review – the relevant circumstances are the governing notions of justiciability, standing, and scope of discretion. Bureaucratic action in the realm of industrial policy is almost always informal. And so it does not create legal rights and duties – it is not then in terms of Article 3 of Administrative case litigation law – justiciable. It is not only a matter of informality: supervisory orders, agency plans or regulations, permissions, approvals within an agency and even within a public body such as the advisory councils are internal governmental acts and so not subject to review; unless they immediately and concretely affect a specific person's legal rights and obligations. The doctrine of standing has been so narrow as to strictly limit entitlement to persons having a legal interest in an administrative disposition. Injury to factual interest is not grounds for standing.[17] In the case of industrial policy convincing a court that an administrative action is illegal is perhaps the hardest obstacle of all and a major barrier to judicial review. To be illegal the act must escape the agency's scope of discretion. Usually in this realm at least this would mean showing that the agency used incorrect criteria or procedures in making the challenged decision or that the decision breached the statute on which it was based. If the goals and purposes of the statute are detailed and precise this is not impossible – as we have seen the court is more likely to be faced with standards as broad, vague, and open to interpretation as 'the smooth functioning of industry X.'

In sum then in the realm of industrial policy the competent authorities benefit from very broad competence couched in very general terms and often without commensurate specific statutory powers. This constrains the agency to favour negotiation and compromise and reliance upon informal arrangements. If the agency confines itself to informal actions then it benefits from enormous freedom from the risk of judicial review because of the current understandings and practices of justiciability and standing and the difficulty of demonstrating that an act exceeds the legitimate scope of discretion of the agency and is at variance with the purposes of the relevant enabling statute. This is an enormous incentive to the agency to reach agreement with its more powerful private sector partners. From the perspective of the latter – the ubiquity of the partner agency (born of the broad jurisdictional competence) is such as to encourage negotiated non-legal agreements.

LEGAL INFORMALITY

Legal informality is a fact of economic life in Japan. Administrative guidance remains a critical means of steering the economy – although of lesser importance after the 1970s than during them (see below). Japanese and Western commentators argue that legal statutes are the *sine qua non* of administrative guidance and that legal informality is the preferred means of exercising broad legal responsibilities which are couched in general terms. The evidence confirms the first of these propositions: administrative guidance in the industrial policy process is exercised by explicit, often written, reference to legal statutes. The second of these propositions is more doubtful. Administrative guidance is not synonymous with the 'informal enforcement' of legal statutes – although Haley is surely right to point to the ubiquity of informal enforcement and of voluntary compliance to legal statutes in the domain of public policy (Haley, 1991). What is enforced is not the law but the positions and agreements of the industrial policy community. These compromises are the result of no easy and readily emerging consensus but of sometimes protracted and difficult negotiations if the problems are not readily tractable. It is the bureaucratic challenge and also the bureaucratic genius to ensure that there is no great gap between these positions and agreements and the law – a task greatly facilitated by the general terms of the law. It might be said that this is not fundamentally at odds with the legal practice of bureaucrats in the US, the UK, and the Netherlands and elsewhere which habitually effects a fit between preferred practice and the law. This would be to underestimate the significance of broad and general formulations of the goals of a law and of the brevity of reference to its ways and means. In the case of the shipbuilding industry law a goal such as that of the smooth running of the industry sets a huge premium upon the judgment of those charged with the implementation of the law, a judgment which is constrained rather more by the politics of the policy community than overarching norms of legal equality, universality, and uniformity.

Let us look a little more closely at the meshing of law and legal informality in the confection of policy. To deal with adjustment in declining industries the 1978 Law on Temporary Measures for the Stabilisation of Specified Depressed Industries was passed. Other dimensions of the adjustment crisis were approached through the Law on Temporary Measures for those Unemployed in Specified Depressed Industries, the Law on Temporary Measures for those Unemployed in Specific Regions and the Law on Temporary Measures for Small and Medium Enterprises in Specified Depressed Regions. It would be wrong to exaggerate the coherence and integrity of this kind of legislative effort. More often than not these were piecemeal ad hoc responses to rapidly evolving political and economic circumstances. It would be wrong equally to think of these measures as evidence of a coherent and sufficient policy response to the problem of industrial decline. The challenge facing the official was to draw upon the body of law which constituted the authority of his agency and the functional non-sector specific legislation defined in line with the visions so as to confect, to weave together a policy solution. The volume of basic legislation for the industry runs to more than one thousand pages. The Shipbuilding bureau within the MOT enacted thirty-two major laws in the post-war period. Three of these are of particular importance in constituting the authority of the Bureau. These are the Shipbuilding Law of 1950, the Temporary Law on Regulation of Shipbuilding 1953, and the law on Temporary Measures for Rationalisation of Production of Small and Medium Sized Ships (1959-64, 1964-6) subsequently the Law Concerning the Production and Operation of Small Ships (1966-). A range of non-shipbuilding specific ancillary legislation could also be drawn upon in the confection of policy. Of relevance here is the permanent legislation such as the Small and Medium Scale Enterprises Organisations Law of 1957, the Small and Medium Enterprise Modernisation Promotion Law of 1963 as well as the temporary response to crisis inter-sectoral legislation we have glimpsed above: including: the Law on Temporary Measures for Business Conversion of Small and Medium Enterprises (1976-86), the law on Temporary Measures for the Stabilisation of Specified Depressed Industries (1978-83), the Law on Temporary Measures for Small and Medium Enterprises in Specified Depressed Regions (1978-83), and the Law on Temporary Measures for Assisting Small and Medium Enterprises to cope with Yen Appreciation (1978-80). The direct controls of the MOT over the industry and specifically its detailed licensing powers by virtue of the Shipbuilding law were an additional and critically important policy resource.

If we trace the legal and legally informal instruments the agency mobilized in its development of a policy response to the difficulties of the industry following the oil crisis when the index of demand for ships in terms of orders received fell from one hundred in 1973 to twenty in 1975 and to ten in 1978, firms began to lay off workers and the profitability of the industry collapsed. We find the following sample:

i) Invoking its licensing powers – sanctioned ultimately by the shipbuilding law which does not specifically and explicitly authorize the MOT to ban parallel construction, MOT used its discretionary powers to ban side by side construction of medium sized ships in large docks in Spring 1975, that is, it implicitly threatened not to issue construction licences for the ships which were to be built in pairs;
ii) Invoking its licensing powers – sanctioned ultimately by the shipbuilding law that does not authorize the MOT explicitly and specifically to set prices, the Ministry of Transport initiated price guidance after autumn 1975;

iii) As the crisis intensified the range and variety of ships subject to price guidance was increased and the terms of the price guidance became more comprehensive (to include specification for the price of the ship's body section, the machine section, the electric section, etc. as well as the different cost structures of small medium and big shipyards). Guidance was informal but the ultimate point of reference was the shipbuilding law;

iv) Joint administrative guidance was announced by MITI and MOT to set quotas and price levels for ship exports so as to satisfy Western demands for the curtailment of what was claimed to be the dumping of Japanese ships in Western markets;

v) On the basis of article 7 of the Shipbuilding Law that permits the ministry to issue guidance to individual firms, the Ministry of Transport recommended curtailment of operations by major firms on the shipbuilding law in November 1976;

vi) A domestic ship price guidance standard was 'formalized' and fixed by administrative guidance in February 1977;

vii) Following the bankruptcy of Hatohama Shipbuilding in December 1977 the MOT sent out 'advice' (administrative guidance) concerning 'Measures which must be taken by the regional shipping bureaux concerning the bankruptcy of shipbuilding as well as shipbuilding related companies;'

viii) From 1976 to 1978 as unemployment developed and the problems of the small and medium companies increased MOT applied for designation of the shipbuilding industry as a designated depressed industry able to benefit from a raft of 'countermeasures' based on new statutes; the law for the Conversion of Small and Medium Enterprises (1976-86), the law on Temporary Measures for the Stabilisation of Specified Depressed Industries (1978-83) the Law on Temporary Measures for Small and Medium Enterprises in Specified Depressed Regions (1978-83) and the Law on Temporary Measures for Assisting Small and Medium Enterprises to cope with Yen Appreciation (1978-80);

ix) In December 1978 MOT changed the terms of operations curtailment which required a move to direct controls. Again this was an instance of administrative guidance (*kankoku sootan*) with the ultimate sanction of MOT's detailed licensing powers enjoyed by virtue of the shipbuilding law;

x) The Fair Trade Commission noted that MOT guidance might constitute an infringement of the Anti-Monopoly Law but agreed that MOT's guidance be viewed as a depression cartel which would then be beyond the jurisdiction of the Anti-Monopoly Law. MOT renewed its guidance;

xi) The shipping industry complained to the FTC about the cartel system since this put upward pressure on prices. The FTC approved an extension of the cartel in April 1980. MOT renewed its administrative guidance in view of cartel formation;

xii) Following criticism from the FTC, MOT desisted from administrative guidance in the guise of *kankoku sotan* and instead issued 'guidelines' with very similar effect although a remove further from the law.

The above is no more than a glimpse of the battery of formal and informal acts of the Ministry of Transport as it endeavoured to manage an economic crisis. It is suggestive of the potency of the licensing powers enjoyed by MOT by virtue of the shipbuilding law to buttress its use of informal agreements in areas and with respect to matters that are not specifically sanctioned by the shipbuilding law. The importance and equally the binding nature of administrative guidance are evident. Academic lawyers are inclined to deny that its importance derives from its legal status and are likely to suggest that it is not binding legally because it is not itself a source of law.[18] On the other hand they note that it is binding in fact and so point to the goods and services (licences, permissions, and other benefits) access to which is controlled by ministries and others. We are emphatically not lawyers and reluctant to play the part of the fools who rush in where (legal) angels fear to tread but simply put a *de facto/de jure* distinction does not do justice to what it is that makes guidance binding. Undoubtedly politics is a part of the equation and the licences and so forth are important but so is law. Indeed throughout the difficult negotiations between MITI and MOT over how to make policy and to implement it for industries that fell variously into their jurisdictions a constant refrain was that 'we (MOT) don't need you (MITI) because we've got a law – the Shipbuilding law' that we have seen affords the ministry a broad competence to act. Without a shadow of doubt (it seems to us) that administrative guidance is the more comfortable the closer it is to law. The interface between law and policy is equally tricky. The sketch hints at the gap between law and policy as MOT is constrained to resort to its own use of whatever legal and legally informal arrangement are available to it to spin the policy web. The success or failure of the endeavour is decided finally neither by the courts, if the matter is viewed from the perspective of the rule of law nor immediately, by the performance of the industrial sector, if the matter is viewed from the perspective of the developmental state but by the ability of the ministry to carry with it the industrial sector, (the individual companies, informal and formal associations of the big, the medium, and the small companies, the whole industry association, the whole industry advisory councils and the labour unions.) Of course the ability of the ministry to do this does relate finally to the economic performance of the sector. If the ministry's efforts are not seen to improve matters they are resisted.

The exercise of discretion is constrained on the same basis. Initially, authority for the exercise of discretion was sanctioned by the national legislature that is in the case of the Depressed Industries Law of 1978, resolutions passed in the standing committees of the Diet explicitly invite the responsible ministry to exercise administrative guidance in pursuit of a specified end at which point administrative guidance comes to resemble 'delegated legislation.' Subsequently, if a player or players in the policy community[19] believes that the ministry's exercise of discretion offends the rules of the game or simply is against their interest they cry 'foul!' Thus the shipping companies were worried lest MOT's administrative guidance to curtail production and to stabilize prices would mean that the shipping industry would have to pay higher prices for ships. Their response was to lodge a formal complaint to the FTC and to MOT itself (Yonezawa, 1988:439).

When no other remedy is available they will appeal to politicians ever alert to the possibility of recruiting new clients – regional politicians ensured that the interests of the smaller shipbuilders were not threatened by MOT's activities. In addition local shipbuilders organized themselves into 'national lobbying groups' to ensure that their problems were well known and that the machinations of MOT were transparent (Boyd and Nagamori, 1991:184; Uriu, 1996:195; Nihon Zosen Shinko Zaidan, 1983:5). The bureaucracy is keen to avoid such developments that compromise the ability of the minister to 'deliver' the sector in inter-ministerial councils, that make ministers angry and officials embarrassed. These pressures and anxieties are encapsulated in the rule of the game 'let there be no outsiders' by which is understood that MOT, the advisory council, and the trade associations were constrained to carry with them all of the principal players. This is clearly revealed in two intriguing developments in the management of the shipbuilding industry. Given the fact of substantial over-capacity some firms had to leave the industry. Accordingly it was agreed that the capacity reductions would be borne by groups of firms which would collectively bear the exit costs of individual firms constrained to cease business, that is the costs of the 'losers' would be shared amongst the 'winners' so as to lessen the distance between winning and losing. To minimize those costs it was important that redundant shipyards be sold. The financial institutions were not sanguine about the marketability of these assets and were reluctant to support the industry in the absence of a guarantee against loss. To resolve the problem groups of firms signed a *nensho* or memorandum, ('pledge' is what it amounted to) 'guaranteeing' to protect the institutions from losses. It is tempting to argue that satisfying the requirement that there be no outsiders was a prerequisite for MOT's legally informal problem solving. Actually there were outsiders. Although the trade unions were represented in discussions and sat as members in the advisory councils the obligation to carry them with the mainstream was less obviously constraining. Indeed, many were vociferous in their dismissal of the depressed industries law as a 'sacking bill.' That employment countermeasures came to figure in the policy solution owes much to the Japanese media and to the Diet itself (see below). Finally, we can note that the dramatic reduction of a huge labour intensive industry such as shipbuilding which has the added problems of a very high degree of geographical concentration that enables one to speak of shipbuilding towns is a tortuous and painful business. As the MOT picked its way through this minefield and endeavoured to find solutions it proposed arrangements and initiated acts, offered guidance, advice, instructions, recommendations, decisions on price, tonnage, market share, permissible orders, cost structures, and exports on the basis, ultimately, of a body of legislation which made little specific reference to these matters but which afforded the MOT a broad competence for the running of the industry and the ultimate sanction of withholding license to build. To the best of our knowledge there was no legal challenge to the MOT throughout (but see the involvement of the FTC below).

THE DEVELOPMENTAL EFFICACY OF ADMINISTRATIVE GUIDANCE

In a chapter concerned at least in part with the legal dimensions of the 'developmental state' it is hard to avoid a brief comment upon the developmental efficacy of administrative guidance. Johnson's position seems to be that the flexibility and discretion which administrative guidance affords is not in itself developmentally efficacious – if we can forgive an ugly phrase. (Johnson, 1982) The key for him seems to be the combination of a talented, insulated, elite, and responsible bureaucracy, and administrative guidance. The latter effectively empowers the official elite – symbolized for some by MITI, which is then free to pursue and to implement its privileged vision of the economy. This seems more than a little naïve particularly in the wake of the economic crisis in East Asia of the late 1990s. If we did not know it then we know now that 'informality' in the absence of other not as yet specified conditions is as functional for rent seeking, cronyism, and outright corruption as it might be effective and efficacious for economic development in different but equally unspecified conditions. Moreover, even were we to concede the incorruptibility, the high intelligence, the wisdom even of the Japanese official we would still need to recognize that MITI is not a single monolithic intelligence. It is no less than a political system itself in which and through which the interests and demands of hundreds of industrial sectors, thousands of industry associations and who knows how many firms are articulated, aggregated, and argued for. Accordingly it would be unwise indeed to expect that the output whether in the form of law or administrative guidance would be anything like an economically rational policy position rather than a political compromise with the characteristics rather of incoherence, facing both ways at the same time and so on. Indeed it is no secret that MITI has recruited academic economists to produce rationales in economic theory post hoc for policies it finds convenient for other reasons (Komiya, 1988). The Depressed Industries Law of 1978 was very much a product of a messy, political process in which economic rationality was no more than one of a number of interests in play.

THE ROLE OF THE DIET

The stranglehold of the ruling Liberal Democrat Party (LDP) on the Diet was broken a decade ago. The absolute majority over the opposition parties commanded by the LDP throughout the preceding forty years had encouraged the view in the West that the Diet was no more than a legislative rubber stamp for decisions reached elsewhere – notably in the inner councils of the Liberal Democrat Party itself. Notwithstanding the popularity of the view it was never the whole case. The opposition parties have long been ingenious in articulating their views and in developing the ways and means to parlay opposition into influence and the power to bargain for amendments to government sponsored legislation. The case of the passage of the Depressed Industries Law very much confirms this view of the Diet as a forum for genuine debate and stands as a corrective to the old Western stereotype. The depressed industries bill was submitted to the Standing Committee on Commerce and Industry in both the upper and lower houses. It was debated six times at the Lower House and seven times in the upper house. The joint investigation committee of the respective standing committees also discussed it on commerce and industry, social and labour affairs, agriculture, forestry and fisheries, and transport in the Lower House and in the upper house. The Fair Trade Commission also investigated the bill. The bill received serious amendments – in article 1 that dealt with the fundamental purpose of the bill and in the articles geared to its implementation. New articles were added as a direct consequence of interventions in the Diet – which proved itself to be very much other than a rubber stamp. This is of interest and importance in itself. It also has a theoretical relevance since the developmental state model is predicated upon the marginality of elected parliaments as the condition for bureaucratic autonomy. That autonomy is conditional in part upon the insulation of the bureaucracy from societal demands – atrophied parliaments are one means to this.[20]

INDUSTRIAL POLICY AND THE FAIR TRADE COMMISSION

Much has been made of the relative ineffectiveness of Anti-Trust Law in Japan. Given the reach and extent of the law itself, it is sometimes held as evidence of bad faith (particularly in trade negotiations and Western appeals for market opening) that the anti trust-law has had relatively little impact upon the conduct in practice of industrial policy. The evidence suggests that the problem is less one of faith and more one of deep-seated structural and procedural incompatibilities that undermine the effectiveness of the law. Let us consider the organization and preparation of industrial policy.[21] The principal architect of industrial policy is the *genkyoku,* that section of the bureaucracy that has the primary responsibility for developing and supervising policies for a given industry. MITI is the single most important *genkyoku* ministry. In the 1970s five of MITI's bureaux acted as *genkyoku*: the Chemical Industries Bureau, the Coal and Mining Bureau, the Heavy Industries Bureau, the Public Utilities Bureau, and the Textile and Light Industries Bureau. The bureau is internally divided into sections with industry specific responsibilities: thus, within the Heavy Industries Bureau there is an iron and steel section, an automobiles section, and so on. Shipbuilding (as we have seen) is the responsibility of the shipbuilding bureau of the Ministry of Transport (MOT). The *genkyoku* is responsible for devising policy and drafting all of the basic legislation concerning its industry. The prime policy goal of the *genkyoku* is neither growth nor profits so much as the smooth running and good order of its industry. It guards its prerogatives jealously and dislikes nothing more than the spillage of conflict into the public arena with the associated risk of intervention and mediation by 'politicians.' Disputes are to be avoided and if unavoidable to be settled 'in house.' These values have led to a particular policy style: distrust of too intensive competition, ('excess competition' in the bureaucratic vernacular), of restructuring, of uncontrolled entry to 'its' industry and, on the other hand, the open embrace of integration, inter-firm operating agreements, mergers, vertical and horizontal firm groupings, and cartels. In short, the preferred *modus operandi* of the *genkyoku* bureaucracy sets it on collision course with the Fair Trade Commission with its responsibilities for the implementation of the Anti-Monopoly Law. Typically, the FTC, faced with such a concentration of bureaucratic muscle has been the loser. This has changed somewhat. The Anti-Monopoly Law was revised and strengthened in 1977. And a landmark judgment in the 1980 petroleum cartel case has made it much harder since then to restrain competition by means of cartels created by administrative guidance. Indeed, a feature of the Law on Temporary Measures for Structural Improvement of Specified Industries enacted in May 1983 to provide assistance for industries caught in the wake of the second oil crisis, is the requirement of the agreement of the FTC for implementing measures that restrict competition (such as the designation of cartels for capacity reduction, inter-firm tie ups and so on) and further, a legal requirement for the reduction of such measures within an agreed time limit.

BUREAUCRATIC CULTURE: CONTINUITY AND ANTI-COMPETITIVE PRACTICE

Where the scope for official discretion is broad the values, preferences, and procedures of officialdom are commensurately significant because these govern how discretion will be exercised subject to the limitations we have noted above. One very senior insider believes that the bureaucratic culture is deeply rooted in the pre-war values we have described. Former deputy prime minister Gotoda Masaru while reflecting on his life's work in the national bureaucracy (where he served as director general of the national police agency and as deputy chief cabinet secretary) observed that despite a fifty year experience of the constitutional reversal of the bureaucrats' position in 1947 from that of agent of the emperor to that of public servant 'bureaucrats have had a hard time changing their mind set ...' What are the core elements in that 'mind set'? They include a strong urge to govern, based on a feeling that they are an elite.

> They are convinced that they always have the national interest at heart; but that national interest is a very subjective thing. They attempt to distance themselves from private sector pressure groups and special interests. In this sense, we cannot say that they are not impartial. But they are also insulated from public criticism … they gaze at the world through the windows of their offices. As a result, they are liable to see the ministry's interests as the national interest.[22]

Kyogoku makes a similar point about the way the bureaucracy looks after its personnel both publicly and privately from the time they are hired until they retire and sometimes literally until they are in their graves. These are conditions conducive to a strong sense of unity and esprit de corps which leads to the identification of the ministry interest with that of the nation ... the expansion of functions, competence, personnel, and budgets of the various ministries' bureaux, departments and sections are the meaning of life so far as bureaucrats are concerned. Planning and advocating new policies and getting the required personnel and funds give those involved meaning as well as a sense of participation and satisfaction (Kyogoku, 1987).

The ministerial interest is not exclusively a matter of the expansion of functions, competence, personnel, and budgets important as these are. There are other facets to the culture of the ministry and other dimensions of the assumptive universe of the Japanese bureaucrat which are significant for his approach to and understanding of competition.

Suggestive is a highly critical piece by a former bureaucrat from the Ministry of Health and Welfare (Miyamoto, 1994) who identifies core values in the MHW. Relevant here is the following:

i. The *harmony* of the ministry is more important than reality;
ii. The major task of the ministry is the *protection of the industry* not the protection of the public;
iii. *Continuity* is a core value and more important than crisis management;
iv. *Seniority* is a value that leads to the muting of criticism and tends to obscure the existence of problems;
v. *Amakudari* – bureaucrats joining related industries in the field upon retirement fosters the status quo and sustains pre-existing regulations.

None of this will astonish students of Japan's bureaucracy.[23] *Harmony* of the ministry: a close identification of the bureaucrat with his ministry is not peculiar to the Japanese bureaucracy whereas arguably the priority attached to the harmony of the 'ministerial home' is. The bureaucrat is encouraged to see his ministry as his family in an exercise which obscures public/private distinctions. The means by which this is done are multiple but perhaps best encapsulated in the ministry marriage club. Quite literally, to reiterate the words of Kyogoku, the ministry looks after its personnel both publicly and privately from the time they are hired with due regard to whom they wed (a bureaucratic senior will typically preside over the ceremonial itself) until they retire and sometimes literally until they are in their graves. The dutiful bureaucrat in turn has as his first concern the harmony of the ministerial family and accordingly a preference for regulation over competition.

The protection of the industry is more important than the protection of the public. The ministry has direct, close, personal, and long standing relationships with its industry partners organized in trade associations and advisory councils which are staffed by ministry bureaucrats and often headed by an ex bureaucrat. The harmony of the ministry itself is dependent upon the harmony of these relations between government and industry. The ministry is responsible to politicians who themselves benefit from massive campaign contributions from industry. The public is a distant and abstract entity in this skein of relations. This practical, *de facto* subordination of the public to the industry interest is celebrated in a national policy that has throughout the twentieth century placed production before distribution. The importance of *continuity* in such a bureaucratic universe can readily be imagined. The internal harmony of the ministry and the 'good order' of its relations with industry are underpinned by a complex of relationships, a web of agreements and understandings which have been evolved over the long run relationship between business and ministry. These have been substantially untroubled, changed, or disturbed by electoral or other fundamental political change over a period of nearly fifty years. In such circumstances a break with continuity is a threat to harmony and good order and to the ministry itself. The practice of post retirement recruitment of civil servants to peak positions in the company hierarchy *(amakudari)* is an important adjunct to these relationships which further encourages continuity as the retiree educates his company in the ways of the ministry and enjoys a privileged vantage point from which to communicate to the ministry the nature of the 'industry interest.'

Paradoxically perhaps, a notoriously ingrained, institutionalized, and ineradicable bureaucratic sectionalism is *energetically favourable to competition in the politico-bureaucratic market place* but *profoundly anti-competitive within the industrial sector.* In the realm of bureaucratic politics intense bitter competition, protracted turf wars, struggles over jurisdiction, anxieties about who gets the best recruits, the bigger budget, the best post-retirement jobs are the norm and the detailed abstruse calculus of the position of the home agency in any number of pecking orders is paramount – the very stuff of life. The coin has an opposite side: it is a culture *profoundly anti-competitive within the industrial sector for which the ministry is responsible.* If the ministry or agency is to be effective in the politic bureaucratic market place it must be able to deliver 'its' industry. Accordingly the ministry has an additional reason for valuing the peace and stability of the industrial sector to the extent that order is always likely to be valued over competition. Within the complex of agency and sector, we have suggested, harmony, continuity, and good order are the priorities and, we can add, regulation the preferred means and the cartel the archetypal and emblematic institution. Inevitably, these values fundamentally inform the use made by the bureaucracy of law. This is the more significant because (as we have seen) the enabling laws which grant the ministries responsibility for their sector(s) are loosely worded and afford the responsible agency great scope for the exercise of its discretion. The unsurprising consequence is the legal containment of what is perceived to be 'competitive excess.'

CONCLUSION

Notwithstanding the current prominence of a rule of law rhetoric, law does not figure prominently in accounts of East Asian economic development. Much the same can be said of the long run economic development of Japan where growth predated the codification of property rights and where the rule of law was challenged by an entrenched tradition which viewed law as the instrument of rule. The legislative efforts of the Meiji period confirm the persistence of this tradition. These were geared at least as much to political as to economic ends as the fledgling state sought to secure its own fiscal foundations, to enhance its capacity and institutional competence and sought more effectively to control and to regulate economic activity. There is little reason to believe that this tradition[24] and the associated practice of law were seriously eroded in the first half of the twentieth century. It proved then compatible with a century or more of sustained economic growth. The constitutional revisions of 1947 undoubtedly went some way to ground the rule of law understood in more conventional terms but here too there is good reason to believe that a very different understanding of the relationship between law and rule, one more readily understood in traditional terms persisted well into the post-war period. When we turn to the conclusions we derive from the sketch of law and industrial policy in the 1970s these prompt a nuanced, complex, and paradoxical account of the significance of law in the promotion and management of economic change in Japan in which property rights, the rule of law and the legal safeguarding of the possibility of economic competition appear to be of substantially less significance than legal instrumentality, legal informality and emblematic and associative usages of law in the embellishment of authority. On the other hand it seems that institutions anticipated by a rule of law discourse are more vital than has often been conceded, here we have in mind above all the Diet and latterly the Fair Trade Commission. At the same time there is a persistent anti-competitive thrust to the organization and values of the industrial bureaucracy in the industrial sector which is offset by an equally insistent, and in a highly regulated economy, an equally significant competitive pulse in the politico-bureaucratic market place. Finally we have suggested that whereas the margin for the exercise of official discretion in the application of the law to industry is very considerable it is not unconstrained and that it must, in fact, secure the support of, or risk challenge by, the principal players (typically firms and their associations) in the relevant policy area. This last requirement guarantees a certain linkage between the official exercise of legal informality and economic outcomes.

NOTES

1 Research on the shipbuilding case to which the second part of the chapter makes reference was funded by the Economic and Social Research Council of the United Kingdom to which we are grateful. Participation in the Workshop was Law and Development in East and Southeast Asia (January 1998) was made possible thanks to the generosity of Leiden University. In so far as I understand the Japanese shipbuilding industry thanks are due to my colleague Professor Seiichi Nagamori of Kokugakuin University.

2 The rule of law has been a constant theme in the 1990s publications and conferences of the World Bank. It was a central theme in the Annual World Bank Conference on Development Economics in 1996, see Bruno Michael and Boris Pleskovic (eds), (1997), in the subsequent conference, see Boris Pleskovic and Joseph E. Stiglitz (eds), (1998). Competition law and policy was a theme in the 1998 conference, see Boris Pleskovic and Joseph E. Stiglitz (eds), (1999). The Bank together with the OECD ran a project 'Framework for the design and implementation of competition law-policy' which led to a publication of the same name in 1998. On the rule of law in central and Eastern Europe see Cheryl W. Gray and associates (1993). Ohnesorge perhaps understates how common is the call currently for rule of law also on the traditional grounds of human rights and individual dignity even from within the World Bank. See for example Dakolias (1999), Sured and Malik (1999).

3 Eight years ago Robert Wade wrote, 'over the past two decades a literature big enough to fill a small airplane hangar has been produced on the causes of East Asian economic success' (Wade 1992:270). Well, now you would need a large airplane hangar to house it all. A good place to catch up on the literature of the 1990s is Aoki *et al.* (1998), Hayami and Aoki (1998), and Yanagihara and Sambommatsu (1997).

4 Cited by Wade (1992:273)

5 For the arguments of the late 1980s Wade (1992) is helpful. See also Yanagihara and Sambommatsu (1997).

6 Johnson (1982) remains the standard work. See also a useful review article by Onis (1991). On the deployment of the concept in a Latin American context see Smith (1998).

7 Aoki *et al.* (1998), Hayami and Aoki (1998), and see also the 1997 World Development report, *The State in a Changing World* published by the World Bank. At a minimum this might be taken as evidence that the Bank has come to recognize the inadequacy of a sharply dichotomized state/market approach in favour of the 'market enhancing' view which looks to state action not only to provide 'pure' public goods but actively to secure market activity.

8 Okazaki and Okuno-Fujiwara (1998).

9 Indeed Okazaki and Okuno-Fujiwara (1998:494) speak of *de facto* property rights 'serving as the basis' for early industrialization and agricultural development in Japan.

10 For a fuller account see David Johnson (1997) on which the present note is dependent.

11 The *mikoshi* is a portable shrine carried by adherents from the neighbourhood, a guild or trade and so on in the course of festivities. It is a burden to carry which symbolizes and sacrilizes those who shoulder the burden. It has been used by Maruyama the doyen of Japan's political commentators to capture the Japanese notion of authority (see Maruyama 1964).

12 Friedman (1988). There are problems with Friedman's work which is not as empirically rigorous as it might be. Equally one could be accused of requiring from Johnson a second book on implementation as good as the first on MITI itself. For a different perspective on the machine tools industry and industrial policy see Calomiris and Hielberg (1995).

13 Trezise (1983), Hadley (1983), and Patrick (1983).

14 Mention might also be made of an economist who set out to answer precisely this question of the effectiveness of industrial policy. He notes with admirable *sang froid* that, 'Assessments of the effectiveness of Japan's industrial policies are not very numerous' and concludes, borrowing the phrase of Trezise, that 'Ultimately, ... any final assessment will remain ... "an expression of faith"' (Boltho 1985:188). More recently still and in the context of Japan's tussle with the World Bank over the justice of its analyses of East Asian growth a consultancy fee of US$10,000 was paid to John Page the author of the resultant report – the East Asian miracle study (World Bank, 1993) with a view to correlate industrial policy with productivity growth in East Asia. The exercise in regression analysis that resulted revealed no significant match between policy and productivity (Terry, 1995:6).

15 In order to clarify our position so that the reader can make his/her own judgments we are sympathetic to the developmental state idea in so far as this asserts that the economic development of Japan is not explicable exclusively in terms of market forces. However doubts remain about

how adequately we understand the role of the state and the precise meshing of the economic and the political.

16 For a range of perspectives see Ramseyer (1985), Haley (1991), and Upham (1987).

17 In recent years there has been some loosening of standing requirements away from the practice of limiting standing to those individual interests that an administrative agency has been specifically charged with protecting by statute.

18 'Administrative guidance by government agencies and local authorities plays a significant role in Japan, although it is usually *not* regarded as a source of law' (Oda, 1992:61), see also Shiono (1984:204), and Young (1984).

19 Yasunori Sone's usage of the term *gyokai* closely parallels the idea of the policy community. Boyd and Nagamori (1991) have also worked with the notion of *gyokai*. See Sone (1993).

20 Caution is in order. Curtis (1993) suggests that the depressed industries law was an exception and that the Diet has not significantly revitalized itself.

21 Here we closely follow Komiya (1988) 'Introduction.'

22 Gotoda (1994). The quote is as translated in Mikuriya (1997).

23 Here too the literatures are enormous particularly in Japanese. A useful starting point of relevance to questions of economic development is Kim, Muramatsu, Pempel, and Yamamura (eds) (1995).

24 Doubtless Upham is right to question 'the easy assumption that the particularism and informality of Japanese law are the result of the continued strength of traditional values. I have argued that these values are maintained, if not created, by legal rules and institutions as well as by social inertia and that this legal structure is the result of conscious choice' (Upham, 1987:220). But note he does not question the fact of such practices.

REFERENCES

Aoki, Masahiko, Hyung-Ki Kim and Masahiro Okuno-Fujiwara (eds) (1996) *The Role of Government in East Asian Economic Development*. Oxford: Clarendon Press.

Boltho, Andrea (1985) 'Was Japan's Industrial Policy Successful?' *Cambridge Journal of Economics* 9/2, June, pp. 187-201.

Boyd, Richard (1989) 'The Political Mechanics of Consensus in the industrial policy Process: The Shipbuilding Industry in the face of crisis, 1973-78,' *Japan Forum* 1/1, pp. 1-17.

Boyd, Richard and Seiichi Nagamori (1991) 'Industrial policy-Making in practice: Electoral Diplomatic and other Adjustments to Crisis in the Japanese Shipbuilding Industry,' in: Stephen Wilks and Maurice Wright (eds) *The Promotion and Regulation of Industry in Japan*. New York: St Martin's Press, pp. 167-204.

Brunetti, Aymo Kisunko and Beatrice Gregory Weder (1997) *Institutional obstacles to doing business: region-by-region results from a worldwide survey of the private sector*. Background paper for World Development Report 1997. World Bank.

Bruno, Michael and Boris Pleskovic (eds) (1997) *Annual World Bank Conference on Development Economics 1996*. World Bank.

Calomiris, Charles W. and Charles P. Hielberg (1995) Government Credit Policy and Industrial Performance: Japanese machine tool producers 1963-91. *World Bank Policy Research Working Paper* no WPS 1434. World Bank.

Curtis, Gerald L. (1999) *The Logic of Japanese Politics*. New York: Columbia University Press.

Dakolias, Maria (1999) Court performance around the World: A Comparative Perspective. *World Bank Technical Paper* 430. World Bank.

Feeney, David (1998) 'Thailand versus Japan: Why Was Japan First?' in: Yujiro Hayami and Masahiko Aoki (eds) *The Institutional Foundations of East Asian Economic Development*. Basingstoke: Macmillan Press, pp. 413-42.

Friedman, David (1988) *The Misunderstood Miracle: Industrial Development and Political Change in Japan*. Ithaca: Cornell University Press.

Gotoda, Masaru (1994) *Sei to Kan* [Politics and Bureaucracy]. Tokyo: Iwanami Shoten.

Gray, Cheryl W. *et al.* (1993) Evolving Legal Frameworks for Private Sector Development in Central and Eastern Europe. *World Bank Discussion paper* 209. World Bank.

Gyosei Kanricho [Administrative Management Agency] (1981) *Gyosei Shido ni kansuru Chosa Kenkyo Hokokusho* [Study Report of Administrative Guidance] Tokyo: Gyosei Kanricho.

Hadley, E.M. (1983) 'The Secret of Japanese Success,' *Challenge* (May-June), pp. 4-10.

Haley, John Owen (1991) *Authority without Power, Law and the Japanese Paradox*. Oxford: Oxford University Press.

Harada, Naohiko (1983) 'Gyosei Shido Ho no Shihai to Nihonteki Gyosei Taishitsu' ['Administrative Guidance: Judicial Control and Characteristics of Japan's Administration'], *Juristo* 29.

Hashimoto, Kiminobu (1963) 'The Rule of Law: Some Aspects of Judicial Review of Administrative Actions,' in: Arthur T. von Mehren (ed.) *Law in Japan*. Cambridge, Massachusetts: Harvard University Press, pp. 239-73.

Hayami Yujiro and Masahiko Aoki (eds) (1998) *The Institutional Foundations of East Asian Economic Development*. Basingstoke: Macmillan Press.

Hughes, Helen (ed.) (1988) *Achieving Industrialization in East Asia*. Cambridge: Cambridge University Press.

Johnson, Chalmers (1982) *MITI and the Japanese Miracle: The Growth of Industrial Policy, 1925-75*. Stanford: Stanford University Press.

– (1987) 'Political institutions and economic development: the business government relationship in Japan, South Korea and Taiwan,' in: Fred Deyo (ed.) *The Political Economy of the New Asian Industrialism*. Ithaca: Cornell University Press.

– (1988) 'The Japanese Political Economy: A Crisis in Theory,' *Ethics and International Affairs* 2/2, pp. 79-97.

Johnson, David (1997) 'Why the Wicked Sleep: The Prosecution of Political Corruption in Postwar Japan,' *Japan Policy Research Institute Working Paper* 34: June.

Kim Hyung-Ki, (1996) *The Civil Service System and Economic Development: the Japanese experience*. EDI Learning Resources Series.

Kim, Hyung-Ki, M. Muramatsu, T.J. Pempel and K. Yamamura (eds) (1995) *Japanese Civil Service and Economic Development: Catalysts of Change*. Oxford: Oxford University Press.

Komiya, Ryutaro (1988) 'Introduction,' in: Ryutaro Komiya, Masahiro Okuno and Kotaro Suzumura (eds) *Industrial Policy of Japan*. Tokyo: Academic Press, pp. 1-22.

Komiya, Ryutaro and Masahiro Okuno, Kotaro Suzumura (eds) (1988) *Industrial Policy of Japan*. Tokyo: Academic Press Japan.

Kyogoku, Jun-ichi (1983) *Nihon Seiji* [Japan's Politics]. Tokyo: University of Tokyo Press.

– (1987) (the above translated by Nobutaka Ike) *The Political Dynamics of Japan*. Tokyo: University of Tokyo Press.

Lapavitsas, Costas (1990) 'The Chalmers Johnson and David Friedman debate – a summary and adjudication,' Unpublished paper.

Magaziner, Ira C. and Thomas M. Hout (1980) *Japanese Industrial Policy*. Berkeley: Institute of International Studies, University of California.

Mansfield, Edwin (1994) Intellectual Property Protection, Foreign Direct Investment, and Technology Transfer, *IFC Discussion Paper 19*. World Bank.

Maruyama, Masao (1964) *Thought and Behaviour in Japanese Politics*. Oxford: Oxford University Press.

Mikuriya, Takashi (1997) 'Introduction,' *Japan Echo* 24, Special issue.

Miyamoto, Masao (1996) 'Mental Castration, the HIV Scandal and the Japanese Bureaucracy,' *Japan Policy Research Institute Working Paper* 23, August 1996.

Nihon Zosen Shinko Kaidan (ed.) (1983) *Zosen fukyo no kiroku; dai-ichiji sekiyu kiki ni taioshite*. Tokyo: Nihon Zosen Shinko Zaidan.

North Douglass C. (1998) 'The Instititutional Foundations of East Asian Development: A Summary Evaluation,' in: Yujiro Hayami and Masahiko Aoki (eds) *The Institutional Foundations of East Asian Economic Development*. Basingstoke: Macmillan Press, pp. 552-60.

North, D. and R. Thomas (1973) *The Rise of the Western World*. Cambridge: Cambridge University Press.

Oda, Hiroshi (1992) *Japanese Law*. London: Butterworths.

Ogawa, Ichiro (1984) 'The Legal framework of Public Administration,' in: Kiyoaki Tsuji (ed.) *Public Administration in Japan*. Tokyo: University of Tokyo Press, pp 13-19.

Okazaki, Tetsuji and Okuno-Fujiwara Masahiro (1998) 'Evolution of Economic Systems: The Case of Japan,' in: Yujiro Hayami and Masahiko Aoki (eds) *The Institutional Foundations of East Asian Economic Development*. Basingstoke: Macmillan Press, pp. 482-522.

Onis, Ziya (1991) 'The Logic of the Developmental State,' *Comparative Politics,* 24 October, pp. 109-26.

Patrick, H. (1983) 'Japanese Industrial Policy and Its Relevance for United States Industrial Policy,' prepared statement before the Joint Economic Committee, US Congress 13 July.

Pleskovic, Boris and Joseph E. Stiglitz (1998) *Annual World Bank Conference on Development Economics 1997*. World Bank.

– (1999) *Annual World Bank Conference on Development Economics 1998*. World Bank.

Ramseyer, J. Mark, (1985) 'The Costs of the Consensual Myth: Antitrust Enforcement and institutional Barriers to Litigation in Japan,' *Yale Law Journal* 94/3, January, pp. 604-45.

Shiono, Hiroshi (1984) 'Administrative Guidance,' in: Kiyoaki Tsuji (ed.) *Public Administration in Japan*. Tokyo: University of Tokyo Press, pp. 295-306.

Sone, Yasunori (1993) 'Conclusion: Structuring Political Bargains: Government Gyookai, and Markets,' in: Gary Allison (ed.) *Political Dynamics in Contemporary Japan*. Ithaca: Cornell University Press, pp. 295-306.

Raphael, James H. and Thomas P. Rohlen (1998) 'How many models of Japanese growth do we want or need?' in: Henry S. Rowen (ed.) *Behind East Asian Growth: the political and social foundations of prosperity*. London and New York: Routledge.

Rowen, Henry S. (1998) *Behind East Asian Growth: the political and social foundations of prosperity*. London and New York: Routledge.

Sured, Andres Rigo and Waleed H. Malik (1999) *Judicial Challenges in the New Millenium: Proceedings of the Second Summit of the Ibero-American Supreme Courts and Tribunals of Justice*. World Bank Technical Paper 450. World Bank.

Smith, Peter H. (1998) 'The Rise and Fall of the Developmental State in Latin America,' in: M. Vellinga (ed.) *The Changing Role of the State in Latin America*. Boulder: Westview Press.

Totten, George O. III (1984) 'The Reconstruction of the Japanese Shipbuilding industry,' in: Robert L. Friedheim *et al.* (eds) *Japan and the New Ocean Regime*. Boulder: Westview Press, pp. 130-72.

Trezise, P.H. (1983) 'Industrial Policy is not the Major Reason for Japan's Success,' *The Brookings Review* 1 (Spring), pp. 13-18.

Upham, Frank K. (1987) *Law and Social Change in Postwar Japan*. Cambridge–Massachusetts–London: Harvard University Press.

Uriu, Robert M. (1996) *Troubled Industries, confronting economic change in Japan*. Ithaca: Cornell University Press.

Wade, Robert (1992) 'East Asia's Economic Success, Conflicting Perspectives, Partial Insights, Shaky Evidence,' *World Politics* 44/2, pp. 270-320.

– (1996) 'Japan, the World Bank, and the Art of Paradigm Maintenance: The East Asian Miracle in Political Perspective,' *New Left Review* 217 (May/June), pp. 3-36.

World Bank, (1993) *The East Asian Miracle in Economic Growth and Public Policy*. Oxford: Oxford University Press.

World Bank and the OECD (1998) *Framework for the Design and Implementation of Competition Law-policy*. World Bank.

Yanagihara, Toru and Susumu Sambommatsu (1997) *East Asian Development Experience*. Tokyo: Institute of Developing Economies.

Yonezawa, Yoshie (1988) 'The Shipbuilding Industry,' in: Ryutaro Komiya (ed.) *Industrial Policy of Japan*. Tokyo: Academic Press, pp. 425-49.

Young, Michael K. (1984) 'Judicial Review of Administrative Guidance: Governmentally Encouraged Consensual Dispute Resolution in Japan,' *Columbia Law Review* 84/4, pp. 923-83.

– (1991) 'Structural Adjustment of Mature Industries in Japan: Legal Institutions, Industry Associations and Bargaining,' in: Stephen Wilks and Maurice Wright (eds) *The Promotion and Regulation of Industry in Japan*. New York: St Martin's Press, pp. 135-66.

CHAPTER 7

INDUSTRIAL POLICY AND INTELLECTUAL PROPERTY IN JAPAN AND BEYOND

CHRISTOPHER HEATH

At the end of the twentieth century, a good part of the Asian continent seemed to have lost confidence in itself. 'Asian values' were not only sceptically discussed in the US and European circles, but also within Asia itself.[1] Even earlier, the limits of Japan's formula of success as one based on bureaucratic intervention were meticulously exposed.[2] While it would be wrong to try to insulate one single factor responsible for the success or failure of industrial development, the system of intellectual property rights – or the absence of such – should not be underestimated, particularly when analysing the Japanese experience.

THE CASE OF JAPAN

Development of Intellectual Property

Being a country of sparse national resources, Japan had to rely on entrepreneurial ingeniousness and the promotion of inventive efforts through intellectual property rights.[3] Turning to intellectual property rights to achieve its goals of '*fukoku kyôhei*' (a rich country and a strong army) and '*shokusan kôgyô*' (increase industrial productivity) was by no means a foregone conclusion for the Meiji state. After all, in 1721 the military Tokugawa regime that ruled the country between 1603 and 1868 had proclaimed a law that prohibited technical innovations.[4] Nevertheless, patent systems that the Japanese had seen operating in the United Kingdom, the United States, and France, were soon identified as the motor of industrial development. During a visit to the US Patent Office around the turn of the century the first President of the Japanese Patent Office, Korekiyo Takahashi, reportedly stated:

> We have looked about us to see what nations are the greatest, so that we can be like them. We said: 'What is it that makes the United States such a great nation?,' and we investigated and we found that it was

> patents, and so we will have patents (US Department of Commerce/-Patent Office 1972:20).

Yet the first Japanese patent law, the *Sembai ryaku kisoku*, enacted in 1871, had to be scrapped when after one year not a single patent application had been made. Just as well, since there would not have been any properly trained examiners for examining patents:

> If someone requests a patent for a supposedly new invention, it is extremely difficult to determine to what extent the invention is really new. In order to conduct a thorough examination, one would have to employ 50 foreigners. In employing 50 foreigners, it would be necessary to employ the same number of translators. This is certainly very expensive. But were there really so many inventions? The only invention that people talked about in these days was the invention of the rickshaw (Tsûsanshô (Ministry of Trade and Industry) 1964:558).

Undeterred, the subsequent Patent Monopoly Ordinance (*Sembai tokkyo jôrei*) was promulgated on 18 April 1885, and was revised in 1888, 1899, and 1909. Only in 1921 and upon the introduction of the first-to-file system had Japanese patent law found a structure similar to that of the Patent Act of 1959, which is still in force today.

So important was the post of President of the Patent Office that Korekiyo Takahashi[5] later on became Minister of Finance and for a couple of months even Prime Minister. In 1885, in the first year of its existence, 425 applications were filed under the new Patent Act, of which 99 were granted. Already in the following year, the number of applications had doubled to 1,384, while 205 patents were granted (Tokkyo Kyoku (Patent Office) 1934:59). In 1900, for the first time the number of patent applications exceeded 2,000 (actually 2,006). In 1920, the 10,000 mark was surpassed (11,017); in 1966, the number for the first time exceeded 50,000 (55,970); in 1972, the 100,000 mark was passed (102,948); and in 1993, a peak was reached with 361,985 patent applications.[6]

An example of successful legislation complying with the domestic needs of a still fledgling industry was the introduction of a utility model system in 1905.[7] After the accession to the Paris Convention, it had become clear that only foreigners were filing inventions that were novel worldwide. Japanese inventive activity, on the other hand, was seriously hampered by the fact that no special protection could be sought for minor improvements. Competitors were keen to imitate any such improvements, with the result that the quality of goods often deteriorated. Thus, the first Utility Model Act (also termed Petty Patent Act, or Sub-Patent Act, depending on the legal system) of 1905 allowed exclusive rights over 'useful developments concerning the shape, arrangement or concept of a commercial object.' With a protection period of six years and the novelty requirement limited to Japan, the Act satisfied domestic needs for short-term, low-level protection without choking the patent register with long-term monopolistic rights over minor improvements. According to statistics, the utility model system has been a success. Unlike patents, utility models never appealed much to foreigners, and over the years less than two per cent of the applications came from abroad. In Japan, the number of filings rose from 2,011 in 1906 to more than 180,000 in 1980. Only by the late 1980s, had the number of patent applications exceeded the number of utility model applications. This in turn led to a significant change in the utility model system in 1994 (Law No 116, 1994). Since utility model protection had apparently outlived its purpose of serving domestic industry, the term of protection was shortened and rights granted without examination. However, examination is still necessary before raising an infringement suit. In effect, the changes have been the death knell of the utility model system (Tamai, 1992), as is also indicated by the application figures which dropped by more than 80 per cent.

The exact application figures are as follows:

Year	*Application*	*Granted*
1906	2,011	985
1910	14,057	4,358
1920	18,543	3,584
1930	33,111	12,060
1940	30,105	16,535
1950	22,426	6,365
1960	68,102	18,208
1970	124,170	29,264
1980	185,455	44,600
1990	138,294	43,300
1993	77,101	53,400
1995	14,886	63,966

No less interesting is the gradual expansion of patentable subject matter. Only in 1975 was patent protection for pharmaceutical substances introduced; as of 1979, micro-organisms were deemed patentable; during the 1980s, resistance against granting patents for genetically engineered products was overcome; and in 1988, the first patent for animals was applied. In 1997, new guidelines of the Patent Office were issued to facilitate the patenting of computer software and biotechnology.

Rules on Technology Transfer

Apart from legal structures, Japan advanced and refined its system of IP rights by institutional structures and administrative competencies. From the start the Patent Office, and thereby the responsibility for preparing legislation in the field of IP rights, fell into the competency of the Ministry of Agriculture and Trade. Subsequently it was the famous or infamous Ministry of Trade and Industry (MITI), rather than the Ministry of Justice that was responsible for preparing legislation in the field of civil law in general.

Institutional control of intellectual property policy has been particularly important for Japan in the field of international technology transfer. The institutionally responsible Fair Trade Commission (FTC) published its first Guidelines on International Licensing Contracts in 1968,[8] and subsequently revised them in 1989 (Iyori and Uesugi, 1994:467) and 1998.[9] Until 1992, all international contracts had to be notified, and until 1997 the notification requirement continued for exclusive licenses only.[10] The FTC was particularly concerned with so-called grant-back clauses, whereby licensees were obliged to transfer improvement inventions to the licensor without proper remuneration.[11]

Both the FTC and the courts have done much to encourage the so-called parallel importation of foreign made goods in order to lower the price level of imports.[12]

Inherent Weakness of Enforcement

According to a survey conducted in 1996, Japan is not a popular place for initiating patent infringement suits. It is placed among the last five countries, along with Italy, Spain, Argentina, and India. Even Indonesia and Brazil enjoyed a better reputation than Japan (*The World Patent Survey*, 1996:19 (20)). Several reasons have been made responsible for this outcome:

1. Due to a very narrow interpretation of the function of the judiciary, very seldom do judges engage in what would be called 'social engineering' in order to solve a case. Rather it is viewed as the task of bureaucratic administration to balance conflicting interests before proposing legislation – the abstract, *ex ante* control is favoured over the *ex post* control.[13] It is thus no coincidence that court decisions discuss the facts of a case very broadly, but attach much less importance to their legal deductions (Rahn 1990:321ff).

2. Access to training for the legal profession is severely limited, thus creating a shortage of attorneys and judges (Henderson, 1997:27).
3. Due to the lack of specialized courts in matters of intellectual property and the frequent transfer of judges, interpretation tends to stick to the letter of the law due to inexperience and uncertainty. And again, granting protection beyond the letter of the law would mean upsetting the industrial policy the law-making bureaucracy had in mind.

Fuzzy Logic and International Obligations

Japan joined the Paris Convention in 1900. Despite pressure from foreign nations, particularly France and the United States, Japan at first did not give foreigners access to its intellectual property system. Japan was well aware that investment would flow into Japan nevertheless.[14] Japan thus used the accession to the Paris Convention as a bargaining tool in revising the so-called 'unequal treaties' the Shogunate had entered into with several Western powers (Russia, the United States, France, and the United Kingdom) in 1858. This exempted foreigners from these nations from the allegedly 'barbaric' Japanese jurisdiction (Rahn, 1983:461). Only upon a revision of the unequal treaties did Japan join the Paris and Berne Conventions. However, Japan refused to join the Madrid Arrangement for the Repression of False or Deceptive Indications of Source on Goods concluded in 1891, despite repeated requests from the French Government to do so, for the following reasons:

> Most Japanese exports go to countries that have not joined the Agreement, while on the other hand misleading indications of origin from member countries are rare. The main export markets of Japan, that is China, the US, and Germany (the latter being the country where most misleading indications of origin have become known, particularly earthenware from China), have not yet joined the Agreement. Japanese industry is still at the stage of copying and imitation. The average domestic consumer prefers foreign goods, for which reason a number of domestic producers label their goods misleadingly as foreign. Japanese industry is still in its infancy and has little experience of exporting, so confidence in its products is low and it is very difficult to find markets for goods labelled as 'Made in Japan'; therefore, misleading indications of origin are not infrequent. For these reasons, to join the Arrangement would be of very little practical use for promoting [the] Japanese economy. On the contrary, it would rather be an impediment.[15]

Only upon the conclusion of the San Francisco Peace Treaty in 1952, was Japan obliged to ratify the Madrid Arrangement.

Given this historical background, it is quite obvious that Japan had joined the Paris Convention for political and economic reasons, rather than for the conviction that 'the inalienable right of the inventor should be protected by the laws of all cultured nations,' as was the driving idea behind the Paris Convention (Ladas, 1930:74). Rather, Japan has always taken the view that 'unlike fundamental human rights, intellectual property rights are not inherent; rather, they are granted in line with certain policy objectives, such as the promotion of industrial development and the stimulation of cultural activities. Because of this, current intellectual property rights protection systems are not absolute in nature; they change as the policy objectives change. However, the present system is based on granting proprietary rights over intellectual property.'[16]

The first unwelcome obligation under the Paris Convention came in 1925, when under the Hague Revision Conference all Member States were obliged to enact measures against unfair competition.[17] Japan was thus put in a quandary because it had always tolerated acts of unfair competition, particularly the copying of foreign goods and piracy applications of foreign trademarks, because these practices were considered to be advantageous to Japanese industry (Tokkyo Chô (Patent Office) 1955:101). When Japan finally appeared to comply with Art. 10bis Paris Convention by enacting an Unfair Competition Act in 1934,[18] the Act proved inapplicable due to the requirement of intentional contravention against fair competition. In addition, one provision exempted acts under registered industrial property rights – most likely a provision to protect trademark pirates.[19]

Until 1950, only one reported case under the Unfair Competition Act went up to the Supreme Court.[20] Japan had thereby found the perfect fuzzy logic formula by enacting laws to avoid foreign sanctions, but declining to apply the law in order to avoid unwelcome results at home (Rahn and Heath, 1994:345). Regarding trademark piracy in particular, Japan was very much against the adoption of Art. 6^{septies} Paris Convention (misappropriation of a trademark by an agent or representative) at the Lisbon Revision Conference in 1958.[21] With regard to piracy applications of trademarks, a Japanese court as late as 1989 held that 'deft use of another's achievements without compensation cannot normally be considered unlawful.'[22] Part of the relative ease with which trademark pirates have been able to avoid persecution in Japan is the apparent incompetence of Japanese courts to recognize bad faith where it so obviously exists. In the above-quoted 'Popeye' case, a Japanese party in 1965 had registered a mark almost identical with the Popeye drawings from Chrysler-Seager. Despite this fact, even the Supreme Court did not find this was a misappropriation in bad faith.[23]

Another contentious issue has always been the proper remuneration particularly of foreign owners of copyright and neighbouring rights in Japan. Although a member to the Berne Convention as early as 1899,[24] collection of user fees did not begin until the mid-1930s. This was when a German lawyer was requested by several collecting societies, both from the US and Europe, to enforce Japan's copyright provisions with respect to foreign musical works such as Ravel's *Bolero* or the works of Puccini.[25] More recently, Japan was brought before the WTO, because she had refused retroactive protection of neighbouring rights for phonogram producers.[26] The issue has now been settled due to a change in Japanese legislation.[27]

ASIA BEYOND JAPAN[28]

Using Japan as a Blueprint: Korea

The intellectual property system of Korea is closest to the Japanese not merely because of geographical proximity, but also because of Japanese colonisation between 1908 and 1945. Bureaucratic structures were either left in place or else adopted from a country whose language was fairly familiar to those shaping the country after the devastating Korean War in 1953. As in Japan, the Ministry of Trade and Industry (MITI, now METI) is responsible for shaping not only industrial policy, but also industrial property. On the legal side, the Korean Unfair Competition Act is little different from the one the Japanese enacted for Korea in 1935. Also other industrial property laws have been closely modelled after those of Japan.[29]

However there are two aspects which distinguish Korean industrial policy from the Japanese. Korea had much less time to develop structures which were not in accordance with international obligations due to increasing pressure from industrialized countries to grant proper protection. A typical example might be the so-called pipeline protection for pharmaceuticals that was first granted to the US and subsequently to European applicants.[30]

In addition, due to a more litigious legal culture in Korea, the Supreme Court is far more active and assertive in its ruling than its Japanese counterpart. In one decision in 1995, the Korean Supreme Court ruled it unconstitutional that there were no proper channels to appeal decisions of the Patent Office.[31] This led to setting up a Patent Court (by the Law of 14 July 1994), which took up its work on 1 March 1998.

Mighty Mandarins: China, Taiwan, and Singapore

The above parameters of the Japanese model of success – viewing intellectual property protection as a chance for the development for domestic industry, while trying to give only limited domination to foreign right owners – have also been adopted in countries whose bureaucratic mandarins were savvy enough to see not only the downside but also the merits of intellectual property rights. Particularly in China, three attributes of the Japanese system, that is, setting up an intellectual property system for the sake of domestic industrial development, preference of bureaucratic institutions over independent courts, and an institutionalized weakness of enforcement, can also be detected:

> As usual, enforcement is not so much a matter of law as of will. At the top, Chinese leaders understand that the country must protect intellectual property rights if it hopes to attract foreign technology and develop its own industry. But enforcement is complicated by what we call the rule of law with Chinese characteristics: Who is going to order the police on raids for the police report to the guilty parties? The interests of the various laws read: 'In These Pirate Firms Further Explain the Lack of Enforcement Here.' We would note however, that China knows how to enforce the law when it wants. Last year, Reebok worked with the Chinese administration for industry and commerce, leading to raids of 45 factories, the confiscation of some 120,000 pairs of counterfeit shoes. China has officially urged consumers to boycott pirated disks and books, the software and entertainment industry losing some 900 million dollars each year to Chinese piracy where demand requires to go after suppliers. ... Finally while the world can do only so much to change China's behaviour, it cannot least maintain the standards of groups like the World Trade Organisation, a powerful reminder to China that while membership has its privileges, it also has its responsibilities.[32]

From 1985, China put enormous efforts into developing an intellectual property system. Apart from having processed 400,000 applications for patents and designs, the Chinese Patent Office amassed 30 million patent documents from twenty different countries in the first ten years of its existence. At the end of 1993, about 400,000 trademarks have been registered in China, while there were about 5,000 qualified patent attorneys.

It comes as no surprise that compliance with international obligations has not been China's first priority: practicing lawyers, for example, complain about unrealistically short deadlines for responses particularly under the Madrid Agreement for the Protection of Trade Marks.

While Taiwan overhauled her intellectual property system between 1992 and 1996, a similar preference for administrative enforcement and lack of proper judicial control can be found. Taiwan and China, and to a lesser degree Hong Kong, are the main offenders when it comes to the application of piracy trademarks, either domestically or in other Asian countries.

Due to the fact that registering patents in the United Kingdom was unattractive to domestic industry, Singapore revamped much of its industrial property system in 1995. Not unlike Japan, Singapore has attached much importance to promoting industrial development through allowing parallel imports.

Intellectual Property is Theft: The Case of Developing Asia

Other countries in the Asian region have viewed intellectual property rights rather as a tool of industrialized countries to dominate their economy (Adelman and Baldia, 1996; Konan *et al.*, 1995:9-12, 13). Opposition against any sort of intellectual property protection has been particularly strong in the most populous Asian countries, such as India and Indonesia.(Antons, 2000; Kaehlig, 1993) The negative approach might have prevented foreign right owners from exploiting their intellectual property rights in general, but has not assisted in developing the certainly vast potential of domestic industry. It may not be completely far-fetched to argue that the ruling classes in these countries have had little interest in upsetting a status quo that was quite favourable to their economic interests. In Indonesia, India, Brazil and a number of African countries, an oligarchy of a few influential families is in many cases primarily interested in perpetuating the structures for political power and self-enrichment.

The Legacy of Colonialism

The former colonial powers, Great Britain and France, dominated different countries in the Asian region. Britannia ruled the waves and valleys of Malaysia, Singapore, Brunei, and India, while the French colonized Vietnam,[33] Laos, and Cambodia. Thailand,[34] through clever diplomacy, remained the uncolonized buffer country between these two. Indonesia was the most important colony of the dwindling Dutch Empire, while the Philippines rid themselves of centuries of Spanish mismanagement in 1898, only to be colonized by the Americans until 1946 (Hooker, 1988). The Japanese occupied Korea, Taiwan, and parts of China, not particularly to these countries' liking.

Colonization had more influence on legal than on religious structures. In many cases, this led to imported legal systems, which clashed with traditional social or religious beliefs. This phenomenon can also be detected in countries that remained uncolonized. Japan and Thailand adopted western legal systems that were ill fitted to their cultural beliefs.

Due to colonization, most Asian countries had no choice when introducing intellectual property rights, as their colonial masters dictated the decision. This was more the case in some countries than in others. While Indonesia was particularly fervent in cutting all links to the legal system of her previous masters, the common law countries of Asia not only retained the system, but even accepted – and in some cases still accept – filings effected in London and having validity in their respective countries. The last remnant of this system is the system of design protection in Malaysia that was governed by 1949 British legislation on that subject until September 1999.

The Remains of Communism

In China and Vietnam, the traditions of intellectual property protection, if any, were discontinued by the advent of Communism. Re-introduction of intellectual property systems that only followed principles of private property and international dialogue had been re-established at the beginning of the 1980s. China joined the WIPO in 1980 and introduced legislation to protect intellectual property rights between 1984 and 1990. Vietnam introduced the first legislation for patent protection in 1981, for trademarks in 1982, and for copyrights in 1986.

WTO/TRIPs – Lead Vest or Silk Gown?

Quite significant numbers of academics view the WTO/TRIPs Agreement as an act of American Imperialism 'overwhelmingly likely to re-instate and perpetuate dependence.'[35] The way the Agreement was rammed through despite fierce opposition from developing countries certainly smacks of imperialism. What is often overlooked, however, are the chances for developing countries to enact a system of intellectual property protection and technology transfer control that serves as an encouragement to domestic industry as well. With due brevity, the following means can be mentioned:

1. enhancing protection of natural and indigenous resources;
2. introducing a utility model system to encourage small and medium-sized enterprises;
3. narrowing interpretation of patent claims so as to enhance legal certainty and prevent the development of improvements;
4. joining international conventions for the particular purpose of reducing the workload of domestic patent offices. The PCT may be cited as the foremost example in the field of patents;
5. increasing awareness as to the professional training of patent attorneys;

6. preventing abuse of intellectual property rights by, e.g., permitting the so-called parallel importation of patented and trademarked products and a tight control of clauses detrimental to technical progress, particularly the limitation of the licensee's freedom to develop improvements.

It would be a pity if the chances the WTO/TRIPs Agreement offers to developing countries is lost due to ignorance or neglect on the side of developing countries and undue pressure from the side of the developed countries, particularly the United States.

There are some developments in the right direction, however. The enhanced protection of natural and indigenous resources, deserving particular mention is the Philippine Act No. 8371 of 28 July 1997, that is meant to 'recognize, protect and promote the rights of indigenous cultural communities/indigenous peoples.' A Plant Variety Protection Act, that includes protection for 'local indigenous plant varieties,' 'common indigenous plant varieties,' 'wild plant varieties,' and any sort of 'genetic material,' was promulgated in Thailand in 2000.

As to a utility model system, after a good deal of deliberation, Thailand with its Patent Amendment Act of 27 March 1999 (enforced since 27 September 1999), introduced a petty patent system in Sec. 65bis-65^{decem} Patent Act. While this is a step in the right direction, Thailand still lacks a proper curriculum for technically trained patent attorneys, a problem that it shares with many other countries in the region.

Intellectual Property as Power to the People

Proper introduction and enforcement of intellectual property rights may also offer opportunity beyond the sphere of industrial development. It may even be a catalyst for social change. As has been mentioned above, reluctance to introduce intellectual property protection in developing countries was often rooted in patterns of power sharing in oligarchic societies. In many Asian countries democratic shortcomings were seen as a trade-off to fast industrial development and sold as 'Asian values.'

> When the economic crisis hit Thailand, its first victim back in July [1997], it was possible for South East Asia's authoritarians to argue that Democracy was part of the problem. They could claim that those Asian countries with short-lived, unstable governments were ill equipped to cope with a crisis and to impose the harsh measures needed to end it. Six months later, the opposite appears to be true: the more democratic countries seem to have the best chance of successful economic reform'(*The Economist* 17 Jan 1998). The grand old man of legal anthropology, Wolfgang Fikentscher, has convincingly

argued that the advent of intellectual property rights may well spearhead the consciousness for subjective, human rights in general. Intellectual property rights from a tool of industrial policy to a catalyst for human rights awareness – Asia comes full circle to the driving motives for drafting the Paris Convention in 1883.

NOTES

1 Periodicals were ripe with titles such as 'Are Asian Values Finished?' as discussed in *Far Eastern Economic Review*, 22 January 1998, p. 32. More to the point, *The Economist*, 17 January 1998, p. 58 could write: 'Indonesia is an extreme case of a phenomenon seen in several Asian countries, where a government derives its legitimacy from its ability to deliver economic success rather than from a truly Democratic mandate... "Asian values" were alleged to place greater weight on social order and deference to authority than did values of the decadent western variety.'

2 Particularly in Baum (ed.) 1997.

3 The emergence of the Zaibatsu-Groups from the 1880s onwards owes less to governmental patronage than to tough competition, hard work and commercial astuteness: Hidemasu Morikawa, 1992, pp. 1-55.

4 Shinkihatto no ofuregaki (Ordinance Prohibiting Innovations), Ordinance of the Military Government of July 1721, reprinted in Tokkyo Chô (Patent Office), 1955, p. 36.

5 On Takahashi, see Etsuji Kotani, [1979]. An interesting insight into the exchange between the American and Japanese Patent Office is also given by the exchange of letters between Korekiyo Takahashi and Schuyler Duryee, as reprinted by Kazuto Sakamoto [1989].

6 Figures by Tokkyo Chô, 1955, p. 134, Tokkyo Chô, 1985, p. 756, and Tokkyo Chô, 1995, p. 345.

7 Jitsuyo Shin'anhô as of 15 March 1905, Law No. 21. An analysis is provided by Nobuo Monya, 1973, p. 159.

8 Reprinted in English in Nakagawa, 1984, p. 124.

9 The 1998 Guidelines can be found in English at the FTC's homepage, http://www.jftc.go.jp.

10 The changes were mostly due to US pressure.

11 According to Iyori/Uesugi (p. 305), about 20 per cent of all contraventions concerned grant-back clauses. The concern is understandable insofar as such improvement inventions were the forte of Japanese industry (see above). About one fifth of all contracts were found faulty by the FTC.

12 The courts have allowed parallel importation of trade marked goods as early as 1970: Osaka District Court, 27 February 1970, 2 IIC 325 [1971] – 'Parker'; the parallel importation of copyrighted goods is permissible unless the copyrighted work enjoys special distribution rights: Tokyo District Court, 1st July 1995, 27 IIC 570 [1996] – 'Beauty and the Beast.' The importation of patented goods is permissible unless notice of the contrary has been given by the patentee: Supreme Court, 1 July 1997, 29 IIC 331 [1998] – 'BBS Car Wheels III.' The FTC has repeatedly taken action against attempts to prevent lawful parallel imports by warning sole import distributors of: Old Scotch Whiskey, Apple Computers and Feinberg Airguns.

13 This has basically been the view in the presentations in Baum, 1997, and in particular: Kono, ibid, p. 69.

14 The connection between foreign investment and intellectual property protection may have been overstated for political reasons. As the Economist, 22 January 1994, 62/63 could write in an article: *Intellectual Property is Theft*: 'In the past, multinationals have invested heavily in countries long before their secrets were safe there. Investment decisions will continue to have more to do with national laws on ownership, market size, and the state of domestic industry than with intellectual property protection.' This, of course, is not what multinationals, particularly pharmaceutical companies, would be keen to admit.

15 This reply is reprinted in Tokkyo Chô, 1955, p. 103-4.

16 Commission on intellectual property rights in the 21st century, *Towards the area of intellectual creation – challenges for break-through*, Tokyo released on 7 April 1997, both in Japanese and English.

17 Actes de la Haye, Den Haag 1925, p. 475: Attempts by the French government to agree to an even more forceful wording of the provision of Article 10bis Paris Convention were rejected particularly by Japan.

18 Law No. 14 of 27 March 1934, in force since 1 January 1935.

19 Joseph Koe Toyosaki, [1971]. Already Yoshinobu Someno, [1959] voiced doubt about the use of this provision. Particularly foreign brand names and brand goods were clad with the image of high class also because of the high tax duties levied on them. It is fair to say, however, that in most cases the application of the provision was rejected as an 'abuse of rights.'

20 Decision of 27 August 1942, 14 Tokkyo Kenkyû 24 [1992].

21 See, e.g., Stephan Ladas, 1975, II, p. 1264.

22 Osaka High Court, quoted and overturned by the Supreme Court, 20 June 1990, 25 IIC 118 (129) [1994] – 'Popeye Scarves III.'

23 Supreme Court, decision of 20 June 1990, 25 IIC 118 [1994] – 'Popeye Scarves III.'

24 Incorporated into the Copyright Act of 4 March 1899, Law No. 39.
25 Dr Wilhelm Plage (1888-1969), who forced particularly Japanese radio stations to pay-up adequate fees, threatening to sue otherwise. Plage (very aptly, the German name means *plague*) was such a pain in the neck for the Ministry of Culture that it swiftly amended its laws to exempt a number of establishments from payments, and later on helped to establish a Japanese Collecting Society in order to outlaw Dr Plage's activitites. For details, see Shigeo Ooie, 1981.
26 The matter was of particular economic significance to Japan because of the high number of foreign phonograms circulated. The discussion centred around the interpretation of Art. 18(3) Berne Convention, that according to Japanese interpretation left the question of retro-activity to national legislation. A similar stance had been taken by the US upon accession to the Berne Convention in 1988 and more recently by Russia in 1994. For details see, Christopher Heath, 1996, p. 677.
27 By Law No. 117/1996 (26 December 1996), the supplementary provisions of the Copyright Act dealing with retro-active protection were amended. Protection now extends retro-actively to the last 50 years insofar as such protection had not already expired under the old Copyright Act (before 1970). However, the amendment does not permit claims for user fees for phonograms sold hitherto, or for phonograms already produced.
28 Brief overviews are provided by Christoph Antons, [1995] and Michael Blakeney, 1996, p. 544. The following books can be mentioned:
Wineburg (ed.), *Intellectual Property Protection in Asia,* Butterworth 1991 et seq., loose-leaf. The volume contains a brief general introduction and country reports on China, Hong Kong, Japan, Korea, Malaysia, Singapore, Taiwan, and Thailand.
Institute of Intellectual Property (ed.), *Asia shokoku ni okeru chiteki zaisan hogo (Intellectual Property Rights in Different Asian Countries),* Tokyo 1995. The work contains a number of useful tables and offers brief country reports (in Japanese) on China, Korea, Taiwan, Hong Kong, Thailand, Indonesia, the Philippines, Malaysia, Singapore, India, and Vietnam.
Asia Law (ed.), 1996 *Intellectual Property Protection in Asia – Practical Strategies.* The book is a compendium on intellectual property in China, Hong Kong, Indonesia, Korea, Malaysia, the Philippines, Singapore, Taiwan, Thailand, Vietnam, Cambodia, and Laos.
Gutterman/Brown (ed.), *Intellectual Property Laws of East Asia,* Hong Kong/Singapore 1997. General introduction on IP rights in general, and particular country reports on Cambodia, Hong Kong, Indonesia,

Malaysia, China, the Philippines, Singapore, South Korea, Taiwan, Thailand and Vietnam.
UCLA Pacific Basin Law Journal, *Special Issue: Intellectual Property in East Asia,* Fall 1994, Vol. 13/1. Aspects of IP protection in Japan, Taiwan, Korea, and China.
International Review of Industrial Property and Copyright Law (IIC), *Intellectual Property Rights in Asia,* June 1997, Vol. 28/3. Articles and court cases on Malaysia, Indonesia, China, Korea, and Japan.
International Review of Industrial Property and Copyright Law (IIC), *Intellectual Property Rights in Asia II,* June 1999, Vol. 30/4. Articles and court cases on Thailand, Taiwan, Korea, Vietnam, and Japan.

29 Another example would be the Utility Model Act that is basically an import from Japan and that in 1998 was revised similar to the Japanese Utility Model Act in 1994.

30 Basic agreement with the United States as of 28 August 1986, and a subsequent list of products that should receive the benefit of such protection as of 28 February 1990 (US) and 27 September 1991 (EC).

31 Korean Supreme Court, decision of 28 September 1995, No. 92 Hunga 11.

32 Pirates Kidnap Walt Disney, *Far Eastern Economic Review* of 19 January 1995, p. 5.

33 For an overview over the intellectual system of Vietnam, see Heath, [1999].

34 For new intellectual property developments in Thailand, see Ariya-nuntaka, [1999].

35 McGrath, 1996 and in similar fashion: Oddi, 1987 and 1996, and many others.

REFERENCES

Adelman, Martin and Sonia Baldia (1996) 'Prospects and Limits of the Patent Provision and the TRIPs Agreement: The Case of India,' *Vanderbilt Journal of Transnational Law* 507.

Antons, Christoph (1995) 'Analysing Asian Law,' *Law in Context* 13/1, p. 106.

– (2000) *Intellectual Property Law In Indonesia.* London: Kluwer Law International.

Ariyanuntaka, Vichai (1999) 'TRIPs and the Specialised Intellectual Property Court in Thailand,' *IIC* 30, p. 360.

Asia Law (ed.) (1996) *Intellectual Property Protection in China – Practical Strategies.* Hong Kong.

Asia Law (ed.) (1996) *Intellectual Property Protection in China – The Law,* Hong Kong.
Asia Law (ed.) *Intellectual Property Protection in Asia – Practical Strategies.*
Baum, Harald (ed.) (1997) *Japan: Economic Success and Legal System.* Berlin: Walter de Gruyter.
Blakeney, Michael (1996) 'The Impact of the TRIPS Agreement in the Asia-Pacific Region,' *EIPR*, p. 544
Carter, Connie (1996) *Fighting Fakes in China.* London: Intellectual Property Institute.
Chang, Soo-Kil (1988) 'Trademark Prosecution Practice in South Korea,' *IIC* 19, p. 302.
Commission On Intellectual Property Rights In The 21st Century (1997) *Towards the area of intellectual creation – challenges for break-through*, Tokyo released on 7 April 1997.
Far Eastern Economic Review 'Are Asian Values Finished?' 22 January 1998, p. 32.
Far Eastern Economic Review, 'Pirates Kidnap Walt Disney,' 19 January 1995, p. 5.
Fei *Country Report on the Judiciary and the IP System in China*, WIPO ASEAN Regional Colloquium 1992, Geneva 1994 (WIPO Publication).
FTC homepage, http://www.jftc.go.jp.
Gao, Lulin (1995) 'Outstanding Achievements and Basic Experience Gained in the Decade Since the Implementation of the Chinese Patent Law,' *Intellectual Property in Asia and the Pacific*, January/March 1995, p. 15 (WIPO Publication).
Guo, Shuokan (1996) 'TRIPS and IP Protection in the PRC,' *GRUR Int.*, p. 292.
Gutterman, Alan and Robert Brown (eds) (1997) *Intellectual Property Laws of East Asia.* Hong Kong/Singapore: Sweet & Maxwell.
Heath, Christopher (1996) 'All Her Troubles Seemed So Far Away,' *EIPR*, p. 677.
– (1999) 'Industrial Property Protection in Vietnam,' *IIC* 30, p. 419.
Henderson, Dan Fenno (1997) 'The Role of Lawyers in Japan,' in: Harald Baum (ed.) *Japan: Economic Success and Legal System.* Berlin: Walter de Gruyter, p. 27.
Hoay, Tan Bok (1995) 'Protection of Intellectual Property in Singapore 1994 – A Survey,' *EIPR*, p. 163.
Hooker, M.B. (1988) *The Laws of South-East Asia*, Volume II: *European Laws in South-East Asia*. Singapore: Butterworths.

Institute Of Intellectual Property (ed.) (1995) *Asia shokoku ni okeru chiteki zaisan hogo* (Intellectual Property Rights in Different Asian Countries). Tokyo (IIP Publication).

International Review Of Industrial Property And Copyright Law (*IIC*), 'Intellectual Property Rights in Asia,' June 1997, Vol. 28/3.

International Review Of Industrial Property And Copyright Law (*IIC*), 'Intellectual Property Rights in Asia II,' June 1999, Vol. 30/4.

Iyori, Hiroshi and Uesugi, Akinori (1994) *The Antimonopoly Laws and Policies of Japan.* New York: Federal Legal Publishers.

Kaehlig, Carl-Bernd (1993) *Indonesian Intellectual Property Rights*. Jakarta: Tatanusa.

Kim, Byung-Il (1997) 'Unfair Competition Prevention in Korea,' *IIC* 28, p. 361.

– (1999) 'The Protection of Trade Secrets in Korea,' *IIC* 30, p. 403.

Konan *et al.* (1995) 'Intellectual Property Rights in the Asian-Pacific Region: Problems, Patterns and Policy,' *Asian Pacific Economic Literature* 11, pp. 9-2, 13.

Kono, Toshiyuki (1997) 'Judges and Mediators in Japan: The Administration as Motionless Mediator?' in: Harald Baum (ed.) *Japan: Economic Success and Legal System*. Berlin: Walter de Gruyter.

Kotani, Etsuji (1979) 'Takahashi Korekiyo kiden no koto (On the autobiography of Korekiyo Takahashi),' *Patent* 32, p. 71.

Ladas, Stephan (1930) *International Protection of Intellectual Property*. Cambridge, Mass: Harvard University Press.

– (1975) *Patents, Trademarks and Related Rights*. Cambridge, Mass.: Harvard University Press, 3 vols.

Legislation

– By-Law No. 117/1996 (26 December 1996).

– Copyright Act of 4 March 1899, Law No. 39.

– Law No. 116/1994.

– Law No. 14 of 27 March 1934.

– Shinkihatto No Ofuregaki (Ordinance Prohibiting Innovations), Ordinance of the Military Government of July 1721, reprinted in Tokkyo Chô (Patent Office) (1955) *Tokkyo Seido 70 nen shi (70 Year History of the Patent System)*, Tokyo.

Leong, Susanna (1996) 'Salient Features of the Patent Act 1994 in Singapore,' *IIC* 27, p. 26.

Liu, Kung-Chung (1999) 'Unfair Competition Law in Taiwan,' *IIC* 30, p. 377.

McGrath, Michelle (1996) 'The Patent Provisions in TRIPS: Protecting Reasonable Remuneration for Services Rendered? Or the Latest Development in Western Colonialism?' *EIPR*, p. 398.

Monya, Nobuo (1973) 'Zur Rezeption des deutschen Gebrauchsmusterschutzes in Japan,' *Mitarbeiterfestschrift zum 70. Geburtstag von Eugen Ulmer*, München.
Morikawa, Hidemasu (1992) *Zaibatsu – The Rise and Fall of Family Enterprise Groups in Japan.* Tokyo: University of Tokyo Press.
Nakagawa, Hiroshi (1984) *Antimonopoly Legislation of Japan.* Tokyo (FTC Publication).
Oddi, A.S. (1987) 'The International Patent System and Third World Development: Reality or Myth?' *Duke Law Journal*, p. 831.
– (1996) 'TRIPS, Natural Rights and a "Polite Form of Economic Imperialism",' *Vanderbilt Journal of Transnational Law*, p. 415.
Ooie, Shigeo (1981) *Nippon chôsakuken monogatari (Tales on Japanese Copyright Law)*. Tokyo Shuppan Kaihatsu Sha.
Pun, K. H. (1995) 'Anti-Unfair Competition Law in China: Still Awaiting Supplements,' *IIC* 26, p. 637.
– (1997) 'Chinese Recent Development in Software Copyright,' *IIC* 28, p. 347.
Rahn, Guntram (1983) 'The Role of Industrial Property in Economic Development: The Japanese Experience,' *IIC* 14, pp. 449 (461).
– (1990) *Rechtsdenken und Rechtsauffassung in Japan.* München: C.H. Beck.
Rahn, Guntram and Christopher Heath (1994) 'What is Japanese about Japanese Unfair Competition Law,' *IIC* 25, pp. 343 (345).
Sakamoto, Kazuto Takahashi Korekiyo to tokkyo gyôsei (Korekiyo Takahashi and Patent Policy), *Tokkyo Kenkyû* 8 (Patent Studies), p. 34 [1989].
Someno, Yoshinobu (1959) 'Fusei kyôsô boshi hô (Unfair Competition Law),' *Tokkyo Kanri* 9, p. 18.
Tamai, Katsuya (1992) 'Mushinsa tokkyo toshite no saisei ka kanman na shi ka (Revival or Slow Death of Unexamined Patents?),' 1007 *Jurist* 63.
The Economist, 17 January 1998, p. 58.
The Economist, 22 January 1994, 62/63 'Intellectual Property is Theft.'
The Economist, 'Political Fall-Out in Indonesia,' 17 January 1998, p. 57.
The World Patent Survey (1996) *Managing Intellectual Property* 6, p. 19.
Tokkyo Chô (1955) *Tokkyo seido 70 nen shi* (*70 Year History of the Patent System*). Tokyo: Hatsumei Kyokai Publishing.
– (1985) *Kôgyô shoyûken seido 100 nen shi (100 Years of History of the Industrial Property System),* 3 vols., Tokyo: Hatsumei Kyokai Publishing.
– (1995) *Kôgyô shoyûken seido kono 10 nen no ayumi* (The Following 10 Years of Industrial Property System). Tokyo: Hatsumei Kyokai Publishing.

Tokkyo Kyoku (Patent Office), (1934) *Tokkyo Kyoku 50 nen shi* (50-Year History of the Patent Office). Tokyo: Hatsumei Kyokai Publishing.

Toyosaki, Joseph Koe, (1971) 'Unfair Competition in Japan,' *IIC* 2, pp. 372 (378).

Tsûsanshô (Ministry of Trade and Industry) (1964) *Shôkô seikaku shi* (History of Trade and Industry), Tokyo, p. 558.

UCLA Pacific Basin Law Journal, *Special Issue: Intellectual Property in East Asia,* Fall 1994, Vol. 13/1.

Union Internationale pour la Protection de la Propriété Industrielle, Actes de la Conférence de la Haye, Den Haag 1925.

US Department Of Commerce/Patent Office (1972) *The Story of the United States Patent Office.* Washington DC.

Wineburg, Arthur (ed.) (1991) *Intellectual Property Protection in Asia,* Butterworth.

WIPO (1996) *Background Reading Materials on IP Rights in Korea,* Geneva (WIPO Publication).

Yang, Meongcho (1987) 'Anti-Trust Aspects of Technology Transfer to South Korea,' *IIC* 18, p. 371.

Yin, Xin-Tian (1991) 'A Patent Invalidation Case in China,' *IIC* 22, p. 513.

– (1993) 'The Newly Revised Chinese Patent Act – Brief Introduction,' *IIC* 24, p. 189.

Young, L.W. (1996) 'Taiwan and WTO Membership,' 1996/6 *East Asian Executive Reports* 9.

CHAPTER 8

JAPAN AS A MODEL? COMPARING LAW AND DEVELOPMENT IN JAPAN, SINGAPORE, AND INDONESIA

CHRISTOPH ANTONS

The subject of this book is the development of commercial law as a regulatory framework for industrialization in East and Southeast Asia. The region has gone from being praised as an 'economic miracle'[1] through a period when it was condemned as plagued by collusion, corruption, and nepotism[2] back to recognition for reforms and renewed promises of a bright future.[3] In July 1997, at a time when the first signs of the Asian crisis were already visible, the World Bank still recommended in its World Development Report (1997) a careful study of many aspects of the Asia–Pacific approach to development. What then, if anything, is so peculiar about this approach? The constituting elements of the 'Asian developmental state' have been summarized by political scientists as follows: long-term economic planning by an efficient bureaucracy, administrative guidance of economic behaviour, the strategic support and use of large conglomerates and weak labour movements (see e.g. MacIntyre, 1993a:253-4). The theoretical question whether there is anything specifically 'Asian' about this approach cannot be raised within the limited space of this chapter. In fact, comparisons with other nineteenth and twentieth century 'late developing countries' ranging from Bismarck's Germany to the likes of Fujimori's Peru are likely to reveal many similarities. Furthermore, to a certain degree industrial policy is also practiced in the EU and even in that high temple of free market economies, the USA (Erber *et al.*, 1997).

This chapter departs from the assumption that developmental policies will be mirrored in the legal systems of the countries concerned. Therefore, rather than to engage in a theoretical debate about terminology, an attempt will be made to look at some of the key strategies used during the industrialization process of Japan, Singapore, and Indonesia and the laws that were used to implement these strategies. The choice of these three countries over others demands an explanation. First, to a varying degree all three countries represent excellent examples of attempts at corporatist development under strong guidance of the state. The experiences of Japan and Singapore have also often been presented as models for other developing countries. Second, the analysis of an OECD country, a so-called newly-industrializing country (NIC) and a large developing country brings the factor of time into the discussion. It allows an examination as to which of the specific elements of these countries are likely to be only temporary features typical of developing countries and which ones are more likely to remain at least for the foreseeable future. The weaknesses of the regulatory framework which were exposed by the economic crisis has added a further aspect: with the more or less stable situation in each of the countries prior to the crisis, the question can be asked which elements of the regulatory framework have contributed to the crisis.

The chapter presupposes that strategies during the industrialization process of the three countries can be related to key areas of commercial law in the following way:

- Enlisting a co-operative workforce: labour law and industrial relations;
- Mobilizing capital: banking laws, financial market and foreign investment regulation;
- Nurturing national enterprises: company and securities legislation; anti-monopoly legislation;
- Technological upgrading: intellectual property law;
- Privatizing successful state companies: company and securities legislation.[4]

No attempt is being made at achieving a complete picture and some of the fields play a role in different stages of the process, e.g. company and securities legislation cannot be separated from foreign investment and capital mobilization. The investigation is confined to a few snapshots of fields of commercial law with both public and private character and cannot cover all of these areas for lack of space. In particular, the intellectual property issue has been omitted because two other chapters in this volume already deal with this topic. Nevertheless, the picture could easily be extended to cover administrative and other laws supporting these strategies, e.g. the role of land law, provision of housing and social security legislation in 'enlisting a co-operative workforce' and at the privatization stage and the provision of educational facilities in 'technological upgrading.' However, in view of the large number of areas discussed, the survey can only be very brief. The aim of the survey is to show that it is advantageous to analyse single fields of law in the context of the political and economic framework of the respective development strategy and that the different fields are, therefore, strongly interrelated. At the same time it needs also to be added that this is not an assessment of the success rates of these policies, which has interested many political scientists and economists (e.g. Hill, 1998:297-323). Legislation is about the 'ought' rather than the 'is' and it allows conclusions about the intentions of those governments that introduce it. Whether these intentions achieve their aim is obviously another matter. However, some comments about the different success rates of these three countries will be made at the end of the chapter.

ENLISTING A CO-OPERATIVE WORKFORCE: THE REGULATION OF INDUSTRIAL RELATIONS

At the initial stages of their development, all three countries surveyed here have relied on abundant cheap labour. This is particularly true for Japan and Singapore, who hardly had other resources to rely on, but to a lesser degree also for Indonesia as a country rich in natural resources. In all three countries surveyed, labour legislation was used to mobilize and pacify the work force in the interest of industrial production.

Japan: The Rise of Enterprise Unions

During the 1980s, the Japanese industrial relations system became the envy of Western managers because of its flexibility. The system is a good example of the manner in which Asian governments often mingle formal and informal mechanisms to achieve strategic purposes. As with anti-monopoly law, the formal labour law of Japan is largely a result of the American occupation and it is often more significant for what it fails to regulate than for what it regulates. This, however, was not always the case. In the early days of industrialization, Japan relied on similar methods to achieve a compliant workforce as her nineteenth century European contemporaries. Attempts to organize skilled labour and strikes were prohibited and prosecuted under the Public Peace Police Act (Matsuzaki, 1994:12). Those relatively few craft guilds that existed and could serve as a basis for the development of a union movement were prohibited in 1872. The 1885 Trade Association Ordinance constituted a further attempt at controlling and discouraging organized labour. Nevertheless, a few unions began to be formed from 1897 on. They were weak and mostly formed as part of a company. However, even these were suppressed under the further Public Peace Police Act of 1900 (Matsuzaki, 1994:14-15; Fukui, 1992:201). Only from 1912 on, the moderate *Yuaikai* (Friendly Society) was allowed to exist, which finally developed into *Sodomei*, the Japanese Federation of Trade Unions, in 1921 (Matsuzaki, 1994:16).

By this time, the attitude of the government had changed from suppressing organized labour movements to encouraging so-called 'factory councils' as rivals of independent unions (Matsumura, 1994:42-3). Other attempts at harmonizing industrial relations included the Factory Law of 1911 which prohibited employment of children under the age of twelve, night work by women and minors while limiting the workday to twelve hours. Additional measures for the protection of employees health and welfare were introduced in the early 1920s. However, when it came to organized unionism and strikes, the government continued to act swiftly. The Peace Police Act of 1900 was replaced in 1924 by a Peace and Security Maintenance Law that was even stricter than the previous legislation (Fukui, 1992:201-2). Especially Marxist influenced organizations were the target of the 1925 Peace Preservation Law which banned all organizations that denounced the principles of imperial sovereignty or private property (Fukui, 1992:206). After the invasion of China, the National Mobilization Law was passed in 1938 giving the government emergency powers to control human and material resources in time of war. Under the umbrella of this law, the government passed ordinances in 1939 which limited labour mobility and controlled wages. Also in 1939, the National Registration System was introduced which required particularly skilled persons to register with the government. A National Workbook Law of 1941 required all workers to carry workbooks which were registered with the Employment Agency and which contained a detailed history of their employment, their current status and wages. This was followed by an anti-turnover ordinance of 1942 which made it almost impossible for workers in heavy industry to move from one factory to another (Matsumura, 1994:44-5). Already in 1940, *Sodomei* had been forced to dissolve itself into the *Sanpo* Federation, a semi-governmental organization which was soon to come completely under the wings of the Welfare Ministry. According to Kazuo Nimura (1994:65) this was not merely a war-related emergency measure but a conscious early effort to carve out the structure of Japanese post-war industrial relations.

After the defeat in World War II, the American occupation brought a thorough reform of the industrial relations legislation. The Trade Union Act and the Labour Relations Act of 1946 and the Labour Standards Act of 1947 gave workers the right to organize, to bargain collectively, and to strike. The legislation improved labour standards, introduced a number of welfare provisions, and set up mechanisms for conciliation and arbitration (Allen, 1981:21; Nimura, 1994:67), in particular the Labor Relations Commission (Komatsu, 1994:120). However, the government once again succeeded in marginalizing the union movement and achieving an industrial relations system that emphasizes harmony. In contrast to the pre-war situation, this was largely achieved through informal means and compromises. The national unions were marginalized through the important role given to 'enterprise unions' so that the national unions became mere co-ordinating bodies at the national level. Wages are split into different sorts of fringe benefits and bonuses for which the unions bargain at the level of the individual enterprise (Allen, 1981:220). The leadership of such 'enterprise unions' is often appointed by the company management and recruited from the ranks of loyal white-collar workers (Nagasawa, 1996:662; Nimura, 1994:81).

Other frequently celebrated features of Japanese industrial relations were lifetime-employment and a wage-system based on seniority. These benefits were important in the eyes of union leaders and they reinforced the trend towards enterprise unionism (Ishikawa, 1998:179). But apart from the fact that these privileges apply only to the increasingly smaller fraction of 'established employees' (Allen, 1981:221; Nimura, 1994:81),[5] the system works in favour of the management in so far, as it allows the shifting of employees in a flexible way to a number of different positions and production sites during the period of their employment (Nimura, 1994:83; Nagasawa, 1996:662, 665-6). The importance of the seniority wage system has waned since the 1970s and it is currently undermined by an increasing stress on meritocracy as a basis for promotion (Nimura, 1994:86-7; Nagasawa, 1996:666). Lifetime employment has also come under pressure because of the economic crisis. Restructuring and staff redundancies are an important prerequisite for Japanese banks to receive government bailout funds (McAlinn, 1999:33 fn. 5). So far, major Japanese companies have attempted to cut their workforce mainly in overseas branches, to transfer excess employees to subsidiaries, or to offer early retirement incentives (McAlinn, 1999:32 and 34 fn. 31 and 32). However, an increasing reliance on temporary contract workers and on foreign workers could herald the end of the Japanese lifetime employment system (McAlinn, 1999: 33 and 34, fn. 15). Since lifetime employment and the seniority based wage system was the price for the smooth relationship with the unions and since an ever decreasing number of employees is unionized (Ishikawa, 1998:191), 'enterprise unionism' as the third pillar of the Japanese industrial relations system might also come under threat and industrial conflicts might become more frequent.[6]

Singapore: Industrial Adjustment via Wage Policies

As in Japan, 'harmonious' industrial relations played an important role in the development strategies of the city-state of Singapore. These have been achieved mainly through a strong government supervision of the trade unions, the establishment of a National Wages Council (NWC) to recommend wage increases, a controlled inflow of foreign workers from the surrounding ASEAN countries and a legislation that leaves considerable discretion to the administration in matters of industrial relations. Similar to the developments in Japan, the Singaporean government initially destroyed confrontational, pro-communist unions and established co-operative, pro-government unions (Anantaraman, 1990:101-5; Lee, 1987:175-6). The links between government and unions was then intensified by appointing politicians of the ruling People's Action Party (PAP) to leading positions in the union movement and vice versa by recruiting union leaders for top level government positions (Anantaraman, 1990:34; Legett, 1993:124; Chew and Chew, 1996:135). Once government domination of the union movement was secured, two omnibus unions were split into nine industry-wide unions which were also given new non-traditional tasks to secure their membership (Anataraman, 1990:111; Lee, 1987:176-7; Tan, 1990:43-4). Finally, Japanese management practices are reflected in the most recent push for enterprise based 'house unions,' a more flexible wage policy that allowed for more differentiation between individual companies, and for an improvement in management-labour relations (Chew and Chew, 1996: 133-5; Lee, 1987:177; Wong, 1992:144-5; Tan, 1990, 46-7).

To break the resistance of confrontational, left-wing unions, Singaporean governments continued to use a strict registration system that was first introduced by the British colonial administration in the Trade Unions Ordinance 1940 (Anantaraman, 1990:101) as amended in 1959. The amended ordinance gave a wide discretionary power to the Registrar whether to register a trade union or not. Under s. 19 of the Ordinance, unregistered unions became unlawful associations and had to be dissolved. Furthermore, the Registrar was also given wide powers to deregister a union, if it was used for unlawful purposes, against the interests of the workers, or if the union 'has failed to show cause ... or which, having shown cause, has failed to satisfy him' (Anantaraman, 1990:106-7).[7] The current Trade Unions Act still allows an appeal against the decision of the Registrar only to the Minister for Labour, whose decision is final and does not have to be accompanied by reasons (Anantaraman, 1990:107-8). A residue from the days of the Emergency[8] are the powers of Registrar and Minister for Labour to freeze union funds (NTUC, 1994:45; Anantaraman, 1990:112-3). During the Emergency, these provisions were used to prevent pro-communist unionists from disappearing with the union's funds (Anantaraman, 1990:102). A further 1966 amendment extended the definition of 'industrial action' which required a secret ballot to include 'any practice, procedure or method of doing work which would limit output or production in any trade, industry and occupation' (NTUC, 1994:42). This extended definition was introduced to cover such practices as go slow and work to rule which would be damaging but not suffice to be regarded as an illegal strike (Ananataraman, 1990:109-10). Finally, s. 2 of the 1982 amendment to the Trade Unions Act shows the current emphasis on improved labour-management relations by defining the purposes of a union as follows:

(i) To promote good industrial relations;
(ii) To improve the working conditions of workmen or enhance their economic and social status; and
(iii) To increase productivity for the benefit of workmen, employers and Singapore's economy. (NTUC, 1994:39; Anantaraman, 1990:114-15).

After successfully using the Trade Unions Act and the Preservation of Public Security Ordinance to achieve a co-operative union movement, the governing

PAP introduced a further set of legislative measures in 1968 which aimed at disciplinizing the workforce in order to increase the attraction of Singapore to foreign investment in low-value added, labour-intensive industries. The Employment Act 1968 for example made fringe benefits dependent upon disciplinized behaviour at the workplace (Anantaraman, 1990:124-5) and the Industrial Relations (Amendment) Act 1968 precluded the unions from bargaining in such areas as retrenchments, promotions, task allocation, recruitment, and transfer of employees (NTUC, 1994:31-2; Tan, 1990:43; Lee, 1987:176; Anantaraman, 1990:127-8).

As important as the legal mechanisms mentioned above was the setting up of the National Wages Council (NWC) in 1972, a tripartite body consisting of unionists, employers, and government representatives. During a period of full employment in the early 1970s, the initial task of the NWC was to recommend policies of wage restraint (Anantaraman, 1990:173-5). While the NWC wage guidelines are actually not legally binding and cannot be legally challenged due to their informal character, they are nevertheless used as guidelines also by the Industrial Arbitration Court (Chew and Chew, 1996:130-1) and achieve thereby a quasi-legal role. After keeping wages low during the 1970s, the NWC's recommendations became an important instrument in forcing employers to technologically upgrade their production as part of Singapore's so-called 'second industrial revolution' starting in 1979. A short period of high-wage recommendations was combined with the creation of an employer-funded skill development fund to train and educate employees for the industries of the future (Wong, 1992:145-6; Lee, 1987:179; Tan, 1990:45; Leggett, 1993:119).[9] Once this shift was achieved, the government concentrated its efforts on achieving better labour-management relations along the lines of the Japanese example. This included the encouragement of enterprise unions, quality control circles and work excellence committees (Lee, 1987:177; Wong, 1992:146-7; Tan, 1990:46-7). Strict recommendations by the NWC now began to be regarded as limiting the flexibility of management. Consequently, the NWC began to adopt much wider margins in its wage recommendations which were sometimes left deliberately vague (Chew and Chew, 1996:133-5). A 1984 amendment of the Employment Act supported these measures by allowing the management far more flexibility in the organization of the work pattern of their employees (Leggett, 1993:120; Anantaraman, 1990:131-6).

Reacting to the Asian crisis, the Committee on Singapore's Competitiveness (CSC) recommended in a report of 1998 in particular to re-position the Skills Development Fund (SDF) to encourage employers to train their workers in certifiable skills to enhance employability and to elevate the Skills Redevelopment Programme (SRP) to a national programme to help minimize the threat of structural unemployment. Further recommendations were made to attract foreign talent through greater flexibility in the eligibility criteria of employment pass holders. It can be assumed that these recommendations are designed to attract especially talented Indian and Chinese information technology workers to Singapore. To make Singapore more attractive to domestic and foreign workers, the CSC also recommended facilitating the use of Employee Stock Option Programmes (ESOPs) (Committee on Singapore's Competitiveness, 1998:81-3).

Indonesia: Pancasila Industrial Relations

In Indonesia, the unions played an important role in the anti-colonial struggle in the first half of this century (Adiwinata *et al.*, 1974:45; Shamad, 1997:52-3). During the Soekarno period, unions tended to be affiliated with political parties (Rinakit, 1999:143). Particularly strong during this period was SOBSI (*Sentral Organisasi Buruh Seluruh Indonesia*), the All Indonesia Workers Organization. This union was dissolved after the events of 1965 and the rise of the 'New Order' Government under Suharto, because of its links to the Indonesian Communist Party (PKI) (Shamad, 1997:57). The 'New Order' swiftly established the Indonesian Workers Joint Action Front (KABI) in 1966, whose pro-Government and developmental outlook is recognizable in its programme: 1. To help to develop the New Order while actively dissolving the Old Order, Sobsi-PKI, Communism, and the teachings of Soekarno and his supporters, 2. To develop a democratic life for labourers and cultivate co-operation among the labourers supporting the New Order; 3. To increase production by helping to make the programme of the Ampera Cabinet a success, especially in the field of economics (Adiwinata *et al.*, 1974:46-7; see also Dittrich and Chalid, 1998:282).

Government plans to simplify the structure of the union movement were supported by the Indonesian Workers Consultative Assembly (*Majelis Permusyawaratan Buruh Indonesia*), which was set up in 1969 and during a seminar in May 1972 drafted the 'vow to reform and perfect Indonesian labour organization' (Adiwinata *et al.*, 1974:48-9). This led to the dissolution of the principal unions into a single All-Indonesian Labour Federation (*Federasi Buruh Seluruh Indonesia-FBSI*) (Shamad, 1997:57-63; Adiwinata *et al.*, 1974:49; Nayar, 1996:3) and to the adoption of the so-called '*Pancasila* Industrial Relations.' In '*Pancasila* Industrial Relations' the stress is on social and industrial harmony and increased productivity in the interest of economic development.[10] The former Director for Industrial Relations and Director for Wages and Social Security in the Ministry of Labour, Yunus Shamad summarizes some of the main principles as follows: '... Pancasila Industrial Relations strive to eradicate differences and to develop similarities for the creation of harmony between the workers and the employers. In the Pancasila Industrial Relations it is believed that every difference of opinion and dispute must be settled through consultation and deliberation and must not be settled through pressure by one party upon the other' (Shamad, 1997:7). To achieve this aim ... the workers and the employers are partners in the production process; this means that both have to co-operate for mutual assistance to smoothen the business of the company and to increase the welfare and productivity' (Shamad, 1997:8). Finally, 'the government ... has the role of the guardian, guide, protector, and peacekeeper which in short means a role as the defender and custodian for all parties related in [the] production process' (Shamad, 1997:9; see also Dittrich and Chalid, 1998:278-80; Rinakit, 1999:144-5).

A further centralization of the Indonesian trade union movement occurred in 1985 when the federalized FBSI changed into the unitary All Indonesian Workers' Union (*Serikat Pekerja Seluruh Indonesia*-SPSI). Also in the middle of the 1980s the now abolished Ministerial Decree No. 342 gave the military a role in suppressing labour unrest (Nayar, 1996:3-4 and 10; Dittrich and Chalid, 1998:280). However, with rising international scrutiny of Indonesia's labour conditions, the government began to encourage the formation of enterprise unions, which are now regulated in the Regulation of the Minister of Manpower No. 1/1994. Such enterprise unions can be set up in companies with at least 25 workers (art 4 of the Regulation). That such enterprise unions are once again guided by the spirit of *Pancasila* Industrial Relations is emphasized in the preamble of the Regulation and in art 3, where the aim of the enterprise union is defined as 'promoting the quality of workers and the welfare of workers and their families; creating a peaceful atmosphere of work and ensuring business continuity; increasing the productivity of work.' An earlier regulation of 1993, which also allowed other unions to receive Ministerial recognition, had little practical impact because of the strict requirements for such a recognition (Nayar, 1996:6 in particular fn. 12; Dittrich and Chalid, 1999:282).

With the most recent Law on Manpower (*UU Pokok Ketenagakerjaan*), the Government is finally giving its concept of *Pancasila* industrial relations a legal basis. Indonesian Unionists and representatives of international labour organizations have criticized the law not only for this reason. The development of a registration system for unions, the creation of a National Tripartite Commission, the centralization of union power in the hands of the SPSI and the prohibition of demonstrations have also attracted criticism (Gantra and Raditya, 1997:30; Rahmanto, Anggraeni, and Gunawan, 1997:70). With the National Tripartite Commission, the system for maintaining harmony in industrial relations has been developed further. It complements already existing bipartite and tripartite co-operation at enterprise level (Shamad, 1997:10-11) and the dispute settlement mechanism of UU No. 22/1957 which foresees compulsory conciliation, mediation and arbitration involving civil servants of the Ministry of Manpower as well as the Regional and Central Labour Dispute Settlement

Committees (Shamad, 1997:12; Uwiyono, 1997:37-8). Given the fact that a strike cannot take place before the acceptance of a strike declaration has been confirmed in writing by the Regional Labour Dispute Settlement Commission (Uwiyono, 1997:38, fn. 8; see also Surowidjojo, 1999:27), the possibilities for a legal strike remain very small. Even this small chance is probably thwarted by the lack of independent funding of unions, since only very few workers can afford to pay union fees (Gantra and Raditya, 1997; Nayar, 1996:7).[11] However, the law has also been criticized from a formal point of view as its details are regulated in not less than eight further laws and thirteen administrative regulations, thereby giving wide discretionary powers to the administration and to the government.[12] The new law was originally due to come into force on 1 October 1998, but because of the political upheaval in Indonesia its implementation has been postponed and it will now become effective on 1 October 2000 (Surowidjojo, 1999:24).

THE MOBILIZATION OF CAPITAL: FOREIGN INVESTMENT AND CAPITAL MARKET REGULATION

Japan: the Peculiarities of the Japanese Banking System

From the early days of her industrialization during the *Meiji* period, Japan had been relatively hostile to foreign direct investment and suspicious of foreign capital. Lockwood remarks about this period:

> Aware of political events elsewhere in Asia, the early Meiji leaders frowned on direct foreign investment in Japanese mining, industry, or agriculture. Even a German farmer who had established a model farm in Hokkaido at the invitation of the Shogunate was immediately bought out by the new regime. Foreigners were restricted by law from owning land or operating mines. Although this did not bar them from participating in Japanese companies so engaged, such investments appeared none too secure under Japanese law (Lockwood, 1954:321-2; cf. also Howe, 1996:153).

Instead, the crucial factors in mobilizing capital for the industrialization process became taxes, the high rate of savings and the peculiarities of the Japanese banking system. The predecessors of the post-war financial system of Japan were created during the 1880s and 1890s after a brief and unsuccessful period of experimenting with national banking. Japan established a central bank in 1882 and a few special banks which were entrusted with tasks such as foreign exchange transactions, mobilizing the savings of the poorer parts of the population, and providing long-term loans for industrial and agricultural development against the security of immovable property. They were soon closely linked to the *zaibatsu*, so that the *zaibatsu* in fact had a financial and an industrial branch at the same time (Allen, 1981:54-7). Besides these, a large number of commercial banks developed. The supervision of these banks by the Bank of Japan was very loose, so that big businesses could easily get finance from banks within the same group. The Bank of Japan confined itself more or less to stepping in in emergency cases (Allen, 1981:60) Around the same time the tax system was reformed and substantially improved and the income from the taxation of land was particularly high (Allen, 1981:49).

One of the few channels for foreign investment was the Industrial Bank of Japan, which dealt with government debentures (Allen, 1981:56). Only in the period from the early 1890s to 1914 was foreign borrowing substantial as Japan had to finance the wars with China and Russia and the colonization of large parts of the Asian mainland which she acquired as a result of these wars (Howe, 1996:153-8). But even then the impact of foreign investment remained limited. Howe states:

> The Japanese carefully selected foreign partners to maximize the favourable effects of technology transfer in Japan, and structured their activities in ways that minimized foreign interference in the economy. So much so that foreigners sometimes complained bitterly of the Japanese sharp practice of taking over foreign investments once the key technologies had been mastered (Howe, 1996:157).

After World War II, the Allied Occupation Authority separated the *zaibatsu* banks from the industrial undertakings and ordered the closure of the special banks (Allen, 1981:204). However, the Cold War interfered and as the relationship with the USSR deteriorated and Communism advanced in China as well, the Occupation Authority became more interested in a speedy economic recovery of Japan than in fundamental structural changes (Allen, 1981:189-99; Pape, 1979:464-5). Slowly, successors to most of the special banks were established, though the concentration in the banking sector remained much smaller than it had been before the war (Allen, 1981:204-5). What emerged finally were the *keiretsu* of the last several decades, which again were large groups of manufacturing companies centred on a bank. The share of the manufacturing companies within such groups was usually rather low and the percentage of ownership by the financial institutions varied during the 1970s and early 1980s between 37 per cent and 41 per cent (Thorn, 1987:19; Caves and Uekusa, 1976:38-9; Argy and Stein, 1997:113). Equally, manufacturing companies in such groups had comparatively little assets and high ratios of borrowing (Thorn, 1987:17). This and the marginal role of the equity stock market (Hamada and Horiuchi, 1987:233-4) allowed the Bank of Japan and the

Ministry of Finance (MOF) to strictly supervise the financial market during the period of high growth that ended in the early 1970s (Hamada and Horiuchi, 1987:235-45). This control over capital markets became the perhaps most important tool of Japanese industrial policy until well into the 1980s (Eads and Yamamura, 1987:431).

However, a combination of growing hostility to Japanese exports abroad, American pressure, and the phenomenon of globalizing financial markets led since the 1970s to a slow liberalization and opening of the Japanese financial market. Important initial steps in this liberalization process were the passing of the amended Foreign Exchange and Foreign Trade Control Law in 1979 and the new Banking Law of 1981. The Banking Law 1981 introduced a number of new instruments, partly removed the formerly rather strict compartmentalization between banks and securities companies, and put foreign banks on equal footing with domestic banks (Thorn, 1987:28; Matsushita and Schoenbaum, 1989:177). Earlier, the Foreign Exchange and Foreign Trade Control Law had liberalized foreign investment and exchange transactions. Capital transactions, however, were free only in 'ordinary cases' and the authorities retained the right to intervene if (1) the foreign exchange market is chaotic, (2) in case of a deteriorating balance of payment or (3) if there is 'financial confusion.'[13] Licensing requirements also remain for so-called 'special methods of payment' (Matsushita and Schoenbaum, 1989:118). The Foreign Exchange and Foreign Trade Control Law reversed the earlier position under which foreign investment, etc. were generally prohibited unless specifically approved by the government authorities. However, as Matsushita and Schoenbaum pointed out in 1989, the various ministries administering the law retained a great deal of discretion:

> There is virtually no case of a formal acceptance or rejection of an application to undertake a transaction under the Control Law. Rulings are generally made by means of the technique of administrative guidance (Matsushita and Schoenbaum, 1989:116-17).

As described by Baum in the preceding chapter, the struggle over the liberalization of Japan's financial market continued during the 1990s. A 1992 reform amended the Securities and Exchange Law, the Banking Law and other related financial statutes and the Securities Fairness Law created a Securities and Exchange Surveillance Commission (Satusky 1999:293), which Baum views as a 'semi-independent body' and 'nothing more than a renamed bureau of MOF staffed with people from the ministry' (Baum, in this volume). Baum described the elements of the Japanese version of the 'Big Bang' in a previous chapter in this volume and it is likely that Japanese financial market and their legal regulation will look more familiar to Western observers in the future than they have in the past (Satusky, 1999:299). Nevertheless, as a Japanese based observer concluded his survey of recent reforms:

> The one reasonably certain thing is that any solution will be a 'Japanese solution' which will work in this environment even if it confounds the logic of its outside observers (McAlinn, 1999:10).[14]

Singapore: Foreign Investment Plus High Savings

Within ASEAN, tiny Singapore in 1987 was second only to Indonesia in the amount of foreign investment it attracted and in 1986, foreign companies accounted for 58 per cent of employment, 68 per cent of valued added and 87 per cent of direct exports (Regnier, 1987:62-4). This emphasis on foreign investment was a feature of Singaporean industrial policies from the start and it was already recommended in three influential reports commissioned by the government between 1955 and 1961. As a result of the 1955 report of the International Bank for Reconstruction and Development (IBRD), an Industrial Promotion Board with still limited powers and resources was set up in 1957. The Lyle Report of 1959 and the election victory of the People's Action Party in the same year led to the Pioneer Industries (Relief from Income Tax) Ordinance 1959 and the Industrial Expansion (Relief from Income Tax) Ordinance 1959 with considerable tax exemptions for expanding companies and those in pioneer industries (Cheng, 1991:188-9; Chong and Yeoh, 1990:103-4). The result of the 1961 Winsemius Report was the first State Development Plan and the creation of the Economic Development Board in August 1961, which was provided with an initial capital of $100 million. It consisted at first of the divisions of Investment Promotion, Finance, Projects and Technical Consultation Service, and Industrial Facilities (Cheng, 1991:191; Low, 1993a:33-5; Hughes, 1993:6-7; Low, 1993c:86-9). These divisions were later partially replaced and partially supplemented by the Development Bank of Singapore (DBS), the Singapore Institute of Standards and Industrial Research (SISIR), and the Engineering Industries Development Agency (Cheng, 1991:191). In line with new tasks, current sub-divisions are the Industry Development Division, the Services Development Division, the Enterprise Development Division, the International Manpower Division, and the Strategic Business Units (Davidson and Ciambella, 1995:189-99). Immediately after the split from Malaysia in 1965, Singapore embraced an export-oriented strategy which was supported by tax relief for export enterprises and concessionary financing. From 1983 onwards, export strategies were further co-ordinated by the Trade Development Board (Davidson and Ciambella, 1995:199 and 210; Abraham, 1985:331-2, 352-3; Woon, 1986:266).

Tax incentives for foreign investors are nowadays provided via the Economic Expansion Incentives (Relief from Income Tax) Act and the Income Tax Act.[15] While some of the incentives require a 50 per cent local ownership and some others are restricted to locally incorporated companies, what is most remarkable about the tax incentive legislation is the large administrative discretion given to different ministries in deciding whether to confer the benefits or not. The decision about the incentives is made by the Minister of Finance who grants them 'if he considers it expedient in the public interest to do so' and 'subject to such conditions as he thinks fit.' However, details about the benefits and industries to be encouraged are decided by the Ministry of Trade and Industry and the Economic Development Board (Fordham, 1988:57). Margaret Fordham sees as common feature of the different parts of the tax incentive legislation:

> The rather vague wording of the basis for granting the benefits (and, where relevant, for dealing with objections to applications) means that it is quite possible for a company which appears to satisfy all the requirements laid down in the Act to be refused a benefit or for an objector's argument to be rejected without explanation ... The Government wishes to retain complete control over its policies for economic development, and over the areas of manufacture or service to be encouraged, without it having to face the possibility of being required to supply detailed explanations of, or justification for, such policies (Fordham, 1988:58).[16]

Closed to foreign investment in Singapore are the sectors of arms and ammunition, air transport, and public utilities. Singapore Telecom's monopoly over telecommunication services was recently phased out seven years earlier than originally projected and the government paid Telecom $1 billion in compensation (Cooper Maysami *et al.*, 1999:65). Licences of the Monetary Authority of Singapore are required for banking, financing, and insurance businesses. They have allowed the government to differentiate between international and domestic financial intermediation (Bryant, 1989:347), as different licences allow for different scopes of activities (as to the details see Cooper Masyami *et al.*, 1999:60). Furthermore, participation of foreigners in the ownership and management of newspapers is narrowly restricted by the Revised Newspaper and Printing Presses Act 1991. Finally, apart from a few exceptions with government approval, foreigners are precluded from owning residential property and commercial real estate (Davidson and Ciambrella, 1995:200-1; Abraham, 1985:329; Woon, 1986:276). Although the Exchange Control Act remains in force, all controls on the transfer of funds and currency have effectively been lifted since 1978 (Woon, 1986:275; Davidson and

Ciambella, 1995:199). The Asian financial crisis and the competition with Hong Kong to become the leading financial services centre in the region (for a comparative analysis see Montes 1999) has led to a further reform of the regulation of Singapore's financial markets with the aim to raise bank disclosure standards, to standardize the reporting of undisclosed reserves and the choice of accounting policies and adopt what has been called a risk-focused approach to bank supervision. This means that the Monetary Authority of Singapore (MAS) will allow greater flexibility for institutions with strong internal control mechanisms while it will continue to strictly supervise institutions without such mechanisms (Cooper Masyami *et al.*, 1999:62-5). While the Committee on Singapore's Competitiveness recommended greater regulatory flexibility, it also requires from domestic financial institutions 'to gear up for greater foreign competition' (Committee on Singapore's Competitiveness, 1998:140-2). Statements by leading government figures such as Deputy Prime Minister, Lee Hsien Long, indicate that the Singaporean government aims to nurture a limited number of internationally competitive banks by encouraging bank mergers and concentrating foreign and domestic talent in these institutions (Cooper Masyami *et al.*, 1999:65-6).

Besides foreign investment, the government has also always encouraged domestic savings, in particular via the Central Provident Fund (CPF). The Central Provident Fund was introduced by the CPF Ordinance of 1953 and started to operate in 1955. Initially established as a fund for security in old age, it is meanwhile used for a variety of objectives including the funding of home-ownership, investments in non-residential properties, approved investments in shares, unit trusts and the like, to finance educational tuition fees and medical insurance. Contributions to the CPF rose from a mere 10 per cent of the monthly wage in 1955 to 50 per cent in 1984 and has since been maintained at a level around 40 per cent (Tay, 1992:264-81). In 1998, investment opportunities for these pension funds were further expanded (Montes, 1999:163). The Committee on Singapore's Competitiveness has further recommended to allow private pension funds to exist alongside the CPF and to offer their services to senior executives with salaries above the CPF limit and to foreign executives who do not contribute to the CPF (Committee on Singapore's Competitiveness, 1998:136).

Indonesia: Shifting Policies and ad hoc Approaches

Besides Korea, Indonesia has been hardest hit by the financial crisis in Asia, exposing severe weaknesses in the financial sector and the regulatory framework. To experienced observers of the political economy of Indonesia, however, these developments have not come as a complete surprise. Andrew MacIntyre, for instance, wrote in 1993:

> The flood of new entrants into the banking sector after 1988 gave rise to intense competition as banks struggled to attract depositors and borrowers. Competition for market share is thought to have led a number of banks to overextend themselves and to have assembled loan portfolios of dubious quality. Concerns about the stability of the banking industry were accentuated by the discovery in 1990 that a leading private bank had suffered massive losses through foreign exchange dealings and mismanagement. In these circumstances, a shake-out of the industry seems quite possible (MacIntyre, 1993b: 162).

The different swings in the economic policy of the Indonesian government before this crisis have been described elsewhere in great detail (Robison, 1986; MacIntyre, 1993b; Hill, 1988; Hill, 1996). They can be mentioned here only briefly as far as they are relevant for the current regulatory framework regarding foreign investment and the financial market. In general, Indonesian policy as to foreign investment and financial market regulation has fluctuated in accordance with the availability of other sources of revenue. Oil and gas in particular financed a large part of the Indonesian budget until the middle of the 1980s. Inheriting the tightly state controlled economy of the final years of the Soekarno government, a period of liberalization followed which lasted roughly until 1973. This was followed by a period of stronger reliance on state intervention after the sharp rise of the oil price, lasting from 1974 to 1982. The oil price began to decline in 1983 and prices fell sharply in 1986 and 1987. Again, a reversal of Indonesian economic policies followed and the accent has since been on liberalization and deregulation. The rise and fall of these different strategies was usually also reflected in the influence of different political camps advocating more liberal or more state interventionist policies. The stronghold of the so-called technocrats centred around a group of US trained economists in the Ministry of Finance and the National Economic Planning Board, whereas state interventionists have been influential in the Ministry of Industry, the Ministry of Science and Technology, the central bank, and the capital investment board (MacIntyre, 1993b:154-5).

As a result of new banking legislation in 1967, the status of Bank Indonesia as central bank was reaffirmed. A number of state-owned commercial banks were given the task to provide services for different sectors of the economy.[17] Compared to the state-owned banks, private and foreign banks played only a minor role. The state kept a strong influence through preferential loans to priority borrowers, a central bank control of the deposit and loan rates of the state banks and preferential refinancing of loans extended by state banks to priority sectors (MacIntyre, 1993b:136-9). The financial sector was, therefore, from the beginning heavily politicized and the system was used for supporting indigenous and small-scale entrepreneurs in competing with Indonesian-

Chinese, for co-opting political allies, and for subsidizing rice farmers to prevent rural discontent. The regulatory mechanisms to oversee the system were weak. For example, Bank Indonesia did not have the administrative capacity to control whether information provided by the commercial banks about the allocation of preferential credits was correct or not. The system invited corruption by bank officials who would allocate preferential credits to non-priority borrowers and share in the difference in interest. Non-indigenous and large scale borrowers manipulated the system with silent approval of the banks by using domestic personnel as straw-men to apply for preferential loans (MacIntyre, 1993b:151-2. For a rather humorous description of these various practices see Kwik Kian Gie, 1999b). The hierarchical structure of Indonesian society facilitated many of these practices as bank employees often felt that their jobs depended more on satisfying their political clients than on the financial performance of their bank. Bennett (1999:21) uses the term 'memo lending' for loans extended to such clients as banks would often decide to grant a loan merely because of a memorandum sent by a high-ranking official or a person in an influential position.

State control of the financial system still increased during the years of high-income from oil[18] until falling revenues from oil showed the need to improve the efficiency of the banking sector and sparked the deregulation of the 1980s. First reform steps were taken in 1983 when credit ceilings were abolished, refinancing and direct commercial lending by the central bank was reduced and restrictions on state bank interest rates were removed. The number of categories of preferential borrowers was also reduced substantially (MacIntyre, 1993b:145 and 158; Sabirin, 1993:67-8).[19] This was followed by the so-called 'Pakto 1988,' the deregulation package of 27 October 1988 that facilitated the licensing of new and foreign banks and the establishment of small-scale credit banks and joint-venture banks. Foreign bank activities were allowed in provincial capitals and, importantly, the minimum reserve ratio was reduced from 15 per cent to 2 per cent.[20] Indonesia's conglomerates set up many of the new private banks as an easily accessible source of finance for their business groups. Bennett (1999:22) calls these banks a 'captive funding source for the conglomerate's businesses.' As a consequence, there was excessive lending to affiliated companies.

A new banking law replaced the 1967 legislation in 1992. The new law distinguished between general or commercial banks and small-scaled credit or rural banks. Only Indonesian citizens or entities were allowed to establish general banks. Foreign banks could form joint ventures with Indonesian banks as long as their participation was limited to 85 per cent of the paid-up capital. A licence of the Ministry of Finance was required for all banking activities in Indonesia. State banks became limited liability companies with shares held by the state. General banks were also allowed to go public and to register their shares at an Indonesian stock exchange, as long as the participation of foreigners remained under 50 per cent.[21] The 1992 legislation also improved legal lending limits to affiliated parties that were originally imposed as part of the 'Pakto 1988.' Under the revised legislation, a bank was not allowed to lend more than 10 per cent of its issued capital to commissioners, directors and other related parties or more than 30 per cent to a group of related parties (Tabalujan, 1999:5). In fact, contraventions of these rules were common. In a report of 1997, the ten worst offenders had lent to related parties between 85 per cent and 345 per cent of their respective paid-up capital (Tabalujan, 1999:6).

Hal Hill summarized the effects of the deregulation of the banking sector as follows:

> Breaking out of the straitjacket of heavy central bank control, few banks had much experience of project appraisal and loan assessment. There was an acute shortage of qualified staff, leading to very high salaries and frequent 'hijackings' of personnel. Accounting and auditing standards continued to be very poor. The closed nature of many of the major business conglomerates and the fact that in many instances they were really lending back to themselves, put further strain on the system. Finally, Bank Indonesia's monitoring and supervisory capacity was still rudimentary. Over this period, there were frequent allegations that sizeable proportions of outstanding loans were either in arrears or in outright default. Yet the central bank appeared not to have accurate data on the extent of these problems (Hill, 1996:37).

As the minimum paid-in capital under the 1992 legislation was only US$5 million (Bennett, 1999:27), the Indonesian banking sector developed an unusually large number of undercapitalized banks.[22] At the beginning of the Asian crisis, Indonesia had over 230 banks whereas Thailand for example had only fifteen and Malaysia and Korea had less than thirty commercial banks (Bennett, 1999:54-6; Tabalujan, 1999:4). Indonesia has also maintained a free foreign exchange system since 1970. Following the deregulation, this led to extensive borrowing by private companies and by the new private banks abroad. Because much of this borrowing was unhedged and with the value of the Rupiah falling, banks and private companies carried an increasingly heavy debt burden (Bennett, 1999:12-16). Once again, Hal Hill has pointed out that many of the 'private sector' projects that had necessitated this external borrowing had in fact a strong government connection and often received preferential access to finance because of real or apparent government guarantees (Hill, 1996:249).

After the onset of the Asian crisis, the Indonesian government announced the closure of the sixteen weakest private banks in November 1997 (Bennett, 1999:31; Tabalujan, 1999:5-6). In January 1998, the Indonesian Bank Restructuring Agency (IBRA) was formed to oversee the reform of the banking system, to administer the government's guarantee programme for bank debts, to take over non-performing assets from banks that were to be liquidated or merged with stronger banks, and to collect the amounts that private banks owed Bank Indonesia in connection with liquidity support received by them (Bennett, 1999:35; Tabalujan, 1999:6). Depending on the amount of liquidity support received from Bank Indonesia, the IBRA divided the most troubled banks into two categories. Category A banks were to be liquidated. Their performing assets were transferred to other banks under IBRA control, whereas their non-performing assets were transferred to an Asset Management Unit (AMU) that the IBRA had established. The operations of ten such banks were suspended in August 1998. In addition, the IBRA took over the management of four somewhat less troubled category B banks (Bennett, 1999:36-7). As a result, at the end of 1998 either IBRA or Bank Indonesia directly controlled about 70 per cent of the total assets held by Indonesia's banks (Bennett, 1999:51).

Also in November 1998, the 1992 Banking Law was amended. Amendments introduced a deposit insurance scheme and relaxed bank secrecy regulations. They broadened the scope of the legal lending limits and required a stricter assessment of prospective borrowers. The tasks of licensing and supervising banks, which were formerly divided between the Ministry of Finance and Bank Indonesia, became now the exclusive responsibility of Bank Indonesia. Foreign Ownership ceilings were abolished and the IBRA's role was formally endorsed by the new law. In January 1999, the closure of another 38 private banks followed (Tabalujan, 1999:7-8).

The field of foreign investment regulation has experienced similar swings of economic policy as the regulation of financial markets. The Foreign Capital Investment Law of 1967 as amended by Law No. 11/1970 re-opened Indonesia to foreign investors by offering tax incentives and assurances against nationalization or foreign exchange restrictions. Joint ventures became the usual vehicles for such investments. At first they were merely encouraged through the granting of tax incentives, but with the more restrictive policies of the 1970s a Resolution of the Cabinet[23] of 22 January 1974[24] made them compulsory. The law attempted to safeguard Indonesian interests by demanding the employment of Indonesian labour, the provision of educational facilities,[25] and a certain Indonesian equity participation, which was originally left to the discretion of the administration, but after the resolution of 1974 was deemed to be 51 per cent. The Decision of January 1974 also began the discrimination between *pribumi* and *non-pribumi* with regards to equity participation without providing a definition of these terms.[26]

Foreign investments are subject to approval by the Capital Investment Co-ordinating Board, which prior to 1977 required on average more than fifty weeks to reach a decision (Himawan, 1980:286-7). In 1977, two Presidential Decrees turned the Capital Investment Co-ordinating Board into a 'one stop' agency for foreign investors by authorizing it to issue most of the necessary permits (Gautama, 1995:367-8).[27] In the same year, the Board issued its first scaled list of priorities for investments. The List distinguished between priority activities, non-priority activities which attracted tax incentives, non-priority activities without such incentives and prohibited activities (Gautama, 1995:368). The criteria for these different designations remained vague and included the ability of the venture to increase production or to absorb employment and a consideration of the location of the venture to ensure an even spread of industrial activities in Indonesia (Himawan 1980:293). Hill cites an Indonesian official with the following remark on the investment legislation: 'The [Foreign Investment] Law is brief and simple, though one should not look at [it] only, but at the 328 kinds of related legislation as well' (Hill, 1996:100).

Major reform of the field began in 1988, when the priority list of investments was replaced by a negative list, automatically allowing all investments not mentioned there (Hill, 1996:100). Important new regulations were introduced in 1994 by Government Regulation No. 20/1994 on Ownership of Shares in a Company established in the Framework of Foreign Investment and in the Decree of the Minister for Investment Procurement/Chairman of the Investment Co-ordinating Board (BKPM) No. 15/SK/1994. The Regulations allowed, among other things, foreign individuals to be shareholders in 100 per cent foreign owned companies or joint venture companies, permitted a maximum of 95 per cent foreign shareholding in companies operating in special sectors of particular interest to the state, dropped the requirement of a minimum investment, and of a divestment to Indonesians in the first fifteen years of the investment, allowed the sale of shares of 100 per cent foreign owned companies without prior approval by the BKPM, and substantially facilitated the acquisition of shares by foreign companies and citizens (Gingerich, 1994:11-15; Mills, 1996:9, 15-19).

NURTURING NATIONAL ENTERPRISES: COMPANY, SECURITIES AND ANTI-MONOPOLY LEGISLATION

Immediately after setting upon the path of industrialization, all three countries surveyed here attempted to nurture successful national companies that would be able to compete on a world market. However, Japan transferred successful state companies into private hands as early as during the 1880s (Lockwood, 1954:15) and from then on relied on its influence over the state banks and on administrative guidance to ensure that its economic policies were followed by the private sector. To strengthen the competitive position of national companies, Japan initially used the usual means of tariffs and subsidies for strategic industries. With foreign direct investment tightly controlled and the lack of anti-trust legislation, the powerful Japanese cartels, the *zaibatsu*, developed. The state encouraged the formation of cartels in particular during the 1920s and 1930s, occasionally even to the point of enacting laws that provided for compulsory membership in a cartel (Pape, 1979:464; Matsushita and Schoenbaum, 1989:139; Caves and Uekusa, 1976:48-9). The important role of these groups in the wartime economy of Japan was one of the reasons why they became targets of the Allied Authority after World War II. After the dissolution of forty-two of the largest holding companies in 1946 and of a further nineteen in 1947, an Anti-Monopoly Law modelled on US lines was introduced to prevent a reemergence of the *zaibatsu* (Pape, 1979:464-5). However, cold war reality quickly led to an overriding concern to strengthen the new ally Japan. In the process, the provisions of the anti-monopoly legislation became diluted. After first amendments in 1949, important changes were introduced in 1952. The general prohibition of cartels was liberalized and so-called 'depressed industry cartels' and 'rationalization cartels' exempted from the legislation. Some further exceptions, e.g. for import and export, were made in additional legislation. The process resulted in the emergence of the *keiretsu*, the post-war successor to the *zaibatsu*. Since then, the Japanese Ministry of Industry and Trade (MITI) and the Fair Trade Commission (FTC) have often been on collision course as to whether to encourage or prohibit mergers. Commentators have argued that MITI's views have mostly prevailed (Pape, 1979:465-6; Matsushita and Schoenbaum, 1989:139-40; Sonneville and Jagtenberg, 1995:159-60). However, as Boyd points out elsewhere in this volume, the strengthening of the Anti-Monopoly Law in 1977 and a landmark judgment of 1980 that made the restraining of competition by means of cartels more difficult should not be overlooked.

Another means to discourage foreign participation in the Japanese economy was the system of interlocking companies by cross-shareholding, which led to the effective withdrawal of large quantities of shares from the stock market (as to this phenomenon elsewhere in Asia see Bowring 2000). In addition, the Securites and Exchange Commission was abolished in 1952 and the securities business was placed under the direct control of the Ministry of Finance. Finally, take-overs could be avoided by issuing additional shares to 'friendly third parties,' if necessary at 'especially advantageous' prices. Only in the latter case would such an allotment need the approval of the shareholders under the Japanese Commercial Code (Sonneville and Jagtenberg, 1995:160, 165-6).

As a result of liberalization measures during the 1980s and 1990s, the stock market has become much more attractive. This has led to a number of revisions of the Securities and Exchange Law and to the re-installment of a Supervisory Commission on Securities Transactions. The Anti-Monopoly Law was again revised in 1992 and in 1997. The revised law allows holding companies in all industries with the exception of banking and finance. Guidelines of the Fair Trading Commission will contain details about those holdings that will continue to be prohibited.

In Indonesia and Singapore, state enterprises have continued to play an important role, in spite of liberalization measures in other sectors of the economy (Hill, 1996:101-7; Tan, 1992:12-19). In Singapore, new strategies have in the past been spearheaded by the statutory boards, in particular the Economic Development Board, the Jurong Town Corporation, the Telecommunication Authority of Singapore, the Public Utilities Board, and the Housing and Development Board. From these have branched off hundreds of private companies, controlled by three major holding companies (Temasek, Singapore Technologies, and MND Holdings) (Tan, 1992:13-16; Pillai, 1983:77-95).[28] Formal compliance with the company law requirement of at least two shareholders is achieved by having two civil servants taking up one share each (Pillai, 1983:89). Directors are appointed by the Ministry of Finance with a relatively small group of permanent secretaries and high level civil servants holding cross-directorships in many government-owned companies (Richardson 2000b). In accounts presented to parliament, investment in state-owned companies is listed as 'other investments' and not further specified. In case of defence related companies, balance sheets and accounts would not even be available to shareholders (Pillai, 1983:116-21). However, following recent criticisms of the role of Singapore's government-linked companies, which account for 10 per cent of economic output and 25 per cent of stockmarket capitalization in Singapore, the government has announced a unit trust to sell more shares in such companies to the Singaporean public (Richardson 2000b).

In Indonesia, the distinction between public corporations and state-owned private corporations was abolished with the State Enterprise (*Perusahaan Negara*) Law No. 19/1960. This law said that 'a *Perusahaan Negara* is any enterprise (*perusahaan*) the capital of which is State's property or belongs to the State's Treasury, except when otherwise stated by law.' The law led to a bewildering implementing legislation to re-introduce differentiation and to the extension of civil servant status to all employees of such companies (Gautama, 1995:336-8). A Presidential Decree of 1967 and the subsequent law No. 9 of 1969 re-established the former distinction, with the *perusahaan umum* (public corporation) still covered by Law No. 19/1960 and the *perusahaan perseroan*, a limited liability company under the Commercial Code, whose shares are wholly or partially owned by the state. Besides this, the Law provided for the possibility of special state enterprises created by statute, as in the case of the state oil-company Pertamina (Gautama, 1995:339-40).

Privatization in Indonesia has been slow. In comparison to Singapore or Japan, it encounters the additional difficulty of taking place in an economy that is divided along ethnic lines (Low, 1993b:168-83; Hill, 1996:106-7). As a result of the Asian crisis, the Indonesian government enacted an Anti-Monopoly and Unfair Competition Law in 1999, that came into effect in March 2000. Responsible for the investigation of monopolistic practices and acts of unfair competition is a new Business Competition Supervisory Committee consisting of seven members that are appointed by the President and approved by the House of Representatives. The new law has been criticized because of the influence that the President retains and because it fails to specify what sort of business practices will be deemed to be 'unfair' or 'detrimental' to society (Abdurrachman and Ryan, 1999).

CONCLUSION

A number of conclusions might be drawn from this survey that concern both content and form of these Asian business laws. While all three countries have to a varying degree relied on cheap labour in the early stages of the development process, it is really at the capital formation stage, that significant differences appear between the 'late developer' Japan and the 'late late developers' in Southeast Asia. Japan remained hostile to foreign investment during that period and relied on a substantial tax burden and the peculiarities of her banking system. In contrast, Singapore developed a peculiar mix of greatly facilitating foreign investment, on the one hand, and maintaining a fairly large state-controlled sector in 'strategic industries' on the other. The high rate of compulsory savings generated by the Central Provident Fund was partly channelled into these sectors. Indonesia's embrace of foreign investment was much more hesitant and the greater available revenue from oil made it possible to maintain a state-centred policy well into the 1980s.

A difficulty of the comparison between Japan and Southeast Asia is the great difference in time between the beginnings of industrialization in the different countries. Japan was often saved by peculiar historical circumstances, beginning with a silk worm disease in Europe early in the Meiji period to the Cold War and Korean War of the 1950s, when the victorious powers of World War II allowed her a quick comeback as a new alley against communism. The genius of Japan has been to seize these opportunities to greatly enhance her technological and educational foundations. The same must be said of Singapore that made the best of its strategic location during a boom period and successfully anticipated future requirements at an early stage. In the case of Indonesia, the government alternated between quite different development strategies, often relying on *ad hoc* solutions to particular problems.

All three countries to a certain extent instrumentalized their imported commercial laws for development purposes. In Japan, Western law was introduced to revise the unequal treaties and litigation for individual goals was never encouraged. Singapore impresses with its formal legal system, but some essential parts of the development strategy have been removed from judicial scrutiny. In Indonesia, the court system has been largely unreliable and Western derived business laws served to appease foreign investors and to justify developmental policies of the government. As far as form is concerned, a few similarities have emerged: the most striking feature of business laws in these three countries has been the explicit or implicit incorporation of the developmental ideology as part of the laws. Judges and administrators were required to assess individual claims taking into account 'the state of the national economy,' 'the interest of development,' etc. even in fields traditionally belonging to private law. The classical distinction between private and public law was, thereby, blurred. There was also a tendency to rely on administrative guidance and to shift essential parts of the legislation to be regulated in a large number of administrative decrees. As these are often difficult to obtain, public scrutiny has remained a problem, especially as these regulations are also easily and frequently changed. Finally, the administration retained a large discretion and there has been at times little hesitation to bend the law and divert from the original purpose, if this was 'in the interest of development.'

With a similar emphasis on a strong state and administrative guidance in the implementation of business laws, success becomes then dependent on the quality of the administrators. Here it is absolutely essential to minimize corruption.[29] This in turn requires that the salaries of administrators and judicial personnel are kept at least as attractive as those in the private sector.[30] This is a major factor that explains the 'English public servant ethos' in the Singaporean public sector and the 'samurai spirit' of its Japanese counterpart. While cases of corruption have been exposed in Japan, too, in comparison to Indonesia's KKN (*korupsi, kolusi, nepotisme*) the lavish entertainment of Ministry of Finance officials must be regarded as petty corruption. Indonesia's failure to develop a coherent industrial policy has also been explained by the constant struggle between competing approaches and interest groups or, as Hal Hill has put it, between Indonesia's character as a hard and as a soft state (Hill, 1998:319-21). What has been missing in Indonesia is what Eads and Yamamura (1987:429), using the analytical framework developed by Zysman (1983) have called 'a prior agreement on basic goals of industrial policy.' Japan's and Singapore's history has been characterized by fear: fear of foreign domination in the case of Japan and fear of invasion by hostile neighbours in the case of Singapore. This has created a constant state of emergency that the government used in cases of economic crisis to make sacrifices more palatable.

While this consensus from fear seems to be waning, it has never existed in the pluralist archipelago of Indonesia, which always had to contend with dissatisfied provinces and vastly different ideological approaches and religious views.

NOTES

1 Most famously in The World Bank (1993). In a similar vein e.g. Root (1996) and Rowen (1998).

2 In particular in Indonesia 'KKN' the acronym for '*korupsi, kolusi, nepotisme*' (corruption, collusion and nepotism) is usually referred to when it comes to discuss the reasons for the crisis (see Kwik Kian Gie 1999a:287-316).

3 Lim (2000:36).

4 For a similar picture covering different areas of law and economic development see Pistor and Wellons (1998:31).

5 Nagasawa (1996:665) puts the percentage of not permanently employed people among the Japanese workforce as high as 20 per cent. Ishikawa (1998:194 fn.1) estimates that only about 20 to 25 per cent of all employees in Japan are covered by the so-called 'three pillars' of the Japanese industrial relations systems (lifetime employment, seniority based wage system, company-based unionism). These are mainly employees in large firms and in the government bureaucracy.

6 As to the substantial drop in the number of labour disputes between 1970 and 1989 see the statistics in Ishikawa (1998:190).

7 Cf. also the current text of the legislation in National Trade Union Congress 1994:45-6.

8 As to the Emergency and the Emergency Regulations declared in 1948 to fight the armed insurrection of the Malayan Communist Party see Yeo and Lau (1991:123-4).

9 As to more background information about the 'second industrial revolution' see Rodan 1989:142-88.

10 *Pancasila* Industrial Relations were created at a National Seminar in 1974 with the following proclamation: 'To carry out the ideals of the 17 August 1945 Independence Proclamation of the Republic of Indonesia in the national development, in order to materialize a just and prosperous society based upon *Pancasila* and to take part in implementing the world law and order based upon freedom, eternal peace, and social justice through the creation of tranquil, peaceful and orderly atmosphere of work and of tranquil atmosphere of business, to increase production, and to promote

workers' welfare and status in conformity with man's dignity,' cited after the translation by Shamad 1997:5-6.

11 Rinakit (1999:146) also alleges that only a small fraction of the actual fee payments of SPSI members is forwarded to SPSI.

12 'Pokok-Pokok Pandangan Komisi Pembaharuan Hukum Perburuhan Terhadap Rancangan Undang-Undang Pokok Ketenagakerjaan,' in: *Diponegoro* 74, 20 January 1997, p. 7.

13 See Thorn, at 28, who remarked in 1987: 'One of these three conditions has been deemed to exist ever since the passage of the law.'

14 As to the speed of reforms see also Delhaise (1998:191): 'The reforms will eventually take place, but their impact – in terms of disclosure more perhaps than in real terms – on some banks will be so severe that it would not be surprising to see the schedule stretched somehow beyond the target dates.'

15 ASEAN Law Association (1995), 351; as to the different tax incentives cf. also Fordham (1988).

16 It nevertheless seems that the tax benefits have been awarded very generously, ibid, 59.

17 ASEAN Law Association (1995), p. 43.

18 Cf ASEAN Law Association (1995), p. 44.

19 ASEAN Law Association (1995), p. 44; MacIntyre (1993b), pp. 145 and 158; Syahril Sabirin, 'Money Market Policy in Indonesia,' in: Ministry of Law/Singapore Academy of Law/Faculty of Law, National University of Singapore, Proceedings of the First Indonesia-Singapore Law Seminar: *Business & Investment Laws in Indonesia*, 26-27 February 1993, pp. 67-8.

20 ASEAN Law Association (1995), pp. 44-5.

21 See ASEAN Law Association (1995), pp. 45-6.

22 Bennett (1999:55) compares the total assets of only US$500 million of the average Indonesian bank with the figures in Korea, where the smallest commercial bank had assets in access of US$2 billion and Thailand, where 12 of the 15 commercial banks had total assets in excess of US$4 billion.

23 Referred to as National Stabilization Council Decision of January 22, 1974.

24 As to the legally doubtful step of overriding the Foreign Capital Investment Law by means of a mere Cabinet Resolution, see Charles Himawan, *The Foreign Investment Process in Indonesia*, pp. 266, 278-88.

25 In the majority of cases, foreign investors preferred to pay a fine instead, see Himawan, p. 272. As to the safeguarding of Indonesian interests see also Gautama, *Indonesian Business Law*, PT Citra Aditya Bakti, Bandung 1995, 371-3.

26 Later decrees preferred to speak about the 'economically weak' and the 'economically strong,' see Himawan, 283-4.

27 Himawan, p. 286, however, mentions a few permissions which cannot be granted by the Foreign Capital Co-ordination Board and require a second step.

28 According to a recent report, such government-linked companies (GLCs) account for 10 per cent of economic output and about 25 per cent of stock market capitalization in Singapore, see Richardson (2000b).

29 See also the recent report of the Political & Economic Risk Consultancy Ltd., as reported in *The International Herald Tribune* of 23 March 2000 (Richardson, 2000a). The report found Indonesia to be the most corrupt country of those surveyed, whereas Singapore, Hong Kong, and Japan were the least corrupt.

30 In an effort to fight corruption, the Indonesian government this year increased the basic salaries of civil servants by 30 per cent, see Richardson (2000a).

REFERENCES

Abdurrachman, Yanti S. and Kerry Ryan (1999) 'Indonesia's Anti-Monopoly and Unfair Competition Law,' *Asia Business Law Review* 25, pp. 3-9.

Abraham, Mohanraj (1985) 'Singapore,' in: Dennis Campbell (ed.) *Legal Aspects of Doing Business in Asia and the Pacific* 3, Deventer–St. Paul: Kluwer Law and Taxation Publishers.

Adiwinata, Saleh, June Katz, and Ronald Katz (1974) *Survey of Indonesian Economic Law: Labor Law*. Bandung: Padjajaran University Law School.

Allen, G.C. (1981) *A Short Economic History of Modern Japan*, 4th ed., Houndmills–London: Macmillan Press.

Anantaraman, Venkatraman (1990) *Singapore Industrial Relations System*. Singapore: Singapore Institute of Management–McGraw-Hill Book Co.

ASEAN Law Association (eds) (1995) *ASEAN Legal Systems*, Singapore: Butterworths Asia.

Bennett, Michael (1999) 'Banking Deregulation in Indonesia: An Updated Perspective in Light of the Asian Financial Crisis,' *University of Pennsylvania Journal of International Economic Law* 20/1, pp. 1-59.

Bowring, Philip (2000) 'New Look for Asian Stock Indexes: Revised Data Illustrate Family Domination of Major Firms,' *International Herald Tribune*, 29 September 2000.

Bryant, Ralph C. (1989) 'The Evolution of Singapore as a Financial Centre,' in: Kernial Singh Sandhu and Paul Wheatley (eds) *Management of Success: The Moulding of Modern Singapore*. Singapore: Institute of Southeast Asian Studies.

Caves, Richard E. and Masu Uekusa (1976) *Industrial Organization in Japan*. Washington: The Brookings Institution.

Cheng Siok Hwa (1991) 'Economic Change and Industrialization,' in: Ernest C.T. Chew and Edwin Lee (eds) *A History of Singapore*. Singapore–Oxford–New York: Oxford University Press.

Chew Soon Beng and Rosalind Chew (1996) 'Industrial Relations in Singapore: Past Developments and Future Challenges,' in: Basant K. Kapur, Euston T.E. Quah and Hoon Hian Teck (eds) *Development, Trade and the Asia-Pacific*. Singapore: Prentice Hall, pp. 122-40.

Chong Li Choy and Caroline Yeoh (1990) 'Multinational Business and Singapore Society,' in: Chong Li Choy, Tan Chwee Huat, Wong Kwei Cheong and Caroline Yeoh (eds) *Business, Society and Development in Singapore*. Singapore: Times Academic Press.

Committee on Singapore's Competitiveness (1996) *Committee on Singapore's Competitiveness*. Ministry of Trade and Industry, Singapore.

Cooper Maysami, Ramin, Lee San San and Ooi Ming Lee (1999) 'An Economic Analysis of Reforms in Singapore's Banking Industry,' *Asia Business Law Review* 26, pp. 58-68.

Davidson, Paul J. and Franca Ciambella (1995) *Investment in Southeast Asia: Policy and Laws*. Singapore: Butterworth–Heinemann Asia.

Delhaise, Philippe F. (1998) *Asia in Crisis: The Implosion of the Banking and Finance Systems*. Singapore: John Wiley & Sons (Asia) Pte Ltd.

Dittrich, Eckhard J. and Pheni Chalid (1996) 'Labour Relations and Labour Unrest in an Indonesian Export Processing Zone,' in: Hing A.Y., C.T. Chang and R. Lansbury (eds) *Work, Organisation and Industry – The Asian Experience*. Singapore: Armour Publishing.

Eads, George C. and Kozo Yamamura (1987) 'The Future of Industrial Policy,' in: Kozo Yamamura and Yasukichi Yasuba (eds) *The Political Economy of Japan, Volume 1: The Domestic Transformation*. Stanford: Stanford University Press, pp. 423-68.

Erber, George, Harald Hagemann and Stephan Seiter (1996) 'Global Competitiveness: Industrial Policy in the Performance of Asia and Europe,' *Journal of Contemporary Asia* 27/3, pp. 338-55.

Fordham, Margaret (1988) *Developing Singapore – Tax Incentives for Investment and Expansion Under the Economic Expansion Incentives (Relief from Income Tax) Act*. Singapore: Longman Singapore Publishers.

Fukui, Haruhiro (1992) 'The Japanese State and Economic Development: A Profile of a Nationalist-Paternalist Capitalist State,' in: Richard P. Appelbaum and Jeffrey Henderson (eds) *States and Development in the Asian Pacific Rim*. Newbury Park–London–New Delhi: Sage Publications, pp. 199-225.

Gantra, Maman and Ronald Raditya (1997) 'RUU Ketenagakerjaan: Demi Buruh Atau Stabilitas' (The Law on Manpower: For Workers or for Stability), *Forum Keadilan* 8, 28 July, p. 30.

Gautama, Sudargo (1995) *Indonesian Business Law*. Bandung: Penerbit PT. Citra Aditya Bakti.

Gingerich, Duane J. (1992) 'New Foreign Investment Rules Scrap Some Key Policies, Allow 100 per cent Foreign Firms,' *East Asian Executive Reports* 15, 7 September, pp. 11-15.

Hamada, Koichi and Akiyoshi Horiuchi (1987) 'The Political Economy of the Financial Market,' in: Kozo Yamamura and Yasukichi Yasuba (eds) *The Political Economy of Japan, Volume 1: The Domestic Transformation*. Stanford: Stanford University Press, pp. 223-60.

Hill, Hal (1988) *Foreign Investment and Industrialization in Indonesia*. Singapore: Oxford University Press.

– (1996) *The Indonesian Economy Since 1966: Southeast Asia's Emerging Giant*. Cambridge-New York-Melbourne: Cambridge University Press.

– (1998) *Indonesia's Industrial Transformation*. Singapore–St Leonards: Institute of Southeast Asian Studies–Allen & Unwin.

Himawan, Charles (1980) *The Foreign Investment Process in Indonesia*. Singapore: Gunung Agung.

Howe, Christopher (1996) *The Origins of Japanese Trade Supremacy*. Bathurst: Crawford House Publishing.

Hughes, Helen (1992) 'An External View,' in: Linda Low, Toh Mun Heng, Soon Teck Wong, Tan Yong Kam and Helen Hughes (eds) *Challenge and Response: Thirty Years of the Economic Development Board*. Singapore: Times Academic Press.

Ishikawa, Akihiro (1998) 'Changing Patterns of Japanese Industrial Relations,' in: Hing A.Y., C.T. Chang and R. Lansbury (eds) *Work, Organisation and Industry – The Asian Experience*, Singapore: Armour Publishing, pp. 176-95.

Komatsu, Ryuji (1994) 'The labour movement and the government in Japan,' in: Jim Hagan and Andrew Wells (eds) *Industrial Relations in Australia and Japan*. St Leonards: Allen & Unwin, pp. 116-22.

Kwik Kian Gie (1999a) *Ekonomi Indonesia dalam Krisis dan Transisi Politik* (The Indonesian Economy in Crisis and Political Transition), Jakarta: Penerbit PT Gramedia Pustaka Utama.

Kwik Kian Gie (1999b) *Saya bermimpi jadi konglomerat* (I dreamt of becoming a conglomerate), Jakarta: Penerbit PT Gramedia Pustaka Utama.

Lee (Tsao) Yuan (1987) 'The Government in the Labour Market,' in: Lawrence B. Krause, Koh Ai Tee, Lee (Tsao) Yuan (eds) *The Singapore Economy Reconsidered*, Singapore: Institute of Southeast Asian Studies.

Leggett, Chris (1992) 'Singapore's industrial relations in the 1990s,' in: Garry Rodan (ed.), *Singapore Changes Guard: Social, Political and Economic Directions in the 1990s*. Melbourne–New York: Longman Cheshire–St. Martin's Press.

Lim, Linda (2000) 'Globalization is the Best Welfare,' *Far Eastern Economic Review*, 20 April 2000, p. 36.

Lockwood, William W. (1954) *The Economic Development of Japan: Growth and Structural Change 1868-1938*. Princeton: Princeton University Press.

Low, Linda (1993a) 'From Entrepot to a Newly Industrialising Economy,' in: Linda Low, Toh Mun Heng, Soon Teck Wong, Tan Kong Yam and Helen Hughes (eds) *Challenge and Response: Thirty Years of the Economic Development Board*. Singapore: Times Academic Press, pp. 27-59.

– (1993b) 'The public sector in contemporary Singapore: in retreat?' in: Garry Rodan (ed.) *Singapore Changes Guard: Social, Political and Economic Directions in the 1990s*. Melbourne–New York: Longman Cheshire–St. Martin's Press, pp. 168-83.

– (1993c) 'The Economic Development Board', in: Linda Low, Toh Mun Hong, Soon Teck Wong, Tan Kong Yam and Helen Hughes (eds) *Challenge and Response: Thirty Years of the Economic Development Board*, Singapore: Times Academic Press, pp. 61-120.

McAlinn, Gerald Paul (1997) 'Japan,' in: 'Employment Law in Asia,' *Asia Business Law Review* 23, pp. 27-34.

– (1999) 'The Financial Crisis in Japan: Reforming a System in Chaos,' *Asia Business Law Review* 23, pp. 3-11.

MacIntyre, Andrew J. (1993a) 'Indonesia, Thailand and the Northeast Asian Connection,' in: Richard Higgott, Richard Leaver and John Ravenhill (eds) *Pacific-Economic Relations in the 1990s: Cooperation or Conflict?* St Leonards: Allen & Unwin, pp. 250-70.

– (1993b) 'The Politics of Finance in Indonesia: Command, Confusion and Competition,' in: Stephen Haggard, Chung H. Lee and Sylvia Maxfield, Ithaca–London: Cornell University Press, pp. 123-64.

Matsumura, Takao (1993) 'Labour relations in Japan between the wars,' in: Jim Hagan and Andrew Wells (eds.), *Industrial Relations in Australia and Japan*. St Leonards: Allen & Unwin, pp. 37-46.

Matsushita, Mitsuo and Schoenbaum, Thomas J. (1989) *Japanese International Trade and Investment Law*. Tokyo: University of Tokyo Press.

Matsuzaki, Hajime (1993) 'Employers and employed in Meiji Japan,' in: Jim Hagan and Andrew Wells (eds) *Industrial Relations in Australia and Japan*. St Leonards: Allen & Unwin, pp. 6-17.

Mills, Karen (1993) 'Indonesia's Ongoing Deregulation of Direct Foreign Investment,' *East Asian Executive Reports* 15 9 January, pp. 15-19.

Montes, Manuel F. (1999) 'Tokyo, Hong Kong and Singapore as competing financial centres,' in: Gordon de Brouwer and Wisarn Pupphavesa (eds) *Asia Pacific Financial Deregulation*. London-New York: Routledge, pp. 151-70.

National Trade Union Congress (1994) *A Guide to Labour Legislation in Singapore*. Singapore: SNP Publishers.

Nagasawa, Takashi (1993) 'Arbeitsbeziehungen in Japan' (Industrial Relations in Japan), *Arbeitsrecht im Betrieb* 11, pp. 661-6.

Nayar (1996) *Indonesian Labor Legislation in a Comparative Perspective: A Study of Six APEC Countries*. Policy Research Working Paper 1673, The World Bank – East Asia and Pacific Country Department III.

Nimura, Kazuo (1993) 'Post-Second World War labour relations in Japan,' in: Jim Hagan and Andrew Wells (eds) *Industrial Relations in Australia and Japan*. St Leonards: Allen & Unwin, pp. 64-91.

Pape, Wolfgang (1979) 'Kartellrecht' (Antimonopoly law), in: Paul Eubel (ed.) *Das japanische Rechtssystem* (The Japanese Legal System), Frankfurt am Main: Alfred Metzner Verlag.

Pillai, Philip N. (1983) *State Enterprise in Singapore: Legal Importation and Development.* Singapore: Singapore University Press.

Pistor, Katharina and Philip A. Wellons (1999) *The Role of Law and Legal Institutions in Asian Economic Development 1960-1995*. New York: Oxford University Press.

Rahmanto, Wahid, Dewi Anggraeni and Arya Gunawan (1993) 'Buruh dan Majikan Bisa Menuntut' (Workers and Employers can sue), *Forum Keadilan* 9, 11 August, p. 70.

Regnier, Philippe (1990) *Singapore: City-State in South-East Asia*, Honolulu: University of Hawaii Press.

Richardson, Michael (2000a) 'Fighting Graft Brings a Net Advantage, Survey Says,' *International Herald Tribune*, 23 March 2000.

– (2000b) 'Singapore Privatization Push Expected,' *International Herald Tribune*, 3 May 2000.

Rinakit, Sukardi (1999) 'Trade Unions and Labour Unrest,' in: Richard W. Baker, M. Hadi Soesastro, J. Kristiadi and Douglas E. Ramage (eds) *Indonesia: The Challenge of Change*. Singapore-Leiden: KITLV Press–Institute of Southeast Asian Studies.

Robison, Richard (1986) *Indonesia: The Rise of Capital*. North Sydney–Wellington–London: Allen & Unwin.

Rodan, Garry (1989) *The Political Economy of Singapore's Industrialization: National State and International Capital*, Houndmills–London: Macmillan Press.

Root, Hilton R. (1996) *Small Countries, Big Lessons: Governance and the Rise of East Asia*. Oxford–New York: Oxford University Press.

Rowen, Henry S. (ed.) (1996) *Behind East Asian Growth: the political and social foundations of prosperity.* London–New York: Routledge.

Sabirin, Syahril (1993) 'Money Market Policy in Indonesia,' in: Ministry of Law/Singapore Academy of Law/Faculty of Law, National University of Singapore, *Proceedings of the First Indonesia-Singapore Law Seminar: Business & Investment Laws in Indonesia*, Singapore, 26-27 February 1993.

Satusky, Elton (1999) 'Japanese Financial Market Reform from a Global Regulatory Perspective: A New Beginning for Market Oriented Regulation or the Status Quo?' *Banking & Finance Law Review* 14, pp. 275-328.

Shamad, Yunus (1996) *Industrial Relations in Indonesia.* Jakarta: PT Bina Sumber Daya Manusia.

Sonneville, M. and Jagtenberg, R. (1995) 'Mergers and Acquisitions in Japan,' in: A.J. de Roo and R.W. Jagtenberg (eds) *Yearbook Law & Legal Practice in East Asia 1995*. The Hague–London–Boston: Kluwer Law International.

Surowidjojo, Arief T. (1996) 'Employment Law in Asia: Indonesia,' *Asia Business Law Review* 25, pp. 24-9.

Tabalujan, Benny S. (1999) 'Indonesian Banking: Recent Legal Developments,' *Asia Business Law Review* 24, pp. 3-11.

Tan Chwee Huat (1990) 'Employees and Trade Unions in Singapore,' in: Chong Li Choy, Tan Chwee Huat, Wong Kwei Cheong and Caroline Yeoh (eds) *Business, Society and Development in Singapore.* Singapore: Times Academic Press, pp. 41-50.

– (1992) 'Public Sector Management: Past Achievement and Future Challenge,' in: Linda Low and Toh Mun Heng (eds) *Public Policies in Singapore: Changes in the 1980s and Future Signposts*. Singapore: Times Academic Press.

Tay Boon Nga (1992) 'The Central Provident Fund: Operation and Schemes,' in: Linda Low and Toh Mun Heng (eds) *Public Policies in Singapore: Changes in the 1980s and Future Signposts*. Singapore: Times Academic Press.

Thorn, Richard S. (1987) *The Rising Yen: The Impact of Japanese Financial Liberalization on World Capital Markets*. Singapore: ASEAN Economic Research Unit–Institute of Southeast Asian Studies.

Uwiyono, A. (1997) 'Pandangan Hukum Dalam Upaya Mengatasi Konflik Ketenagakerjaan Dalam Sistem Hubungan Industrial Pancasila' (Legal Perspectives in the Efforts to Contend Industrial Conflicts within the System of Pancasila Industrial Relations), *Hukum dan Pembangunan* 1, pp. 33-40.

Wong, Evelyn (1990) 'Labour Policies and Industrial Relations,' in: Linda Low and Toh Mun Heng (eds) *Public Policies in Singapore: Changes in the 1980s and Future Signposts*. Singapore: Times Academic Press.

Woon, Walter C.M. (1986) *Commercial Law of Singapore: An Introduction*. Cambridge: Woodhead-Faulkner.
World Bank (1993) *The East Asian Miracle: Economic Growth and Public Policy*. New York: Oxford University Press.
– (1996) *The State in a Changing World*. Oxford: Oxford University Press.
Yeo Kim Wah and Lau, Albert (1990) 'From Colonialism to Independence, 1945-1965,' in: Ernest C.T. Chew and Edwin Lee (eds) *A History of Singapore*. Singapore-Oxford-New York: Oxford University Press.
Yuasa, Kyozo and Hanamizu, Yukukazu (1985) 'Japan,' in: Dennis Campbell, *Legal Aspects of Doing Business in Asian and the Pacific* 3, Deventer–St. Paul: Kluwer Law and Taxation Publishers.

PART THREE

LAW IN A 'SOCIALIST MARKET ECONOMY': THE CASE OF CHINA

CHAPTER 9

POLICY AS LAW AND LAW AS POLICY
THE ROLE OF LAW IN CHINA'S DEVELOPMENT STRATEGY

JIANFU CHEN

Since 1978, the growth of law in China, like that of the economy, has been remarkable. When the post-Mao reforms began in 1978, there were virtually no law or any functioning legal institutions in China; the only 'laws' were a few statutes and some provisional regulations or orders drawn up in the 1950s. Today, a relatively independent legal system exists and functions throughout China. In terms of lawmaking, from 1979 to the end of 1998, the National People's Congress (NPC) and its Standing Committee had promulgated 351 statutes and resolutions. During the same period of time, the State Council had adopted more than 800 administrative regulations while over 6,000 local rules were issued by local people's congresses and their standing committees (People's Daily, 1999).

Government by law has been a constant and consistent theme in post-Mao China. The Third Plenary Session of the Eleventh Central Committee of the Communist Party of China (CPC) in 1978 was seen by Chinese officials and scholars as a new epoch in modern Chinese history and a turning point in legal development in China. It declared not only that large-scale nationwide mass political campaigns should be stopped and 'the emphasis of the Party's work should be shifted to socialist modernization as of 1979,'[1] but also that a legal system was a necessity for socialist modernization (Liu and Wu, 1986:569). Such a need for economic development and for law was summarized by Deng Xiaoping as a 'Two-Hands' policy. On the one hand, the economy must be developed; and on the other hand, the legal system must be strengthened (Wang *et al.*, 1996:7).

This new policy under the leadership of Deng Xiaoping, and now under the third generation of leadership of the CPC, contrasts sharply with the practice under the leadership of Mao Zedong who was reported to have declared that '[we must] depend on rule of man, not rule of law' (Leng, 1977:356). This apparent difference in policy and practice raises an important question: is the role of law in China today fundamentally and qualitatively different from that during Mao's leadership?

In this chapter I will argue that the changing fate of law in China is inexorably tied to the need, as perceived by the Party leadership, for national development. In this regard, law serves as a tool and tool only; its usefulness depends largely on the Party's policy of the time. The Rule of Law *per se* is not seen as having much value. While this may be so, after twenty years of reform and practice, legal discourse in the 1990s in China is qualitatively different from those in the first forty years of the People's Republic of China (PRC). If legal theories developed by Chinese scholars are to be translated into practice, there is hope that China may abandon the ideology of legal instrumentalism and begin to see law as more than a means to an end. To support this argument, I will first briefly examine the troubled fate of law under Mao's leadership. I will then focus on analysing the changing perceptions of the role of law in present China and the broad trends in the rapid legal development in the 1980s and 1990s.

POLICY AS LAW – THE ROLE OF LAW UNDER MAO'S LEADERSHIP[2]

The PRC's legal system was established on the basis of the pre-1949 experience of communist justice and on the Soviet model (Chen, 1999a:ch.2). Although the pre-1949 communist legal developments were largely experimental and localized in nature, certain features of 'people's justice' were emerging and being shaped during these years. To start with, the Marxist concept of law as being a tool to remould the society and to suppress class enemies, to enforce party policy rather than protecting individual rights, was taking its root. Secondly, justice was politicized (such as the enforcement of class justice in which distinction was made according to the class elements in administering justice) and popularized (such as the implementation of a mass line under which mass trials were organized not so much for the administration of justice but for political education and indoctrination). Thirdly, extra judicial organizations and procedures and extralegal measures were often utilized to impose sanctions and to settle disputes (Leng, 1967:ch.1; Tay, 1969:165-72; Brady, 1987:ch.4).

It is then clear that the legal system of the PCR under Mao's leadership was established on a rather shaky foundation. It is also well recognized that Soviet influence or Marxist theories of law did not lead to any significant activities in lawmaking or institution-building in China. Instead, the main features of law in the first thirty years of communism in China differed little from those of the pre-1949 communist experiences (Tay, 1969, 1973, 1976; Butler, 1983; Leng, 1967; Leng and Chiu, 1985). There was, however, another face to the experience, one that has not been well recognized.

The first three to four years was a period for the new government to consolidate its newly gained powers and gain control of China through political campaigns. However, the need to make new laws and to establish a new judicial system was recognized by the new government from the moment the Six Codes of the Nationalist Government (the KMT) were abolished.[3] Indeed, no less than 376 'legal documents' were issued by various central government departments and commissions during that period of time (Wu, 1983:8).

Towards the end of 1952 when the period of consolidation had passed, the Party began to shift its focus towards economic construction. Mao first proposed a general line for the transitional period to the Central Committee of the CPC, and elaborated this in June 1953 at the Politburo of the CPC. This stipulated that:

> During the transition the general line and fundamental task of the Party is to bring about, step by step, over a fairly long period of time the socialist industrialization of the country and to accomplish, step by step, the socialist transformation of agriculture, handicraft and capitalist industry and commerce (Mao, 1986:704).

This policy was first adopted by the Party in 1953 and then incorporated into the 1954 Constitution of the PRC.[4] The conditions necessary to a planned economy and a gradual transition to socialism were deemed to have been created after large-scale political campaigns in the previous three years (Preamble to the 1954 Constitution). The first Five-Year Plan was thus adopted in 1953.

More important for legal development was the official recognition of the inadequacy of the pre-1949 experience of law for the establishment of a socialist legal system by the Party. Liu Shaoqi, then the President of the State, in his Report to the Eighth National Congress of the CPC in 1956, declared:

> Now, ... the period of revolutionary storm and stress is past, new relations of production have been set up, and the aim of our struggle is changed into one of safeguarding the successful development of the productive forces of society; a corresponding change in the methods of struggle will consequently have to follow, and a complete legal system has become an absolute necessity (Liu, 1985:253).

In the same Report, Liu stressed that one of the urgent tasks of the state was to start systematically making laws and perfecting the legal system (Liu,

1985:253). The then President of the Supreme People's Court, Dong Biwu, in his speech to the same Congress, specifically pointed out that:

> The problem today is that we still lack several urgently-needed, fairly complete basic statutes such as a criminal code, a civil code, procedural laws, a labour law, a law governing the use of land and the like (Dong, 1986:481).

The first serious efforts to rebuild a legal system and to draft comprehensive codes began,[5] marking the commencement of what the Chinese scholars called the 'golden period' of the 1950s.

With this policy in place, the Constitution, organic laws for courts and procuracy as well as regulations covering arrest and detention were duly adopted in 1954. Drafting work on major codes, including the civil code and criminal code, also started. And before the completion of these major codes, no less than 4,072 individual laws, regulations, and decrees, though unsystematic, incoherent, and inconsistent, were issued from October 1949 to October 1957 (Tay, 1976:411).

This first effort to draft comprehensive codes was, however, abruptly ended by what are now termed 'leftist errors' or 'communist wind' by scholars in China, i.e. the Anti-rightist Movement of 1957 and the 'Great Leap Forward' of 1958 (Wu, 1983:11; Zhang and Wang, 1989:328; Zhao, 1990:232).[6]

After these upheavals the political climate changed again in 1961. After the disaster of the 'Great Leap Forward' of 1958, a policy of 'readjusting (Tiaozheng), consolidating (Gonggu), strengthening (Chongshi) and enhancement (Tigao)' – a policy basically advocating a better controlled and more realistic economic plan for national economic development, and in today's terminology, economic reform – was adopted by the Party's Central Committee in early 1961. More importantly, at an enlarged meeting of the Central Committee of the CPC in February 1962, the necessity for the development of a commodity economy was recognized (Gu, 1989:102). In Communist ideology, this means the need for law and social order (Hazard, 1975:145-75). With it, again, was the demand for law. It was under these circumstances that Mao was reported to have said in 1962 that '[l]aw was needed – not only a criminal code, but also a civil code' (Gu, 1989:102; Zhang and Wang, 1989:328).

The second effort to make laws and rebuild a legal system was fated to share a similar fate as the first attempt.[7] It was first interrupted by the so-called 'Four Clean-ups' Movement of 1963-5 (clean up of politics, the economy, organization, and ideology, also called 'Socialist Education').[8] This was then followed by the so-called 'Cultural Revolution' of 1966-76 during which virtually all laws and the legal system were destroyed (Tay, 1976:417-23). The words of individual leaders and policies of the Party, as Chinese scholars often reminded us, acquired binding force and took the place of that of law in running and ruling the state.

LAW AS POLICY – THE ROLE OF LAW UNDER DENG'S LEADERSHIP

Under Deng's leadership in the 1980s and 1990s, China has witnessed massive and rapid enactment of laws and regulations, particularly laws and administrative rules regulating economic and commercial relations, as well as a swift re-establishment of legal institutions including the courts and the procuracy.

One must however not be misled by the apparent difference between Mao and Deng. The different attitudes must be understood in their 'historical' context. When Mao occasionally advocated for law, it was at the time the 'storming revolution' was perceived as being over and an orderly economic development was considered necessary. When he repudiated law, it was at the time when he was advocating the 'uninterrupted revolution' which aimed at destroying 'old' orders. When Deng took over leadership, the 'uninterrupted revolution' had pushed the Chinese economy to the verge of collapse; the legitimacy of the Party leadership had to be rebuilt upon economic development. For him, therefore, law must be used to establish stability and order for economic development (Deng, 1984:335-55; Liu and Wu, 1986:574). It was against this background that the Party declared in 1978 the now famous phrase:

> There must be laws for people to follow; these laws must be observed; their enforcement must be strict; and law-breakers must be dealt with...

From Deng's various speeches on law, it is clear that both Mao and Deng unambiguously regarded law as an instrument of the Party policy; neither has taken the establishment of the Rule of Law as an end in itself. One of the most prominent and influential jurists, Zhang Youyu, once clearly spelt out the rule of law in the PRC:

> Socialist democracy and the legal system [*fazhi*, sometimes translated as 'Rule of Law'] are inseparable; both of them are [to be used] to consolidate socialist economic bases and to enhance socialist development. At present, they are powerful tools for promoting the

> Four Modernizations. Neither of them is an end but both of them are means (Zhang, 1984:41).

If law is to facilitate economic development, an obvious question then arises. Why does China need law in addition to Party policies since it is the Party policy that decides the direction of economic reform? Well, according to Peng Zhen, then the Chairman of the Standing Committee of the NPC, law is an important and necessary tool for implementing Party policies:

> Law is the fixation of the Party's fundamental principles and policies, that is the codification of the Party's fundamental principles and policies. These fundamental principles and policies are those that have in practice proven effective and correct (Peng, 1984:160-1).[9]

That is, policy is the foundation of law and law is the mature form of policy (Keller, 1989:658; Foster, 1982:395-413). In other words, law is, to a large extent, to be used to generalize and institutionalize Party and state economic reform policies and measures. To many Chinese lawyers and scholars, law is only a better tool than policy, capable of securing and institutionalizing *ad hoc* policies in a more universal manner; of providing stability and order through state coercive forces for economic development and of defining rights and duties in relation to the state as represented by various administrative authorities (Law Department of Beijing University, 1984:212-21; Wu and Shen, 1987:165-77). Rule of Law *per se* has no virtue. As such, the nature and the extent of legal developments essentially depend on the parameters set by the reform programme.[10]

As the economic reform had no clear direction,[11] it was not surprising that legal development had taken an *ad hoc* and piecemeal approach. This then produced a large system of law consisting of many individual statutes, decisions and orders, and administrative regulations and rules made under different *ad hoc* policy orientations.

In short, Party policies were to be transformed into state policy through legislative procedures. Law, as such, embodies only vague and general principles; it lacks the fundamental elements of clarity, certainty, universality, and stability.[12] It offers few solutions to legal and practical problems; and its enforcement has been largely selective and various, depending on the prevailing policy consideration.[13] The difference between law and policy under Deng is thus more a matter of formality than of substance.

A RULE OF LAW FOR A MARKET ECONOMY?

Although law was ruthlessly used by Deng as an instrument for political domination, particularly in the immediate aftermath of the 1989 Tiananmen Square event, and for economic development, 1992 appeared to show evidence of the start of an apparent new period in legal development in China. In that year, the Party decided on a long-term direction of economic reform – to establish a 'socialist market economy.'[14] The adoption of such a policy then began to change the practice in legal construction, at least in rhetoric.

As I have argued elsewhere (Chen, 1999d:73-6), there is little new in the notion of 'socialist market economy' as far as reform measures are concerned; the real significance lies with the justification for introducing the notion, rather than with the notion itself. That is, the significance lies in the abandonment of the requirement for ideological correctness in introducing reform measures. Hence, the notion of 'socialist market economy' introduced a practical licence to use capitalism in the economic sphere and to introduce capitalist mechanisms and measures (including legal measures) that will facilitate economic development.

It is under the new policy parameters that we have seen some bold theoretical discussions in Chinese legal circles, arguing for a rights-based approach towards legal construction, the separation of public and private law, equal treatment of all economic participants, universality of legal norms, and freedom of contract (Chen, 1999d:73-6). Market economy, for Chinese scholars, means an economy under the Rules of Law and demands 'rational' law in the sense defined by Max Weber.

This 'new' understanding of the role of law in society then soon led to a renewed discussion and debate on the difference between Rule by Law and Rule of Law.[15]

The recent discussions began in early 1996 when Jiang Zemin initiated a seminar, given by prominent Chinese scholars to Party and state leaders, on the topic of 'Ruling the Country by Law' (Yifa Zhiguo). At the conclusion of the seminar, Jiang made a speech entitled To Rule the Country By Law and To Guarantee Long-Term Stability of the Country.[16] Thereafter, the Ninth Five-Year National Economic and Social Development Plan and the Long-Term Goals to the Year 2010, first proposed by the Party and then dutifully adopted by the Fourth Plenary Session of the 8th NPC on 17 March 1996, formally decided that 'Ruling the Country by Law' is to be a long-term development strategy.[17] More importantly, the notion was further elaborated in the Political Report to the 15th Party Congress in September 1997. The main text on 'Ruling the Country by Law' as contained in the Report states:

> Developing democracy must go hand in hand with the efforts to improve the legal system so that the country is ruled by law. Ruling the Country by Law means that the broad masses of the people, under the leadership of the Party and in accordance with the Constitution and other laws, participate in one way or another and through all possible channels in managing state affairs, economic and cultural undertakings and social affairs, and see to it that all work of the state proceeds in keeping with law, and that socialist democracy is gradually institutionalized and codified so that such institutions and laws will not change with changes in the leadership or changes in the views or focus of attention of any leader. Ruling the Country by Law is the basic strategy employed by the Party in leading the people in running the country. It is the objective demand of a socialist market economy, an important hallmark of social and cultural progress, and a vital guarantee for lasting political stability of the country. The Party has led the people in drawing up the Constitution and other laws, to which it confines its activities. In ruling the country by law, we can unify the adherence to Party leadership, development of people's democracy and doing things in strict accordance with the law, thus ensuring, institutionally and legally, that the Party's basic line and basic policies are carried out without fail, and that the Party plays the role of the core of leadership at all times, commanding the whole situation and coordinating the efforts of all quarters (Political Report (1997)).

There was little discussion of democratization, political reform and the protection of human rights.

The adoption of the terminology of 'Ruling the Country by Law' (*Yifa Zhiguo*), and hence the change of terminology from 'legal system' (*fazhi*) to 'ruling the country by law' apparently has aroused great enthusiasm and strong interest among scholars in China. To Chinese scholars, such a formal adoption of the phrase 'Ruling the Country by Law' means the final acceptance of the notion of Rule of Law and, thus represents a new landmark in legal construction (Liu *et al.*, 1996:73). Official propaganda machines also emphasize that the adoption of such a term indicates a deeper understanding of the socialist political system, imposes a higher standard for socialist democracy and a socialist legal system, and signifies a new era in socialist democracy and legal construction (People's Daily, 1997; Lin, 1997; Xue and Wang, 1997).

The discussions on the phrase 'Ruling the Country by Law' have all been based on the Western notion of Rule of Law. It embraces the concepts of supremacy of law, judicial independence, equality before the law, separation of powers, checks and balances, a parliamentary system, and the protection of human rights (Liu *et al.*, 1996). Thus one scholar argues that the 'Rule of Law' is not just a means to rule the country; 'Rule of Law' demands judicial fairness as well as power control and supervision (Lin, 1999). Other scholars declare that to establish a 'Rule of Law,' supremacy of law, judicial fairness and impartiality, and protection of human rights must be first firmly established as its fundamental principles (Zhao and Guo, 1998). Clearly, the language in legal discourse is qualitatively different from those embodied in the Party policy statements.

The renewed discussion seems to indicate that Chinese scholars have now finally admitted that China under Deng Xiaoping was a country under the Rule by Law. Their suggestion that present-day China under the 'Third Generation of Community Party Leadership with Jiang Zemin as Its Core' is moving towards a Rule of Law is dubious. The Chinese scholars seem to have forgotten that the term 'Ruling the Country by Law' was not an invention of Jiang Zemin nor indeed was first used by him; other leaders (including Deng Xiaoping) and official documents had on occasion used this term (Liu *et al.*, 1996:46-7). In reality, however, the Party's Political Report says little about Rule of Law: the supremacy of law (over and above the Party and its policies), the independence of the judiciary, and checks and balances are all missing from the Political Report. The Report was talking about Rule by Law, not Rule of Law. The Chinese scholars' belief, it seems to me, is divorced from reality and, at best, wishful thinking without much foundation.[18]

Despite all these ambiguities inherent in the phrase 'Ruling the Country by Law,' it was formally incorporated into Article 5 of the Constitution during the 1999 revision of the Constitution.[19] The incorporation of this phrase is emphasized as being an important guarantee for the country's long-term stability (Tian, 1999).

SOME CONCLUDING REMARKS

Under the banner of the 'Socialist Market Economy,' the Chinese legal discourse and legislative practice accord more with Max Weber than with Karl Marx. However, one again must not be misled by appearances. In terms of the movement towards the Rule of Law, it is important to distinguish the role of law in economic development and that in political domination. In modernizing Chinese law and building a legal system for a socialist market economy, Chinese scholars and lawmakers are constantly reminded not to forget the 'Four Fundamental Principles' in making and implementing laws (Gu, 1989:42-3). The implications of upholding these principles should not be underestimated. Under these principles, as explained by Gu Angran,[20] firstly, important principles of all legislation have to be approved by the Party and secondly, the Party line, its guiding principles and policies, must be written into law (Gu, 1989:42; Gu, 1999). Under the guidelines for establishing a 'socialist market economy,' Marxism may be out of fashion, 'socialism' is not, at least when it is useful. Indeed, as some Chinese scholars have argued, the socialist 'Rule of Law' demands that 'ruling the country by law' must be carried out under the leadership of the Communist Party and through the principle of 'people's democratic dictatorship' in which democracy is allowed to the people and dictatorship exercised on the enemies (Sun and Huang, 1998:12-13).

Nevertheless, the present search for 'rational' law and jurisprudential discussions have clearly moved Chinese law away from the dogmatic ideologies imported from the former Soviet Union and made the Chinese legal theories much more sophisticated. It has accelerated the law reform processes and facilitated the mutual understanding of legal cultures internationally (though not without a real danger of mutual misunderstanding). It also has the potential of leading the Chinese reform to some fundamental political changes and the establishment of a Rule of Law in China.[21]

However, the strong instrumentalist approach still taken to law has ensured that the Rule of Law is far from being established after half a century of struggle. The core problem is that it has never been seen as an end in itself. In other words, under the name of upholding the Party leadership has been a clear authoritarian attitude towards reforms. The obvious and constant lag between political and economic reforms, the reluctance to participate in international human rights dialogue by hiding behind the shield of national sovereignty, and the insistence on human rights as being a Western idea are just a few of the examples of the instrumental and authoritarian approach to law.[22] The fundamental danger of such an approach to law is to use law cynically as a weapon both to 'legitimate' and to enforce repressive policies against attempts at democratization. The declaration of martial law 'according to the Constitution' in May 1989 in Beijing is only one of the recent examples of this cynical use of law. The insistence by the Chinese Premier, Li Peng, and the Party Secretary-General, Jiang Zemin, that the 1989 Beijing Massacre was a correct measure follows this instrumentalist and authoritarian logic closely.[23] Similarly, the massive crackdown on the Falun Gong – basically a non-political organization – carried out in the first half of 1999 clearly revealed the role of law in China, that is, it is simply a powerful tool for the ruling elite. With this attitude towards law prevailing, Chinese scholars are rightly concerned that China might end with a Rule by Man in the name of Rule by Law (Guo, 1994:2). Chinese scholars are also rightly concerned that, without rejecting the ideology of legal instrumentalism, it would be very difficult for the Rule of Law to be realized in China (Yu, 1989; Xie, 1994).

One of the serious consequences resulting from such an approach to law is the lack of respect for law. The tremendous difficulties being experienced by Chinese courts in enforcing court judgments or decisions are but one example of such consequences. If law cannot be enforced independently, as one Chinese scholar has questioned (Zhao, 1994:5), it is doubtful whether it is important to have law at all.

On the whole, it seems to me that the notion of 'socialist market economy' is one under which an ideological breakthrough can be made by adopting measures for economic and hence legal development. It has however not led to a fundamental departure from legal instrumentalism as an ideology and from the practice of using law as a tool, and tool only, for political domination and economic development. What remains hopeful is the current theoretical effort being made by Chinese scholars, as evidenced in the present jurisprudential discourse. If legal theories developed by Chinese scholars, instead of party policies, are to be translated into practice, there is hope that China may abandon the ideology of legal instrumentalism and begin to see law as more than a means to an end. If the experience in the 1980s provides any guidance,[24] it might be reasonable to be optimistic that, once academic discussions and debates start, they may well gain their own momentum. With the increasing involvement of legal experts in lawmaking, such a translation of theories into practice may not be a mission impossible. Let us hope that day will not be too far away.

NOTES

1 See the Communiqué of the Third Plenary Session of the Eleventh Central Committee of the CPC. An English translation of the Communiqué appears in Liu and Wu (1986), pp. 564-77.

2 In this chapter, we take 'law' to mean normative documents adopted and promulgated by legislative authorities through formal legislative procedures, whereas 'policy' means normative documents, issued, publicly or otherwise, by other authorities having no formal legislative power. In the Chinese context, in which legislative powers are granted to many authorities (including administrative authorities) and 'law and regulations' are issued by a variety of authorities (not all of them having the formal legislative authority), the difference of the two notions also lies in the binding force, backed by the state apparatus, of the documents.

3 See the Common Program of the Chinese People's Political Consultative Conference, which served as a provisional constitution until 1954. An English text can be found in Blaustein (1962:34-53).

4 See the Preamble to the 1954 Constitution. An English text of the Constitution can be found in Blaustein (1962:1-33). The only change in the Constitution was the word 'State,' replacing the word 'Party.'

5 As the pre-1949 experience was seen as inappropriate to the prevailing circumstances, Soviet models were taken as the main sources. Indeed, many young students were sent to study in the Soviet Union and many Soviet scholars came to lecture in China. A large number of Soviet law textbooks and codes were also translated into Chinese. By 1957, 165 foreign legal texts and monographs had been translated into Chinese. Among them, the great majority were from the Soviet Union. See Zhang and Wang (1989:5).

6 For a brief discussion of these movements, see Brugger (1981a:174-206); and Liu and Wu (1986:215-43).

7 No significant laws were issued during this period of time, though some provisional measures or regulations on technical standards, forest protection, and economic contracts were issued by the State Council. See Lan (1982:5-6).

8 For a brief discussion of the political situation during the period between 1962-5, see Brugger (1981:21-42).

9 Identical views were echoed by prominent Chinese scholars. See e.g. S. Chen (1988:196). Chen was one of China's most prominent scholars. His article was originally published in Chinese in *Studies of Law* (*Faxue Yanjiu*), (no.1, 1980), and later reprinted in *A Collection of Articles on Chinese Legal Science*, Beijing: Press of the Masses (1984), pp. 13-31. See also Yu (1989:46-7).

10 I have discussed elsewhere, in detail, the relationship and interaction between legal development and economic reform in the context of civil and commercial law. See Chen (1995a:ch.3).

11 This is characterized by the Chinese phrase 'Crossing the river by touching the stones underneath (*Mozhuo Shitou Guohe*).'

12 Few Chinese laws issued in post-Mao China contain sufficient details for implementation purposes. Almost without exception, laws are supplemented by various 'implementing rules' issued by different administrative or judicial authorities at a later stage according to the prevailing policy considerations. Such supplementation frequently fragments Chinese basic laws, making these laws truly 'policy guidelines.' The most comprehensive codes in China today are the comprehensively revised Criminal Procedure Law (1996) and Criminal Law (1997). However, in less than three years, both codes have been

supplemented several times by various authorities, such as the Provisions on Certain Issues relating to the Implementation of the Criminal Procedure Law (1998), Supreme People's Court, Supreme People's Procuratorate, Ministry for Public Security, Ministry for State Security, Ministry of Justice, Legal Affairs Committee of the Standing Committee of the NPC), Provisions on Determining Names of Crimes in Implementing the Criminal Law (1997), Supreme People's Court. Similar provisions were also issued by the Supreme People's Procuratorate), Interpretations on the Supreme People's Court of Relevant Issues concerning Specific Application of Laws for Hearing Criminal Cases involving Fraudulent Purchasing and Illegal Trading of Foreign Exchanges (1998), Decision on Punishing Crimes of Purchasing Foreign Exchange by Cheating, Evasion of and Illegal Sale and Purchase of Foreign Exchange (1998), Standing Committee of the NPC), Explanations of the Supreme People's Court on Certain Issues concerning the Implementation of the Criminal Procedure Law (1998), Interpretation of the Supreme People's Court on Relevant Issues concerning Concrete Application of Laws in Handling Criminal Cases Committed by Units (1999), Provisions on Certain Issues Relating to Bails (1999), Supreme People's Court, Supreme People's Procuratorate, Ministry for Public Security, Ministry for State Security, Provisions on Standards for Filing and Investigation of Cases Directly Conducted by People's Procuratorates (1999), Supreme Procuratorate, and many other individual implementing rules. With practices like this, there is little to talk about certainty, clarity, universality, and stability of Chinese law.

13 Political and legal campaigning targeting specific 'crimes' has been a constant feature in both Mao and post-Mao China. During these campaigns, severe and quick 'justice' is often applied to the targets according to policy guidelines, as the Chinese law frequently leaves large scope for discretionary powers in the law for implementation and enforcement purposes.

14 For detailed discussion on the evolution of economic reform policies and the background in which the policy to establish a 'socialist market economy' emerged, see Chen (1995a:Ch.3 and pp. 280-6); Gao (1993:40); *People's Daily* (1992:1 and 3).

15 This debate is not new, it was one of the contentious issues extensively debated in the late 1970s in China. That debate, however, did not lead to any substantial consensus among scholars nor did it provide much guidance for legal development. More recently, the debate and discussions have resumed. Nevertheless, the phrase *Fazhi* (which literally means: legal system) began to be used in official documents

and by scholars fairly consistently, referring to efforts for establishing a legal system in China. See Keith (1994).

16 The Speech has not yet been formally published, but the main contents were published in *People's Daily* (*Renmin Ribao*), internet edition, 9 February 1996.

17 The text of the Ninth Five Year National Economic and Social Development Plan and the Outline of Goals by Year 2010 can be found in *Guangming Daily* (*Guangming Ribao*), 20 March 1996, p. 1.

18 This divorce of theories from reality has not passed totally unnoticed by some Chinese scholars. See e.g. Ma (1999:29).

19 For a discussion on the 1999 constitutional revision, see Chen (1999b).

20 Gu is the Chairman of the Legislative Affairs Committee of the Standing Committee of the NPC.

21 The rapid development of an administrative law system, including the recent adoption of the Law on Administrative Penalties (March 1996), and the recent comprehensive revision of the Criminal Procedure Law (March 1996) and the Criminal Law (March 1997) which now incorporates some fundamental 'due process' principles (such as the presumption of innocence) and abolishes certain controversial provisions (such as the counter-revolutionary crime provisions) carry a great potential to cause some fundamental changes in the Chinese legal system, for the protection of human rights, and for establishing a Rule of Law in China, if they are to be properly implemented. Also, the above-mentioned jurisprudential debates present unequivocal evidence of a strong rebellious flavour against authoritarianism and totalitarianism. For detailed studies on these aspects, see Chen (1997, 1999c, and 1999e.

22 For further detailed studies on inconsistent Chinese international behaviour, see Feinerman (1995). For the Chinese official attitude towards human rights and international human rights dialogue, see the White Paper issued by the Information Office of the Chinese State Council, *Human Rights Situation in China*, 1991. For a recent analysis by Amnesty International on China's human rights policies and legal aspects of the violation of human rights, see Amnesty International, *No One Is Safe*, AI Index ASA 17/01/96.

23 Li Peng made this insistence during his visit to Germany in July 1994. See 'Li Peng defends '89 crackdown,' *The Age*, 7 July 1994, p. 9. A similar statement was made by Jiang Zemin during his talk with Malaysian Prime Minister, Dr Mahathir, in Beijing in May 1994. See *People's Daily* (*Renmin Ribao*) (overseas edition), 13 May 1994, p. 1.

24 I have discussed, in detail, the relationship between theoretical efforts and legal development in Chen (1995a:Ch.7).

REFERENCES

Amnesty International, *No One Is Safe*, AI Index ASA 17/01/96.

Blaustein A.P. (ed.) (1962) *Fundamental Legal Documents of Communist China.* New Jersey: Fred B. Rothman and Co.

Brady, J.P. (1982) *Justice and Politics in People's China: Legal Order or Continuing Revolution?* London–New York: Academic Press.

Brugger, B. (1981a) *China: Liberation and Transformation 1942-1962.* London: Croom Helm.

– (1981b) *China: Radicalism to Revisionism 1962-1979.* London: Croom Helm.

Butler, W.E. (ed.) (1983) *The Legal System of the Chinese Soviet Republic 1931-1934.* New York: Transnational Publishers Inc.

Chen, J. (1995a) *From Administrative Authorisation to Private Law: A Comparative Perspective of the Developing Civil Law in the People's Republic of China.* Dordrecht–Boston–London: Martinus Nijhoff Publisher.

– (1995b) 'China: Constitutional Changes and Legal Development,' in: Alice E-S. Tay and Conita Leung (eds) *Greater China: Law, Society and Trade*. Sydney: Law Book Co.

– (1997) 'A Moderate Step in a Right Direction – The revision of the Criminal Procedure Law in the PRC,' *Journal of Chinese and Comparative Law* 3, p. 139.

– (1999a) *Chinese Law: Towards an Understanding of Chinese Law, Its Nature and Development.* The Hague–London–Boston: Kluwer Law International.

– (1999b) 'Conceptual Evolution of "Socialism with Chinese Characteristics" – The Revision of the Constitution in the PRC,' *China Perspectives* 24, p. 66.

– (1999c) 'Legalism with Chinese Characteristics – The Revision of the Criminal Law in the PRC,' *China Perspectives* 21, p. 5.

– (1999d) 'Market Economy and the Internationalisation of Civil and Commercial Law in the PRC,' in: Kanishka Jayasuriya (ed.) *Law and Legal Institutions in East Asia.* London: Routledge.

– (1999e) 'The Development and Conception of Administrative Law in the PRC,' *Law in Context* 10, p. 72.

Chen, S. (1988) 'A Review of Thirty Years of Legal Studies in New China,' *Journal of Chinese Law* 2, p. 181.

– (1994) 'Our Legislative Trend in the 1990s,' Guangming Daily (*Guangming Ribao*) 9 March 1994, p. 5.

China Law Society (1992) 'Further Emancipating Minds and Making Great Efforts for the Prosperity of Legal Science – A Discussion in

Commemorating the 10th Anniversary of the Re-establishment of the China Law Society,' Legal Science in China (*Zhongguo Faxue*) 4, p. 13.

Deng, X. (1984) 'Implement the Policy of Readjustment, Ensure Stability and Unity,' in: *Selected Works of Deng Xiaoping* (1975-82). Beijing: Foreign Languages Press.

Dong, B. (1986) A Collection of Works of Dong Biwu on Politics and Law (*Dong Biwu Zhengzhi Falü Wenji*). Beijing: Publishing House of Law.

Fang, L. (1992) 'The Company Examination and Approval System and Administrative Monopoly,' Legal Science in China (*Zhongguo Faxue*) 4, p. 56.

Fang, S. (1993) 'On Correcting Civil Legislation Deficiencies,' (no.1) Legal Science in China (*Zhongguo Faxue*) 1, p. 29.

Feinerman, J.V. (1995) 'Chinese Participation in the International Legal Order: Rogue Elephant or Team Player?' *The China Quarterly* 141, p. 186.

Foster, F.H. (1982) 'Codification in Post-Mao China,' *American Journal of Comparative Law* 30, p. 395.

Gan, Z. (1991) 'How to Secure the Legitimacy of Reform – From Reliance on Policy to Reliance on Law,' Studies in Law (*Faxue Yanjiu*) 6, p. 3.

Gao, L. (1993) 'The Emergence of the Notion of "Socialist Market Economy",' Xinhua Digest (*Xinhua Wenzhai*) 1, p. 40.

Gu, A. (1989) Socialist Legal System and Legislative Work (*Shehui Zhuyi Fazhi He Lifa Gongzuo*) Beijing: China University of Political Science and Law Press.

– (1999) 'Great Achievements in Socialist Legal System and Democracy,' a special collection in http://www.peopledaily.com.cn/electric/hh50/2/-2_0_0.html.

Guo, D. (1994) 'Market Economy and the Changes in Legal Theory and Legal Thought,' Jurisprudence (*Faxue*) 2, p. 2.

Hazard, J. (1975) 'The Abortive Codes of the Pashukanis School,' in: Donald D. Barry, F.J.M. Feldbrugge and Dominik Lasok (eds) *Codification in the Communist World*. Leiden: A.W. Sijthoff.

Human Rights Situation In China (1991) (a White Paper issued by the Information Office of the Chinese State Council).

Keith, R.C. (1994) *China's Struggle for the Rule of Law*. New York: St. Martin's Press.

Keller, P. (1989) 'Legislation in the People's Republic of China,' *U.B.C. Law Rev.* 23/3, p. 643.

Lan, Q. (1982) Thirty Years of Development of Law and Regulations in Our Country (*Sanshi Nian Lai Woguo Fagui Yange Gaikuang*) Beijing: Press of the Masses.

Law Department Of Beijing University (ed.) (1984) Basic Theories of Legal Science (*Faxue Jichu Lilun*) Beijing: Beijing University Press.

Leng, S. (1967) *Justice in Communist China: A Survey of the Judicial System of the Chinese People's Republic.* New York: Oceana Publications, Inc.

– (1977) 'The Role of Law in the People's Republic of China as Reflecting Mao Tse-tung's Influence,' *Journal of Criminal Law and Criminology* 68, p. 356.

Leng, S. and H. Chiu (1985) *Criminal Justice in Post-Mao China: Analysis and Documents.* Albany: State University of New York Press.

Li, F. (1997) 'Characteristics and Trends of Recent Law-making in China,' Jurisprudence Frontiers (*Faxue Qianyan*) 1, p. 182.

Li, J. (1992) 'On the Significance of and Current Barriers to the Making of a Civil Code,' Law Science (*Falü Kexue*) 5, p. 37.

Li, M. (1995) 'The Legal Controversy Concerning the Separation of Public and Private Law,' Seeking Truth (*Qiushi*) 22, p. 44.

Liang, H. (1992) 'To Make a Perfect and Modern Civil Code,' in 'Further Emancipating Minds and Making Great Efforts for the Prosperity of Legal Research – A Discussion on Deng Xiaoping's Talk during His Southern Tour,' Studies in Law (*Faxue Yanjiu*) 5, p. 5.

Lin, C. (1997) 'The Development of Democracy Must Be Closely Linked with the Improvement of Legal System,' People's Daily (*Renmin Ribao*) Internet Edition, 18 October 1997.

Lin, F. (1999) 'The Meaning of "Rule of Law",' Legal Daily (*Fazhi Ribao*) internet edition, 16 September 1999.

Lin, J. (1994) 'A Question on the Proposition "Market Economy Is an Economy Under the Rule of Law",' Legal Science in China (*Zhongguo Faxue*) 1, p. 68.

Liu, H. *et al.* (eds) (1996) To Rule the Country by Law and to Establish a Socialist Country Ruled by Law (*Yifa Zhiguo Jianshe Shehui Zhuyi Fazhi Guojia*) Beijing: Press of Chinese Legal System.

Liu, J. (1995) 'Globalisation: An Historical Process Full of Paradoxes,' Pacific Studies (*Taipingyan Xuebao*) 1, p. 70.

Liu, S. and Q. Wu (1986) (eds) *China's Socialist Economy: An Outline History (1949-1982)* Beijing: Beijing Review Press.

Liu, S. *et al.* (1993) 'Market Economy and Changes in Legal Ideologies,' Legal Science in China (*Zhongguo Faxue*) 4, p. 3.

Liu, S. (1985) 'The Political Report of the Central Committee of the CPC to the Eighth National Congress of the Party,' in: Selected Works of Liu Shaoqi (*Liu Shaoqi Xuanji*) II, Beijing: People's Press.

Lu, Y. (1994) 'The Transformation of Legal Models: A Deep Revolutionary Change,' Legal Science in China (*Zhongguo Faxue*) 1, p. 27.

Ma, X. (1999) 'An Historical Investigation into and Some Thought on the Notion of Rule of Law,' CASS Journal of Law (*Faxue Yanjiu*) 2, p. 22.

Mao Z. (1986) Selected Readings of Mao Zedong's Works (*Mao Zedong Zhuzuo Xuandu*) vol. 2, Beijing: People's Press.

Min, X. (1994) 'Socialist Market Economy Is Naturally an Economy Under the Rule of Law,' (Special Issue) Journal of Shandong Normal University (*Shandong Shifan Daxuebao*), p. 93.

Peng, Z. (1984) 'Several Issues Concerning Socialist Legality,' in Selected Materials on Introduction to Law (*Faxue Gailun Ziliao Xuanbian*) Beijing: Publishing House of Law.

People's Daily (1992) 'Great Practice, Bright Chapter – the Birth of the Political Report of the 14th Congress of the Party,' People's Daily (*Renmin Ribao*) (overseas edition) 24 October 1992, pp. 1 and 3.

-(1997) 'To Greatly Push the Process of Ruling a Country by Law,' People's Daily (*Renmin Ribao*) Editorial, Internet Edition, 17 October 1997.

– (1999)'Fifty Glorious Years: Law-Making,' People's Daily (*Renmin Ribao*) internet edition, special collection.

Political Report (1992) 'Accelerating the Reform, the Opening to the Outside World and the Drive for Modernisation, so as to Achieve Great Successes in Building Socialism with Chinese Characteristics,' a Political Report delivered by Jiang Zemin to the 14th Congress of the CPC, in People's Daily (*Renmin Ribao*) (overseas edition) 21 October 1992, pp. 1-3.

– (1997) 'Holding High the Great Banner of Deng Xiaoping's Theory for an All-round Advancement of the Cause of Building Socialism with Chinese Characteristics to the 21st Century,' a Political Report delivered by Jiang Zemin at the 15th National Congress of the Communist Party of China on 12 September 1997. A Chinese version of the Report can be found in People's Daily (*Renmin Ribao*) Internet Edition, 25 September 1997; an English version of the Report can be found in China Daily, Internet Edition, 10 October 1997.

Project Group (Law Institute, Chinese Academy Of Social Sciences) (1993) 'Some Theoretical Considerations and Practical Suggestions Regarding the Establishment of a Legal System for a Socialist Market Economy,' Studies in Law (*Faxue Yanjiu*) 6, p. 3.

Qiao, S. (1994) 'Speech at the 2nd Session of the 8th NPC, delivered by Qiao Shi on 22 March 1994,' Economic Daily (*Jingji Ribao*) 23 March 1994, p. 1.

Qiao, X. (1997) 'To Make a Law on Law-making and to Promote Rule by Law,' Journal of Administrative Law (*Xingzhengfa Yanjiu*) 3, p. 1.

Seidman, A. and R. Seidman (1994) *State and Law in the Development Process: Problem-Solving and Institutional Change in the Third World.* New York: St. Martin's Press.

– (1996) 'Drafting Legislation for Development: Lessons from a Chinese Project,' *American Journal of Comparative Law* 44/1, p. 14.

Sun, G. and W. Huang (1998) 'On Socialist Principle of Ruling the Country by Law,' Legal Science in China (*Zhongguo Faxue*) 6, p. 10.

Sun, G. and B. Zeng (1996) 'On the Definition of Law by Vyshinsky,' Jurists (*Faxue Jia*) 2, p. 38.

Tay, A. E-S. (1969) 'Law in Communist China – Part I,' *Sydney Law Review* 6, p. 153.

– (1973-6) 'Law in Communist China – Part II,' *Sydney Law Review* 6, p. 335.

– (1976) '"Smashing Permanent Rules": China as a Model for the Future,' *Sydney Law Review* 6, p. 335.

Tian J. (1999) 'Explanation on the Constitutional Amendment Bill,' People's Daily (*Renmin Ribao*) internet edition, 9 March 1999.

Wang, C. and W. Liu (1993) 'Market Economy and the Separation of Public and Private Law,' Legal Science in China (*Zhongguo Faxue*) 4, p. 28.

Wang, J. *et al.* (1996) 'On the Rule of Law,' Studies in Law (*Faxue Yanjiu*) 2, p. 3.

Wen, Z. (1995) 'Some Legal and Philosophical Thoughts on Market Economy,' Legal System and Social Development (*Fazhi Yu Shehui Fazhang*) 4, p. 1.

Wu, D. and Z. Shen (1987) A Basic Theory of Chinese Socialist Legal Science (*Zhongguo Shehui Zhuyi Falü Jiben Lilun*) Beijing: Publishing House of Law.

Wu, J. (1983) 'Building New China's Legal System,' *Colum.J.Transnat'l.L.* 22, p. 1.

Xiao, Y. (1994) *Market Economy and Legal Construction.* Beijing: Publishing House of Law.

Xie, G. (1994) 'Market Economy and the Separation of Public and Private Law,' Studies in Finance (*Caimao Yanjiu*) 1, p. 62.

Xie, H. (1993) 'On Establishing a Civil-Economic Law System Appropriate to the Needs of Socialist Market Economy,' Studies in Law (*Faxue Yanjiu*) 1, p. 12.

– (1994a) 'An Analysis and Comment on Legal Instrumentalism,' Legal Science in China (*Zhongguo Faxue*) 1, p. 50.

– (1994b) 'From a Planned Economy to a Market Economy: A Revolution in Legal Theory,' Gansu Journal of Theoretical Research (*Gansu Lilun Xuekang*) 4, p. 53.

Xinghua Digest (1991) 'Jurisprudential Debate on the Relationship Between Rights and Duties,' Xinhua Digest (*Xinhua Wenzhai*) 4, p. 16.

Xue, J. and J. Wang (1997) 'Towards Ruling the Country by Law,' People's Daily (*Renmin Ribao*) Internet Edition, November 1, 1997.

Yang, Z. (1995) 'The Central Point for Chinese Legal Reform is the Civil Law,' Journal of China University of Political Science and Law (*Zhangfa Luntan*) 1, p. 48.

Yu, X. (1989) 'Legal Pragmatism in the People's Republic of China,' *Journal of Chinese Law* 3, p. 29.

Zhang, J. (1994) 'Market System and Private Law in China,' Journal of China University of Political Science and Law (*Zhangfa Luntan*) 6, p. 34.

Zhang, W. (1993) 'Three Points on Market Economy and Legal Construction,' Legal Science in China (*Zhongguo Faxue*) 3, p. 12.

– (1995) 'Market-oriented Economy and the Spirit of Modern Law,' a paper presented to the 1995 International Sociological Association Conference, Tokyo, 1-4 August 1995.

Zhang, Y. (1984) 'On Strengthening the Socialist Legal System,' (no. 6, 1981) Social Sciences in China (*Zhongguo Shehui Kexue*) reprinted in: A Collection of Articles on Chinese Legal Science (*Zhongguo Faxue Wenji*) Beijing: Press of the Masses.

Zhang, Y. and S. Wang (eds) (1989) Forty Years of the PRC's Legal Science (*Zhongguo Faxue Sishi Nian*) Shanghai: Shanghai People's Publishing House (1989).

Zhao, S. (1994) 'On Rule of Law in Market Economy,' Economic Daily (*Jingji Ribao*) 2 May 1994, 5.

Zhao, X, AND GUO X. (1998) 'An Outline of the Principle of the Rule of Law,' Law Review (*Faxue Pinglun*) 4, p. 20.

Zhao, Z. (ed.) (1990) Forty Years of the Chinese Legal System (*Zhongguo Fazhi Jianshinian*) Beijing: Beijing University Press.

Zhou, Y. (1993) 'Market Economy Demands Equality in Legislation,' Legal Science in China (*Zhongguo Faxue*) 4, p. 16.

CHAPTER 10

THE CLONABILITY OF THE SINGAPORE MODEL OF LAW AND DEVELOPMENT: THE CASE OF SUZHOU, CHINA*

CONNIE CARTER

The re-emergence of the 1960s' Law and Development movement (LAD) in the 1980s accelerated after the demise of Soviet communism and the end of the Cold War. However, as discussed elsewhere (Carter, 2000) this rebirth is more than a reworking of the old American paradigm, which was abandoned – at least in part – in the early 1970s after it suffered criticisms for being ethnocentric, naïve, and imperialistic (Trubek and Galanter, 1972; Merryman, 1977). In its 1990s' guise, and in the model set for notoriety in the twenty-first century, the movement has metamorphosed into an instrument wielded by supra-national institutions,[1] regional aid agencies such as the Asian Development Bank, various non-governmental organizations (NGOs),[2] and individual countries seeking to enhance their trade preference or leverage in emerging economies. One such country is Singapore. Indeed, Singapore's entry into this field is, in itself, evidence of a departure from the 1960s' model, which was a purely north-south dialogue between the US and west European countries on one side and newly decolonized nations in Africa, Asia, the Caribbean, and Latin America, on the other. As a successful late-industrialized country, Singapore's rapid economic development during the past four decades can be said to have benefited from aspects of the first LAD movement, while in the 'new' movement Singapore is a facilitator rather than a recipient. Thus the experience analysed in this chapter is probably one of the first examples of a professional south-south dialogue in law and economic development.

This chapter explores aspects of the economic development programme, which the Singapore government, at the invitation of the Chinese government, sought to introduce into a small, clearly defined geographic area of China: the China–Singapore Industrial Park in Suzhou. It argues that legal transplants or Singapore 'software' and 'technical assistance' seem to be resulting in the emergence of a new species of local administrative and regulatory legal measures within the Chinese national legal system. In the pragmatic day-to-day hubbub of life in the Suzhou Industrial Park, this sub-system of laws seems to be taking on a life of its own although none of the measures purport to establish a legal regime which is separate or distinct from China's national legal system. However, it is clear that the Singapore model of law and development is neither the same as its western 1960s' predecessor nor the reborn, post-Cold War, 1990s' version.[3] This chapter first characterizes the nature of the Singapore model of law and development. It argues that far from converging with laws of the west and becoming a replica of western law, the Singapore model has diverged from its western roots into a more holistic and communitarian version in response to local political, economic, and developmental imperatives. The nature of Singapore law may also be described as 'westernistic' and syncretistic.[4] First, because it seeks to give an appearance of a western form in order to assuage the possible apprehension of foreign investors. Secondly, because it borrows from far and wide, combining the characteristics and practices of differing legal systems to form its own. The chapter then explores aspects of the 'transfer' that seems to be taking place in Suzhou and concludes by speculating on whether the Suzhou experience is evidence of the replicability of the Singapore model of law and economic development.

SINGAPORE'S MODERN SYNCRETISTIC LEGAL CULTURE

The roots of Singapore's legal culture are planted firmly in the tradition of the English Common Law. For when Stamford Raffles (later 'Sir') alighted there in 1819, he transported with him, as his birthright, all the laws of England. This custom, entrenched in the Common Law (e.g. *Cooper v Stuart* (1889) 14 AC 286), was further supported by colonial legislation, a sophisticated English court system and administration, which ensured formal reception (Bartholomew, 1985:3-24). However, the English law which took root in Singapore was not necessarily Lord Ellenborough's 'law of liberty,' of respect for the dignity of the individual, her entitlement to life, liberty, and property. Arguably what had taken root was a particular species of English law designed *primarily* to facilitate the smooth running of a profitable colonial regime. Law became a set of rules and practices that underpinned the predominantly economic goals of the colonial state.

The development of this variant of English law accelerated and was transformed into a development tool after Singapore won self-rule in 1959 and particularly after independence in 1965 following Singapore's expulsion from the Malaysian Federation. Indeed the failure of the Federation was the catalyst that created modern Singapore, for it dictated the potent strategy to 'go it alone' and fight for economic survival at any cost. From 1965, the development of law in Singapore was determined by the decision of Singapore's leaders, led by Lee Kuan Yew, to embrace a pragmatic ideology, which prioritized economic development and nation-building as their sole strategic focus. All government policies and actions were harnessed towards achieving these goals.

Acknowledging its vulnerability as a small nation lacking in profitable natural resources, except for its large natural harbour, its geographic location at the crossroads of Asia and the industriousness of its predominantly Chinese but multiracial population, the Singapore government opted for export-oriented foreign investment as its ticket to economic development. It was a courageous decision at a time when just about every newly independent nation sought to free itself as much as possible from the perceived greed and tyranny of foreign actors. To implement this policy the government set out to nurture a degree of social discipline, socio-cultural, political, and racial cohesion, and work ethic among its multiracial population, which it considered would be conducive to making the nation an attractive manufacturing paradise for foreign investors. Consequently, from a conceptual point of view, both Singapore's colonial and post-colonial experiences coincide with Damaska's proposition that the nature of a state's ideology and its political organization plays a crucial role in shaping the development of its legal institutions (Damaska, 1986). In both the colonial and the post-colonial states, economic success was the all-consuming, if not the sole objective. Economic prosperity was the state's *raison d'être*. Indeed during the 1980s, and perhaps earlier, Singapore technocrats began to refer to the venture as 'Singapore Inc.'

Singapore's experience of law and economic development therefore also mirrors relationships that Oakeshott (1975) recognized in the distinction between rules in *civic* societies and those in *enterprise* associations. According to Oakeshott, the rules of a civic association derive their authority from the association itself and not from any goal outside of the association or their use to create desirable outcomes. In contrast, the rules of an enterprise association [such as Singapore Inc.] gain their validity not from the association itself but from its goals or purposes [self-reliance and economic prosperity]. Since the government defined economic success as the only option for Singapore, this enterprise association also gave rise to and provided legitimacy for the rules which were necessary for achieving this goal.

Economic Development and Singapore Law

Singapore is probably the best example of a successful, modern, growth-oriented, interventionist, capitalist state (World Bank, 1993, 1996, 1997). In terms of economic prosperity and quality of life, Singapore remains among the top rank of developed societies irrespective of which measuring tool is employed. For instance, in 1995, per capita GNP was US$24,800 against

US$18,700 for the UK, Singapore's past colonial masters. Scores for life expectancy, infant mortality, persons per physician, literacy rate, and so on are equally impressive (see Statistics Singapore: www.singstat.gov.sg). All these have been achieved within three to four decades of independence. Naturally, the regional economic setback from 1997 to 1999 took its toll. But true to form, the government took radical steps to minimize the effects of contagion.[5]

Economists, development theorists, and others vie to posit theories that might explain 'the economic miracle'. An apt summary might be that, right from the start and consistently for the four decades of its life so far, the Singapore government[6] resolutely promoted economic development through an eclectic mix of:

- Providing selected free market access;
- Establishing and maintaining efficient infrastructure;
- Orchestrating and investing in key export-led sectors of the economy;
- Disciplining and educating the workforce; and
- Creating an ideology and delivering social justice and tangible benefits that secure the acquiescence of the people to the activities of the state and its elite group of bureaucrats.[7]

The scenario that has unfolded during the decades is an example of what Wade (1990) called 'governing the market,' although Singapore, which he dismissed as a minnow state, was not included in his study. 'Law,' as mature government policies, seems to have been the facilitator, the glue that bound these disparate elements together and helped supply the discipline for sustainable growth (Carter, 2000). Legislation, both primary and an abundance of secondary or subsidiary rules, was the main vehicle. It is therefore apt to refer to Singapore's law as administrative in nature (Thynne, 1990). However, it is more than that. For at the core of the emerging species of developmental law one finds the government's determination to shape the lives and behaviour of the people so that they conform to the larger goals of the community as a whole rather than to individual whims and private privilege. During the years, law was used to nurture, build, and coerce a communitarian ideology in which individuals as well as associations (like labour unions) were urged to sacrifice individual rights in the name of the public interest. Among the areas of law that clearly demonstrate this philosophy are those that regulate labour and industrial relations, land and housing, education and industry-specific skills training, investor incentives and so on. Legal regulation was deemed necessary even in areas that many westerners would regard as private, sacrosanct, or petty. Indeed, nothing that the PAP government perceived as a mischief – however small – was left unregulated: from adverse comment by NGOs, lawyers, church leaders or foreign journalists (Maintenance of Harmony Act, No 26 of 1990, ss8-19; Internal Security Act, cap 143, 1985 rev ed., ss8-19; Newspaper and Printing Presses (Amendment) Act, No 22 of 1986) to having too many children, but later for having too few (failure of the educated elite to perpetuate their genes); failure of career women to marry and settle down; smoking in public; drug-trafficking; firearms possession; secret societies; silent defendants; traffic jams in the city; crooked lawyers; traditional Malay villages (*kampong*); official and corporate corruption; litter; chewing gum; graffiti; failure to look after one's parents; and even unflushed public toilets (Harding, 1996). Harding calls these 'smart laws' by which he seems to mean laws which are designed to produce not just in general, but rather precisely, the *exact result* desired by their creators.

But precision is a characteristic of Singapore's social engineering and other regulatory laws, even though some are drafted widely to enable discretion in interpretation. Overall, many of them have succeeded in providing highly desirable consequences. For instance, the virtual abolition of corruption, the provision of affordable, universal public housing, health care and education, the reduction of environmental pollution, high levels of savings, disciplined labour relations, and social and political stability. The latter were considered necessary to attract and retain foreign investors, which help maintain the island-state's economic prosperity. The former were vehicles for providing a more equal distribution of the rapidly accumulating national wealth. However, as Harding argues (ibid) these benefits might have been achieved at the expense of freedom of speech, judicial passivism, individual civil liberties, and true democracy.

It is, however, noteworthy that when asked what kind of government they have, many Singaporeans unhesitatingly reply 'democracy'. This is factually correct as it reflects the existence and practice of the procedures of free, regular elections, unencumbered by vote buying or fraud, and a Westminster-style parliament. Besides, although statutes may limit some individual rights, there is, in general, due process of law, equality of opportunity and social justice. Nevertheless, viewed through western eyes, Singapore's legal and political systems with their emphases on law and order, communitarianism, corporatism, and conformity are more authoritarian and instrumentalist than the establishment would find acceptable. Ironically, these are likely to be the very qualities that attracted the admiration of Deng Xiaoping, China's supreme leader from 1976 to 1997, and paved the way for the government-government joint venture in Suzhou.

THE CHINA–SINGAPORE SUZHOU EXPERIMENT

During his famous south China tour in 1992, Deng Xiaoping had openly praised Singapore's 'good social order' and its management style. He seems to have considered Singapore's model for rapid economic development more disciplined and thus superior to the extreme, laissez faire free-for-all adopted from Hong Kong by the early 1980s' special economic zones (SEZs) in nearby Guangdong and Fujian provinces. In the spirit of 'crossing the river by feeling for stones under foot,' Deng urged yet another experiment, this time the Singapore model. The undisclosed bilateral economic development agreement, which was signed by Deng Xiaoping and Singapore's senior minister, Lee Kuan Yew in February 1994, suited Deng's wish for rapid, vigorous but more disciplined economic growth as well as Singapore's ambitious regionalization policy. China was a natural candidate in this deliberate push to go beyond the Malaysia-Indonesia-Singapore triangle.

Suzhou is an ancient imperial city in Jiangsu province, lying in the Yangtse Delta some 80 km west of Shanghai along the rail line to Nanjing. The China–Singapore Suzhou Industrial Park is located a few kilometres west of the old city of Suzhou. The Park comprises a gross development area of 144 square km^2, with a projected core business and residential area of 70 km^2 (against 178 km^2 for the old city). The express intention of the joint venture partners was to build a modern industrial 70 km^2 town capable of supporting a population of 600,000 and one that essentially would replicate Jurong, Singapore's 1980s model town. If successful, the model could then be cloned in suitable areas of the mainland's inner provinces, acting as 'stones' for crossing the river from command to capitalist economy.

The accessible project descriptions[8] do not refer explicitly to the Suzhou experiment as an exercise in legal transplantation. Nevertheless joint documents continually refer to the transfer of Singapore 'software' and 'technical assistance' in contexts that leave one in no doubt that the successful implementation of a 'Jurong-clone' involves the borrowing of well-tried, enabling statutory laws, rules, procedures and regulations.

China's Eclectic Experimental Legal Culture

Following Deng's unprecedented announcement of a comprehensive economic reform programme in 1978, the so-called 'Open-door Policy,' China enacted a raft of laws which aimed to stabilize society and initiate the development of a socialist market economy based predominantly on foreign trade and investment. These laws also signalled the re-establishment of China's legal institutions after their forced absence during the decade of chaos, the Cultural Revolution, which lasted from 1966-76 (Gellhorn, 1987; Dicks, 1989). The new laws borrowed heavily from western jurisprudence as well as from earlier Chinese laws. For instance, the 1979 Criminal Law, the Criminal Procedure Law and laws for reorganizing the People's Courts and the People's Procuracies drew heavily on 1950s Chinese laws, which in turn were based on Kuomintang laws. The latter had been inspired by Soviet laws, which were borrowed from European codes, particularly German Civil law. Commercial laws, such as the 1981 Economic Contract Law, laws for protecting trademarks, the environment, joint ventures, and the 1986 General Principles of Civil Law were inspired by both European and North American laws. Thus civil as well as common-law influences were combined to form a new species of Chinese domestic law.

The enactment of these and later laws, especially during the late 1980s, marked the beginning of China's transformation from a strict command economy to a mixed market economy, albeit with Chinese characteristics. Right from the start China's leaders rejected the neo-classical Big Bang approach to economic development, which was touted by economists such as Sachs (1993:44-8). Instead China's leaders chose an incremental, some would say a trial-and-error approach, in which law was used as a step-by-step restructuring of institutions designed to underpin the move from command to market economy. Thus far, the results contrast starkly with the Russian scenario, which has suffered greatly from the chosen Big Bang shock method (Nolan, 1995). The Sino–Singapore experiment in Suzhou is an example of the implementation of an incremental approach to economic development. The sections below describe the experiment's political and administrative platform, before analysing key aspects of the implementation of Singapore software and technical assistance in the Park.

Political and Administrative Platform

At the basis of the support and administrative structure of the government-to-government project is a holding company, China–Singapore Suzhou Development (CSSD), which was incorporated at the project's inception. Shares were held in the ratio of 35 per cent–to–65 per cent by two companies, China–Suzhou Industrial Park Corporation (CSIPC) and Singapore–Suzhou Trade and Development (SSTD), each representing the China and Singapore authorities, respectively.

The Suzhou Industrial Park Administrative Committee (SIPAC) is the project's governing body. The Major of Suzhou City heads this body. Members of SIPAC include representatives of Singapore's Economic Development Board (EDB), which has a special office at the Suzhou Centre, and the Singapore Software Project Office. A Joint Working Committee, in which the EDB chairman and the Suzhou Mayor also sit, supports this

governing body. Finally, there is a Joint Steering Council comprising representatives from ministries of both governments, headed by Chinese Vice-president Mr Li Langing and Singaporean Deputy PM Lee.
The main areas covered by the bilateral agreement include:

- Land use planning and development;
- Environmental planning and regulation;
- Building construction management;
- Planning and management of industrial estates;
- Management of new towns and public utilities;
- Labour management; and
- Social security.

According to Singapore's Economic Development Board (1995:np)[9] the bilateral agreement 'involves a "software transfer" co-operation project between the two countries'. Furthermore (ibid),

> software transfer refers to the sharing of Singapore's successful public administration and economic management experiences ... so that [the Chinese] authorities can formulate and implement pro-business policies in the China–Singapore Suzhou Industrial Park.

To assist in this transfer, a Singapore Software Project Office (SSPO) under the jurisdiction of Singapore's EDB has been established in the Park. Together, the Park's governing body SIPAC and SSPO identify the relevant type of 'software' which is to be shared. Both agencies decide on how the software designated for transfer is to be adapted. Adaptation is effected mainly through visits and training projects in which Suzhou and the Park's officials are taught the procedures in Singapore. The Singapore government also sends officials to Suzhou to assist in this adaptation process. SSPO is itself staffed mainly by Singaporeans and is supervised by the EDB's established office in Suzhou. The responsibility for drafting and redrafting the transferred software is shared by SSPO, under the guidance of SIPAC and the Singapore EDB.

SIPAC has established special departments or bureaux, which are responsible for project approval, administration, implementation and control. The eight main bureaux comprise Economic and Trade Development, Planning and Construction, Finance Taxation, Social Development, Local Development, Organisation and Personnel, Secretariat and Foreign Affairs, and a controlling Council for Economic and Social Development.

Facing the Legal Challenges in Suzhou, China

The legal challenges facing the Park, and indeed the rest of China, can be summarized by the complaints expressed by foreign investors.[10] The majority of these reflect the state and nature of laws in China. The most frequent complaints are that Chinese laws are often either incomplete or secret (*neibu*), that they lack transparency, they are often vague and ambiguous, and there are uncertainties and inconsistencies between substantive provincial and national laws and their interpretation. Furthermore, inconsistencies and uncertainty are increased by the wide discretion given to administrative agencies, and the traditional Chinese practice of *guanxi* or favouring of personal connections. The result is a larger than usual opportunity for and practice of corruption, graft, confusion, bureaucratic red tape, lack of predictability in decision-making and interference in corporate management autonomy. These are the ills which the Singapore 'transfer' and home-grown experiences are meant to cure in the Park. In addition, the Singaporeans are responsible for creating and improving overall infrastructure, including human resources, and for packaging and marketing the Park so that it attracts investment of US$20 billion, within 10–15 years.

So far the Singapore magic seems to be working. After five years, the Park has attracted in excess of US$3.76 billion invested by 133 projects (*Straits Times,* 29 June 1999:1). About 8 km^2 have been built and occupied. American corporations dominate (39 per cent of the total), followed by 12 per cent Singaporean and 10 per cent from Europe (EDB, 1999). The electronics industry is represented by the largest share of investments (36 per cent) followed by chemicals (23 per cent) and food and beverages (20 per cent). Furthermore, unscientifically conducted interviews with foreign investors in the Park reveal that Singapore's EDB has managed to simplify application procedures for project implementation so that they are on a par with those in Singapore: a one-stop shop is able to process business licenses in one month. This includes the usually onerous environment impact assessments and site location stipulations. The reason for the ease and speed is that written environmental guidelines incorporate a self-assessment regime adapted from Singapore, and site location is regulated through an agreed master plan, that is, 'zoning' rather than the whim of bribable administrators. Customs can be cleared in Suzhou instead of at the Shanghai port. And happily, all administrative fees are published. They have also been reduced from over 300 to only 27 items! The rules about how, when, and why fees are levied have also been published.

Social security reform has also been modernized and made transparent by adopting a scheme that is similar to Singapore's Central Provident Fund. The introduction of this compulsory savings element into the wage package seems to benefit both employees and employers in the Park. At the time of writing it seems to be unique to Suzhou and is not practised elsewhere in China. Like all the other 'software transfers,' laws or rules were required to implement and legitimize them.

But laws in China are a complex affair, and the law-making process even more so (Seidman *et al.*, 1997; Chen, 1999). First, most laws in China are categorized as administrative law. They are designed to serve many purposes, among them to regulate behaviour, promote economic modernization, and preserve the one-party political system. Special commercial laws, which are adapted from the West, are called economic laws. They form a sub-set of administrative law. Foreign investment laws are a sub-set of economic law. Secondly, in theory, the sole source of national administrative law is legislation passed by the Standing Committee of the National People's Congress (NPC). However, in practice, other legal bureaucracies such as the State Council's Legal Affairs Bureau, the NPC's Legislative Work Committee, the Ministry of Justice, and law departments in various State Council ministries and commissions also have legislative powers. In turn, they are all dominated by the Party's political-legal committee system (*zhengfa xitong*). During the first thirty years of the People's Republic of China (PRC), the NPC acted mainly as a rubber stamp, which gave legislative form to Communist Party policy directives (Potter, 1999:675). In line with Deng's modernization policy, the NPC's legislative duties were extended by the 1982 Constitution to include the enactment of basic national statutes, amendments to the Constitution and review of decisions made by the State Council and the NPC's Standing Committee. The powers of the latter were also expanded to include supervision of the State Council's work as well as supervision of other administrative bodies. But the crux, as far as the Singapore-China Suzhou experiment is concerned, is that the State Council and the NPC's Standing Committee also are empowered to *delegate* administrative law-making powers to local, regional bodies either in an 'authorized administrative law-making capacity' (*shonquan xingzheng lifa*) or an 'entrusted administrative law-making capacity' (*weituo xingzheng lifa*).

Thus the Park's governing body, SIPAC, received, from the State Council, powers to create rights and obligations and other legal norms that have never been touched by state organs. The only limitation seems to be that these rules and regulations must not infringe 'the spirit of national applicable law and the Constitution,' and they must be reported to the authorizing body (the State Council). In addition, the Constitution confers inherent legislative power (*zhiquan lifa*) on regional entities, which must comply with similar conditions about not infringing the spirit of national law.

Consequently, the rules and regulations that relate to administrative matters in the Park, whether locally formed or adapted from Singaporean 'software transfer,' are recognized as 'law' in their own right as long as they do not infringe the spirit of China's national laws or the Constitution. In considering the content and nature of these rules and regulations, the imprint of Singapore's developmental law is evident. One of the most obvious cases is the Central Provident Fund Act (cap 36, 1997 ed.) which governs social security and aspects of labour relations. But other areas such as environmental protection, town planning, and personnel skills training also reveal 'software transfer'. In general, these regulations are more narrowly drafted than their Chinese counterparts, which are usually very broadly drafted and intentionally ambiguous to allow flexibility, discretion and weak implementation. The Singapore 'software'-inspired regulations reflect greater clarity and precision. They are less ambiguous and aim to achieve precisely defined economic goals, as desired by their creators. They exhibit the communitarian, syncretistic, and westernistic characteristics of Singapore law as discussed above. They are also the kind of rules that are limited by a general ambivalence towards the full liberal norms of western economic law that protect individual property rights and the restraint on state power which inform true western law – or the rule of law. However, there is sufficient 'transfer' to ensure that western investors, especially American investors, feel comfortable about their investment commitments, despite the obvious gaps and instrumentality of law. This interpretation of the nature of modern Chinese law is underpinned by a 1999 amendment to the Chinese Constitution. According to Potter (1999:674) to denote the concept 'rule of law' the amendment incorporated the Chinese characters that express the term '*yifa zhiguo*'. The phrase actually denotes 'rule *through* law' whereas scholars prefer the characters that express '*fazhi grojia*' to convey the 'rule of law' ideals. However, even the term '*yifa zhiguo*' is met with resistance in many circles because it implies the potential autonomy of law and subservience of the state to law.

As is also the case in Singapore, the version of the rule of law that the local Chinese authorities prefer does not extend to making law exert limiting powers on the state. Rather, law, as Singapore has shown, is used to entrench the powers of the state. It seems more apt to call this version 'rule *by* law'.

REPLICABILITY OF THE SINGAPORE MODEL

It is clear from the foregoing that the Suzhou project has enjoyed a great degree of success. It has provided the right infrastructure and conditions that have attracted foreign investments in excess of US$3.76 billion. But all is not well in Suzhou. In June 1999, it was announced that:

> the Singapore Government will hand over control of the Suzhou Industrial Park (SIP) project to the Chinese government in eighteen months' time ... Singapore will cut its stake in the massive project to 35 per cent from 65 per cent and hand over the management of the park on Jan 1, 2001 (*Straits Times*, 29 June 1999:1).

The explanation that has been given involves Singapore's displeasure with the fact that the Suzhou municipal government got involved in the development of a rival park nearby, the Suzhou New District *The Economist*, 3 January 1998:55.).

But other issues may also have played a role. For instance, the political climate might have changed after the introduction of the new Chinese administration under Jiang Zemin following Deng's death in 1997. Even more significantly for this study, changes in China's national laws might have affected the project. For example, the 1997 Administrative Supervision Law authorized the amendment or repeal of regulations that were deemed inconsistent with laws and regulations issued at higher levels. Could any of the transferred software have fallen into this category? Also, the Administrative Procedure Law enacted in 1998 allows for the challenging of bureaucratic rule-making, just as the earlier Administrative Litigation Law 1991 provided for judicial review of administrative decisions. At the time of writing, a Legislative Law remains in the drafting stage, as its progress has been thwarted by bureaucratic conflicts concerning rule-making authority in China (Potter, 1999:677). Thus the potential curtailment of the ability to 'transfer' and implement 'software' freely might have played a role in the joint venture's partial failure, or at least the variation of the contract. This is pure speculation as there are no published facts. However, it is hoped that the authorities of both China and Singapore will co-operate and allow legal and economic analyses of the entire experiment at a later date. Useful lessons can be learnt by both parties as well by as others seeking to engage in south-south dialogue.

CONCLUSION

At the outset, it would appear that Singapore's model of law and economic development suited well the aspirations of China's supreme ruler Deng Xiaoping in the early 1990s. The model followed a soft authoritarian approach, 'governing the market' with a brand of legal instrumentalism, which was dedicated to the primacy of state power, an incremental approach to economic growth, low or no corruption, and social justice in which the fruits of the rapidly accumulating national wealth would be shared equitably among the wealth-creators.

The joint venture between China and Singapore required Singapore to transfer 'software and technical assistance,' which would enable Suzhou Industrial Park to attract foreign investment and transform it into a Jurong-clone. As discussed in the foregoing, 'software and technical assistance' are euphemisms for key elements of the special brand of regulatory laws and rules, which comprise the Singapore model for law and economic development. The study finds that some of these were transferred successfully. The reasons for Singapore's premature variation of the contract and the apparent failure of the idea of the Park are unknown. Officially, the reason seems to rest on unclear objectives regarding competing interests in Suzhou municipality. However, other reasons might also have played a part, including changes in the political climate, new national laws restricting local law-making processes, and the difficulties of 'two systems not being able to completely mesh with each other' (Lee Kuan Yew, *Straits Times*, Overseas Edition, 2 October 1999:24). According to Lee (ibid) the Singapore government 'will continue to train Chinese officials on software in Singapore for as long as Suzhou deems it useful'. As the governments have agreed to terminate the experiment in mid-flow, it is premature to say with certainty that the Suzhou experience is evidence of the replicability of the Singapore model of law and economic development. Even though, at the time of writing, the 8 km^2 of fully functioning industrial park work unmistakably as if they were located in Singapore. It is therefore hoped that both governments will allow academic researchers to uncover freely the lessons that might be learnt from their experience for the benefit of both parties and of others seeking to engage in south-south economic development dialogues.

NOTES

* I am grateful to Dr Andrew Harding, Professor of Law in the University of London and Head of the Law Department at the School of Oriental and African Studies (SOAS), who commented on this chapter and gave unstintingly of his time and enormous regional knowledge.

1 For instance, the western-dominated financial aid agencies like the IMF and World Bank, and also the United Nations Development Programme (UNDP).

2 NGOs such as the Ford Foundation, the American Bar Association, and the Asia Foundation.

3 For information about the 1960s-70s Law and Development movement, including discussions of the 1970s-80s issue about an international right to development, see A. Carty (ed.) (1992), S. Adelman and A. Paliwala (eds) (1993). For a discussion of the role of law in Asian economic development (selected countries not including Singapore), see K. Pistor and P. Wellons (1999). As yet, there seems to be no anthology of the 1990s' movement. In comparison with the 1960s' movement, the agenda of the 1990s' movement is more explicitly the transplant of the rule of law and democracy (sometimes called 'good governance'). These are often packaged as conditions for financial aid, whereas in the 1960s' model they were regarded as the *result* of economic development. The chief protagonists of this 1990s' model are the United Nations organizations: the World Bank, the IMF, UNDP, etc., the European Union, and individual Western countries such as the US.

4 This term probably derives from Buzan and Segal (1998).

5 For a discussion of the Asian economic setback, see A. Booth (1999).

6 The People's Action Party (PAP) has formed Singapore's governments ever since 1959, when the island-state gained self-rule from the British. Lee Kuan Yew was its Prime Minister until 1990, when he made way for Goh Chok Tong, and became Senior Minister in the new PM's office.

7 The content of this mix is synthesized from the work of economists, development theorists, and others. I am particularly indebted to Mirza (1986), Tan Chwee Huat (1989), Tan Kong Yam (1995), Hanna *et al.* (1996), Huff (1997), the World Bank (1993, 1997), and Low (1998).

8 Neither an MOU (Memorandum of Understanding) nor a bilateral treaty was available. However, I gained access to comprehensive commercial materials written by Singapore's Economic Development Board (EDB) and project descriptions, press releases and guides published by the China–Singapore Suzhou Industrial Park Development Co. Ltd. (CSSD) and/or the Suzhou Industrial Park Administrative Committee (SIPAC).

9 This section draws heavily on commercial literature and press releases distributed by the EDB and/or SIPAC from 1994 to 1998. As a rule, the pages of this literature are unnumbered. All literature is on file with the author.

10 For a comprehensive overview, see Foreign Investment Consultancy Corporation (1991).

REFERENCES

Adelman, S. and A. Paliawla (eds) (1993) *Law and Crisis in the Third World*. London: Hans Zell.

Bartholomew, G. (1985) 'English Law in Partibus Orientalium,' in: A. Harding (ed.) *The Common Law in Singapore and Malaysia*. Singapore: Butterworths.

Booth, A. (1999) *Social Consequences of the Asia Crisis*. Asia–Pacific Economic Literature.

Buzan, B. and G. Segal (1998) *Anticipating the Future: Twenty Millennia of Human Progress*. London: Simon & Schuster.

Carter, C. (2000) *Law and Economic Development in Singapore 1959-1999*. London: Kluwer.

Carty, A. (ed.) (1992) *Law and Development*. Aldershot: Dartmouth.

Chen, J. (1999) *Chinese Law: Towards an Understanding of Chinese Law, Its Nature and Development*. London: Kluwer Law International.

Damaska, M. (1986) *The Faces of Justice*. New Haven: Yale University Press.

Dicks, A. (1989) 'The Chinese Legal System: Reform in the Balance,' *China Quarterly* 119, p. 540.

Economic Development Board, various years 1994-9, Commercial documents and promotions literature, some with no date. All on file with the author.

Foreign Investment Consultancy Corporation (1991) *Zhongguo Touzi Huanjingzhong Cunzai de Wenti* (Problems with respect to investing in the PRC) 4 January 1991:25, quoted in P. Corne (1997) *Foreign Investment in China*. Hong Kong: Hong Kong University Press.

Gellhorn, W. (1987) 'China's Quest for Legal Modernity,' *Journal of Chinese Law* 1, p. 1.

Hanna, N., S. Boyson and S. Gunaratne (1996) *The East Asian Miracle and Information Technology:Strategic Management of Technological Learning*. Washington, DC: World Bank.

Harding, A. (1996) 'Smart Laws in Singapore,' in: L. Palmier (ed.) *State and Law in Eastern Asia*. Aldershot: Dartmouth.

Huff, W. (1997) *The Economic Growth of Singapore*. Cambridge: Cambridge University Press.

Low, L. (1998) *The Political Economy of a City-state*. Oxford: Oxford University Press.

Merryman, J. (1977) 'Comparative Law and Social Change: On the Origins, Style, Decline & Revival of the Law & Development Movement' *American Journal of Comparative Law* 25, pp. 457.

Mirza, H. (1986) *Multinationals and the Growth of the Singapore Economy*. London: Croom Helm.

Nolan, P. (1995) *China's Rise, Russia's Fall*. London: Macmillan Press.

Oakeshott, M. (1975) *On Human Conduct*. Oxford: Clarendon Press.

Pistor, K. and Wellons P. (1999) *The Role of Law and Legal Institutions in Asian Economic Development 1960-1995*. New York: Oxford University Press.

Potter, P. (1999) 'The Chinese Legal System: Continuing Commitment to the Primacy of State Power,' *China Quarterly* 159, p. 673.

Sachs, J. *et al.* (eds) (1997) *Economies in Transition: Comparing Asia and Eastern Europe*. Cambridge, MA: MIT Press.

Seidman, A., R. Seidman and J. Payne (1997) *Legislative Drafting for Market Reform: Some Lessons from China*. London: Macmillan Press.

Tan Chwee Huat (1989) 6th ed. *Financial Markets and Institutions in Singapore*. Singapore: Singapore University Press.

Tan Kong Yam (1995) 'Economic Development and the State: Lessons from Singapore,' in: R. Fitzgerald (ed.) (1995) *The State and Economic Development: Lessons from the Far East*. London: Frank Cass & Co.

Thynne, I. (1990) 'The Administrative State,' chapter 3 in: W. Woon (ed.) *The Singapore Legal System*. Singapore: Butterworths.

Trubek, D. and M. Galanter (1974) 'Scholars in Self-estrangement: Some Reflections on the Crisis of Law and Development Studies in the United States,' *Wisconsin Law Review* 4, p. 1062.

Wade, R. (1990) *Governing the Market*. Princeton, N.J: Princeton University Press.

World Bank (1993) *The East Asian Miracle: Economic Growth and Public Policy*. Washington DC: Oxford University Press.

– (1997) World Development Report 1997: *The State in a Changing World*. New York: Oxford University Press.

PART FOUR

SOUTHEAST ASIAN APPROACHES TO LAW AND DEVELOPMENT

CHAPTER 11

PROSPERITY AT A PRICE: REGULATION OF ORGANIZED LABOUR IN MALAYSIA

JESSE WU MIN AUN

Since attaining independence in 1957,[1] Malaysia's relentless drive towards economic prosperity has been remarkable by any standard. A productive and inexpensive labour force is, among other things, an important contributing factor. In 1999, most reports suggest that the Malaysian economy is emerging from the financial and economic convulsion that had engulfed Asia. Malaysia adopted some home-grown remedies rather than seek assistance from the International Monetary Fund. The home-grown measures included the imposition on 1 September 1998 of the much criticized regime of capital controls to ward off currency speculators and the easing of interest rates to help over-leveraged companies.

The unorthodox medicine is showing results. Gross domestic product is expected to grow by more than 3 per cent in 1999, albeit from a low base after the economy contracted by 7.5 per cent in 1998. The GDP growth rate may touch 5 per cent in the year 2000. Remarkably, the result has been achieved without the initial pains experienced by other stricken Asian countries. Indonesia, Thailand, and South Korea, were compelled to shut down companies and lay off workers as part of the mandated policies demanded by the International Monetary Fund which co-ordinated the multi-billion-dollar rescue packages (Toh, 1999).

Malaysia has largely used the breathing space provided by capital controls to effect some restructuring in the economy, particularly in the banking sector. A newly created asset management company, Danaharta, mopped up non-performing loans in the system, while a recapitalization agency, Danamodal, injected funds into weak financial institutions.[2]

On the road to post-independence prosperity, the availability of reliable and inexpensive labour played a pivotal role in attracting foreign direct investment to selected industries although it came at a price. Now, labour appears even 'cheaper' following the 1998 financial crisis, which resulted in a dramatic plunge in the value of the ringgit. Once again, the country is attracting the attention of foreign investors eager to capitalize on any advantage. It is reported, for instance, that a US company, KOMAG Inc., is so eager to tap the cheap Malaysian work force that it is shutting two plants near its headquarters in San Jose, California, and re-locating all of its production to Malaysia. The maker of parts for computer disk drives says the move will slash payroll costs by 67 per cent, or US$80 million (S$134 million) a year. While Malaysia became something of a pariah in international financial markets because of slapping controls on capital flows in September 1998, it is now quietly luring more foreign investors like KOMAG to make their products in Penang and even in the town of Kuching, on the island of Borneo.[3] The country's move to peg its currency, the ringgit, at 3.8 to the US dollar, appears to be the key motivation for the foreign investors; it has made Malaysia one of the cheapest places in the region to make almost anything.[4] The cost of workers, land, and buildings has fallen, relative to its neighbours – effectively giving Malaysia a competitive advantage compared with countries such as Thailand and the Philippines, where currencies have strengthened.

Economic prosperity owes much to the availability of a cheap and compliant labour force secured mostly by severe regulation of industrial activities often justified on the grounds of either national integration or economic imperative. Laws governing industrial behaviour are largely restrictive and keenly enforced, with the government and the bureaucracy often quick to intervene in the face of a perceived threat to economic prosperity.

Central to this paper is an account of the regulatory framework of organized labour and the exercise of discretionary power by authorities to ensure that capital is well supported, by the availability of reliable and generally inexpensive labour for developmental goals. Particular attention is given to the legal regulation of trade unions and their ability to take industrial action in protection of their interest, highlighting, where relevant, the unusually wide discretionary power of the executive and public servants with respect to these matters. Particular attention is given to the two principal instruments of legal regulation, namely the *Trade Unions Act* 1959 and the *Industrial Relations Act* 1967.

BACKGROUND

The initial character of trade unions and their activities were largely moulded by considerations of security, politics, and race relations during the colonial and early post-colonial periods. The following significant events dictated the direction of the trade union movement and industrial relations:

1. Violent communist upheaval that erupted in colonial Malaya (as it was then called) in 1948. It led to a declaration of emergency by the colonial authority,

the imposition of restrictions on civil liberties, a ban on the Malayan Communist Party and its activities and the enactment of laws providing for detention without trial. These and related events impacted heavily on the labour movement which was then closely associated with communism. The law relating to detention without trial has remained in the statute book in an extended version ever since and on one occasion, was utilized in an industrial strike.[5]

2. Ethnic tension, in particular the racial riots of 1969, caused a change in socio-economic strategy. On the political front, the federal government imposed restrictions on various freedoms, including the ability of workers to freely organize. Racial polarization is exacerbated by religious differences, where race is often identified with religion, and in employment. To be classed a Malay, one must also be a Muslim. In relation to employment, the public sector (public service, defence forces, and police) is dominated by Malays largely through a race-based preferential system. Chinese predominate in private enterprises and small businesses. Despite the ostensible appearance of ethnic harmony, tensions do surface from time to time. The New Economic Policy introduced in the aftermath of the racial riots of May 1969 was in part intended to redress the identification of race with economic activities, in particular to promote greater Malay ownership and participation in the private sector. Unfortunately, the preferential policies and their implementation have also fuelled resentment among non-Malays who perceive an injustice, given that they continue to be shut out of the public sector and public tertiary education while inroads are made into their traditional areas of activities.[6]

3. Laws prohibiting trade unions from participating in or financing political parties and their activities and vice versa isolating organized labour from the political arena.

In the immediate post-war period, organized labour in the form of the General Labour Union (hereafter referred GLU), was heavily infiltrated by communists. It opened its head office in Singapore soon after the Japanese ended their occupation of Malaya and Singapore in 1945. The GLU quickly assumed a pre-eminent role in the labour movement through rapid expansion into all major towns in Malaya to the north of Singapore. The immediate postwar period was plagued by chronic inflation and acute food shortages – ideal breeding conditions for labour disputes. The grievances were genuine enough. The newly liberated territories were engulfed in a state of socio-political sickness stemming from a lack of economic planning, absence of democratic labour institutions and the mistrust of communalism in a multiracial society. The GLU skilfully exploited the situation by taking on the pre-eminent role of leader and organizer of workers. A state of intensified general unrest soon ensued. The colonial administrators, through either general indifference or ineptitude, had unwittingly caused workers to fall victims to the political ambition of the GLU. Strikes and demonstrations intensified and coupled with popular demands for more rice, freer movement of food, exemption from water and electricity bills, higher prices for tin and rubber, etc., the territories slowly descended into chaos and industrial strife.

Trade union laws in Malaya lagged well behind those of the United Kingdom. No trade union legislation existed in Malaya until 1940. The colonial view was that unlike home, there was no need for such laws in the territories. After all, employed labour was largely comprised of immigrants and any labour unrest could be quickly dealt with by a combination of police action, arrests, and banishment, if a migrant participated. The local police could always be relied upon to break strikes. The colonial authority, influenced mostly by local British interests, did not see the need for trade union law in that environment. If anything, organized labour was regarded as a pain and promptly discouraged. What was desirable in the mother country was not necessarily regarded as appropriate in colonial possessions.

The first trade union law enacted in 1940 was motivated largely by financial considerations. The United Kingdom Parliament had earlier passed the *Colonial Development and Welfare Act* 1940, which contemplated various schemes for long term financial assistance by the mother country to the colonies, on the condition, that there were laws protecting trade unions, fair wages, children in employment, and related matters. The lure of money seems to have stirred the minds of an otherwise lethargic colonial authority in Malaya.

The *Trade Union Enactment* 1940, originally enacted for the Federated Malay States, was not at the time implemented as the Japanese invaded the territories soon after. Upon British reoccupation, the law was extended in 1946 to cover the whole of the Malay Peninsula which had been reconstituted[7] into a new political entity called 'Malayan Union.' It consisted of 9 Malay States and the colonies of Penang and Malacca. Singapore was excluded from the short-lived Union.

The law introduced a scheme of compulsory registration for all trade unions. A Department of the Registrar of Trade Unions was created for the purpose of registering and supervising trade unions and their activities. A Trade Union Adviser's Department was added, whose purported duties were to foster the growth of trade unions, to assist them in negotiations with employers and to advise them on how best to build up their membership, finance, and leadership. In respect of employers' organizations, the Adviser's responsibility was limited to providing assistance upon request in respect of negotiating procedures and settlement of disputes.

Compulsory registration of trade unions under the law began in earnest in 1947. By the end of the year, the figures revealed the existence of 289 unions with a total membership of 195,113. It was estimated that nearly half the membership was under communist control exercised through the successor of GLU, the Pan-Malayan Federation of Trade Unions ('PMFTU') (ILO Report, 1962:30). Communist and trade union activities in the private sector were largely associated with the Chinese community with a smattering of Malays and Indians[8] but in the public sector communist influence was relatively insignificant.

The year 1948 marks the turning point in the Malayan trade union movement. Heightened frequency and momentum of strikes, many of which had political overtones, caused the colonial government to react with repressive measures, presumably in the conviction that British colonial interests were under threat. Control over trade unions and their activities was tightened through amendments to the *Trade Union Enactment* in June 1948. Registration of federations of trade unions became compulsory and their membership restricted to trade unions whose members were employed in similar trades, occupations, or industries.[9] The restriction of membership to similar trades, occupations or industries spelt an end to federations of a general nature – in practical effect, an end to large federations of trade unions. Henceforth, they would be broken up into smaller units. Another amendment made it compulsory for trade union officials, other than the secretary, to have at least three years' experience in the industry of their unions. The intent being to remove outside influences and 'infiltration,' thus ensuring that only genuine workers would hold office.

The PMFTU reapplied for registration as required by the new law. Along with about a hundred other unions, their applications were predictably rejected given the requirement that a federation must also be comprised of trade unions whose members were employed in similar trades, occupations or industries. The rug was swept out from under their feet. The new law ended their agenda of using trade unions as a front for securing political power.

The Malayan Communist Party, finding its activities through trade unions drastically curtailed, altered strategy and embarked upon a violent campaign of guerilla warfare. That strategy changed the course of Malaysian contemporary history, which had, until then, been relatively free of violent political activities. Prior to taking to the jungle, the Malayan Communist Party quietly spirited away whatever trade union funds it could lay its hands on. In response to the growing violence, the government banned the Malayan Communist Party and declared a state of emergency on 16 June 1948. The impact of the events on trade unionism may be summarized from the Report of the International Labour Office on the trade union movement:

> ... their sudden disappearance left thousands of the rank and file leaderless, bewildered and disillusioned. Realising that many of their sacrifices had been in vain and that they had been made the plaything of political parties, a large percentage of the workers began to lose faith in trade unionism and all it stood for. As the Emergency dragged on, this attitude became more widespread and it was a long time before the effects of the 'let down' began to wear off (ILO Report (1962).

Although Malaya attained Independence in 1957, the state of emergency declared by the colonial authority remained in place. It did not formally end till 1960 but self-rule effectively ended the main communist platform of anti-colonialism. Despite the formal ending of the state of emergency in 1960, pockets of insurgency continued for a while, particularly in the regions bordering Thailand. It was only in 1993 that the communists formally abandoned their struggle and signed an agreement in return for certain amnesty.

Given that background, it is not surprising that successive post-independence governments were suspicious of trade unions. They adopted a fiercely anti-communist policy. While recognizing the need for trade unions, they took the view that labour policies should not be liberal, given that until the end of the Cold War, the nation had remained under the threat of communism, and in light of their past experience with communists.

Apart from the communist factor, two other major events in the 1960s impacted heavily on the nation and came to dominate its life. The first event was the merger in 1963 of the States of Sabah, Sarawak, and Singapore with the Federation of Malaya into an enlarged federation, renamed 'Malaysia.' It triggered Indonesia into hostility in an undeclared war (called '*Konfrontasi*'), publicly proclaiming the new federation as neo-colonialism. That undeclared war went on from 1964 to 1967. The second event was the 1969 race riots when race relations were shattered. Both events caused successive emergencies to be declared. The 1969 emergency has remained in force since, despite the cessation of the circumstances of its declaration. New laws that were introduced during this period diluted various freedoms, including that of organized labour.

With respect to industrial relations, these events mapped out its future direction. The already strict legislative controls over trade unions were further tightened in several areas. The government hardened in its view that trade unions must continue to be isolated from political activities, their main function limited to the protection of workers for economic advancement. In political speak, it intends to ensure a compliant labour environment for developmental goals.

The restrictive nature of industrial relations law in contemporary Malaysia owes much to this backdrop. Since independence, Malaysia has taken a relentless path towards the twin objects of nationalism and economic prosperity, and in respect of the latter, the attainment of a fully industrialized status by the year 2020,[10] despite the setback of the 1997/1998 recession.

REGULATION OF TRADE UNIONS

Trade unions affairs and industrial conflicts are tightly regulated. The government exercises wide administrative discretion, to support legislative controls, in its efforts to secure industrial harmony. The regulation of trade unions and industrial activities is relatively simple because federal law and not a plethora of state laws govern trade unions and industrial relations. Two pieces of federal legislation, viz the *Trade Unions Act* 1959 (hereinafter referred to as TUA) and, to some extent, the *Industrial Relations Act* 1967 (hereinafter referred to as the IRA), cover the whole area.

The TUA was first enacted as *F M Ordinance No. 23 of 1959* and revised on 21 November 1981 as *Laws of Malaysia Act 262*. Since its revision, substantial amendments have been made to the Act from time to time.[11]

REGISTRATION OF TRADE UNIONS

The right of both employers and employees to form trade unions and to engage in their legitimate activities are embodied in the IRA. In particular, s 4(1) of the IRA declares:

> No person shall interfere with, restrain or coerce a workman or an employer in the exercise of his rights to form and assist in the formation of and join a trade union and to participate in its lawful activities.

The right exists in respect of registered trade unions. Unregistered trade unions are treated as illegal organizations so that persons involved in their activities become liable to criminal sanctions.

Strict statutory guidelines govern the process of registration. An application for registration must be made to the Director General within one month from the date of the establishment of a trade union although this period may be extended at the Director General's discretion, but such an extension must not exceed six months in the aggregate (TUA s 8). A trade union is deemed to have been established on the first date on which any employees or employers agree to become or create a trade union (TUA s 9(1). This necessarily assumes that the body is established in furtherance of any one or more objects specified in the definition of a trade union contained in s 2(1).

For the purpose of prosecution for non-registration, unless proven otherwise, the date of establishment is presumed to be:

(a) the date on which any person is proved to have been accepted or admitted as a member of that trade union; or
(b) the date on which any act is proved to have been done by that trade union in furtherance of any one or more objects of a trade union; and
(c) in a case where proof is available of both dates referred to in items (a) and (b) above, the earlier of such dates TUA s 9(2).

Upon registration, a trade union is entitled to certain rights, immunities, and privileges, for example, it could bargain for and withdraw labour without the threat of such common law action as breach of contract of employment or other tortious actions.

To be eligible for registration, trade unions must be organizations (permanent or temporary) that consist wholly of either employees or employers of one establishment or of one or more descriptions. Unions of a general nature are not registrable under the Act except perhaps within a particular establishment. Any association of employees or employers that is caught by the statutory definition is regarded as a trade union even though it may not have been registered under the law as such.

Membership of a trade union is restricted to workers or employers, as the case may be, 'within any particular establishment, trade, occupation or industry or within any similar trades, occupations or industry.'[12] A prospective union is not registrable if its membership includes unrelated establishments, trades, occupations, or industries. In other words, unions of a general nature are not registrable except in a particular establishment.

The same rule applies in respect of federations of trade unions where membership consists of constituents or affiliations of trade unions. Each federation must consist only of trade unions whose members are employed in a similar trade, occupation, or industry.[13]

The restriction was first enacted, by the colonial authority, in 1948 in respect of federations of trade unions as part of a wider strategy to break up and control the labour movement. The same was later extended to trade unions in 1959. The application of this provision has both a positive and a negative impact on the trade union movement: Positive in that membership of particular trade unions is largely homogeneous but negative in that trade unions are generally fragmented, small and resources rather limited. Emerging also is an increasing number of in-house unions. Their strength as bargaining units is relatively weak by comparison with trade unions in industrialized nations and the weakness seems to serve the purpose of government public policies.

Regulation through Administrative Discretion

The exercise of administrative discretion in public affairs is a familiar theme in Malaysian administrative law. Its application in relation to trade unions and industrial relations fits snugly into this pattern. As mentioned earlier, to qualify for registration (whether of workers or employers, as the case may be) a trade union must be 'within any particular establishment, trade, occupation, or industry or within any similar trades, occupations or industry.' The decision as to whether a trade, occupation, or industry is 'similar' is vested in the Director General of Trade Unions. According to the TUA s 2(2), for the purposes of the definition (and several other purposes) the word 'similar' means 'similar in the opinion of the Director General.'[14] Although any person dissatisfied with the opinion of the Director General on the issue of similarity may appeal to the Minister within thirty days from the date of the opinion, the exercise of power in the negative amounts to a veto by a public servant. On appeal, the decision of the Minister is 'final and conclusive' (TUA s 71A).

The Act is silent on the question of judicial appeal or review in relation to an opinion of the Director General or the Minister on the similarity or otherwise of a trade, occupation or industry. It would appear that the intention is to shut out the courts. Under current practice, courts will not normally intervene before statutory procedures are exhausted, and even when they do intervene, it is on rather limited grounds. This judicial approach in respect of the former is well illustrated in the case, *Metal Industries Employee Union v Registrar of Trade Unions* [1976] 1 MLJ 80, where the Registrar expressed an opinion under s 2(2) of the 1959 Ordinance. That opinion was challenged in the High Court by way of an application for a *declaration.* Though the High Court agreed that there was a question of interpretation, it declined to intervene on a procedural ground; that there was an alternative statutory remedy by way of an appeal to the Minister.

How the Director General applies his or her mind to the test of 'similar trade, occupation, or industry' is far from clear. One can only hazard a guess, that the process for its determination involves interpretation of facts. 'Similar' is a question of degree. It is a subjective determination, and ordinarily, it is made by reference to the trade, occupation, or industry and the membership rules of the union concerned. In *Tanjong Jaga Sdn Bhd v Minister of Labour & Manpower* [1987] 1 MLJ 124, the argument was put that it was incumbent on the Registrar (as the officer was previously referred to) to make due inquiry by considering evidence from both sides. Abdoolcader SCJ, rejecting that suggestion, said:

> There is no provision or requirement for due inquiry as such and all that was necessary was a fair and reasonable decision arrived at by the Registrar in the exercise of his discretion. ... In exercising his functions in this regard, the Registrar had an unfettered discretion which was subject to a duty to act responsibly (p. 129).

His Lordship, however, conceded that a decision could be challengeable but only if the '... decision making body comes to its decision on no evidence or comes to an unreasonable finding so unreasonable that a reasonable person would not have come to it – then the court will interfere' (In *Tanjong Jaga Sdn Bhd V Minister of Labour & Manpower* [1987] 1 MLJ 124 p. 129).

In the electronics industry, the Director General seemed to take a narrow view and ruled that employees could not be represented by a union of electrical workers. In his view, the electronics industry is not similar to the electrical industry. Lee Hun Hoe CJ in *Electrical Industry Workers Union v Registrar of Trade Unions* [1976] 1 MLJ 177 p. 179 said:

> Whether a person in a related or similar industry becomes a member of a particular union is squarely a matter for the decision of the Registrar of Trade Unions. If a particular union could say it is for the union to decide whether those in another industry might be absorbed as members of the Union, a dangerous situation would develop whereby each and every union in the country would do the same ... It is for the Union to satisfy the Registrar of Trade Unions that the Monsato Electronics Workers Union belongs to the same or similar industry as the Union (Electrical Industry Employees Union).

The electronic industry has traditionally been dominated by direct foreign investments. Close control of trade union activities certainly gives encouragement to foreign investors given that the workforce will be largely docile and free of industrial strife. Investments in such industries fit neatly into official perception of national interests.

Restriction of Trade Union Activities

The TUA limits the range of trade union activities, for example, political activities are banned. Restriction is achieved by listing a number of objectives and requiring a trade union to have, among its objectives, one or more of them and nothing else. These objectives are enumerated in s 2(1)(c) as follows:

1. The regulation of relations between employees and employers for the purposes of promoting good industrial relations between them, improving

the working conditions of employees or enhancing their economic and social status, or increasing productivity;
2. The regulation of relations between employees and employees, or between employers and employers;
3. The representation of either employees or employers in trade disputes;
4. The conducting of or dealing with trade disputes and matters related thereto;
5. The promotion or organization or financing of strikes or lock-outs in any trade or industry or the provision of pay or other benefits for its members during a strike or a lock-out (TUA s 2(1)).

It may be noted that none of the above objectives relate to political or related activities. By way of comparison, in some European countries such as Sweden, the relationship between political parties and trade unions are so close that the latter would have political wings. Malaysia has deliberately isolated trade unions from political parties and their activities. In practical terms, political aspirations are prohibited in the trade union movement. In addition, TUA s 52(1) expressly provides that trade union funds 'shall not be applied directly or indirectly in any payment whatsoever to a political party or in furtherance of any political object.' That rules out political donation.

The expression, 'political object,' is comprehensively defined in s 52(2),[15] culminating in a 'catch all' clause – 'any object which the Minister may by notification in the *Gazette* specify.' The Act is silent on criteria, norms, or standards that may provide a guide to the Minister in the exercise of his discretionary power in this area. It is a classic case of unfettered executive power.

Such unfettered executive power may seem extraordinary to the uninitiated. In Malaysia, it is unremarkable given its regular use. The Malaysian statute book is littered with clauses conferring discretionary power to be exercised by the executive or his/her delegate. One is inclined to question why the legislature has provided such wide powers on the executive. The answer behind s 52 is easily traceable to the emergence of strong executive government. Moreover, in the past, trade unions outside the public sector have more often than not supported opposition parties rather than the ruling coalition for a variety of reasons, which it is not necessary to speculate upon for the purpose of this chapter. Given that the same coalition party in different permutations has governed since independence in 1957, the motivation for insisting that trade union activities be totally separated from political activities becomes obvious. It should also be recalled that in the early development of the labour movement in peninsular Malaysia, trade unions were heavily infiltrated by communists. Despite the ending of the Cold War, the government remains anti-communist. Consciously or otherwise, it is much influenced by the old spectre of communist dominated organized labour. Until 1955, trade unions were allowed to use funds for political purposes. So why should this right 'be abolished in 1980, when the Government is freed of Communist threats.'[16] The answer lies not in the strength of the question but in the fact that a government long used to exercising power is not likely to surrender it or see it wrestled away by its opponents.

It may also be noted that s 28(1) of the TUA prohibits an officer-bearer or employee of a political party from holding office in a trade union, including a branch and a federation of trade union. Where the Director General certifies in writing to the executive of a trade union, or a federation of trade unions, that a member of the executive is disqualified from holding office, the person immediately ceases to be a member of such executive. There appears to be no provision in the Act for appeal against the decision of the Director General.

Persons may be exempted from the operation of the above disqualification but such exemption is granted by the Minister through an order exempting either the trade union or officers of a trade union (TUA s 30).

Disqualification of office bearers and employees of political parties from holding offices in trade unions had its origins in the 1969 *Essential (Trade Unions) Regulations,* a law made under emergency powers in the wake of racial riots. These provisions have since become entrenched. They are now sections 28 and 29 of the Act. Prior provisions for separate political funds in trade unions were repealed. In the result, it is now unlawful for any union to use any of its funds for political objectives (TUA s 52). The overall impact of the change means that political parties and trade unions have become almost completely separated[17] with no formal links between them.

Public Sector Union

Trade unions in the public sector are also separated from those in the private sector. Employees of statutory authorities are prohibited from joining or becoming members of any trade union 'unless the membership of that union is confined exclusively to persons employed by that particular statutory authority' (TUA s 3(a)). This restriction means that employees of a statutory authority cannot join private sector unions even if they belong to the same trade or occupation. In addition, they are restricted to a union of 'that particular statutory authority' (*Essential (Trade Unions) Regulations* 1969). It would seem that 'in-house' unions are the only type of organized labour allowed in statutory bodies (A732 *Trade Union (Amendment) Act 1989).*

As an exception, an employee of a statutory authority may join an outside union provided that the trade union's 'membership is confined exclusively to employees of one or more financially autonomous local authorities' and only with approval of the Minister of Human Resources. It is intended as a concession to statutory authorities too small to form separate bodies. There appears to be no guideline provided to the Minister in considering an application for such approval. Presumably, the Ministerial authority is completely discretionary in nature.

Given the various legal constraints, it is not surprising that statutory authority employees unions are generally small in membership.

The general rule as stated in s 27 of the TUA prohibits public officers from joining or becoming members of any trade union unless exempted by the Yang di-Pertuan Agong (the King). The Yang di-Pertuan Agong may allow an exemption by notification in the *Gazette* but subject to such conditions as may be specified. Such exemption was given by the *Trade Unions (Exemption of Public Officers) Order* 1971 which permits public officers to organize on the condition that union membership is confined to public officers within a particular occupation, department or ministry.

Ministerial Power to Suspend a Trade Union

The Minister of Human Resources possesses the power, exercisable at his 'absolute discretion,' to suspend for a period not exceeding six months any trade union, or any class or description of trade unions, which 'in his opinion' is or is being used for purposes prejudicial to or incompatible with the interests of the security or public order of Malaysia or any part thereof (TUA s 18). The discretionary power is exercisable subject to certain constraints, namely:

a. the concurrence of the Minister responsible for internal security and public order; and
b. the publication of the suspension order in the *Gazette*.

The need to publish is merely procedural and a condition precedent to its enforcement. Its real value is illusory, given that the procedure may be dispensed with 'where in the opinion of the Minister the exigencies of the situation so require.' Hence the Minister may suspend a trade union immediately upon an order being made and before its publication but 'after publicising it in such manner as the Minister thinks fit,' for example, by a press statement or an announcement in the mass media. It is indeed an extraordinary discretionary power.

It is also provided in the Act that the Minister's order is 'final and conclusive' (TUA s 18(7)). In practical terms, it is not normally amenable to judicial review except perhaps for the most blatant error of law. It has been argued that the power is needed to meet grave situations that are likely to threaten security or public order. It is an unconvincing argument. In reality, it is yet another illustration of an authoritarian approach to government taken through force of habit. Such power is superfluous given the extraordinary powers that already exist under Articles 149 and 150 of the *Federal*

Constitution, and the laws made thereunder, to deal with activities that have the potential to threaten security or public order.[18]

The Minister's authority to suspend is not restricted to a particular trade union. It is exercisable in respect of any class or description of trade unions. It is conceivable that a Minister, for instance, may decide to suspend all trade unions in the whole industry, if he/she is of the view that they are being used for purposes prejudicial to the interests of public order. Such suspension may occur despite the legitimacy of trade union claims and the fact that they have followed all procedural requirements prior to industrial action. The power of government over trade unions seems almost limitless.

Upon the making of an order of suspension, the Minister has authority at any time to give further directions of an ancillary or consequential nature as he may deem necessary or expedient. A direction so given is valid, notwithstanding anything inconsistent with the TUA and it is also 'final and conclusive.' Again, no guideline or criterion is prescribed for the exercise of this power. The most significant aspect of a ministerial direction is the fact that it is 'valid and have full force and effect' even though it may be contrary to the statute from which the power originates (TUA s 18(4)(b)). In a democratic society, it must surely rank as one of the most undemocratic of powers. It would seem that the legislature has abdicated its responsibility.

The current state of the law is a demonstration of blatant executive power over trade unions and their activities.

The tendency of the legislature, under executive direction, to confer wide discretionary powers to administrative authority to decide matters according to its subjective satisfaction is now legendary. From the foregoing discussions, this approach is amply illustrated. The discretionary nature of the power is demonstrated by the use of such terms as 'he is of the opinion,' 'if he is satisfied,' and 'in his absolute discretion.' All the above expressions are found in the TUA. While it is administratively efficient, it also erodes democratic principles and creates a climate conducive for abuse of power, particularly where the traditional authority of courts to review is ousted at the same time. Clearly when an administrative authority is vested with discretionary powers to be exercised according to its subjective satisfaction, the courts are loath to inquire into the merits. Generally it is regarded as a non-justiciable matter.[19]

REGULATION OF STRIKES

A strike is perhaps the most dramatic manifestation of overt industrial conflict. In a civil society, the freedom of workers to combine and to withdraw their labour is widely recognized as a legitimate form of industrial action. It is seen as the ultimate safeguard against the inherent imbalance of power between capital and labour.

A strike involves a concerted temporary withdrawal of labour by a group of workers for the purpose of protecting or promoting their interests. Workers' interests normally relate to the terms and conditions of employment of the strikers or in an industry but in countries with a liberal democracy such as Australia and the United Kingdom, other interests that may be sought to be protected or promoted through strikes and other industrial actions do not necessarily relate to employment matters alone but may involve other issues such as political or environmental concerns. Modern trade unions often take on wider agendas, including politics, but in the case of Malaysia, that is not the practice given that the law prohibits workers from engaging in strikes unrelated to their employment. In consequence, their concerns are far narrower and limited.

Control of Strikes

Embarking on strike action in Malaysia is similar to running the marathon. It is long, hard, and a test of endurance.

Strike is strictly controlled by legislation through various techniques. In the first instance, the word 'strike' is given an expansive statutory meaning; thus snaring a multitude of actions that might be employed by trade unions in furtherance of industrial conflicts, within the ambit of strike laws. Section 2 of the IRA and s 2(1) TUA define a 'strike' in similar terms to mean:

> The cessation of work by a body of workmen acting in combination, or a concerted refusal or a refusal under a common understanding of a number of workmen to continue to work or to accept employment, and includes any act or omission by a body or workmen acting in combination or under a common understanding, which is intended to or does result in any limitation, restriction, reduction or cessation of or dilatoriness in the performance or execution of the whole or any part of the duties connected with their employment.

Three elements are present in the above definition: (a) cessation of work; (b) action less than cessation of work but which results in a limitation, restriction, reduction, or dilatoriness in the performance of work and (c) concerted action. Thus industrial acts such as 'go slow,' 'work to rule,' overtime ban, and so forth, which do not involve a complete cessation of work, are caught by s 2. They are regarded as strikes and therefore subject to various controls. Trade unions cannot resort to 'go slow' or 'work to rule' and claim that they are not on strike. Given this wide definition of what constitutes a strike, not surprisingly strike action in general is not particularly widespread.

Is there a Right to Strike?

There is no statutory provision expressly conferring on workers the right to strike. The right to strike is inferred from several provisions of both the TUA and IRA. The relevant provisions are as follows:

1. TUA s 2(1) provides amongst the objects of a trade union 'the promotion or organisation or financing of strikes or lock-outs in any trade or industry or the provision of pay or other benefits for its members during a strike or lock-out;'
2. TUA s 21 provides a registered trade union with legal immunity from civil suit in respect of any act done in contemplation or furtherance of a trade dispute. Trade disputes include strike action;
3. TUA s 25A provides for a mandatory procedure, including the taking of a secret ballot, before strike action can commence;
4. IRA s 4(1) provides that 'No person shall interfere with, restrain or coerce a workman or an employer in the exercise of his rights to form and assist in the formation of and join a trade union and to participate in its lawful activities.' The lawful activities of a trade union include the promotion, organisation and financing of a strike as indicated in item (1) above;
5. IRA s 42(1) and (2) prevents persons acting in combination in contemplation or furtherance of trade unions from being prosecuted or sued for their actions;
6. The *Employment Act* 1955 s 8 provides that nothing in any contract of service must restrict the right of any employee from participating in the activities of a registered trade union. Such activities would presumably include strikes.

The right of workers to strike is supported by judicial pronouncements. For instance, Raja Azlan Shah FJ in *South East Asia Fire Bricks* [1976] 2 MLJ 67 p. 19, citing with approval a statement of Lord Wright, which says:

> It is declaratory of present day industrial relations that management should encourage workmen to join a union and to play an active part in its work, … such as the freedom to strike. 'The right of workmen to strike is an essential element in the principle of collective bargaining' *per* Lord Wright in *Crofter Hand Woven Harris Tweed Company, Ltd and Ors v Veitch & Anor*. That is a truism. There can be no equilibrium in industrial relations today without the freedom to strike. If workers could not, in the last resort, collectively withhold labour, they could not bargain collectively.

His Lordship elaborated, 'the freedom to strike appears in the form of immunities from criminal prosecution and from civil action,' provided the actions are taken in contemplation or furtherance of trade disputes. The same case is also authority for the proposition that workers who go on lawful strike have not terminated their contracts of service but are merely suspending it for the duration of the strike. Consequently, an employer cannot, by issuing warning notices, convert the absence from work of those workers, who are on strike, into abandonment of their service contract.

Mandatory Requirements for Lawful Strikes

While the right to strike seems settled, the road towards it is long and arduous. Firstly, only registered trade unions may go on lawful strike, and second, the strike must be in contemplation or furtherance of a trade dispute between the workers on strike and their employer. A strike in support of other workers is illegal, given that a trade dispute must involve a dispute with their employers. Thirdly, strikes for political, economic, social, or related purposes such as environmental concerns are illegal and persons so participating are liable to prosecution.

Sections 25A and 40 of the TUA impose certain compulsory procedures to be observed before a trade union can commence a lawful strike (or a lock-out in the case of an employer). Failure to observe the prescribed procedures can lead to prosecution and, in the event of a prosecution for infringement, the burden of proof is reversed.[20]

In a criminal case, the prosecution is normally required to prove the guilt of the defendant beyond reasonable doubt. It is quite puzzling that in relation to a breach of the law relating to strike, the burden of proof is reversed. Surely industrial disputes are not a greater threat to the community as a whole than criminal activities. Shifting the burden of proof to a defendant places a heavy burden of responsibility on trade unions, their officers and members. The government conveys the impression that it is less tolerant of unlawful industrial action than of other criminal activities. Given the already tight regulation of strikes, it is draconian to treat industrial law violators more harshly than criminal offenders.

Among the several mandatory procedures of a lawful strike is the taking of a secret ballot in a decision on 'all matters relating to strikes and lock-outs' (TUA s 40(1)). It is a condition precedent to a lawful strike (or lock-out). Secret ballot is an issue of union democracy and reduces incidence of intimidation. By and large, it is generally agreed that it is an appropriate procedure: for a decision to strike being tested democratically on the floor through a secret ballot. Other methods of determining support such as a show of hands and associated methods at open forums are not satisfactory.

However, before a secret ballot can be taken in relation to any matter concerning a strike or lock-out, a proper resolution must be circulated setting out clearly the issues leading to the proposed strike or lock-out and a description of the nature of the industrial action, which is contemplated, in the course of such a strike or lockout. A secret ballot not conducted correctly is invalid and of no effect, and 'no strike or lock-out shall be carried out on the basis of such secret ballot.' It is clear that industrial actions such as wildcat strikes, where members walk out off their jobs without notice, are illegal.

A strike decided by secret ballot must be supported by at least two-thirds of the total number of union members, who are entitled to vote, and in respect of whom the strike is to be called. The same is required of employers in the case of a lock-out (TUA s 25(1)(a)). A simple majority of members in support of a strike is insufficient.

Role of the Director-General in Strikes

The Director General of Trade Unions plays a major role in matters relating to strike action. Pursuant to s 40(5) of the Act, the results of a secret ballot on a strike or lock-out must be submitted in triplicate by the secretary of the trade union to the Director General within fourteen days of the taking of the ballot. The secretary is under a legal duty to take all steps to ensure that all ballot papers and documents used in connection with the secret ballot are kept at the registered office of the union for a period of not less than six months after the completion of the ballot (TUA s 40(7)).

Upon receipt of the results of a secret ballot calling for a strike or a lock-out, the Director General is empowered by s 40(6) of the Act to 'carry out all such investigations as he may deem necessary.' For the purpose of satisfying himself that a secret ballot taken by a trade union has been properly conducted according to law and the rules of the union concerned, he may act in the following manner:

1. require any person to deliver to him any ballot papers, envelopes, lists, or other documents, which have been used in connection with the secret ballot;
2. inspect any such documents; and
3. retain them for such period as he deems necessary.

Other than the Director General, as provided in the rules of the union, no other person 'shall be allowed to inspect or copy any document relating to a secret ballot.'

The Director General may decide as follows:

1. take note of the secret ballot calling for strike or lock-out;
2. declare the secret ballot taken to be invalid if he is satisfied that the union has contravened any provision of the Act or its regulations, or any of its own rules in carrying out such secret ballot (TUA s 40(9)); or
3. direct the union not to commence any strike or lock-out where he is satisfied that the proposed action if carried out would contravene the Act or any other written law (TUA s 40(6)).

The power of the Director General under item (3) above is exercisable at his subjective discretion. It is unclear whether the Director General can direct that a proposed strike be aborted because in his subjective view, the proposed strike would contravene the Act or 'any other written law,' regardless of a secret ballot in favour of a strike or lock-out, with no ostensible flaw in its conduct. If the answer is affirmative, the Director General's power is indeed far reaching. Is the Director General an appropriate person to decide subjectively whether an industrial action has contravened or is likely to contravene a written law? Surely that is a function of the court rather than a public servant. The provision as it stands gives far too much authority to a public servant.

Cooling Off Period

A 'cooling off' period is also prescribed by law. Following the submission of the results of a secret ballot in favour of a strike to the Director General, at least seven days must elapse before a strike or lock-out can actually commence (TUA s 25A(1)(b)). A strike or lock-out carried out or declared in contravention of s 25A(1) is illegal. Any trade union and every member of its executive who commences, promotes, organizes, or finances such illegal strike or lock-out is liable, on conviction, to a fine not exceeding two thousand ringgit, or to imprisonment for a term not exceeding one year, or to both. There is a further fine of one hundred ringgit for every day the offence continues (TUA s 25A(2)). This prescribed 'cooling off' period is probably intended to provide some breathing space for both protagonists to reach a settlement.

Restriction of Strikes in Certain Circumstances

In certain circumstances, strikes are completely prohibited, namely:

1. Recognition of trade unions: s 10(1) prohibits a worker from taking strike action for 'whatever reason during the pending of proceedings under section 9, or after the decision of the Minister thereunder by reason of any dissatisfaction with such decision.' Section 9 concerns a claim by a union for recognition from an employer. It would appear that once a trade union

has served a claim for recognition on an employer, a statutory process is put in train and during that period, workers are prohibited from going on strike. Employers are likewise prohibited from declaring a lock-out or from terminating the services of their employees;

2. Essential industries: s 43 places restrictions on strikes and lock-outs in 'essential industries.' A prescribed period of notice is required before a strike can commence;
3. Other miscellaneous circumstances: s 44 prohibits workers and employers from resorting to strikes and lock-outs respectively in any of the following circumstances:
   (a) during the pendency of the proceedings of a Board of Inquiry appointed by the Minister in respect of a trade dispute involving such workers and employer, and seven days after the conclusion of such proceedings;
   (b) after a trade dispute or a matter involving such worker or employer has been referred to the Industrial Court for settlement, and the parties concerned have been notified of such reference;
   (c) in the case of a trade dispute relating to any public service or the service of a statutory authority, after the Yang di-Pertuan Agong has withheld consent to a reference of the dispute to the Industrial Court under s 26(2), and the parties concerned have been notified;
   (d) in respect of any of the matters covered by a collective agreement that has been taken cognizance of by the Industrial Court in accordance with s 16 or by an award; and
   (e) in respect of any of the matters pertaining to management's prerogatives that are not to be included in a union's proposal for a collective agreement covered by s 13(3).

Where a trade dispute relates to the public service or a statutory authority, workers may have no means of redress if the Yang di-Pertuan Agong or the relevant state authority refuses to give its consent for a dispute to be referred to the Industrial Court. In practical terms, these workers are denied the benefits of either compulsory arbitration or the right to strike in order to force a settlement of their grievances. In this respect, workers in the public sector are at a relative disadvantage in comparison with their counterparts in the private sector. By virtue of s 45(1), strikes and lock-outs are deemed to be illegal if they are carried out in contravention of s 43 or s 44 or 'of any provision of any other written law'; likewise, if strikes have any objective other than the furtherance of a trade dispute between the workers and their employer. A strike that is declared in response to an illegal lock-out is not deemed to be illegal (IRA s 45(2)).

Penalties for Unlawful Strikes

In general, penalties imposed on workers participating in illegal strikes including instigators and financial supporters are severe. They include imprisonment for up to a year. Offences relating to illegal strikes (and lock-outs) are treated as 'seizable' offences for which a person may be arrested without a warrant. Bail may not be granted to an accused person or a person charged if the 'Public Prosecutor certifies in writing that it is not in the public interest to grant bail to such accused person' (IRA s 50). A prosecution cannot be instituted except with the consent of the Public Prosecutor but the proviso does not affect the rule with respect to arrest, remand, or bail other than the fact that the case 'shall not be further prosecuted until that consent has been obtained' (IRA s 51(1)).

Punishment extends beyond mere prosecution. Any member of a trade union of workers who commences, participates, or otherwise acts in furtherance of a strike in contravention of TUA s 25A(1) 'shall forthwith cease to be a member of the trade union, thereafter such member shall not be eligible to become a member of any trade union except with the prior approval of the Director General in writing' (TUA s 25A(3)). The trade union of which he is no longer a member must remove his name from its membership register, inform the Director General of Trade Unions and the member concerned of the removal, and exhibit conspicuously in its registered office a list of members whose names have been removed. In certain situations, widespread participation in an unlawful strike can wipe out the whole union.

Again, the Director General possesses almost unbridled power to order the removal of members' names from the membership register, regardless of a prosecution or conviction for an offence (TUA s 25A(5)). By virtue of section 25A(4) the Director General may, 'where he is satisfied' that a contravention has occurred and the trade union concerned has failed to remove the names or where there is undue delay, order the union concerned 'to remove forthwith the names of the members concerned from its membership register' (TUA s 25A(4)). The power is discretionary although exercisable only after he has conducted 'such investigation as he deems necessary.' It is remarkable that such power is conferred on a public servant; a power that is exercisable despite the insufficiency of evidence to bring a person to court for trial. A failure to comply with the order of the Director General is an offence.

PIONEER COMPANIES

Direct foreign investments are attracted to industries in Malaysia where they are able to secure pioneer company status under the *Promotion of Investments*

Act 1986. The conferment of such status gives rise to certain privileges, including tax advantages and strict statutory control of labour.

The *Employment Act* 1955 contains minimum conditions of employment of workers. It is provided in the IRA s 15 that no collective agreement in relation to pioneer companies 'shall contain provisions with regard to terms and conditions of service that are more favourable to workmen than those contained in Part XII of the Employment Act 1955' with the qualification that the Minister may approve any variation. Clearly, the intention is to encourage investments in certain industries and one of the incentives is to ensure that labour costs associated with employment are sufficiently attractive for investors. Lower labour cost is achieved at the expense of workers in this instance when an artificial lid is imposed on conditions of employment, including wages for a period of 5 years which may be extendable by the Minister.

In the longer term, manipulation of labour costs is bound to affect the competitiveness of the company or industry when market forces are restored after the expiry of the 5-year honeymoon period. Of course, the honeymoon period may be indefinite given that it is elastic. The Minister may extend it 'from time to time by notification in the Gazette' and 'for such further period or periods.'

CONCLUDING REMARKS

Hallmarks of Malaysian industrial law include tight regulations of trade unions, their activities and the conduct of industrial relations. Control is secured mainly by restrictive laws and vesting wide discretionary powers in the Minister and the two Director Generals (the Director General of Trade Unions and the Director General of Industrial Relations). The absence of statutory direction for the exercise of these powers, coupled with a diminished ability of the judiciary to intervene, leads inevitably to a very timid trade union movement often unable to adequately protect the legitimate interests of its workers. The law as it currently stands is loaded in favour of employers. The current low level of industrial strife is predictable enough given the legal controls engineered by the government. It is not a reflection of a genuine partnership between employers and workers.

NOTES

1 First as Federation of Malaya comprising 11 states and later as Malaysia in 1963 to include the states of Singapore, Sabah and Sarawak. Singapore left the federation in 1965 and became a sovereign nation.

2 The Deputy Finance Minister reportedly informed Parliament that Danaharta had taken over non-performing loans worth 39.3 billion ringgit (10.3 billion US dollars) from financial institutions as of 15 October 1999.
http://www.afp.com/ext/english/nst/malaysia/991025083313.qivf30qm.html

3 Reported on 16/10/99 in http://business-times.asia1.com.sg/6/nmsia/-nmsia01.html

4 For an account of capital controls, see R. Gengatharen (1999) Destablishing Financial Capital Controls: Are Capital Controls the Solution, *Lawasia Journal,* 12.

5 In 1978 in response to industrial action by employees of Malaysian Airline System, the Minister of Home Affairs detained several union officers under the *Internal Security Act*, which was a law enacted under Article 149 of the Federal Constitution. The Act provides for detention without trial. The minister said that he had detained them on the grounds, amongst others, that some employees were tampering with airplanes belonging to the airline. In any event, detention of the employees broke the back of the industrial action.

6 A limited study by Associate Professor Sheela Abraham reported in late 1999 that racial polarization at Universiti Malaya, Malaysia's oldest University, has reached a level where there is almost no interaction among the communities outside classes. While it is common knowledge that the level of social interaction among Malay, Chinese, and Indian students has decreased over the years, the paper says that racial segregation on campus is now almost complete. The survey found that 98 per cent of Malay students did not mix socially with students of other races. The figures for Chinese and Indian students were equally alarming: 99 per cent and 97 per cent, respectively. See http://straitstimes.asia1.com.sg/reg/mal1. Also reported in *The Sun*, 12 October 1999.

7 The Malayan Union was created after British reoccupation and comprised of 11 states. It was soon abandoned in the face of strong Malay opposition, to be replaced by the Federation of Malaya.

8 The government of contemporary Malaysia remains staunchly anti-communist but adopts a pragmatic approach in its dealings with

communist or ex-communist countries in matters relating to trade and commerce.

9 That provision has been carried over to the current law and in consequence caused the federations of trade unions to remain small and weak though homogenous.

10 For an account of industrial relations law generally, see Wu Min Aun (1995) *The Industrial Relations Law of Malaysia*. Petaling Jaya: Longman Malaysia.

11 By the Act A717 *Trade Unions (Amendment) Act* 1989; Act 732 *Trade Unions (Amendment) Act* 1989 and Act A798 *Trade Unions (Amendment) Act* 1991.

12 See Part xii of the *Trade Unions Act* 1959 in respect of the legal requirements of trade unions. S 75 of the TUA makes it clear that the law relating to trade unions applies equally to a federation of trade unions. It reads:

The provisions of this Act relating to trade unions (including the provisions as to penalties) shall apply, so far as the same may be applicable, to a federation of trade unions as if such federation were a trade union.

13 See Part XII of the *Trade Unions Act* 1959 in respect of legal requirements of federation of trade unions. Section 75 of the TUA makes clear that the law relating to trade unions applies equally to a federation of trade unions. It reads:

The provisions of this Act relating to trade unions (including the provisions as to penalties) shall apply, so far as the same may be applicable, to a federation of trade unions as if such federation were a trade union.

14 The power to determine similarity also applies for the purposes of s 32 (amalgamation of trade unions). s 33 (transfer of trade unions), s 72 (formation of federation of trade unions) and s 74 (affiliation with registered federation of trade unions).

15 'Political objects' referred to includes:

1. The payment of expenses incurred either directly or indirectly by a candidate or prospective candidate for election to either Houses of Parliament;
2. The holding of any meeting or the distribution of any literature or document in support of any such candidate or prospective candidate;
3. The maintenance of any person who is a member of either House of Parliament;
4. The registration of electors or the selection of a candidate for membership of either House of Parliament; and

5. The holding of political meetings of any kind or the distribution of political literature or political documents of any kind.

16 See Sharifah Suhana Syed Ahmad (1992) Trade Unions in Malaysia: Organs with 'Bark or Bite?' *Developments in Malaysian Law*, Petaling Jaya: Pelanduk Publications 358.

17 Reported in the *Star* (22 May 1991) the Minister of Human Resources emphasized that trade unions should not involve themselves in politics as there would be a danger of them 'losing of sight of their original objectives,' p. 4.

18 See note no. 5.

19 See *Loh Chin v The Registrar of Trade Unions* [1957] MLJ243 and *Electrical Industry Workers Union v Registrar of Trade Unions* [1976] 1 MLJ177; in *Minister of Human Resources Ors v National Union of Hotels, Bar and Restaurant Workers, Semenanjung Malaysia and Another* [1997] 3 MLJ377 the Court of Appeal held that the Director General of Trade Unions was under no duty to provide reasons for his decision; in *Petaling Jaya v Lee Kian Chan* [1994] 1 SCR325 the Supreme Court reaffirmed the well established principle that judicial review is available in respect of jurisdictional error despite the presence of an ouster clause. For recent case law on judicial review, see *Roma Chandran v The Industrial Court of Malaysia & Anor* [1997] 1 MLJ145.

20 Section 25A(7) provides that 'in every prosecution for an offence under this section the onus of proving that the requirements specified … have been complied with shall be on the trade union, the member of its executive or the member of the trade union, as the case may be.'

REFERENCES

Gengatharen, R. (1999) 'Destablishing Financial Flows: Are Capital Controls the Solution?' *Lawasia Journal* 12.

Ilo Report (1962) Geneva 30.

Industrial Relations Act 1967.

Sharifah Suhana Syed Ahmad (1992) 'Trade Unions in Malaysia: Organs with 'Bark or Bite?' Developments *in Malaysian Law*. Petaling Jaya: Pelanduk Publications 358.

Toh, E. (1999) 'Will M'sia Scale New Heights Into the Future' *The Business Times Singapore* 30th September.

Trade Unions Act 1959.

Wu Min Aun (1995) *The Industrial Relations Law of Malaysia*. Petaling Jaya: Longman Malaysia.

CHAPTER 12

THE LEGAL REGULATION OF TECHNOLOGY TRANSFER ARRANGEMENTS WITHIN ASEAN

MICHAEL BLAKENEY

THE ASEAN FRAMEWORK AGREEMENT ON INTELLECTUAL PROPERTY CO-OPERATION

On 15 December 1995 ASEAN member countries[1] adopted a Framework Agreement on Intellectual Property Co-operation (Framework Agreement Z, 1996 35 ILM 1072). Emulating the European model, the Framework Agreement envisages the establishment of an ASEAN patents and trademarks system, including ASEAN Patent and Trademarks Office (Framework Agreement Z, Art 1.4 and 1.5). Intellectual property co-operation is envisaged for the fields of 'copyright and related rights, patents, trademarks, industrial designs, geographical indications, undisclosed information, and layout designs of integrated circuits (Framework Agreement Z, Art 3.1). The Framework Agreement recited the obligations of Member States to implement intra-ASEAN intellectual property arrangements in line with their international intellectual property obligations, in particular, their obligations under the WTO Agreement on Trade Related Intellectual Property Rights (Blakeney, 1996). Among the co-operative measures to enhance the enforcement of intellectual property rights, the Framework Agreement proposes co-operation in cross-border protection and the networking of ASEAN judicial authorities and enforcement agencies (Framework Agreement Z, Art. 3.3.1). Additionally, the Framework Agreement proposes the networking of training facilities and the exchange of personnel (Framework Agreement Z, Art. 3.3.4). Prior to the 1995 Bangkok Summit, ASEAN had hesitated to involve itself in intellectual property matters, taking the view that intellectual property rights tended toward the perpetuation of trade imbalances between developed and developing countries (Sirat, 1997).

The Bangkok Declaration was accompanied by expressions of the importance of the interrelationship between trade, investment and intellectual property. The first proposal for co-operation on intellectual property was made to the ASEAN Senior Economic Officers Meeting (SEOM) in Jakarta in August 1994. Thailand chaired the first meeting of

ASEAN's Working Group on Intellectual Property, which met at Chiang Mai in September 1994. Thailand as chair, proposed the first draft of the Framework Agreement. The Framework Agreement was proposed in the context of the establishment of an Asian Free Trade Area ('AFTA'). The Bangkok Summit Declaration, which accompanied the Framework Agreement, acknowledged 'the importance of intellectual property in intra-ASEAN and world trade' (Bangkok Summit Declaration 1995 Art 8 35 ILM 1067).

In the Special Meeting of ASEAN in July 1997, which welcomed the admission of Laos and Myanmar into ASEAN, the intention of members to establish an ASEAN intellectual property union, as part of a commercial union, was reiterated. The First Informal Leaders' Summit, held in Jakarta on 30 November 1996, endorsed the Basic Framework of the ASEAN Mekong Basin Development Co-operation, to promote the economic integration of economies of the ASEAN and non-ASEAN riparian states.

INTELLECTUAL PROPERTY CO-OPERATION BETWEEN MEKONG RIVER BASIN COUNTRIES

Parallelling the Thai intellectual property initiatives within ASEAN, have been comparable initiatives by Thailand among the countries of the Mekong Valley Basin: Cambodia, Laos, Myanmar, and Vietnam, as well as with China. This initiative commenced with a Memorandum of Understanding on Bilateral Co-operation in the Field of Industrial Property, which was signed by Thailand and Vietnam on 22 April 1994. This MOU, which predated Vietnamese membership of ASEAN,[2] contained many of the ingredients of the Framework Agreement. It proposed bilateral co-operation in the exchange of information and staff, comparative studies of procedures and practices, and the use of automation and dissemination of information on industrial property (Weeraworawit, 1996). The MOU was followed by a Co-operation Programme, which was promulgated on 17 February 1995 and which was initiated with a joint working group to determine common criteria on well-known marks. On 7 December 1996 Thailand and Vietnam signed an MOU on Copyright and Neighbouring rights, which proposed a plan of co-operation, similar to that proposed for industrial property.

Similar bilateral arrangements in relation to industrial property were made between Thailand and Laos by memorandum in 1994. A Plan of Actions on Industrial Property was agreed between Laos and Thailand on 30 January 1996 proposing information exchanges and linkages between the Thai Department of Intellectual Property and the Lao Science, Technology and Environment Organization. Preliminary consultative meetings have also been held between Thailand and Myanmar and between Thailand and Cambodia to establish arrangements for intellectual property co-operation.

Thailand has also been conducting negotiations on intellectual property co-operation with the People's Republic of China. Memoranda of Understanding were signed between Thailand and China in the fields of trademarks (6 April 1995), patents (7 April 1995), and copyright (1 December 1995). A major objective of these MOUs was the promotion of regional co-operation in intellectual property.

The Thai architect of these bilateral intellectual property arrangement identified it as 'the most significant development,' the 'clear determination to co-operate closely and endeavour to reach common positions in both bilateral and ASEAN contexts' (Weeraworawit, 1996). The various bilateral arrangements which Thailand has negotiated with the Mekong Basin group of countries will no doubt strengthen its position as the leader in this field in ASEAN. For example in the 1996 meetings of the Paris and Berne Unions, Thailand was elected Chair of the Asia group of developing countries. A regional consultative meeting convened by Thailand in Chiang Mai formulated an Asian position for the WIPO Diplomatic Conference on copyright in December 1996. The leadership which Thailand has assumed in regional intellectual property arrangements will inevitably enhance its position in the negotiations which will ensue concerning the location of the ASEAN patent and trade mark offices.

INTELLECTUAL PROPERTY AND TECHNOLOGY TRANSFER

The close inter-relationship between intellectual property and technology transfer underpins most national and international legislative regimes (Blakeney, 1989). For example, a principal objective of the ASEAN Framework Agreement is the exploration by Member States of 'appropriate intra-ASEAN co-operation arrangements in the field of intellectual property contributing to … the transfer and dissemination of technology (Framework Agreement Art. 1.3).' Among the principles animating the Framework Agreement is 'the adoption of measures necessary for the promotion of the public interest in all sectors of vital importance to the Member State's socio-economic and technological development, which are consistent with international obligations (Framework Agreement Art. 2.4).' To this end, Art. 2.5 refers to the necessity for Member states to 'adopt appropriate measures to prevent the abuse of intellectual property rights by right holders or the resort to practices which unreasonably restrain trade or adversely affect the international transfer of technology.'

Similar provisions are contained in the TRIPs Agreement.[3] The preamble to the Agreement recognizes 'the underlying policy objectives of national systems for the protection of intellectual policy, including developmental and technological objectives.' Article 7 recites the objective that:

> The protection and enforcement of intellectual property rights should contribute to the promotion of technological innovation and to the transfer and dissemination of technology, to the mutual advantage of producers and users of technological knowledge in a manner conducive to social and economic welfare, and to a balance of rights and obligations.

Article 40 permits Members to enact measures to eliminate provisions in intellectual property licences which 'may have adverse effects on trade and may impede the transfer and dissemination of technology.'

The assumption of the efficacy of intellectual property protection in promoting the transfer and acquisition of technology is reflected in the priority which ASEAN has given to the introduction of intellectual property and technology transfer regimes. However, ASEAN, particularly with the admission of Laos, Myanmar, and Vietnam and the proposed admission of Cambodia, comprises a group of countries at diverse developmental stages and with diverse political and legal traditions. Consequently, the approaches within ASEAN to the regulation of technology transfer reveal this background diversity. Within ASEAN, these approaches range from the laissez faire attitude of Singapore, which allows an unregulated free market in technology, through the partial regulation which applies in Indonesia and Malaysia, to the comprehensive technology transfer code enacted in Vietnam. For countries such as Cambodia, Laos, and Myanmar, emerging from periods of recent isolation and turbulence, technology transfer legislation is yet to be enacted, as only preliminary intellectual property arrangements are in place.

Surveyed below, as a recent exemplar of the detailed prescription of technology transfer arrangements within ASEAN, is the technology transfer regime adopted by Vietnam. This is contrasted with the recent legislation of the Philippines, which considerably dilutes the formerly prescriptive technology transfer regime.

Vietnam

Doi Moi and Technology Transfer

A central aspect of the policy of Doi Moi, or modernization of the Vietnamese economy, which was inaugurated in the late 1980's was the encouragement of the importation of foreign capital and technology. Three legal instruments were promulgated to facilitate the transfer of technology. An Ordinance on the Transfer of Foreign Technology to Vietnam was promulgated by the State Council in December 1988. This was accompanied by an interpretative Decree on Licensing which was promulgated by the Council of Ministers. In March 1991, a further Decree on the Transfer of Foreign Technology was promulgated by the Council of Ministers and this was amplified in January 1994 with a Circular on Transfer of Foreign Technology into Vietnam which was issued by the Ministry of Science Technology and Environment (MOSTE), which was the Government authority entrusted with the administration of technology transfers. A subsequent Circular on Licensing Contracts was issued by MOSTE in April 1994 to provide guidelines for the implementation of regulations on the approval and registration of the licensing of industrial property and know-how.

In addition to these technology transfer instruments in February 1989 an Ordinance on Industrial Property Rights was promulgated by the State Council and this was supplemented by an Ordinance on Author's Rights, which was promulgated in February 1987 and substantially amended by a similar Ordinance in December 1994.[4] Finally A Law on Foreign Investment, which was promulgated in December 1987 and amended in June 1990 and December 1992 contained provisions dealing with technology transfer in the context of foreign investment projects.

By the mid 1990s it was perceived that there were a number of problems with the implementation and appropriateness of these technology transfer laws. These included the following:

- The various statutory instruments were overlapping and inconsistent in effect. Different regimes were established for technology transfer transactions and for licensing agreements and for the transfer of technology within the context of foreign investment transactions;
- Different evaluation authorities administered technology transfer agreements applying different approaches to the approvals process. Technology transfer and licensing fell within the purview of MOSTE, but the evaluation of foreign investment projects was undertaken by the State Committee for Co-operation and Investment, an instrumentality of the Ministry of Finance;
- A number of the regulations were considered to be unnecessarily harsh on transferors. For example, clause 6 of the Licensing Circular made licensors responsible for intellectual property breaches of third parties. Also the 1994 Circular provided that the recipient of technology within a foreign investment project could defer payments until such time as the project became profitable. The obligation of transferors to transfer

improvements free of charge to transferees was perceived to be particularly unrealistic;[5]

- Some regulations were considered to be confusingly vague, for example the 1991 Technology Transfer Decree in Article 4.2 required transferor's to guarantee that technology would not result 'in any effects which may be detrimental to the environment such as "... damage to the cultural and social aspects of populated areas;'"
- Another problem was that a number of provisions were considered to be commercially unrealistic in that they mandated contract terms which were usually the subject of negotiation between commercial parties. For example the 1994 technology Transfer Circular stipulated the precise content of conditions and warranties;
- The remuneration provisions of the various instruments were considered to be unnecessarily complex, as well as conflicting;
- The gradual liberalization of the Vietnamese economy following Doi Moi rendered inappropriate some of the restrictions placed upon the permissible forms of commercial organization. For example, the prohibition against the appointment by a transferor of a sales agent and distributor was recognized as being an obstacle to manufacturing arrangements; and
- Finally, the difficulties which foreign investors experienced with the technology transfer regime was reflected in the declining number of approvals of foreign investment projects in the country. For example, in Hanoi 62 projects were approved for 1994; 59 in 1995; and 35 for the first 10 months of 1996, a rate of decline of 38 per cent (*Viet Nam News* 15 November 1996).

During 1995 and 1996 Vietnam prepared three drafts of a Memorandum of Understanding to support its application for membership of the WTO. As the corollary to this membership was the obligation to conform its intellectual property laws to TRIPs standards, the time was opportune for a review also of the technology transfer laws of Vietnam.[6] On 28 October 1995, a Civil Code was promulgated by the National Assembly of Vietnam. In Part 6 of the Civil Code, chapters were included on the subjects of Copyright, Industrial Property and Technology Transfer. The Civil Code, which came into force in July 1996, replaced the scheme of technology transfer and intellectual property laws which preceded it. As the Civil Code is a necessarily general pronouncement on these subjects, supplementary explanatory legislation is required.

Intellectual Property Under the Civil Code

(1) Copyright

The first copyright protection measure in Vietnam was the 1994 Ordinance on Copyright. This was replaced from 1 July 1996, with the copyright provisions of the Civil Code. Protection is given under chapter I of Part Six of the Code to the creators of original literary, artistic, scientific, and technical works. However in the technology transfer provisions, contained in chapter 1H of the Part, copyright is not identified as an object of technology transfer, beyond the reference in that chapter to computer software and drawings (Civil Code Art.806.1.b).

(2) Industrial property

Article 781 identifies as the objects of industrial property protected by the State: 'inventions, utility solutions, industrial designs, trademarks and names of origin of goods.' Systems for the registration of these industrial property objects is established under the Code and Art.806.2 provides that 'if the objects of industrial property are protected as objects of industrial property, then the transfer of ownership or the right of use thereof must be carried out in accordance with the law before the technology is transferred.'

Technology Transfer under the Civil Code

Technology

Article 806 of the Civil Code identified the objects of technology transfer as:

(i) objects of industrial property attached to or separated from the machines or equipment permitted by law to be transferred;
(ii) know-how, technical knowledge in the forms of technology processes, technological solutions and processes, computer software, drawings, formulas, technological data, technical plans with or without attached machines and equipment;
(iii) technical services, training of technicians and information concerning the transferred technology;
(iv) methods for rationalizing production.

A criticism which had been made of the earlier technology transfer regime is that it was confined to objects of industrial property and had not included technology embodied in copyright, such as computer programs and technology which was contained in *sui generis* intellectual property categories such as the layout designs of integrated circuits and plant variety rights. The principal expansion effected by Article 806 of the Civil Code is through the inclusion of computer software in the list of items of know-how and technical knowledge which are objects of technology transfer.

Article 806 also requires that if the relevant technology involves the use of an industrial property right, its transmission or use must comply with the industrial property laws of Vietnam.

The Technology Transfer Decree seeks to expand the Code provisions by supplying a definition of 'technology' as meaning 'a systematic combination of solutions generated by the implementation of scientific knowledge' being used to settle problems 'arising in production and business activities.' This definition is in line with that recommended by the World Intellectual Property Organization in its Licensing Guide for Developing Countries (WIPO 1977 Geneva 28).

Transferable Technology

Article 5 of the Decree prescribes the requirements of transferable technology. In summary, these include the requirement that: the technology has to enhance production capacity, create new jobs, increase product quality, reduce production costs, facilitate import substitution or assist in the expansion of exports. Improved environmental protection and production safety, are also included as criteria.

Prohibited from transfer are:

- technologies which do not meet legal requirements on labour safety, labour sanitation and environmental protection;
- technologies with negative impacts with respect to culture, society and security; and
- technologies prohibited by law from transfer

The Approvals Authority

Article 31 of the Technology Transfer Decree provides that MOSTE is the primary body entrusted with the approval of technology contracts under the Decree. A potential source of confusion is the fact that where the transfer of technology occurs within the context of a foreign investment project, as a contribution towards the capital of a joint venture under the Vietnamese Law on Foreign Investment, it may be the subject of an over-riding approval from the Ministry of Finance. This problem can be resolved if Vietnam adopts a solution similar to that in the Philippines where the approval of technology transfers is entrusted to an approvals body which comprises representatives from all relevant ministries, government and non-government authorities, and from universities and research institutes. In this way the limited pool of approvals expertise in the country can be shared by relevant ministries.

Article 33.3 of the Decree provides that contracts with a value of below US$50,000 do not have to be submitted to MOSTE for approval, unless they are funded from the State budget. Otherwise, Art. 33.1 requires that MOSTE approves technology transfer contracts:

i. with a value above US$500,000;
ii. involving the transfer of foreign technology to Vietnam;
iii. involving the transfer of Vietnamese technology outside the country;
iv. involving industrial property rights; and
v. management contracts with training and technical support and a foreign investment component.

The Approvals Process

The application for consideration and approval of technology transfer contracts by MOSTE requires the submission of a dossier comprising the form of application, the contract with relevant appendices, and an explanation of the objectives and feasibility of the relevant technology. Article 34.3 of the Decree suggests that this explanation can comprise a feasibility study, a justification of the contract, analyses of the market, raw material requirements, and financial and efficiency aspects of the technology.

An application fee for consideration and approval of a technology transfer contract is levied under Art. 30 of the Decree. This is graduated according to the value of the project and ranges between US$100 and US$10,000. Where the technology transfer involves a contribution to foreign investment capital it is exempt from this fee.

The approvals body is obliged by Art. 35 to issue its decision within 30 days. It may require amendment of documents under the Article and a further 60 day period is prescribed within which this has to be achieved. This limitation of the time during which the approvals process must be finalized, will, if achieved, involve a significant improvement in Vietnamese practice in this regard. The experience of transferors to date is that delays in obtaining approvals have been extremely lengthy.

The Technology Transfer Contract

Article 809 of the Civil Code requires that all technology transfers be effected by written contract. Article 11 of the Decree permits the contract to involve multiple documents. The particulars of this contract are prescribed in Art. 812 of the Civil Code and amplified in Art. 16 of the Decree. These include:

- particulars of the transferee and transferor;
- definitions of contractual terms;
- description of the technology to be transferred;

- documentary evidence of industrial property rights;
- a schedule of the transfer timetable;
- a statement of the rights and obligations of contracting parties;
- details of technical training and support;
- price and payment particulars;
- undertakings as to the quality and reliability of technology,
- confidentiality, environmental protection and work safety,
- non-breach of third party rights and terms of payment;
- obligations of the parties to co-operate and exchange information;
- conditions on amendment and termination;
- duration; and
- applicable laws

Article 17 of the Decree requires the contract to be prepared in Vietnamese and a common language agreed by the parties. Both languages will have equal validity. The commencement date of the contract is stipulated by Art. 811 of the Civil Code and Art. 21 of the Decree to be the date on which approval is obtained from the approvals authority.

Price

Article 17.2 of the Decree provides that 'subject to the modernity, contents and exclusivity of the relevant technology' the price of the technology shall be equal to:

(i) from 0 per cent to 5 per cent of the net sale price of products; or
(ii) from 0 per cent to 25 per cent of after-tax profits from products sole or services provided; or
(iii) from 0 per cent to 8 per cent of total invested capital, less the land value, provided that the latter does not exceed 20 per cent of the registered capital of the project.

In the case of high technology, technology of significance to Vietnamese development, or technology contributing to the development of products for export, Art. 26.3 permits the price to account for up to 8 per cent of the net sale price of products or to 30 per cent of after-tax profits.

'Net sale price' is defined in Art. 2.13 of the Decree to mean the total sales price of products or services produced utilizing the technology from which is deducted: indirect taxes, prices and taxes for component parts and semi-finished products, and packing, transportation and advertising costs.
The method of payment permitted under Art. 27 of the Decree is:

(a) capital contribution of the transferred technology;

(b) periodic payment according to the percentage of after-tax profit;
(c) payment in lump-sum, by installments or in kind; or
(d) a combination of the above.

Under Art. 29 of the Decree the proceeds from the technology transfer may be subject to a scheduled tax.

Warranties
(i) Quality
Article 8 of the Decree enshrines the obligation within Art. 815 of the Civil Code that the transferor warrants the quality of the transferred technology. The Code in Art. 814 takes the objectives of the contract, together with product specifications and environmental factors into account in defining this warranty.
(ii) Title
Article 8.3 of the Decree requires the transferor to warrant that third party rights are not infringed by the contract. This is emphasized by Art. 12 of the Decree which, in the case of industrial property rights requires the transferor to warrant entitlement to use such rights.

Remedies for breach
Article 815.3 of the Code requires the transferor to make good any breaches of warranty as to quality or title. In the event that these breaches are not cured, Art.8.4.c of the Decree permits the transferee to seek settlement or to terminate the contract with compensation.

Duration
Article 810.1 of the Civil Code prescribes a maximum seven year duration for technology transfer contracts, commencing from the date that the contract takes effect. In 'extraordinary circumstances' the Article makes provision for the extension of that term. The Decree, in Art. 19, identifies three such extraordinary circumstances. These are: (a) where upon the expiry of the contract, the technology remains a globally advanced technology; (b) the technology has great significance for socio-economic development; and (c) the technology transfer involves the maintenance to international standards of the quality of goods produced under the contract. In the case of technology transfer under foreign investment contracts, Art. 810.2 provides that the duration of any technology transferred under the project will be computed according to the term of the investment.

This duration provision has attracted considerable criticism from practising lawyers within Vietnam as inadequate for many technology projects (Counsell in Blakeney & Sinden (eds), 1996). In any event it ought not be too difficult for a contract not to satisfy one of the requirements of Art. 19.2 to secure an extension at least to a 10 year term.

Prohibition of Restrictive Terms

In common with most systems for the statutory regulation of technology transfer, the Vietnamese legislation proscribes the inclusion of a number of restrictive provisions. These include:

(a) the supply of technology to which is tied the supply of unwanted goods, labour and industrial property rights;
(b) forcing the transferee to comply with limits in relation to the scale of production, price, scope of consumption, and the appointment of product agents;
(c) restricting exports by the transferee;
(d) inhibitions on research by a transferee;
(e) compulsory assignment of improvements; and
(f) unreasonable prohibitions on the use of technology after the termination of the agreement.

Article 9 of the Decree confers a positive right upon transferees to develop and improve technology on the basis of 'equality and mutual benefit'.

Confidentiality

Article 820 of the Civil Code permits the imposition of confidentiality obligations and in Art.820.2 provides for the compensation of a transferor if this term is breached. This is an important obligation in a country which does not yet have an unfair-competition law dealing with this issue or a general law confidentiality requirement.

This protection is useful as Art.36 permits agreements to be submitted to appropriate experts for their comments during the approvals process.

Avoidance of Technology Contracts

Article 23 of the Decree renders null and void technology contracts which:

(i) breach Art.3 in that the transferor is not legally capable of transferring the technology or where the transferor of industrial property rights cannot make good its title to those rights;
(ii) the objects and contents of the contract are otherwise inconsistent with the Decree;
(iii) the contract is not in a written form and registered under the Decree; and

(iv) the transferor loses any relevant industrial property rights during the currency of the contract.

In the event of voidness Art. 24 provides that the contract may not be enforced or completed and each party shall be liable for any damages arising from defaults which lead to voidness. In the case of partial invalidity, Art. 24.2 provides for the severance of invalid portions.

Amendment and Termination

Article 37 permits the amendment or modification of technology contracts. In the event of such alteration the Article requires the altered contract to be submitted to the approvals authority. Article 825 of the Civil Code obliges parties to inform each other about new scientific and technical information which may affect the performance of a technology contract and must consider the possibility of alteration of the technology contract to take this into account. Article 825.3 imposes the expense of any alteration in these circumstances upon the transferor. This may be considered a trifle harsh and commercially unrealistic, particularly as the transferor is likely to be the source of relevant new information.

Termination of the contract is provided for in Art. 25 upon expiry or according to the agreement of the parties. Where the parties agree to terminate the contract, they are required to notify the approvals authority and to make good any damages which may be caused to third parties. Termination may also result from force majeure or from an irremediable breach of the contract.

In the event of termination caused by expiry or force majeure, Art. 25.2 provides that all provisions concerning the settlement of disputes and claims shall continue to be in force. Where, however, the contract is terminated due to the breach of one of the parties, Art. 25.3 provides that all damages will be borne by the defaulting party, unless otherwise provided in the contract.

Types of Technology Transfer Contracts

The Civil Code and its implementing Decree provide specific provisions for particular types of technology transfer contracts.

(i) Industrial property licences

Where a technology transfer contract involves an industrial property right, Art. 821 of the Civil Code prohibits the exclusive transfer of such rights to third parties. Where the transfer of an industrial property right involves a transferee in liability, the Article provides for indemnification of the transferee. Article 12.3 of the Decree limits the duration of a licence of an industrial property right to the term for which that right is registered in Vietnam.

(ii) Trademark licences
Article 822 of the Civil Code and Article 13 of the Decree permit the insertion of quality control provisions in trademark licences. This recognizes the requirement in most trademark laws that a trademark owner controls the use of that mark so that its use by a licensee can be imputed to an owner, thereby avoiding deception as to the origin of goods and services supplied under the mark.
(iii) Technical services and consultancy agreements
In contracts for the supply of technical consultancy and supplementary services, Art. 824 of the Civil Code requires inclusion within technology contracts of the qualification of the persons rendering the services and the results to be achieved under the contract. In the event that the parties cannot agree on a warranty of quality of the services, Art. 824.2 provides that the party rendering the services has satisfied the obligations of the contract if those services are rendered 'with due care, with proper qualifications and within the stipulated time.'

Article 14 of the Decree provides in effect that the quality of the services which are provided under the contract will be measured against the standard of competence to which the transferee aspires under the contract to ensure product quality and the technical and economic criteria set out in the contract.

Dispute Resolution
Article 39 of the Decree encourages the resolution of disputes through negotiation and then arbitration. In the event that a dispute under the contract cannot be settled in this way, Art. 39.3 provides for judicial resolution. Where the dispute is between Vietnamese parties, the applicable law will be the law of Vietnam. Where a foreign party is involved, Art. 39.4 permits the parties to make their own choice of law.

Penalties for Breach of the Decree
One of the final matters to be settled under the Decree is whether to impose criminal penalties for breaches of its provisions. Early drafts of the Decree provided for a range of fines and pecuniary penalties, which were related to the value of the technology contract. The Drafting Committee is currently considering the removal of these criminal sanctions, thereby instituting a more commercially acceptable technology transfer regime.

The Philippines

Overview

Unlike Vietnam, which is fairly new to the business of technology transfer regulation, the Philippines has had a regulatory structure in place since 1978. Presidential Decree No. 1520 of that year, established a Technology Transfer Board which was obliged to scrutinize technology transfer transactions to ensure that they complied with a catalogue of mandatory and advisory contractual terms, along the lines of the approach which has now been adopted in Vietnam. In 1986 the Technology Transfer Board was merged with the Philippines Patent Office to create the Bureau of Patents Trademarks and Technology Transfer (BPTTT). The regulations governing the import of technologies were incorporated into the Rules of Procedures of the Technology Transfer Registry (TTR) of the BPTTT.

As part of a policy of deregulation inaugurated in the Philippines at the end of 1992, the Rules of procedure of the TTR were amended on 9 November 1992, to permit the automatic registration of technology transfer arrangements, providing for royalty payments in an amount less than 5 per cent of net sales.

Further liberalization followed with the Republic Act 8293 of 6 June 1996, which introduces the Intellectual Property Code of the Philippines (IPC), which took effect on 1 January 1998. Under the IPC, technology transfer arrangements which do not contain any prohibited clauses and which complies with certain mandatory provisions, are not required to be registered. No cap is placed on royalties and a mechanism to resolve disputes arising from technology transfer payments is established.

Technology Transfer Arrangements

Under s 4.2 of the IPC, the term 'technology transfer arrangements' refers to contracts or arrangements involving the transfer of systematic knowledge for the manufacture of a product, the application of a process, or rendering of a service, including management contracts; and the transfer, assignment or licensing of all forms of intellectual property rights, including licensing of computer software, except software developed for a mass market. Previously, technology transfer arrangements which were examinable under the legislation were confined to industrial property licences between foreign and domestic companies. It now includes those entered into between domestic companies and includes copyright and integrated circuits.

Prohibited Clauses in Technology Transfer Arrangements

Under s.87 of the IPC, the following restrictive clauses are not allowed in technology transfer arrangements:

(i) Export restrictions
Clauses which directly or indirectly restrict the export of products manufactured by a technology recipient under a technology transfer arrangement are not acceptable under the IPC, unless justifiable for the protection of the legitimate interests of the parties. This may include restrictions obliged to prevent the infringement of another person's intellectual property rights;

(ii) Post-expiry restrictions
Restrictions on the use of technology supplied after the expiry of technology transfer arrangements are not permitted, except where the early termination of an agreement is attributable to the technology recipient. Similarly the IPC prohibits the continued payment for intellectual property rights after their expiration, termination, or invalidation;

(iii) Improvements made by licensee
The IPC invalidates clauses which require that major improvements made by a technology supplier should be supplied free of charge, or that they should be patented in the name of the supplier, or required to be exclusively assigned to the technology supplier;

(iv) No-contest clauses
The IPC prohibits clauses which prevent a technology recipient from contesting the validity of licensed patents;

(v) Exclusive dealing clauses
Provisions which prohibit a technology recipient from dealing with competitors of the technology supplier are invalidated by the IPC. Such provisions include prohibitions on obtaining patented technology from competitors of the technology supplier and provisions, which tie-in the supply of raw materials, components and equipment from the technology supplier. Such tie-ins may be permitted where the selling price of tied-in items is based on the international market price for those items and there are no other cheaper sources of supply and where the tie-in requirement is necessary to maintain the quality standards prescribed by the technology supplier;

(vi) Restrictions on research and development
The IPC prohibits clauses which restrict the activities of a technology recipient in absorbing and adapting the transferred technology to local conditions; and

(vii) Exemption from liabilities
Finally, the IPC prohibits provisions which exempt the technology supplier from liability for non-fulfilment of his responsibilities arising under the technology transfer arrangement and/or liability arising from third party suits brought about by the use of the licensed technology.

Mandatory provisions
Prescribed by the IPC as mandatory provisions to be included in technology transfer agreements are:

(i) the choice of Philippines law in governing interpretation of the contract, with the venue for litigation being the courts in the place where the technology recipient maintains its principal office;
(ii) a commitment from the technology supplier to provide continuing access to the acquirer of improvements to the technology;
(iii) in cases of arbitration, the arbitration procedure of the Arbitration Law of the Philippines or the internationally accepted rules of arbitration, such as those of UNCTRAL or the ICC, shall apply and the venue of arbitration shall be the Philippines or a neutral country; and
(iv) section 88.4 of the IPC provides that Philippine taxes on all payments relating to the technology transfer arrangements shall be borne by the licensor.

Remuneration
The IPC having abandoned the previous policy of regulating the amount of royalty which may be imposed, provides an administrative mechanism for the resolution of disputes involving royalty rates. Jurisdiction to resolve these disputes is conferred on the Documentation and Information Technology Transfer Bureau (DITTB).

Exceptional Cases
Section 91 of the IPC provides that in exceptional or meritorious cases, where substantial benefits will accrue to the economy, exemption from any of the above provisions may be allowed by the DITTB after evaluation on a case by case basis. Such benefits to the economy may include: increase in foreign exchange earnings, employment generation, regional dispersal of industries, substitution with and use of local raw materials, high technology content of a transaction and registered companies with 'pioneer status' granted by the board of Investments.

Mekong Basin Group
A central assumption underpinning technology transfer and intellectual property laws is that technological development is a precondition for economic development and that an intellectual property system is indispensable to the acquisition of technology. The perceived significance of the role of intellectual property in economic development probably explains the establishment of the World Intellectual Property Organization (WIPO) in 1970 as a specialized agency of the United Nations Organization. The

preamble to WIPO's Model Law for Developing Countries on Inventions states:

(a) the importance of new technology for economic development and in particular the industrialization of the country;
(b) the necessity of creating new technology in the country and of adapting existing technology to the needs of the country; and
(c) the necessity of having access to foreign technology (WIPO Model Law for Developing Countries on Inventions 1979).

Similarly WIPO's Licensing Guide for Developing Countries commences with the assertion that:

> Industrialization is a major objective of developing countries as a means to the attainment of high levels of the well-being of the peoples of such countries. The attainment of science and the development of a technological base are the essential conditions of industrial growth. The development of a technological base in a developing country depends on the existence of indigenous technological capacities and the acquisition of selected technology from abroad .... (WIPO Licensing Guide for Developing Countries 1977).

This reasoning explains the endeavours of the new members of the Mekong Basin group to promulgate intellectual property laws as an early priority.

Cambodia

In August 1991, the Cambodian Ministry of Commerce established a Trade Mark Registry and an informal procedure for the registration of trade and service marks. The period of protection is 10 years, with the opportunity for renewals. A mark is vulnerable to cancellation for non-use if it is not used during a five-year period. Where infringements occur, a complaint may be lodged with the Ministry of Commerce, which may require the Economic Police to investigate the complaint. Following this process, civil enforcement may ensue or the complaint may be passed on to the Customs authorities for action.

As part of the upgrading its legal system to facilitate democracy and to encourage the development of the economy, the Royal Government of Cambodia has issued three draft intellectual property statutes: the Patents and Designs Act, the Marks Protection Act, and the Copyright and Related Works Act. In 1995 Cambodia became a member of WIPO.

Laos

From 1986, Laos has been moving towards a free market economy. Decree 104, issued in 1987, recognizes the need to protect intellectual property rights in Laos. Although this decree was not a substantive intellectual property statute, Laos government ministries have relied upon the authority granted in the decree to permit the registration of industrial property rights. A Department of Industrial Property (DIP) was established under Decree 104 and it currently attends to the registration of trade marks. The DIP is authorized to call upon other relevant government ministries to assist where necessary in the enforcement of trade mark rights.

Myanmar

Following the admission of Myanmar into ASEAN, four intellectual property statutes have been prepared by the Myanmar Attorney General's Office (Finch & Myint, 1997). Until these laws are enacted, there are no IP laws in the country. However, some protection can be obtained under the Myanmar Registration Act, which provides that documents not required by law to be registered, may be registered with the Office of Registration of Deeds. Direction 13 of the Registration Act provides that trade marks may be registered by means of a declaration of ownership. In practice, registrations are renewed every two years and in case of infringements, both civil and criminal actions may be brought (Finch & Myint, 1997). In the case of other categories of industrial property, the Patents and Designs (Emergency Provisions) Act 1946 provides that the India Patents and Designs Act of 1911 is still in force in Myanmar.[7]

The Copyright Act of Myanmar came into force in 1914. This is an adaptation of the UK Copyright Act, 1911. The copyright period for works first published in Myanmar is 10 years from the date of first publication. The Act envisages the possibility of establishing a copyright registration system, but this has never been implemented.

With the accession of Cambodia, Laos, and Myanmar to the Mekong Basin Group, under the tutelage of Thailand, close co-operation in intellectual property measures has been established, with a view to the harmonization of their intellectual property laws.

NOTES

1 ASEAN then comprised Brunei, Indonesia, Malaysia, the Philippines, Singapore, Thailand, and Vietnam.

2 Vietnam became a member of ASEAN at the Bangkok Summit December 1995.

3 For a comprehensive discussion of this agreement see M. Blakeney *Trade Related Aspects of Intellectual Property Rights: A Concise Guide to the TRIPs Agreement* 1996.

4 See Dr Vu Khae Trai, Legislative Framework for Intellectual Property Rights in Vietnam Blakeney and Sinden (eds 1996) *Proceedings of the National Symposium on the Role of Intellectual Property Rights in the International Trade and Business 23.*

5 Ibid, 6.

6 For the influence of TRIPs on the intellectual property law reform in Asia see Blakeney (1996) *The Influence of TRIPs on Intellectual Property Laws in the Asia Pacific Region* EIPR.

7 Myanmar was officially separated from India in 1937.

REFERENCES

Blakeney, M. (1989) *Legal Aspects of Technology Transfer to Developing Countries*. Oxford: ESC.

– (1996a) *Trade Related Aspects of Intellectual Property Rights: A Concise Guide to the TRIPs Agreement*. London, Sweet & Maxwell.

– (1996b) 'The Impact of the TRIPs Agreement in the Asia Pacific Region,' *European Intellectual Property Review* 110, p. 544.

Civil Code of Vietnam (1996).

Counsell, Debra (1996) 'Foreign Investment in Vietnam,' in: M. Blakeney and P. Sinden (eds) *Proceedings of the National Symposium on the Role of Intellectual Property Rights in International Trade and Business.* Hanoi, May 1996, IIPTI, 23.

Finch & Myint (1997) 'Myanmar Moves Forward, but IP Lags Behind,' *IP Asia*, p. 36.

Framework Agreement on Intellectual Property 1996 35 ILM 1072).

Sirat 'Intellectual Property Co-operation among Association of South East Asian Nations (ASEAN) Present and Future Plans', WIPO Sub-Regional Round Table on the Implications of the ASEAN Free Trade Area (AFTA) on the Intellectual Property System, Jakarta, 9-10 May, 1997 Bangkok Summit Declaration of 1995, Art.8, 35 ILM 1067 (1996).

Trai, V.K. (1996) 'Legislative Framework for Intellectual Property Rights in Vietnam,' in: M. Blakeney and P. Sinden (eds) *Proceedings of the National Symposium on the Role of Intellectual Property Rights in: International Trade and Business.* Hanoi, May 1996, IIPTI 23.

Viet Nam News, 15 November 1996, p. 1.

Vu, K.T. (1996) 'Legislative Framework for Intellectual Property Rights in Vietnam,' in: M. Blakeney and P. Sinden (eds) *Proceedings of the National Symposium on the Role of Intellectual Property Rights in International Trade and Business.* Hanoi, May 1996, IIPTI, 23.

Weeraworawit, Weerawit (1996) 'The Rising Tide of Regional Cooperation on Intellectual Property: Thailand's Role and Initiatives,' Department of Intellectual Property, Annual Report 1996, 45, p. 48.

World Intellectual Property Organization Licensing Guide for Developing Countries 17 & 28,Geneva, 1977, WIPO.

– Model Law for Developing Countries on Inventions vol. 1, Geneva, 1979, WIPO.

PART FIVE

LAW AND DEVELOPMENT AND THE REGION

CHAPTER 13

RESOLVING TRADE DISPUTES IN ASIA: AN ESSAY ABOUT THE LAWS, INSTITUTIONS, AND CULTURES[1]

ROBERT E. LUTZ[2]

THE MILIEU FOR PUBLIC AND PRIVATE DISPUTE-RESOLUTION IN ASIA

'It is better to enter a tiger's mouth than a court of law,' so an ancient Chinese proverb states (Theroux, 1976:124; Maher, 1980:260 note; Koa, 1991:439). While it is difficult to generalize, the Asian experience in resolving international trade disputes of both private and public nature tends to confirm this reputed Asian aversion to adversarial processes where parties move from dispute toward resolution of their disputes. The hallmarks of this aversion are well known and frequently described:

1. the overriding concern for harmony so that the goal of resolving a dispute is focused on the restoration and maintenance of the relationship rather than punishing the wrongdoer;
2. the concern for *face* (we often call it 'saving face');
3. the general concern for the total context of the human relationship rather than the functionality of the relationship (Donahey, 1995:74).

Logically, persons influenced by such Asian cultural imperatives would view dispute resolution in a person-oriented, non-adversarial way. The natural inclination of Asians is to lean toward the *softer ADRs*[3] namely, negotiation, consultation, mediation, conciliation. By contrast, Westerners have a cultural tendency to prefer litigation in the settlement of disputes and, to the extent they employ arbitration, tend toward its more adversarial forms making it barely distinguishable from litigation (Coombe, 1996:708). However, cultural predisposition with respect to dispute-resolution must be seen in a larger context of forces both internal and external – operating in Asia today. These forces are, and will be, driving the direction and pace of legal development of regimes designed to resolve public and private trade disputes for the foreseeable future.

The first of these cultural forces suggests that despite the cultural underpinnings described, the rigidity of cultural preference in Asia is not what it used to be. A cultural fusion between Eastern and Western models is gradually occurring. This cultural fusion is making Asian traders more amenable to adversarial dispute-resolution processes, long the domain of the West. As a leading commentator has expressed:

> [T]he traffic on trade, investment, information, aviation, cultural, and educational highways is increasing by leaps and bounds. [T]he explosion of contacts must eventually lead to a two-way process of cultural osmosis (Mahbubani, 1995:111).

Thus, while the preference for less adversarial dispute resolution methods, such as mediation, is certainly still alive, Asians engaged in international trade are increasingly willing to accept arbitration, and even litigation, depending on the hospitality of the forum. In that same respect, as Westerners increase their involvement with international trade in Asia, they are more accepting of the less adversarial, traditionally Asian dispute resolution techniques (Donahey, 1995:77; Coombe, 1996:708).

Second, the sweeping developments in communications and transportation are minimizing the importance of global location. Advances in communication and technology together with the harmonization of legal structures of dispute-resolution have made the site where dispute resolution processes occurs less important than it used to be.[4] A party can agree to arbitrate in almost any Asian country, and expect to be subject to basically the same arbitration laws and rules that would govern arbitration in another Asian country.[5]

Third, the shift towards privatization (and away from socialist and statist economies) in Asia, coupled with the decline of developed-country foreign aid and, a corresponding replacement with private capital,[6] will provide a breeding-ground for increased private trade disputes. The prospect of an increased number of private party disputes is likely, given the increased number of private traders and financiers who are wholly concerned with the bottom line. Furthermore, this prospect of an increased number of private party disputes is enhanced by the current economic *malaise* in Asia today.[7]

To appreciate how these forces are guiding Asian dispute-resolution development, a survey of current Asian dispute-resolution institutions and methods follows. This survey will provide a baseline from which to assess some of the emerging issues contained in the final section of this essay.

NATURE OF DISPUTE RESOLUTION IN ASIA: THE BASELINE

Parties and Fora

Trade disputes can occur between private parties[8] between private and public entities,[9] and between states. Depending upon the relationship of the parties, very different institutions and legal procedures for resolving disputes apply. Most Asian countries have a legal structure for international arbitration and conciliation in-place for private party disputes.[10] Virtually all Asian nations have publicly-financed or privately-financed institutions to administer the dispute resolution processes.[11] In addition, most Asian nations are party to the United Nations *Convention on the Recognition and Enforcement of Foreign Arbitral Awards* – the New York Convention – ((1958) 21 *U S T* 2517, 330 *U N T S* 38), the major multilateral convention on the enforcement of arbitral decisions.

For private disputes, many Asian nations[12] provide an array of alternative dispute mechanisms for foreign parties to resolve their disputes with nationals of the forum country. In addition, many Asian nations function as a neutral (third party) forum to resolve commercial disputes between nationals of other countries.[13] In both types of fora, three basic methods of alternative dispute resolution are employed: consultation, conciliation/ mediation, and arbitration, or a combination of the three.[14]

Consultation between disputing parties appears as the preferred first step of dispute-resolution. Following consultation, the parties engage in conciliation or mediation.[15] If the parties fail to agree on a settlement during this stage, the dispute often proceeds to arbitration. Throughout the dispute resolution process, many Asian arbitrators continue to encourage conciliation. In fact, many Asian nations allow either a blending of the conciliation and arbitration processes or a conjoined procedure (*infra* discussion at III, C). Most Asian countries allow for *ad hoc* arbitration[16] in addition to institutional arbitration. *Ad hoc* arbitration is becoming an increasingly popular alternative for parties which find institutional arbitration not as expedient nor as inexpensive as in the past (Arkin, 1990:502; Wolf, 1995:196-8; Karalis, 1992). Litigation, especially in China, India, and Japan, is definitely a last resort for private disputes.

When a dispute involves both private parties and governmental entities or state enterprises, there are major limitations that restrict dispute resolution through alternative dispute resolution mechanisms. These limitations arise from concerns about state sovereignty. One facility which does provide a forum for the settlement of private party/government entity disputes is the International Center for the Settlement of Investment Disputes of the World Bank (ICSID).[17] In addition, many Asian countries provide fora for private party/government entity disputes and enforce the awards rendered (Nafziger, 1987:642).

Where disputes arise between states within the Asian region, several regional economic organizations are available for dispute resolution, having recently developed that capability. On a global scale, the establishment of the World Trade Organization (WTO) has provided a forum for the resolution of state-to-state trade-related disputes (GATT, 1994).

Regional Economic Institutions

A number of Asian regional organizations provide dispute-settlement facilities for member-states and some (but limited) assistance with respect to private-investor member-state disputes.[18] The Association of Southeast Asian Nations (ASEAN), founded in 1967, currently incorporates nine countries: Thailand, the Philippines, Malaysia, Singapore, Brunei, Vietnam, Indonesia, Laos, and Myanmar.[19] ASEAN was originally conceived as a defensive arrangement for Asian nations to combat communism. Presently, ASEAN exists to promote economic co-operation and social interests of this region (Stephenson, 1994:439; Koh, 1996:844).

The ASEAN Free Trade Area (AFTA) (see generally Haas, 1994:809; Kenevan, 1993:224) was created by the original six ASEAN countries with the Singapore Declaration of 1992 (1992, 31 *ILM* 498). Its purpose was to dismantle intra-regional trade barriers and achieve a free trading area by 2007. This framework agreement further prescribed the following with respect to dispute-settlement mechanisms: 'Any difference between the Member States concerning the interpretation or application of the agreement shall, as far as possible, be settled amicably between the parties, and whenever necessary, an appropriate body shall be designed for the settlement of disputes (ibid).' The process ensures that AFTA disputes, if not resolved by the parties, are ultimately resolved by the Economic Ministers. AFTA Ministers are able to retain maximum flexibility in dispute resolution by shielding disagreements between AFTA members from the public, while maintaining discretion to select what issues are addressed and what decisions are publicly revealed (Kaplan,1996:176).

The Asia–Pacific Economic Cooperation (APEC)[20] came into being at the 1989 ministerial conference in Canberra, Australia, and initially included the ASEAN countries, the US, Korea, Japan, Canada, Australia, and New Zealand (Kodama, 1995:368). Although APEC was originally intended to be an informal consultative forum regarding economic matters, it has since taken on a more formal nature (ibid).[21] In 1994, discussion commenced regarding the formation of a dispute-settlement mechanism for ASEAN member economies (Green, 1995:719; Cardenas and Buranakanits, 1995:67-9). Since APEC is not a rules-based organization, it lacks the competence to establish a formal binding dispute-settlement mechanism (APEC, 1994; Cardenas and Buranakanits, 1995:68). APEC nations felt that trade and other types of disputes between APEC economies have negative implications for the implementation of agreed co-operative agreements. The leaders of APEC nations agreed that, whatever specific arrangements are adopted within APEC, they should supplement the World Trade Organization's dispute settlement mechanism, which will continue to be the primary channel for resolving trade disputes in the region (Kodama, 1995:381-2).

At this time, the APEC dispute mediation process is focused by ways in which disputes can be solved through dialogue and increased understanding. The approach taken is one of practical problem-solving as an effective means to reduce, avoid, and resolve disputes in the APEC region (Davidson, 1997:24). The goal of the APEC dispute mediation process is to find ways in which disputes can be addressed at an early stage by both or all of the involved economies so that member economies may avoid confrontation and dispute escalation, which would entail involving the WTO and other formal agreements to resolve disputes between member economies (Cardenas and Buranakanits,1995:68).

International Institutions

GATT/WTO

Established in 1995, the World Trade Organization's General Council convenes as the Dispute Settlement Body (DSB) to deal with disputes arising from any agreement contained in the GATT Uruguay Round (WTO, 1999). The Dispute Settlement Body (DSB) of the World Trade Organization has sole authority to establish panels, adopt panel and appellate reports, maintain surveillance of implementation and authorize retaliatory measures, if required in cases of non-implementation (ibid; Aldonas, 1995:76; Mota, 1999:75).

The first stage of settling disputes under the World Trade Organization's Dispute Settlement Body requires bilateral consultation between the governments (parties) concerned (WTO Annex 2 Art. 4). If the parties fail to come to an agreement, the establishment of a panel to hear the case may be requested (WTO, 1999). The Panel's report is adopted by the Dispute Settlement Body unless one party notifies the DSB that it intends to appeal a decision, or a consensus among the WTO members forms against adoption of the report (WTO, Annex 2 Art. 16). Either party may appeal to the DSB's Appellate Body (ibid Art. 17; WTO, 1999).

The Dispute allows a 'reasonable period of time' (set by the DSB) to delay implementation of the recommendation (WTO Annex 2 Art. 22; WTO, 1999). Ultimately, some form of compensation is prescribed and paid, or the complainant may request to suspend concessions or obligations to the other party (WTO Annex 2 Art. 22). In the about five years of operation of the WTO's Dispute Settlement Body, Asian countries have actively employed the dispute settlement process of the WTO to complain about trade infractions; they have also been the respondent in numerous cases. However, on only a few occasions has an Asian country filed a complaint against another Asian country.

The effects of the regional co-operatives – such as ASEAN, AFTA and APEC – on the WTO in settling Asian trade disputes are not yet known as these organizations have only recently implemented dispute resolution mechanisms for member countries. The existence of regional economic organizations with dispute resolution mechanisms for intra-member disputes will likely shift away member state reliance from the World Trade Organization's Dispute Settlement Body towards these regional co-operatives.

Both ASEAN and APEC have created their settlement procedures based on the WTO dispute resolution process, and require that the first step between disputing parties be consultations; the same first step is also required by the WTO (Annex 2 Art. 4). Although the initial steps to be followed are the same, the regional co-operatives of ASEAN and APEC are set up so that member parties can avoid resorting to the more public and legalistic procedures that the DSB utilizes. With this in mind, Asian nations which are members of a regional co-operatives and are involved in a dispute have the option of meeting *behind closed doors*. Since these regional co-operatives incorporate regional cultural values, regional co-operative decisions may be rooted in Asian cultural values of harmony and justice, rather than what may be *legally* correct. This type of regional co-operative dispute resolution is, arguably, better suited to the Asian concept of dispute resolution.

WIPO

The World Arbitration and Mediation Center was established in 1994 as part of the International Bureau of the World Intellectual Property Organization (WIPO). WIPO offers arbitration and mediation services for the resolution of commercial disputes between private parties involving intellectual property (WIPO, 1999). The Center offers mediation, arbitration, and expedited arbitration and mediation (ibid). Parties to a dispute may select their own arbitrators, or may leave the choice to the Center. The Center maintains an index of mediators and arbitrators, including a comprehensive list of their qualifications and areas of expertise. Currently, the list is comprised of approximately 650 persons from 61 countries (ibid).

Law of the Sea

The UN Convention of the Law of the Sea (UNCLOS) (1982, 21 *ILM* 1261) which now has about 120 states parties (with the notable exception of the United States), requires that Parties to the Convention settle any dispute between them concerning the interpretation or application of the Convention by peaceful means in accordance with article 2(3) of the UN Charter and by the means indicated in UN Charter article 33(1).[22] Pursuant to UNCLOS article 286, when no settlement is reached, the dispute must be submitted to a court or tribunal having jurisdiction. Those courts with jurisdiction in such matters are: The International Tribunal for the Law of the Sea, including the Seabed Disputes Chamber (recently established in Hamburg, Germany); the International Court of Justice; an arbitral tribunal constituted in accordance with arbitration rules in UNCLOS Annex VII; and a special arbitral tribunal constituted in accordance with Annex VII (Special Arbitration Rules) of the Convention (United Nations, 1999B).

Some important Asian territorial disputes are brewing and may be submitted to this process: the Spratly Islands (claimed by China and four ASEAN countries, Brunei, Malaysia, the Philippines, and Vietnam). Each claim part of the islands, which are believed to be rich with minerals and which straddle strategic sea lanes in the South China Sea. Other potential or existing disputes include: a fishing zones disagreement between Japan and the Republic of Korea related to ownership of small islands in the seas between those countries; and China's continued oil exploration in the South China Sea that is protested by Vietnam (United Nations, 1999A).

ICSID

The International Centre for the Settlement of Investment Disputes (ICSID) was created by the 1965 Washington Convention on the Settlement of Investment Disputes between States and Nationals of Other States to provide accessible facilities for the conciliation and arbitration of international investment disputes (World Bank, 1999). ICSID provides institutional facilities and performs related administrative functions for resolving investment disputes between contracting states and non-state entities. Under Article 25 of the Convention, ICSID's jurisdiction extends to 'any legal dispute arising directly out of an investment between a contracting state (or any constituent subdivision or agency of a Contracting State designated to the Centre by that State) and a national of another Contracting State, which the parties to the dispute consent in writing to submit to the Centre.' (1965, 4 *ILM* 532, 536)

The Centre maintains a roster of qualified potential panelists who may at the request of the parties conduct conciliation or arbitration pursuant to ICSID's rules. Appeals are not allowed, but either party may apply to the ICSID Secretary-General for interpretation, revision, or annulment of the award. Enforcement, however, depends upon the enforcement regime of the country in which enforcement is being sought (ibid; also Koa,1991:464 note).

TRENDS AND ISSUES

In Asia, arbitration awards are more predictably obtained and more readily enforced than court judgments (Burton, 1995:637). Several trends have emerged with regard to alternative dispute resolution in Asia revealing that international alternative dispute-resolution of trade disputes has come of age in Asia.

Emergence of the Chinese ADR Regime

As of 1 January 1989 the Chinese government officially adopted new arbitration rules under the auspices of the China International Economic and Trade Arbitration Commission.[23] The rules, known as '1989 CIETAC Rules' were based upon the UNCITRAL Model Law (1985). A number of fundamental changes were brought on by the CIETAC adoption. The jurisdiction of CIETAC was significantly expanded from the earlier Chinese arbitration framework found in the Foreign Trade Arbitration Commission of China (FTAC Rules) (Fishburne and Chuncheng, 1997:306). In addition, the CIETAC rules allowed for foreign nationals to be appointed to CIETAC's Panel of Arbitrators (ibid). These changes have brought Chinese law in line with international standards (Brown and Rogers, 1997:339). Statistically, according to reports available, Chinese nationals and foreigners are equally successful when using CIETAC (Volz and Haydock, 1996:902).

The enactment in 1995 of the *Arbitration Law of the People's Republic of China* (August 31, 1994) significantly altered the structure of China's alternative dispute resolution process. Under the new Chinese arbitration law, the Chinese government established two separate arbitration systems. Depending upon the origins of the parties and the nature of the contract, disputes can be held in a forum dedicated to domestic economic disputes or one dedicated to foreign-related economic disputes (Cheng, 1996:291). This new Arbitration Law establishes independent, centrally governed arbitration commissions in provincial capitals and large cities which deal with domestic disputes (Brown and Rogers 1997:338; Fishburne and Chuncheng, 1997:306; Cheng, 1996:291). The establishment of provincial arbitration commissions does not have any direct effect on international arbitration (Cheng, 1996:291).

A major concern for foreign participants involved in alternative dispute resolution proceedings abroad is the independence of an arbitration institution from its host government. In China, the work of arbitration commissions is overseen by the Chinese Arbitration Association (CAA), a separate legal entity. As a non-governmental organization, the CAA has jurisdiction over provincial arbitration commissions (Fishburne and Chun-cheng, 1997:306). The Arbitration Law provides that 'an arbitration commission shall be independent of administrative bodies and shall have no subordinate relationships with [administrative authorities] (ibid Art. 14).' Although the Chinese Arbitration Association is not yet financially independent of the Chinese government, it acts as a self-regulatory organization overseeing provincial commissions (ibid Art. 15; Burton, 1995:637). The development of an independent self-regulatory committee to oversee commission work and the adoption of new arbitral rules by the Chinese government have served to legitimize the arbitration process as recognized by, but independent of, the Chinese government (Brown and Rogers 1997:338).

Enforcement Difficulties

Arbitration Awards

One potential hazard of international arbitration is the difficulty in judicial enforcement. The mechanism of enforcing arbitral awards in Asia is accomplished through the courts as in most countries, not through arbitral institutions. Although an arbitral award has the same effect as a court judgment, in most Asian nations, a party seeking enforcement of an award must either file an application with the appropriate court (usually in the defaulting party's home forum), or ask the court to stay litigation in violation of the arbitration agreement or award. What follows is a brief overview of enforcement of arbitral decision in Asian nations.

The majority of Asian nations have now acceded to the Convention on the Recognition and Enforcement of Foreign Arbitral Awards (New York Convention) of 1958. Signatories to the New York Convention have agreed to recognize arbitral awards rendered by another contracting state and exclude any judicial review of the merits of an arbitral award when enforcement is sought (Craig, 1996:3). Most states have also adopted the reciprocity and commercial reservations of the New York Convention.[24] Under the reciprocity reservation in Hong Kong, Japan, and Malaysia, enforcement of awards in non-Convention countries will depend on local rules of comity and bilateral treaties.

China

Once CIETAC has rendered its decision, CIETAC, itself, has no authority to enforce an award against a party (Volz and Haydock, 1996:903; Ge and Alexander, 1995:563-5). Due to local protectionism in China, it is often difficult for a foreigner to enforce an arbitration award against a Chinese national (Volz and Haydock, 1996:904). 'To minimize enforcement dilemmas, the Supreme People's Court in China has directed the local courts not to interfere with such awards, requiring that any review be done in Beijing (ibid). Judicial enforcement of CIETAC arbitral decisions is subject to procedural rules contained in the People's Republic of China Procedure Code, Article 195 (Volz and Haydock, 1996:903; Liu and Alexander, 1995:563-5). The Arbitration Law of the People's Republic of China (Art. 15) lists six conditions where Chinese courts may refuse to enforce arbitration decisions (Wang, 1996:5):

(1) There is no arbitration agreement;
(2) The arbitration is beyond the scope of the agreement or the arbitration institute has no jurisdiction;
(3) The composition of the arbitral body or the arbitration procedures violate statutory procedure;
(4) Evidence is concealed resulting in an unfair hearing;
(5) An arbitrator seeks or accepts a bride, misbehaves, or bends the law;
(6) The award violates public policy (Volz and Haydock, 1996:904-5).

Japan

With the United States and Japan as major trade partners, arbitration is frequently selected by corporations when transnational disputes develop. Consistent with this policy to promote trade, arbitral decisions are relatively easy to enforce in Japan (Volz and Haydock, 1996:907). 'The Japanese Code of Civil Procedure, Article 800, provides that an arbitration award has the same effect as a judgement and is conclusive between the parties.'(ibid)

Indonesia

Until 1990, legal mechanisms were not in place to comply with the New York convention (ibid). To enforce an award in Indonesia, the award must be made by a country-party to the New York Convention and the dispute must be considered commercial under Indonesian law (Volz and Haydock, 1996:908). Further, a party which seeks to enforce an arbitration decision in Indonesia must obtain a writ of execution from the Indonesia Supreme Court. It is unclear whether foreign arbitral decisions are enforced, despite Indonesia's ratification of the New York Convention (ibid).

Singapore

Singapore has passed the International Arbitration Act, which is based upon UNCITRAL Model Law (Volz and Haydock, 1996:909). Singapore is also party to the New York Convention.

Thailand

Thailand has not ratified the New York Convention, but it generally follows the terms of the Convention (Volz and Haydock, 1996:910). Under the Arbitration Act of 1987, the Thai courts can deny the enforcement of a foreign arbitral award '[i]n case[s] where the court is of the opinion that an award is contrary to the law governing the dispute, is the result of any unjustified act or procedure, or is outside the scope of the binding arbitration agreement or relief sought by the party.'(ibid) As a result of the broad number of defenses available to vacate decisions under the Arbitration Act, many disputes eventually must be tried under the Thai legal system (Raissi, 1992: 105).

Foreign Judgment Enforcement

Many Asian countries provide, in their laws, for judicial enforcement of foreign judgments on the basis of international agreement or reciprocity. As usual in Western countries, jurisdiction over the defendant is necessary and often problematic, and the defense of contrariness of the foreign judgment to the forum's public policy are frequent issues. Given such impediments, most trade disputants tend to prefer trying to enforce arbitral awards via the more developed and internationally accepted N.Y. Convention route (see generally Pryles, 1997).

Combining Conciliation and Arbitration

As previously discussed, Asian cultures tend to favour conciliation where the preference in Western nations is to favour arbitration. As the two cultures have interacted, a combination of the two procedures has developed merging the best of both worlds (Sagartz, 1998:700(note)). Utilizing this hybrid form of dispute resolution combining consultation and arbitration has proven to be attractive to parties of many cultures (ibid). 'Asian parties to international contracts have learned to accept the possibility of arbitration when all negotiations and conciliations efforts have failed and the parties are no longer "friends." Meanwhile, Western parties can hedge their bets on conciliation with arbitration as an option' (Burton, 1995:637; Sagartz, 1998:700).

There are two primary ways to proceed with the hybrid form of consultation and arbitration. First, the blended method where the dispute resolution process shifts between consultation to arbitration and back again without defined boundaries (Sagartz, 1998:701). Second, the conjoined method may be utilized as a hybrid method of alternative dispute resolution. 'With a conjoined method, a conciliation may be arranged as an initial stage to occur within a fixed time. When that time period expires, conciliators would be required to acknowledge the failure of their efforts. This event would then trigger the right of the parties to embark upon arbitration or litigation' (Lecuyer-Thieffry and Thieffry, 1990:577; also Sagartz, 1998:700).

Whatever the formula, the most practical advantage of combining conciliation and arbitration is that arbitration can impose a final and binding resolution, while conciliation helps to preserve the business relationship. Thus this concept has been most widely accepted by dispute resolution centers in Asia and is gaining support from Westerners doing business in the Pacific Rim (Donahey, 1995:74-8).

Foreign Lawyer Representation before Arbitration Tribunals

A distinctive trend in Asian international commercial arbitration is allowing and encouraging foreign arbitrators and foreign counsel to participate in arbitral proceedings. Australia, China (in 1995), Hong Kong, Japan (in 1996), Malaysia, and Singapore (in 1995) now permit foreign lawyers to appear as legal counsel in arbitrations or act as arbitrators in their respective institutions.[25] The number and percentage of foreign arbitrators participating in Asian dispute resolution continues to increase (Stevens, 1997).

Ethics Concerns Regarding Arbitrators and Representatives

A major concern for international parties concerning foreign arbitration is that of arbitrator impartiality (Carter, 1988:141). Most alternative dispute resolution processes require disclosure to combat impartiality concerns. For example, Rule 7.3 of the CPR Rules for Non-administered Arbitration of International Disputes requires nominees to disclose 'circumstances that might cause doubt regarding the arbitrator's independence or impartiality. Such circumstances include bias, interest in the result of the arbitration, and past or present relations with a party or counsel' (UNICRAL, 1992:Rule 7.3; also Silver, 1995:37). Similarly, The *International Bar Association Rules of Ethics for International Arbitrators* (1992: Rule 4) compels disclosure of past relationships between the arbitrator and any party which is more than trivial (Silver, 1995:37).

New Rules and Laws

There is a distinctive trend for most Asian nations to revise its arbitration laws and institutional rules to conform to the international standards of the UNCITRAL Model Law and the UNCITRAL Arbitration Rules. This trend is toward harmonization and a convergence of arbitration laws. For example,

India, Korea, and Singapore have recently adopted, in large part, the Model Law and Arbitration Rules, as many other Asian countries did earlier. The Model Law, was designed to assist States in reforming and modernizing their laws on arbitral procedure. The Model Law takes into particular features and needs of international commercial arbitration, concentrating specifically on the powers of the arbitrators, the conduct of the arbitrators and the scope of judicial supervision (Kwatra 1996:86; Gerardi, 1995:686).

AN EMERGING INTERNATIONAL DISPUTE RESOLUTION CULTURE

Despite the recent Asian economic down-cycle, the incredible amount of economic activity in Asia – linking its trade and investment with the Americas and Europe – has spurred the development of transnational and regional institutions to facilitate such activity. Closely related has been the growth of legal infrastructure in the form of laws and institutions to provide for the effective and fair resolution of disputes between trade and investment participants.

This has led inevitably to a shift away from the traditional, stereotypical role of dispute-resolution in Asia, often characterized as 'non-adversarial.' While cultural typologies are almost always risky, it is safe to say that the stereotype that Asians abhor adversarial processes and strongly favour conciliatory approaches is gradually eroding with the rise of foreign trade and investment in this region. It may be too much to suggest that Asian traders have embraced the more adversarial approaches of the West, but the old reluctance to participate in these processes is clearly an attitude of the past. The open acceptance of arbitration institutions to conduct international arbitrations, the speedy development of legal and institutional frameworks to implement the resolution process, and the growth in willingness to resort to the use of such facilities to settle disputes evidences a cultural turn away from the 'softer' co-operative resolution approaches formerly associated with Asian countries and commercial entities.

Another sign of a changing Asian legal culture is the gradual move toward uniformity and harmonization of the legal framework for international dispute resolution. The UNCITRAL Arbitration Law and the New York Convention are legal models being adopted all over the Asian region. Acceptance and use of the many other 'public' and 'quasi-public' forms of dispute-resolution by most countries in the region reflect a worldwide trend toward building into trade institutions various dispute-resolution capabilities. And yet a cautionary note about this development needs to be advanced: despite the surface-level uniformity, substantial resistance to the enforcement of foreign-made judgments and arbitral awards still lies at the core of many national legal systems in Asia.

Finally, the emergence of a capability to resolve disputes of a public, quasi-public, and private nature in Asia raises fundamental questions about whether such a legal regime will succeed. A commitment of governments and private participants to making the system independent and fair is necessary. Much like the commercial arbitration process has been challenged in the US for not providing basic due process, (Reuben,1998:31) processes for resolving international trade and investment disputes must meet the criteria of being fair and transparent. Similarly, appropriate enforcement of foreign judgments and arbitration awards needs to be possible in a system that purports to provide a viable trading regime governed by the rule of law.

There is much reason to applaud the developments in Asia, however. A transnational legal trading culture is being constructed, and, eventually, a rule of law will prevail to offer all international traders and investors a fair and efficient way of resolving their differences.

A Mexican proverb expresses it best: 'The joy of disputes is in making peace.' As long as 'making peace' remains a goal of our international trading system, the rule of law – in a transnational sense – will prevail for the benefit of all those involved in the Asian trading process.

NOTES

1 This essay is drawn from the remarks of the author to the Symposium on *Trade with Asia: Legal Challenges for the Next Century,* presented on 20 September 1997, at the University of California at Berkeley School of Law (Boalt Hall), and his participation in Leiden in the International Institute for Asian Studies' Conference on 'Law and Development in East and Southeast Asia,' on 30 January 1998, in Leiden, the Netherlands.

2 Paul E. Treusch, Professor of Law, Southwestern University School of Law. The author is grateful for the outstanding research work of Tanya Garza (Southwestern Class of 1998), Pak Kouch (Southwestern Class of 1999), and Jason Gundel (Southwestern Class of 2000). He is indebted to Southwestern for its financial support via Southwestern's Summer Research Program.

3 ADR is an abbreviation often used to refer to 'alternative dispute resolution' processes, which include, but are not limited to, negotiation, mediation, conciliation and arbitration.

4 See generally, Knoke (1997), who suggests that with the revolutions in communication and transportation technologies have created a kind of 'placeless' society.

5 Location, however, is still important with respect to a number of aspects. For example, the experience and qualifications of arbitrators, their legal training, the legal culture of the country and how it influences judicial processes that might be involved.

6 Richer countries, feeling strapped for cash themselves, have cut back their foreign aid. At the same time, however, many of the impoverished nations have abandoned socialism and embraced capitalism. As a result, private capital has become the economic mainstay in many poorer countries (Pine, 1997; Wang, 1999:131).

7 See Holley (1997) and Wysocki (1997) who states: 'In Southeast Asia, this year's currency crises will slow economic growth to an annual rate of 4 per cent or less from 8 per cent or more. The aftermath of that abrupt slowdown will be bankrupt companies, bad loans and falling consumer spending.'

8 'Private Parties' are defined as non-governmental, commercial entities.

9 'Public Parties' are defined as governmental entities or state enterprises.

10 Meaning there is a national law that specifies the procedure to be followed for arbitration and concilliation/mediation.

11 Most Asian arbitration institutions are operated as private or quasi-public institutions of the judicial process. However, these are often partially financed by the Chamber of Commerce or other semi-publicly funded agency.

12 The Asian nations studied include Australia, Cambodia, China, Hong Kong (an autonomous administrative unit of China), India, Indonesia, South Korea, Japan, Malaysia, Philippines, Singapore, Thailand, and Vietnam.

13 While Hong Kong, Singapore, and Kuala Lumpur are the leading sites for neutral arbitration, the most popular alternative non-Asian venue is the Stockholm Chamber of Commerce in Sweden. The Stockholm Chamber of Commerce is especially favoured by the Chinese.

14 The Asian countries studied utilizing the dispute resolution mechanisms of consultation, conciliation/mediation, and arbitration – both institutional and *ad hoc* – include: Australia, Cambodia, China, Hong Kong, India, Indonesia, Japan, Korea, Malaysia, Philippines, Singapore, Thailand, and Vietnam.

15 The terms, 'conciliation' and 'mediation,' are generally used interchangeably in the international context.

16 *Ad hoc* arbitration refers to arbitration that is administered by the parties themselves (sometimes called, 'non-administered'), pursuant to the rules

established by the parties. 'Institutional arbitration', on the other hand, refers to arbitration that is administered by an organization which is in the business of arbitration administration.

17 Approximately 130 countries have satisfied the *Convention on the Settlement of Investment Disputes between States and Nationals of other States* (the 'Washington Convention') (1965) 17 *U S T* 1270, *U N T S* 159 which created ICSID. See *infra* discussion of ICSID at II.C.4. Also <http://www.worldbank.org/icsid>

18 For example, a 'Protocol on Dispute Settlement Mechanism' amended in December 1995 and finalized in 1996, sets out a procedure of consultations, good offices, conciliation, or mediation which is followed by the establishment of a panel, and contains provisions for a report, appeal and compensation/suspension of concessions – quite similar to the WTO Dispute-Settlement Body's procedures. An ASEAN Framework Agreement on Intellectual Property Cooperation was signed specifying a consultation process for resolving intellectual property disputes among member states in 1995. In November 1996, ASEAN ministers approved a Dispute Settlement Mechanism to cover all economic agreements in ASEAN.

19 Malaysia, the Philippines, and Thailand formed the predecessor of ASEAN, the Association of South-East Asia, in 1961. ASEAN was formed in 1967, when three founding members were joined by Indonesia and Singapore. In 1984, Brunei was added, and Vietnam, Laos, and Myanmar joined in the 1990s. Cambodia has observer status as of 1998 (Stephenson,1994:439).

20 The eighteen members of APEC are: Australia, Brunei, Canada, Chile, Hong Kong, Indonesia, Japan, China, Republic of Korea, Malaysia, Mexico, New Zealand, Papua New Guinea, Republic of the Philippines, Singapore, Taiwan, Thailand, and the United States. The 'three Chinas' (China, Hong Kong, Taiwan) joined in 1991.

21 In 1992, a secretariat was established in Singapore, marking the first major step towards becoming a fully-fledged regional trade institution.

22 See *Settlement of Disputes, Oceans and Law of the Sea.* (visited on 3 Sept. 1999) <http:www.un.org/Depts/los/los_disp.htm#htmSD>. Article 2 (3) of the UN Charter status: 'All Members shall settle their international dispute by peaceful means in such a manner that international peace and security and justice, are not endangered.' UN Charter Art. 33 (1) states: 'The parties to any dispute ... shall ... seek a solution by negotiation, inquiry, mediation, conciliation, arbitration, judicial settlement, resort to regional agencies or arrangements, or other peaceful means of their own choice.'

23 China's Foreign Trade Arbitration Commission (FETAC), which later became the Chinese International Economic Trade Arbitration Center (CIETAC), was established in 1954 by the government. In September 1997, China's New Arbitration Law made CIETAC and other arbitration institutions in China independent from administrative authorities.

24 N.Y. Convention, Art. I. 3: '...[A]ny State may, on the basis of reciprocity declare that it will apply the Convention to the recognition and enforcement of awards made only in the territory of another Contracting State. It may also declare that it will apply the Convention only to differences arising out of legal relationships, whether contractual or not, which are considered as commercial under the national law of the State making such declarations' (Redfern and Hunter,1986: 344-5).

25 Singapore has a history of inhospitality toward foreign lawyers. The High Court prohibited foreign lawyers from arbitration in 1988. Legislation which would have permitted foreign counsel to participate in arbitration when foreign law was applicable was tabled by the Law Minister in 1991, but finally accepted in 1995.

REFERENCES

Aldonas, Grant D. (1995) 'Revolution in International Trade Dispute Settlements,' [July] *Disp. Resol. J.*, p. 76.

APEC (1994) 'Trading Arrangement in the Pacific Rim: ASEAN and APEC,' in: *Selected Documents, APEC Meeting of Ministers Responsible for the Environment, Vancouver, March 1994*, p. 1.

Arbitration Law of the People's Republic of China, August 31, 1994.

Arkin, Harry (1990) 'New Opportunities for Arbitration in East/West Trade,' 3 *Transnat'l Law,* p. 495

Brown, Frederick and Catherine A. Rogers (1997) 'The Role of Arbitration in Resolving Transnational Disputes: A Survey of Trends in the People's Republic of China,' 15 *Berkeley J. Int'l L.,* p. 329.

Burton, Steven (1995) 'Combining Conciliation with Arbitration of International Commercial Disputes,' 18 *Hastings Int'l* and *Comp. L. Rev.*, p. 637.

Cardenas, Lorraine C. and Apaporn Buranakanits (1995) 'The Role of APEC in the Achievement of Regional Cooperation in Southeast Asia,' 5 *Ann. Surv. Int'l.* and *Comp. L.*, p. 49.

Carter, James H. (1988) 'A Code of Ethics for International Commercial Arbitration,' in: Emmanuel Gaillard *et al.* (eds) *International Commercial Arbitration: Recent Developments*. New York Law Journal, p. 141.

Cheng, Yuan (1996) 'Legal Protections of Trade Secrets in the People's Republic of China,' 5 *Pac. Rim L* and *Pol'y J.*, p. 261.

Coombe, George W. Jr. (1996) 'The Resolution of Intellectual Property Disputes Involving East Asian Parties,' 19 *Hastings Int'l* and *Comp L Rev*, p. 707.

Craig, Laurence W. (1996) 'Some Trends and Developments in the Laws and Practice of International Commercial Arbitration,' 30 *Tex. Int'l L. J.*, p. 1.

Davidson, Paul (ed.) (1997) 'The Osaka Action Agenda: Implementation of the Bogor Declaration – APEC Economic Leaders' Meeting, Japan, Nov. 1995,' in: *2 Trading Arrangements in the Pacific Rim: ASEAN and APEC*, Oceana, p. 24.

Donahey, M. Scott (1995) 'Seeking Harmony: Is the Asian Concept of the Conciliator/Arbitrator Applicable in the West,' [April] *Disp. Resol J.*, p. 74.

Fishburne, Benjamin P. III and Chuncheng Lian (1997) 'Commercial Arbitration in Hong Kong and China: A Comparative Analysis,' 18 *U. Pa. J. Int'l Econ. L.*, p. 297.

Framework Agreement on Enhancing ASEAN Economic Cooperation, done Jan. 28, 1992. 'Singapore Declaration' (1992) 31 *ILM*, p. 498.

GATT Secretariat (1994) *The Results of the Uruguay Round of Multilateral Trade Negotiations: The Legal Texts*, 3 *ILM* II, especially 'Agreement on Dispute-Settlement' <http:www.wto.org/wto/dispute/dispute.htm.>

Gerardi, Melissa (1995) 'Jumpstarting APEC in the Race to Open Regionalism: A Proposal for the Multilateral Adoption of UNCITRAL's Model Law on International Commercial Arbitration,' 15 *Nw. Int'l L.* and *Bus.*, p. 686.

Green, Carl (1995) 'APEC and Trans-Pacific Dispute Management' 26 *Law* and *Pol'y Int'l Bus*, p. 719.

Haas, Deborah A. (1994) 'Out of Other's Shadows: ASEAN Moves Toward Greater Regional Cooperation in the Face of the EC and NAFTA,' 9 *Am U J Int'l* and *Pol'y*, p. 809.

Holley, David (1997) 'Unfinished Business Troubles Thailand,' 10 September, *L.A. Times*, A-1, col. 4.

Kaplan, Jeffrey A. (1996) 'ASEAN's Rubicon: A Dispute Settlement Mechanism for AFTA,' 14 *Pac Basin L J*, p. 148.

Karalis, John P. (1992) 'Resolving Joint Venture Disputes' in *International Joint Ventures, A Practical Guide*, Saint Paul, Minnesota: West Publishing Co.

Kenevan, Peter and Andrew Winden (1993) 'Comment: Flexible Free Trade: The ASEAN Free Trade Area,' 34 *Harv Int'l L J*, p. 224.

Knoke, William (1997) *Bold New World: the Essential Road Map to the Twenty-First Century*. Kodansha America, Inc.

Koa, Christopher (1991) 'The International Bank for Reconstruction and Development and Dispute Resolution: Conciliating and Arbitrating with China through the International Centre for Settlement of Investment Disputes,' 24 *N Y U J Int'l L* and *Pol.*, p. 439.

Kodama, Yoshi (1995) 'Asia Pacific Region: APEC and ASEAN,' 30 *Int'l Law*, pp. 367-389

Koh, Parlie M.C. (1996) 'Foreign Judgments in ASEAN – A Proposal,' 45 *Int'l* and *Comp L Q*., p. 844.

Kwatra, G.K. (1996) *The New Arbitration* and *Conciliation Law of India: A Comparative Study of the Old and New Law*. New Delhi: Indian Council of Arbitration.

Lecuyer-Thieffry, Christine and Patrick Thieffry (1990) 'Negotiating Settlement of Dispute Provisions in International Business Contracts: Recent Developments in Arbitration and Other Processes,' 45 *Bus. Law*, p. 577.

Liu, Ge and Lourie Alexander (1995) 'International Commercial Arbitration in China: History, New Developments, and Current Practice,' 28 *J. Marshall L. Rev.*, p. 539.

Mahbubani, Kishmore (1995) 'The Pacific Way,' *Foreign Affairs*, p. 100.

Maher, Kevin (1980) 'Foreign Investment in the People's Republic of China: Compensation Trade, Joint Ventures, Industrial Property Protection and Dispute Settlement,' 10 *Ga J Int'l* and *Comp L*, p. 233.

Mota, Sue Ann (1999) 'The World Trade Organization: An Analysis of Disputes,' 25 *N C J of Int'l Law* and *Comm'l Reg*, p. 75.

Nafziger, James A.R. (1987) 'Chinese Methods of Resolving International Trade, Investment, and Maritime Disputes,' 23 *Williamette L Rev*, p. 619.

Pine, Art (1997) 'Private "Foreign Aid" Offers Challenge to United States,' 9 September, *L. A. Times*, A-1.

Pryles, Michael (ed.) (1997) *Dispute Resolution in Asia*. Kluwer Law International.

Raissi, Jahan P. (1992) 'Arbitrating in Thailand,' 16 *Hastings Int'l* and *Comp. L. Rev*., p. 99.

Redfern, Alan and Martin Hunter (1986) *Law and Practice of International Commercial Arbitration*. London: Sweet and Maxwell.

Reuben, Richard C. (1998) 'Reforming ADR–Private Justice Requires Public Rights,' [February], *California Lawyer*, p. 31.

Sagartz, Andrew (1998) 'Resolution of International Commercial Disputes: Surmounting Barriers of Culture without Going to Court,' 13 *Ohio St. J. on Disp. Resol*., p. 675.

Silver, Carolene (1995) 'Models of Quality for Third Parties in Alternative Dispute Resolution,' 12 *Ohio St. J. on Disp. Resol.*, p. 37.

Stephenson, Sherry M. (1994) 'ASEAN and the Multilateral Trading System,' 25 *Law* and *Pol'y Int'l Bus.*, p. 439.

Stevens, Charles R. (1997) *Foreign Lawyer Advocacy in International Arbitrations in Japan, Problems and Approaches to Dispute Resolution in Asia.* Chicago: American Bar Association, Section of International Law and Practice.

Theroux, Eugene (1976) 'Exporting to China: Practical Legal Problems,' in: Holtzman H. (ed.) *Legal Aspects of Doing Business in China*, New York.

UNCITRAL (1985) *UNCITRAL Model Law on International Commercial Arbitration*, U N GAOR, 40th Sess., Supp. No.17, Annex I, pp. 81-93, U.N. Doc. A/40/17, reprinted in (1985) 24 *ILM*, p. 1302.

United Nations (1958) *United Nations Convention on the Recognition and Enforcement of Foreign Arbitral Awards* 21 *U S T* 2517, 330 *U N T S* 38.

– (1999a) *In the News, Oceans and Law of the Sea.* (visited on Sept. 3 1999) <http://www.un.org/Depts/los/los_news.htm>

– (1999b) *Settlement of Disputes, Oceans and Law of the Sea.* (visited on Sept. 3, 1999) <http:www.un.org/Depts/los/los_disp.htm#htmSD>.

Volz, Jane L. and Roger S. Haydock (1996) 'Foreign Arbitral Awards: Enforcing the Award against the Recalcitrant Loser,' 21 *W M Mitchell L Rev.*, p. 867.

Wang, Guiguo (1996) 'The Unification of the Dispute Resolution System in China – Cultural, Economic and Legal Contributions,' 13 *J of Int'l Arb.*, p. 5.

Wang, Guiguo (1999) 'Reform or Privatization of State-Owned Enterprise? Opportunities and Challenges,' 2 *J. World Intell Prop.*, p. 131.

WIPO (1999) *Introduction: 11 Basic Questions About the Center and its Services*, WIPO Arbitration and Mediation Center (visited on Sept. 3, 1999) <http://www.wipo.org/eng/arbit/arbit.htm>.

Wolf, Kevin M. (1995) 'The Legal Framework for Joint Development of China's Onshore Resources: Negotiation Strategies and Future Prospects.' 9 *J. Chinese L.*, p. 141.

World Bank (1965), *Convention on the Settlement of Investment Disputes between States and Nationals of other States* (the 'Washington Convention') 17 *U.S.T.* 1270, *U.N. T.S.* 159 also at (1965) 4 *I L M.*, p. 532 <http://www.worldbank.org/icsid>.

– (1999) *About ICSID, International Center for Settlement of Investment Disputes* (visited on Sept. 3, 1999) <http://www.worldbank.org/icsid/-about/about.html>.

WTO (1999) *How the WTO Resolves Trade Disputes, Dispute Settlement* (visited Sept. 3, 1999) <http://www.wto.org/wto/dispute/webds.htm>.

WTO, Annex 2 'Understanding on Rules and Procedures Governing the Settlement of Disputes' from *World Trade Organisation Agreement*, available online (visited July 22, 1997) <http://www.wto.org/wto/-dispute/dsu.htm>.

Wysocki, Bernard Jr. (1997) 'Beyond the Markets, Asia's Woes will Exact a Toll on Many Lands,' 30 October 1997, *Wall St. J.*, A1, col. 6.

CHAPTER 14

ASIAN ECONOMIC CRISIS AND LEGAL INSTITUTIONS: A TALE OF TWO CITIES*

ROMAN TOMASIC

The Asian and world financial crisis of the late 1990s has shown the limits of governments as the sole or even primary contributors to policy debates regarding the development of commercial law and economic development. Non-governmental scholarly and professional groups, such as the Asia Pacific Economic Law Forum (APELF), have an important contribution to make, especially in the current policy vacuum. The Asian financial crisis presents opportunities for further collaborative endeavour. These possibilities are beginning to be recognized in governmental bodies such as APEC and the Asian Development Bank.

This theme will be explored here. This area could also serve as the focus for further comparative research and analysis by socio-legal scholars interested in economic phenomena such as the process of economic law reform in Asia and its relationship to economic crisis and economic development. There is a major opportunity for 'retooling' legal institutions and bodies of commercial law across the Asian region. The enhancement of the commitment to the rule of law and the provision of access to justice are important goals which are relevant to all countries in the region, even those which already express a commitment to such values. This chapter will also argue that there is a need to keep an eye on broader issues when devising research questions in this field.

Recent attacks on corruption and crony capitalism have shown the need for a further economic law reform effort. It should also be noted that, as many in the region have also noted, there are also problems in other parts of the world, such as with US hedge funds (as many in the Asia–Pacific region such as Malaysia's Prime Minister Mahathir Mohamad, the Governor of the Reserve Bank of Australia, Ian Macfarlane (Henderson, 1998:1) and the head of the HK Monetary Authority have noted). This chapter seeks to approach the task of analysis through a number of Asian socio-legal stories (and their storytellers) as they may tell us much about the issues facing the region and which remain to be fully explored by socio-legal researchers interested in economic law issues.

Firstly, I would suggest that our research can achieve much by focusing upon some of the big issues or the big picture, rather than the microscopic focus which has dominated so many of our concerns as scholars and researchers. We have only had relatively slight success in adopting such an approach, although many socio-legal and economic disciplines clearly lend themselves to such a broader focus. This is not to suggest that we should avoid detailed research, but that we should be looking at some of the bigger issues and themes which abound. The 'stories' that will shortly be discussed in this chapter are good illustrations of this kind of broad ranging approach. All too often we have been content to look at narrow issues or themes without seeking to challenge prevailing orthodoxies or to take on board major themes.

Events during the late 1990s have shown us how fragile the economic order is and how easy it has been to delude ourselves by uncritically accepting prevailing myths and ideologies about such matters as Asian values, the so-called Asian century, Asian tigers, and other such comforting illusions or stereotypes. Scholars and researchers interested in legal themes have an obligation to be more critical of concepts such as these and to be less timid in formulating research objectives and in devising research questions.

TWO HIGH-PROFILE STORYTELLERS AND THEIR EPIC TALES

We can begin by looking at two recent efforts by two very well known public figures who have contributed to our understanding of some large questions affecting Asia today; one may be called the Hong Kong Story while the other is called the Singapore Story. Hong Kong and Singapore are frequently seen as rivals. These 'stories' have been written respectively by former British Hong Kong Governor Chris Patten (1998) and the former Singapore Prime Minister (Harry) Lee Kuan Yew (1998). Each book in different ways tells a story of law and political development, although their authors have each reached different conclusions in regard to the distinctiveness of Asian values.[1]

Patten's book (1998:20) could have been entitled the 'Hong Kong Story'; he even uses this phrase at various points.[2] In contrast, Lee's story is a highly personalized and detailed account of key political episodes which arose in the 25 years prior to Singapore's independence in 1965. The reader has to search carefully for generalizations in Lee's story, whilst in Patten's they are to be found on almost every page. However, Patten is more comfortable in seeking to address larger questions than Lee, as is most apparent from a phrase in the subtitle of his book, *East and West*, namely,

'On Power, Freedom and the Future.' Patten (1998:85) also observes that his Hong Kong experience 'raised more profound questions about politics and economics – questions that went well beyond the story of Hong Kong.'

That Lee has his eyes on a similarly broad goal is immediately suggested when one opens his book to find 28 extraordinary admiring statements from former Presidents and Prime Ministers (of the US (2), the UK (4), Germany (2), France, Thailand, Japan, New Zealand, (2) and Australia (3)), as well as a variety of statements from other senior Ministers and Secretaries of State (like Henry Kissinger, George Schultz, and James Baker). These testimonials seem to be directed to entrenching Lee in our minds as a great thinker and as someone who speaks for Asia.[3] One way of looking at these statements is to see them merely as extravagant efforts at self-promotion, but that is probably unfair. In any event, Lee's book emphasizes the extremely pragmatic nature of his politics which have shifted with the needs of the times, from an alliance with communists and Malays to successful efforts to oust communists and exit from Malaysia.

These two 1998 books and their authors, Chris Patten's *East and West* and Lee Kuan Yew's *The Singapore Story*, have been tremendously successful in their different ways. It is therefore legitimate to ask whether scholarly efforts have any hope of matching the influence and scope of these publishing endeavours or whether there is something to learn from their success. It is also legitimate to ask if statements of the kind made here by Lee and Patten can be supported through research efforts. These questions will be pursued later in this chapter. In the meantime something can be said about these two books, to give those who have not read them closely a flavour of their arguments.

There are many similarities and differences of view in these two books, although each is compelling reading and each takes on big themes. Patten's 340 page book is in many respects more complete than Lee's 664 page book; and the latter's book is but the first of a two volume memoir by its author. However, the detailed nature of Lee's analysis tells us a great deal about the nature of Lee as a politician and of the political, ethnic, and cultural forces which have been at work in Singapore during a critical period in the history of this city state. Patten does not look as closely at Hong Kong's own internal politics, except in so far as this relates to the lead up to the 1997 handover of sovereignty over Hong Kong to China. Whilst Patten seeks to provide a comprehensive treatment of a number of themes, as well as telling a story in ten chapters, the 43 short chapters in Lee's book are more constrained by their factual context of dealing with Lee's version of historical episodes and battles for ascendancy or control in Singapore and Malaysia.

Baroness Thatcher is quoted (in the introductory pages of Lee's book) as saying of the analyses in Lee's speeches while he was in office that '[h]e was never wrong.' Now, Chris Patten in his book tells us that he sometimes disagreed with Mrs Thatcher (Patten supra, pp. 61-2, 316-17). He certainly takes a different view of the supposed uniqueness of social values from those espoused by Mr Lee in his concern for Asian values, such as when Patten says that '[v]alues are universal' (ibid:4) and he goes on to point to the 'absurdity of arguing that there is a fundamental difference between the personal standards and moral principles of Asians on the one hand and Europeans and Americans on the other' (ibid:61). Patten enjoys emphasizing, for example, that loss of face is not only something which Chinese politicians worry about, this is also something which Western politicians are also concerned about.[4] Patten also notes that Lee Kuan Yew:

> ... thought I was wrong – wrong about Hong Kong, about China, about freedom and democracy in Asia (perhaps everywhere), and about their relationship to economic success and human decency and satisfaction. I think that what I did in Hong Kong and what I said there and elsewhere were regarded by Mr Lee as an almost personal affront, an attack on the very foundations of his philosophy of government ... Hong Kong's vitality was a sign that social engineering and an iron fist were not essential to success in a city of Chinese migrants (ibid:147).

It is not appropriate to deal here with all of the wide range of issues raised by each of these two authors in their richly diverse discussions. Two or three issues raised by them would suffice for present purposes. Those that stand out are the importance of the rule of law, the significance of Asian values and the effects of globalization on Asian and other economies. Mr Patten is more direct and expansive in dealing with these issues than Mr Lee.

The Rule of Law

Firstly, both Lee and Patten devote considerable attention to the importance of the rule of law, although each writer sees the application of this ideal in very different terms. While Patten is a defender of the rule of law ideal, Lee is a practitioner of the rule by law philosophy. One commentator notes that Lee's memoirs 'provide a glance at his early tactics that foretell of behaviour such as the deft use of law to obtain political advantage: rule by law rather than rule of law' (Lingle, 1989:23). At the outset, Lee tells us that when Singapore came into being in 1965, it was 'founded upon the principles of liberty and justice' (Lee supra, p. 13) although it is never really quite clear from his later discussion what this statement of principles actually means.

For example, Lee is far from enthusiastic about the jury system. Surprisingly, for an experienced lawyer, Lee reveals that in his first trial, in which he successfully defended a number of Muslims accused of the murder of an English serviceman (named Ryan), he considered that justice had been thwarted as he 'had no doubt that ... [his] ... four clients did kill Ryan.' Lee had achieved this acquittal result by casting many doubts in the minds of the jury about the prosecution case. Lee adds that he 'had no faith in a system that allowed the superstition, ignorance, biases, prejudices, and fears of seven jurymen to determine guilt or innocence ... I had seen juries in British courts. I did not think they deserved the reverence that lawyers and jurists ritually accorded to their collective wisdom.'[5] Of course, Lee may well be correct in this assessment.

Lee seems to have much greater reverence for the role of the Special Branch; a police force which monitored political opposition groups over many years in Singapore. Lee's relationship with the Internal Security Department is not discussed by him as much as it might be, although this Department played an important role in destroying the leadership of Lee's political opponents and his critics in the media (Rodan, 1989:23).

Mr Lee continued to support such internal security groups after he became Prime Minister, such as by the creation of the Corrupt Practices Investigation Bureau in 1960 (Lee supra, p. 346). A major priority for Lee in the discussions leading up to the formation of Malaysia was to ensure that the Corrupt Practices Investigation Bureau and the Prevention of Corruption Ordinance in Singapore were carried over into the federation (ibid:479). The use of law to seek to prevent corruption is one kind of commitment to the rule of law. However, it is far from constituting a comprehensive commitment to this ideal.

A clue to Lee's approach to policing also comes from this time. This is evident from his observation that after becoming Prime Minister at the age of 35, '[a]t the street level, I wanted the police to be disciplined, but also firm, decisive and robust once we decided to break up a demonstration or an incipient riot' (ibid:328). Law and legal institutions are seen primarily in terms of the maintenance of order rather than as guarantors of the expression of individual rights. Law and order has clearly been a principal concern for Lee from his earliest days, as is evident from his discussion of the Japanese occupation of Singapore where he observed that 'law and order [were] in suspended animation' (ibid:49).

Twenty years later, the same concerns for law and order were evident, as is apparent from Lee's discussion of the race riots that took place in Singapore in 1964. In regard to this episode, Lee observes: '[d]eep inside, I felt frustrated for I had lost control of the instruments of law and order and could not deal with these blatant racists' (ibid:559). He goes on to suggest that those in UMNO responsible for fanning racist sentiments amongst the Malays in Singapore should have been prosecuted for sedition by 'those in authority in Kuala Lumpur', but that they were not (ibid:562). Although Lee was probably correct in regard to the responsibility for the riots, this statement illustrates Lee's perception of the use of the law as an appropriate instrument for dealing with dissent and political rivals.

Subsequently, Lee initiated legal proceedings for libel against an UMNO opponent who had published a statement (which Lee quotes) that the 1964 'riots were started by *agents provocateurs*, who may even have been in the pay of Lee Kuan Yew. Lee's intention is to create disorder in Singapore ...' (ibid:606). Lee notes that his critics became more circumspect '[n]ow that those words would be scrutinized in a court of law...' (ibid). This libel action was subsequently settled (in 1966) after Singapore separated from Malaysia. As seen in more recent years, defamation and libel actions have been used effectively in Singapore to restrain political opponents.

Interestingly, Lee denied the claim made by Tun Abdul Razak that he had ever suggested that the 'Malays were not the indigenous people of Malaysia' (ibid:607). Whilst this may have been correct, strictly *speaking*, Lee himself does acknowledge that on a visit to Australia he had told Prime Minister Menzies that: '... the three major races in Malaysia the Malays, Chinese, and Indians – had the wellsprings of their culture outside Malaysia, in Indonesia, China, and India' (ibid:595). This looks very much like suggesting that the culture of the Malays was foreign to Malaysia and by implication that the Malays were themselves foreigners in their own country. But, of course, Lee did not say this directly, although it is hardly surprising that the Malays interpreted his words in the way that they did.

Furthermore, Mr Lee acknowledges that compliance with the law should not be seen in isolation and that the achievement of wider objectives may depend on the use of non-legal means. Thus, he observes that in the 1950s, '[m]y way of constitutional opposition, working within the law, was in marked contrast to that of the communists, and I got results. But without the communists going beyond the law and using violence, my methods would not have been effective' (ibid:211). It should be noted that during this period Lee worked closely, if secretly, with the communists, even if he was politically opposed to them.[6] Lee's penchant for law and order seems to be related to what may be an obsession with tidiness. His somewhat emotional statement in relation to untidy conditions in 1964 suggests this:

> But morale in Singapore had sagged. The city looked scruffy. With the weakening of law enforcement, Indian herdsmen had allowed

> their cows and goats to graze on playing fields and even on grass verges of roundabouts. A lawyer drove his car into a cow one night just outside the town centre and was killed. From my office window, I could see cattle on the Esplanade. After two riots, the place was slovenly, with more litter, more cows and goats meandering on the streets, more stray dogs, more flies, more mosquitoes, more beggars. Even the grounds of the Singapore General Hospital were unkempt. I was determined to check this decline. I called a meeting at the Victoria Theatre of all officers concerned with public health, and with full press and television coverage urged them to restore standards of cleanliness and tidiness ... This had a salutary effect. The city spruced up.

Singapore was clearly being prepared for a future as a tidy town maintained by the force of law.

In contrast, Chris Patten frequently emphasizes the central role of the rule of law in explaining economic prosperity in Hong Kong and the United Kingdom. For example, Patten (1998:4) notes that '[f]reedom, democracy, the rule of law, stability and prosperity are found most frequently in one another's company.' He adds that '[g]ood government, the rule of law and market economics transformed the battered and beggared community of the post-war years into one of the greatest trading centres on earth ...' (ibid:22). Noticeably absent from this list of qualities essential for prosperity was a thoroughgoing commitment to democratic values.[7]

The rule of law is thus a major theme in Patten's analysis of the sources of prosperity and freedom. This of course has been a concern of socio-legal scholars over the years. For Patten, liberty and the use of the law by the citizen against the state are important principles, as illustrated by the concept of *habeas corpus*; that no one can be imprisoned or accused of an offence without having the opportunity of being brought to trial.[8] As Patten (1998:78) notes: '[w]e can use the law to defend ourselves against anyone, however powerful.' This becomes increasingly important where a nation or community seeks to achieve what Patten described as 'quality growth' as opposed to 'quantity-based growth.' He observes that the former places a

> ... premium on inventiveness, creativity and technological flexibility. The communities best able to unleash these qualities, in Asia as in other continents, will be those that provide their citizens with political liberty as well as economic, those communities that nurture their citizens' talents through pluralism (ibid:202).

Chris Patten goes on to add that:

> Tolerance of dissent, genuinely representative government, the rule of law and the free press bestow real comparative advantages in the race for quality growth (ibid).

Curiously, Patten's most impassioned statements about the importance of the rule of law are made in a chapter entitled 'How to Make Money,' pointing to the close link between the rule of law and the growth of markets. Thus, Patten argues passionately that:

> A market place free and fair to all and an economic system purged of or at least resistant to graft are incomparably more likely where there exists the most important of all software in a free society, the rule of law. What does that mean? First, it means that everyone is subject to the law, however mighty they may be. The rule of law is not some convenient justification for coercion by the powerful, a legalistic cover for locking up or shooting people that the government does not like. It applies equally to those who govern and those who are governed, to lawmakers and law abiders. In a free society under the rule of law, with a fairly elected legislature that itself makes the laws, the ruled are also the rulers. It is vital to understand this. Rules and laws which may or may not apply impartially to everyone are different from the rule of law, majestic, comprehensive and wholly impartial (ibid:259).

Patten notes that the rule of law does not only cover commercial life, but covers all other areas of society. He notes, for example, that the case of James Peng, an Australian citizen who was imprisoned in China for alleged economic crimes, is a notorious example of politics becoming intertwined with commercial disputes; this case remains an important illustration of the failure of the rule of law in China,[9] as Patten also emphasizes:

> The law is not a ceremonial hulk. It lives and breathes. Without it, there is no market economy but a jungle economy, every one for himself or herself, a bracing environment for the brave but not a place where most of us would want to invest much if any of our pension funds. The rule of law underpins prosperity and sustains the most acceptable and profitable way of doing business. ... The law constrains just as it enables. It acts as a brake, so that liberty does not slide and slither into anarchic licence. It draws lines in the sand, protects the weak from the strong, defines the public interest in an

> orderly and balanced way, and ideally acquires the moral authority to do all that by the extent to which it can demonstrate its own even handedness and by the manner in which it is made (ibid:260-1).

These are two quite different conceptions of the rule of law; both are popular in different parts of Asia and both may be criticized in different ways. If anything, Mr Lee's view may be criticized for being overly austere and instrumentalist, whilst Mr Patten's may be criticized for verging on idealism and for failing to take into account the major obstacles which undermine the achievement of the rule of law, East and West.

The Pursuit of Asian Values and Chinese Culture

Another major theme which runs through these two books is the question of Asian or Chinese values. Although Lee Kuan Yew is often closely identified with the idea of Asian values, it is interesting to note how infrequently he uses this phrase in his discussion of his rise to power in Singapore. This is not to say that Lee was not determined to ensure that the Chinese community was not alienated and that it did not fall under the influence of the communists. During the period of time that he covers in this book, Lee was clearly very interested in being accepted by the Chinese-speaking community and in being able to relate to Chinese cultural values.

Lee therefore went to some trouble to learn to speak Mandarin and Hokkien languages and he even sent his children to Chinese schools so that the Chinese population of Singapore could be assured of Lee's Chinese identity. Lee notes that in the early 1950s '[i]t was often embarrassing because my Chinese was totally inadequate' (ibid:152). Lee also notes that his 'spoken Hakka and Hokkien were pathetic, almost negligible. I vowed to make up for past neglect' (ibid:183). As was to happen in later years, the adoption of Chinese values or manners was done for strategic or pragmatic purposes. During the Japanese occupation, he even started to learn Japanese for similar reasons (ibid:61-2).

As Lee tells us, the Chinese are a very pragmatic people. He observes that '[t]he Chinese-speaking in Singapore, like the Chinese-speaking everywhere in Southeast Asia, traditionally preferred to sit on the fence until they saw clearly which way the wind was blowing' (ibid:390). However, Lee emphasizes the importance of manipulating language and culture for the purposes of political control when he tells us that he recognized that:

> The biggest single theme that galvanised the Chinese-speaking was Chinese culture, and the need to preserve Chinese traditions through

> the Chinese schools. It was not a proletarian issue; it was plain, simple chauvinism' (ibid:185-6).

Elsewhere, Lee notes that he:

> ... never allowed the communists to exploit Chinese language, education and culture, and in this I gained strength from my children being educated in Chinese. Thus I denied the communists a powerful weapon against me. They could attack my bourgeois middle-class background but could not demonise me ... as an enemy who was a destroyer of Chinese culture (Lee supra, p. 409).

Lee's success depended greatly upon his capacity to relate to different ethnic groups, as he notes that in the early 1960s:

> Speaking in Hokkien and Mandarin, I had convinced the Chinese that I was not a stooge of the British, that I was fighting for their future. The Malays backed me because they saw me fighting the Chinese communists. The Indians, as a smaller minority, were fearful and therefore reassured to find me completely at home with all races, speaking bazaar Malay and English to them and even a few words of greeting in Tamil (ibid:487).

Turning to Chris Patten's book, Patten argues that Chinese culture is not incompatible with the rule of law, as can be seen from the operation of the rule of law in Hong Kong and Taiwan. Interestingly, he does not mention Singapore as a bastion of the rule of law. It could also be argued that the rule of law is increasingly becoming a part of the official language of Mainland China itself, although for the present its focus is mainly upon rule by law (*South China Morning Post* 1 December 1998).[10] That a commitment to the rule of law was not incompatible with traditional Chinese values is emphasized by Patten when he remarks of Hong Kong in the years after the Second World War, 'Hong Kong had a competent government, pursuing market economics under the rule of law. It was a government that fully met the Confucian goal, 'Make the local people happy and attract migrants from afar' (Patten supra, p. 21).

However, he also notes of Hong Kong that 'Confucian values did not seem to have led to the establishment of adequate services for the elderly, of whom there were growing numbers' (ibid:50). In any event, Patten cites the well known Sinologist, Simon Leys, when he argues that the more essential humanistic side of Confucian teaching has tended to be downplayed by governments whilst those aspects of his teaching that emphasized submission to authority have tended to be exaggerated by governments over the years. As Patten explains:

> Given how often one is told that Asians in general, and the Chinese in particular, are not really concerned about politics, it is interesting to note that Confucius regarded his true vocation as politics and was disappointed ... that he could not find anyone who would let him put his political ideas and sense of mission into practice. His views on politics have a universal appeal and force ...
>
> The discovery of Confucius as the reason for Asia's economic success would have puzzled some of his most faithful followers as well as earlier European philosophers and historians. Humanism is rarely analysed in terms of GDP per capita ...
>
> ... In order to use Confucianism to justify unswerving obedience to the state, you have to turn a blind eye to many passages in the *Analects* that endorse personal liberty (ibid:162-4).

Somewhat caustically, Patten notes that China's rediscovery of how to draw upon the Confucian legacy had to rely upon insights from Lee Kuan Yew, 'to tell them how Confucius would teach them the way to yoke political control to capitalist success' (ibid:164). Patten remarks that Lee Kuan Yew '...was the most intellectually rigorous of the exponents of this faith [that Asia's success was as much a cultural as an economic phenomenon], its high priest if not its most obvious exemplar' (ibid:93). Patten concludes that:

> Claims about Asianness and the Asian way, and about the contrasts between Asian and other societies, are customarily rhetorical or anecdotal; not very much has been done to try to establish with any modest degree of social-science measurement exactly what the differences may be. Evidence has not been sought or demanded for what is generally seen as an essentially political set of propositions (ibid:165).

To support his argument, Patten relies upon some empirical work undertaken by David Hitchcock in 1995, based on interviews with a range of Asian leaders, intellectuals and experts, and a smaller number of interviews with Americans. This research showed that there was little unanimity amongst Asian leaders regarding the so-called Asian values that they shared and that economic success was sometimes accompanied by increasing self-confidence (ibid:165).

However, as Patten frequently notes, '[t]he very diversity of Asia questions the concept of Asian values' (ibid:155). He adds that present political leaders of Asian polities are on different sides of the debate on Asian values. This is evident from different approaches to politics and dissent in India, the Philippines and Hong Kong when compared to other places such as Singapore, Myanmar, and China. Despite this diversity, Patten does however conclude that there is an underlying similarity between the situations of peoples in East and West, when he observes that:

> The more that I have looked at all these questions, the more it seems to me that we all face similar problems, face them to different degrees according (partly) to how we have developed, and will discover similar solutions rooted in the same respect for human decency and in the same regard for an economic philosophy that maximises the opportunity for the individual to excel. Some of the challenges cast at Western societies by Asians are wholly fair ... though I believe that the sweeping condemnation of the West [by Lee Kuan Yew] and the commendation of the East are overdrawn ... Men and women are political animals and not just economic machines and commercial appetites (ibid:170-1).

Not surprisingly, Patten acknowledges that there is a need for a new balance in the way that the East and the West are seen. He argues that those in the West can learn something from the East about the importance of order, harmony, partnership, and responsibility; whilst those in the East can learn from the West about the provision of more respect for citizens as persons who actually do possess rights (ibid:172).

There are many empirical questions raised by both Lee Kuan Yew and Chris Patten about the importance of Asian and other values and these are useful vehicles for an assessment of the role of law and legal institutions in Asian societies. However, they are ideas which are increasingly having to contend with the influence of global forces, which are perhaps seeing a process of Americanization sweeping the world; this is certainly the case at the level of cultural values and the mass media which influence the young. However, one should not overlook the influence of Japanese values and models across the Asia Pacific region; they are certainly very strong in Korea and Taiwan, and China itself has not been unknown to borrow legal ideas from Japan.

The Impact of Globalization

Although Lee Kuan Yew does not contribute to the emerging debate about globalization, this is a crucial issue for Singapore due to the heavy exposure of Singapore to the international economy. Chris Patten relies heavily upon the concept of globalization. However, he repeatedly takes issue with the current use of this idea, arguing wrongly that the concept is not a new one as international trade and the movement of peoples and technologies across borders is not a recent phenomenon (ibid:209-13). In contrast, as Malcolm Waters (1995) has pointed out in his excellent review of the concept of globalization, we need to distinguish between internationalization of trade and commerce and the phenomenon of globalization. Globalization has been seen as 'the making of the world into a single place' (Robertson, 1990). Internationalization never did this. The international securities market and the global corporation are two of the best illustrations of this kind of globalization, which seems to limit spatial and temporal constraints.

Nevertheless, globalization occupies a central place in Patten's analysis. He observes that '[o]ne of the most spectacular casualties of globalization has been the delusion that governments are all-powerful' (Patten 1998:211). He concludes that:

> It is in this debate about globalization and its ethics that I see the main lesson to be absorbed from the Asian experience. The idea that there is some off-the-shelf Asian model which can be bought as it stands by growth-minded Western governments was always absurd, and now that the model – such as it was – appears to have fallen off the shelf and on to the floor the argument is even more preposterous. What I take from the Asian experience, and from the changes in the developed world that helped to make Asian growth possible, is the importance of three fundamental issues, the first two of which in particular are central to any discussion about globalization (ibid:213).

Patten's three explanations for Asia's success over recent decades are, firstly, free trade and open markets (as opposed to pressures for protectionism, especially in the US) (ibid:213ff); secondly, the role and size of governments and their involvement in regard to economic performance (ibid:225ff); and thirdly, encouraging greater individual self reliance in the face of increasing welfare burdens being placed on the state.

It is clear that globalization has been one of the key factors which have affected Asian and other financial markets. This is clear from the emergence of electronic commerce and the extent to which stock exchanges, securities trading, and investment flows have become internationalized. This is not to say that it is impossible to influence the effect of these global forces, as

Hong Kong has shown in its very successful efforts at defending the Hong Kong dollar and the value of securities traded on the Hong Kong Stock Exchange. However, such efforts cannot be sustained in the longer term.[11]

The ongoing pressure arising out of China's pursuit of membership of the WTO, and the influence of bodies such as the IMF and the World Bank, are evidence of the continued effect of the forces of globalization. However, legal systems are probably less likely to be affected by the forces of globalization than are financial and banking systems; this is because of the extent to which local cultural factors underlie the operation of legal systems.[12] Nevertheless, in regard to commercial law, there are increasing pressures to achieve uniformity in areas of law such as contract law, insolvency law, securities law, company law, etc. International regulatory bodies, international financial institutions, and international legal and accounting firms have probably contributed to this process of globalization, although the impact of these bodies in this regard remains to be quantified by researchers.

SOME OTHER (LESS WELL KNOWN) STORIES

Much can be gained from comparative socio-legal analysis of economic institutions and behaviour. A number of studies can be examined which may be seen as exemplars of the kind of analyses that are most illuminating and which examine fundamental issues which are discussed by more high profile commentators, such as Messrs Patten and Lee. Clearly, the rule of law, the effects of cultural traditions and the effects of globalization are issues which are fundamental to an understanding of financial crises and systemic change.

Three such studies may be examined here, although a number of others might have been examined.[13] The three studies that will be briefly referred to are firstly, Anthony Woodiwiss's 1998 book, *Globalisation, Human Rights and Labour Law in Pacific Asia*; Tomasic and Little's 1997 book on *Insolvency Law and Practice in Asia* and (very briefly) the 1997 report for the Asian Development Bank (and subsequent book) by Katharina Pistor and Philip Wellons, on the *Role of Law and Legal Institutions in Asian Economic Development 1960-1995*. Each of these works deal with major issues of contemporary concern in the late 1990s and seek to draw upon detailed research to support their findings. None have however had the impact or generated the publicity of the works by more high profile political figures such as Mr Patten or Mr Lee.

Woodiwiss's Globalisation, Human Rights and Labour Law in Pacific Asia

Anthony Woodiwiss, a sociologist from the University of Essex, has previously written books on labour law in the United States and Japan. In his important new study, *Globalisation, Human Rights and Labour Law in Pacific Asia,* he examines human rights and labour law as these have emerged in four Asian legal systems: The Philippines, Hong Kong, Malaysia, and Singapore. Woodiwiss notes that human rights ideas drawn from socialist and liberal traditions (as reflected in the UN Covenants) have now been supplemented by a patriarchal model of human rights. Whilst the socialist tradition emphasized social and economic rights, the liberal tradition emphasized civil and political rights. Patriarchalism can be seen as a form of traditional authority (as Weber has noted) with a strong familialist focus. This is to be distinguished from paternalism or patriarchy, which refers to male dominance over females. Woodiwiss examines the nature of patriarchalism as reflected in the labour laws of four Asian legal systems, with Japan providing a model against which the labour laws of these four legal systems are compared.

Woodiwiss goes on to refer to what he calls the mendicant patriarchalism of the Philippines; the authoritarian patriarchalism of Malaysia; the patriarchalist individualism of Hong Kong, and the active patriarchalism of Singapore (Woodiwiss 1998:4). Patriarchalist systems find it difficult to accept individualist and universalistic norms, preferring heteronomy to autonomy as a social value. Such systems also find it culturally unacceptable to rely upon the 'cold' techniques of the law as having a place within 'warm' and flexible patriarchalist social relations. However, Woodiwiss argues that in the absence of the rule of law 'there is no reliable or effective means of enforcing respect for any rights ...' (ibid:7). His theory of law is broadly Marxist-inspired seeing law as characterized by a relative autonomy from the structures of the state (ibid:45). For Woodiwiss, and other law and society theorists, such as Roberto Unger, the rule of law is primarily concerned with the reduction of arbitrariness and is not merely a reflection of liberalism (ibid:47).

In addition to the importance of the rule of law, we are told that it is essential to seek to understand human rights from a transnational perspective. Woodiwiss seeks to do this by looking at labour law issues. In particular, he focuses on human rights that are most relevant to labour, such as civil and political rights of freedom of association and the social and economic rights to work, to enjoy just and favourable conditions, to enjoy trade union membership, the right to collective bargaining, and a living wage (ibid:9). It can be argued that any broadly based sociology of law needs to focus upon one substantive area of law in the way that Woodiwiss now proceeds to do.[14] However, he does not provide the kind of detailed judicial case law and statutory analysis that one would expect of a lawyer; instead, he draws upon the work of others for this purpose. He argues that:

> ... the best strategy for ensuring the effectiveness of labour and human rights regimes in Pacific Asia is likely to be one that seeks to articulate indigenous patriarchalist discourses with the rule of law and so reintroduce elements of internal critique and substantive mutuality into such discourses (Woodiwiss 1998:13).

Woodiwiss seeks to determine whether a viable model for effective labour and human rights regimes in Asia can be found in post-war Japanese ideas. In that country, Woodiwiss tells us:

> a just labour law regime came to be seen as one wherein employee loyalty and cooperation had to be rewarded, albeit more by employer benevolence, specifically in the form of lifetime employment, than state welfare (ibid:14).

He adds that Japan has become increasingly enmeshed in global structures, becoming the leading investor in the region, and that it is the Japanese rather than the American style of capitalism which is becoming archetypal in the Asia Pacific region (ibid:56). This is an interesting and logical argument, although finding the empirical evidence to support it may not be easy. Woodiwiss goes on to argue that Japan is important not only because of the merger of patriarchalism and capitalism, but also because of 'the potentially equally powerful symbiosis of patriarchalism and the rule of law' (ibid:83). These issues are examined in each of the country studies which Woodiwiss provides in the latter part of his book; two of these, Singapore and Hong Kong, will be discussed here as they can be related to the books by Patten and Lee discussed earlier.

Woodiwiss criticizes proponents of Asian values on a number of grounds; firstly, he notes that the contemporary forms of patriarchialism are quite varied and that some of these are not Asian at all; secondly, he points out that whilst patriarchalism is not essentially antagonistic to human rights, its effectiveness in supporting human rights depends on the State and it also depends on the powerful being prepared to live by their own values; that is, the latter need to accept both the rule of law and that the less powerful should continue to enjoy certain irreducible liberties (ibid:16-17). Woodiwiss goes on to castigate those who rely upon rationalizations, such as Asian values, when he observes that:

> ... what one sometimes encounters in Hong Kong, as in Japan ... Taiwan and Singapore, is a *post hoc* attempt to rationalise and dignify practices undertaken for decidedly more mundane political and economic, or what I term 'ordinary patriarch
> ialist', reasons by referring to them as Confucian or indeed Chinese.[15]

In his Singapore case study Woodiwiss makes the interesting observation that:

> ... the Confucianism that the government for a time urged upon the population was not so much that of Japan, let alone China, but that to be found in a set of texts written by American social scientists such as Herman Khan and Ezra Vogel, who had developed a Confucianist twist to Modernization theory (Woodiwiss 1998:228).

Unlike Chris Patten, who subscribes to a form of convergence theory, based on similar approaches to technological problems, Woodiwiss concludes that the societies of Pacific Asia will remain different from those of the West. However, he does suggest that there is a positive side to globalization which may see the emergence of some mutual learning, whereby the West learns some lessons from the East and vice-versa (ibid:17-18).

Looking firstly at Hong Kong, Woodiwiss notes that as Hong Kong has become more fully localized it has become more patriarchialist. He argues that Hong Kong illustrates what a labour law and human rights regime would look like in a patriarchialist social structure of the kind found in the Pacific form of capitalism (ibid:143-4). He argues that a dominant discourse, with a shared appreciation of the meaning of the rule of law, has developed in Hong Kong as 'the "citizenry" have become ideologically more or less what the state has wanted them to be, whilst the state has become ideologically more or less what the citizenry has wanted it to be.' Expressed differently, this has seen the transformation of individualistic patriarchalism into patriarchialist individualism (ibid:156-7).

Woodiwiss notes that Hong Kong's middle class is relatively small and its history has produced a striking imbalance between the respective powers of labour and capital, leading to the inhibition of labour action and solidarity (ibid:158). He also notes that, when compared to England, an examination of judicial statements in Hong Kong labour law cases shows that Hong Kong has tended to favour the interests of capital. This may also be seen by the existence of a relatively high number of industrial accidents.

He concludes that in Hong Kong individual owners of capital 'have remained relatively unencumbered in their relations with each other, with their employees, with the general public, and with the overseas owners of intellectual property' (ibid:164). This conclusion is supported by a discussion of the legal history of labour laws in Hong Kong which shows that these laws adopted a very restrictive approach to industrial action and the activity of unions in Hong Kong (ibid:167-75). Trade unions were marginalized or excluded in many circumstances after 1967 as:

> the state increasingly took up the role of labour's protector – access to the valuable protections afforded to individuals by the Labour Tribunal is normally on referral from the Labour Department, which will first attempt conciliation. Here, then, is where the state's assumption of the patriarchal role became both explicit and very hard to resist on labour's part (ibid:175).

The rights and claims which can arise under the 1968 Hong Kong Employment Ordinance seem largely to be premised on the existence of a 'continuous contract', or employees who have worked for a period of four weeks for at least three days a week. This has the effect of excluding persons in short term or temporary employment. This is seen by Woodiwiss as being patriarchalist as rights seem to be reserved for employees who have developed some loyalty to an employer.

He adds that the passage of the Employment Ordinance may be seen as the time from which the state in Hong Kong assumed the responsibilities of a patriarch. This has meant that the form of the law and legal rights under Hong Kong labour law may be characterized as 'enforceable benevolence' (ibid:177-80). Woodiwiss concludes his case study of Hong Kong's labour laws by observing that:

> Thus the net result of the coexistence of capitalism, patriarchalism and the rule of law in Hong Kong is a labour law system that, despite the absence of any formal borrowing from the Japanese system, may nevertheless be described as an embryonic form of 'enforceable benevolence'. 'Immunities' rather than 'liberties' have been exchanged for enforceable, albeit lesser, industrial 'claims', supplemented by some significant though still insufficient improvements in social provision with respect to education, housing and welfare (ibid:182).

The labour law rights position in Hong Kong may be compared with the position in Singapore, as described in Woodiwiss's Singapore case study. This Singapore case study is a little disappointing, being the shortest of the four in this book. Whilst Malaysia is described as having a system of authoritarian patriarchalism, Singapore is described in terms of the possibility of achieving 'enforceable benevolence.' However, at present,

Woodiwiss sees Singapore as representing 'an instance par excellence of Pacific capitalism, that Singapore is an island of rampant patriarchalism.' Having said this, he acknowledges the flexibility and self-discipline of Singapore's population in the face of transnational forces and observes that:

> In sum, I wish to argue that for all of the undoubted civil oppressiveness of the current structure of Singaporean society, the republic is structurally closer to representing a model of what a human rights regime premised upon 'enforceable benevolence' might look like than any other society in the region, including Japan. (ibid:216).

One might recall that Lee Kuan Yew began his legal career in Singapore by representing trade union figures. However, soon after the landslide victory of the People's Action Party (PAP) in the 1959 elections, the Singapore government moved to deregister left-wing unions and political and sympathy strikes were banned. After independence in 1965, the National Trade Union Congress (NTUC) was drawn closer to the PAP and the government by being given a voice in the PAP's decision-making processes as well as by being given financial and administrative support by the government.

In return for this support, the government was able to impose restrictions on the NTUC's freedom of action and to have control over the appointment of the NTUC's secretary-general. The PAP also nominated a number of NTUC officials as parliamentary candidates. Woodiwiss concludes that 'the most important single change of all these developments was that prime minister Lee appears to have come to regard himself as the unchallengeable patriarch of his people' (ibid:220-2). As the government took measures to make Singapore more attractive to foreign capital, Woodiwiss notes that 'labour was ... required to give up some of its means of enhancing its autonomy in favour of future, loyalty-dependent benefits' (ibid:227).

As in Hong Kong, the primary labour laws of Singapore were based on English colonial labour legislation which was based on labour's rights in immunities which related only to the achievement of approved economic objectives; however, these laws only applied to trade unions and their officials. The introduction of an Arbitration Court in 1960 constituted a grant of 'powers' to Singapore's trade unions in return for forgoing liberties and immunities (ibid:236-8). However, Singapore has not seen a strengthening of its trade unions, despite the many benefits which were provided to them and Singaporean employees by their government.

Woodiwiss observes that 'all the state's benevolence and therefore the "attachment" of labour and human rights to their supposed bearers remain discretionary and hence instance a paternalism, albeit a highly generous one' (ibid:241). However, he concludes somewhat optimistically, noting that it would not be difficult to amend some of Singapore's laws (such as by strengthening the independence of the judiciary), so as to radically enhance the legitimacy of the state and lead to a more pluralistic approach to the public interest. This seems to be an unrealistic expectation, for as Woodiwiss acknowledges, this would require the paternalistic PAP to sacrifice some of its political security in the national interest. As he adds, '[a]ll that is required is a little more liberty' (ibid:242-3).

Woodiwiss has sought to apply a theoretical model to a set of very diverse societies and legal systems. His theory is quite rich in its explanatory possibilities, although some of Woodiwiss's arguments might have been better supported by further empirical evidence. While his work is not as readable as it might be, due to its occasional lapses into overly technical sociological jargon, it stands as a landmark highlighting the possibilities for comparative research of key areas of economic law in the region.

Tomasic and Little's Insolvency Law and Practice in Asia

Turning now to discuss another kind of comparative analysis of economic law related issues which provide another model for further research in the region, it is appropriate to discuss 'Asian Insolvency Law and Practice' written by Roman Tomasic, Peter Little, and others.[16] The book is primarily based upon six detailed case studies of insolvency law and practice in the PRC, Hong Kong, Taiwan, Singapore, Malaysia, and Indonesia. In each of these six jurisdictions, detailed interviews were conducted with insolvency practitioners, bankers, and regulators. In addition to background library research, a total of 115 interviews were undertaken, or a little less than an average of twenty interviews in each jurisdiction. Whilst these numbers are relatively small, the interviews were conducted with very experienced or elite informants who were able to provide extensive information and opinions which were confirmed by other sources. This served as a rich data source for later analysis.

The book also contains an overview of insolvency laws in six other Asian legal systems, although this discussion will concentrate on the six empirical case studies which drew upon the fieldwork conducted for this study. It is interesting to note in passing that when the interviews were being conducted, in late 1996, the researchers were repeatedly told that insolvency was not an issue of any significance as an economic or legal problem in Asia. As we all now know, this was soon to change. Soon after the publication of the book in early 1997 the Asian financial crisis appeared, leading an Australian High Court judge and the Australian *Business Review Weekly* to suggest that the researchers might have been indirectly responsible for this turn of event; if only academic studies could have such an impact!

The study sought to examine the extent to which traditional Asian values, such as ideas drawn from Confucian and Islamic traditions, had an impact on insolvency administration in different parts of Asia. Indonesia and Malaysia provided two Muslim societies which allowed the researchers to pursue this theme, whilst the remaining four jurisdictions allowed the researchers to examine the impact, if any, of Confucian ideas in predominantly Chinese-speaking societies. The research also examined the effect of globalization upon insolvency law reform in Asia.

Not surprisingly, it was found that there were some differences between jurisdictions in regard to the impact of traditional values. What was perhaps surprising was that in Singapore, where Asian values have been so much discussed, there was very little if any overt impact of Confucian ideas on insolvency administration. Instead, what was found in Singapore was almost a strict and efficient legalism. However, before insolvency proceedings are commenced in Singapore, informal pressures might be placed on debtors and the potential loss of face caused by insolvency would be a factor to be considered (ibid:159). These responses were clearly driven by traditional concerns.

However, as in Hong Kong, the influence upon insolvency administration in Singapore of an English derived legal system has been very strong. Efforts to encourage compromise and negotiation in dealing with debt problems have also been encouraged, but these are not uniquely Asian responses, as similar strategies are built into many western bodies of insolvency law and practice. Sometimes, the Singapore government has indirectly sought to support the rescue of enterprises, but by and large, the government has sought to stay out of this process.

In contrast to Singapore, in China the researchers found that Confucian ideas provided an undercurrent to discussion of insolvency issues. For example, respondents frequently said that bankruptcy was a capitalist idea and was alien to the Chinese tradition which valued the preservation of friendships. It was also said that an underlying Confucian influence remained strong in China; as one informant remarked: 'deep in the heart of every Chinese there is a Confucian influence in their daily life' (Tomasic and Little (eds) 1997:48-9).

In an insolvency context, it therefore became difficult to impose winding up procedures, except as a last resort; this was because there was a preference for resort to other remedies, such as mergers of two or more enterprises or reorganizations. As one PRC interviewee explained in this context, '[t]he Confucian idea is to choose the middle way; to find the balance.' Another said that 'Confucianism encourages balance and harmony. Unless there is no other choice, people will try to keep their friendships and relationships intact' (ibid:49).

Having said this, it should be noted that Confucian ideas are but one set of many influences which are at work in relation to insolvency administration in China. In practice, Confucian influences are probably less significant than other contemporary influences, such as the political implications of causing unemployment through the bankruptcy of enterprises, the massive size of China's state owned enterprise debt problems, the operation of the legal system itself, and the influence of over four decades of communism.

It should also be noted that China is passing through a period of rapid change in regard to the acceptance of ideas such as bankruptcy and this is likely to see a greater acceptance of bankruptcy as a way of dealing with debt. In Shenzhen, for example, one government lawyer characteristically observed that 'bankruptcy law is in fact a good thing in China – it affects competition and improves the standard of enterprises' (ibid:52).

In contrast to the more traditional attitudes found in Taiwan, on the mainland there was relatively little stigma associated with bankruptcy; as one senior PRC official stated: 'bankrupted people may feel a bit shameful. But they don't feel too bad' (ibid:55). In the meantime, China is moving slowly to enact a very modern new insolvency statute and the form of this law is likely to be more influenced by international best practice (such as the need to put in place a corporate rescue regime) and China's capacity to deal with related problems, such as unemployment and welfare support for those who lose their positions as a result of the bankruptcy of a state owned enterprise.[17]

In contrast, in regard to Taiwan, one lawyer reported that '[i]n Taiwan, Confucian ideas see bankruptcy as something to be ashamed of' (ibid:49, 93). A Taipei based insolvency practitioner (an accountant) observed that in Taiwan '... what happens is that people try to find a solution and not to push for bankruptcy – despite what the law says' (ibid:90). Taiwanese seem to be most reluctant to use legal processes in dealing with debt problems. This research found that the tendency to engage in informal workouts outside of the formal legal process and the application of traditional concepts (such as *tao-hao*) was still a large part of the commercial practice in response to insolvency in Taiwan (ibid:90). At the same time, the court system was seen as expensive, slow and inefficient and this did not encourage the use of legal mechanisms for dealing with debt problems. The law was also seen as being very archaic. This was akin to the situation that was found to exist in Indonesia up until the recent reforms to its bankruptcy laws.[18]

Finally, reference may be made to research findings in Hong Kong where it was found in this study that attitudes to insolvency differed depending on whether the case involved small Chinese businesses or debts between internationally oriented firms. Stigma was still seen to be a factor in attitudes to insolvency amongst the Chinese in Hong Kong, but its significance seems to be waning (ibid:126). In contrast, Western companies operating in Hong Kong were said to be much more fearful of the effects of insolvency upon their reputations. There is however a well recognized Chinese tradition that people will be expected to pay their creditors when they can. The Chinese system of dealing with debts was also seen as being one of self-reliance (ibid:128).

Although background cultural attitudes are present in regard to the handling of debt problems in Hong Kong, the research found that these factors play little if any part in the way that the legal system handles insolvency cases. There was clearly a perception that this British derived legislation did not reflect local cultural values. Nevertheless, in general terms, as one interviewee observed of Hong Kong, 'the Confucian social tradition has a huge influence on the way individuals interact and deal with each other in the corporate environment.' Having said this, the legal system is very much governed by the application of British legal ideas (ibid:129). This may explain the relatively small number of insolvency cases coming before the courts in Hong Kong.

This study of 'Insolvency Law and Practice in Asia' provides some lessons on comparative commercial law research in Asia and the social context in which these laws operate. Of course, all law is part of a social context and is constructed by that social context. Laws may be more or less out of date or irrelevant, especially if they have been imposed upon unwilling communities.[19] However, this context is somewhat more complex than it might seem, being subject to international and local influences. Although undertaking fieldwork of the kind that occurred with this study can be exhausting and frustrating, the end result can be quite illuminating, allowing one to assess some of the big contemporary debates, such as those which emphasize the importance of Asian or Confucian values. In the process, the research also induced the researchers to adopt a more critical view of their own legal system by comparing it with others of the kind examined in this book.

PISTOR AND WELLONS'S *ROLE OF LAW AND LEGAL INSTITUTIONS IN ASIAN ECONOMIC DEVELOPMENT 1960-95*.

Finally, reference should very be made to an important study by Katharina Pistor and Philip Wellons of Harvard University which was undertaken for the Asian Development Bank. The authors come from the Harvard Institute for International Development and their report sought to examine the Role of Law and Legal Institutions in Asian Economic Development from 1960-95. This is a very ambitious project that asked whether law matters for purposes of achieving economic development and whether Asia was different in this regard from other parts of the world.

The project draws upon data from a sample of six Asian jurisdictions, the PRC, India, Japan, the Republic of Korea, Malaysia, and Taiwan. The study is based on macro-economic data and socio-legal analyses. The report examines legal transplants in a number of different areas of law: such as competition law, environmental and consumer protection law, intellectual property law, and securities law. Also considered are laws protecting security interests in the face of bad debts.

The authors note that in Asia, economic law developed before economic development had begun to accelerate and that economic development caught up with law much later. However, until this happened, the authors found that law only marginally affected economic behaviour. They note that the enactment of new laws over the last three decades has seen the state take a more active role in the economy which provided a decisive influence on shaping further economic and legal development. As the authors also note: '[t]his suggests that law is not irrelevant for economic development, but that for law to have a positive impact it must be congruent with the prevailing economic policies' (Pistor and Wellons unpub. report 1987:15). Pistor and Wellons also observe that there are elements of both convergence and divergence in Asian legal systems. As they explain:

> With the move towards market-oriented economic policies, the legal system in all countries became more market-allocative and more rule-based. Despite the overall trend towards market-allocative and rule-based legal systems, the remaining differences in legal processes and institutions lead us to conclude that legal systems are partly converging, and partly diverging (ibid:15).

Finally, Pistor and Wellons also assess the fundamental question of cultural influences on Asian legal systems and conclude that:

> Cultural factors my have played a role in the evolution of law and legal processes. Our findings suggest that legal behavior responded to changes in economic policies. Cultural factors may have determined the nuances of this response or even helped explain the change in policy, but they did not stop the legal system from adapting to changing economic strategy and environment (ibid).

This is a rich and broad ranging study which deserves closer analysis than has been possible here.[20] It does however show the value of using cross-jurisdictional economic and legal data as a means of seeking to develop models and make general observations about law and economic development in Asia.

CONCLUSION: BIG PICTURES AND THE SEARCH FOR NEW STORIES TO TELL

Many challenges await socio-legal researchers seeking to make a contribution to improving understandings of major contemporary issues, such as the late 1990s Asian financial crisis, the place of the rule of law, human rights, nation building, and the effects of globalization. Finding the time, resources, skills, and energies to undertake such work will provide some challenges in this regard. However, these challenges are not insurmountable, as some of the studies discussed above have shown.

Although efforts should be made to contribute to the understanding of bigger questions, this is not to suggest an abandonment of research methods which look at issues from the 'grass roots', such as case studies, interviews with key actors, and economic modelling. After all, one of the first lessons of good research is ensuring manageability or the use of research methods, which are appropriate to research objectives, time-scale, and resources. There are great virtues in collaboration in research of this kind as this may help to compensate for deficiencies experienced by any one researcher. Collaboration between researchers also has other merits, which should not be ignored, such as maintaining momentum in large research projects through mutual support of members of the research team. Others, such as John Braithwaite, have also written of the advantages of group research activity when undertaking fieldwork or interviews of the economic, legal, and official elite.

This chapter has sought to examine a number of very different ways of looking at the key issues of law and economic development in Asia. The stories of Chris Patten and Lee Kuan Yew are quite illuminating and their messages have been very influential. They do however call for closer analysis and critique by researchers. What is interesting to note is the extent to which the concerns of these two authors mirror those which can be found in the academic literature, if the three academic studies discussed above are taken as reflecting trends in that literature.

Legal researchers are only beginning to develop the tools and experience to undertake the kind of further research and analysis in legal and related economic issues that is called for in the region. There is no shortage of possible areas in which such further work can be undertaken, as this is a relatively unploughed field of endeavour. There are therefore many more 'stories' to tell. However, these should provide for a balance of theory and data, which is essential for the reliability and usefulness of such studies.

NOTES

* This chapter is based on a paper delivered in 1998 at the Hong Kong annual conference of the Asia Pacific Economic Law Forum. A selection of papers from that conference are published in (1999-2000) Vol. 4 (Nos 1-2), *Journal of Chinese and Comparative Law*, pp. 1-198.

1 Lee Kuan Yew's book is the first book of memoirs by Lee and described the years leading up to the independence of Singapore in 1965. A subsequent Lee memoir dealing with the following 25 years has recently been published.

2 Patten supra, p. 20. He also refers to what he calls the '[t]he Empire Story of the most humane and well-intentioned of the colonial powers – a story that at its best encompasses scholar-administrators who knew and loved the distant lands they governed more than the country in whose name they served ...' (supra, p. 6).

3 For example, former Australian Prime Minister, Bob Hawke, (who opened the first APELF conference held in Brisbane) is quoted as saying that '[w]hether one agrees with all the attitudes, decisions and analyses of Lee Kwan Yew, this book is a must for anyone who wants to understand the mind-set of Asia.' Similarly, Former German Chancellor, Helmut Schmidt, is quoted as saying of Lee that '[m]any American and European leaders have profited from his wisdom, particularly by his evaluation of China as a world power and by his analysis and explanations of Asian values.'

4 See for example ibid:53 and p. 67. Patten also quotes (p. 290) George Kennan's remark that 'the Chinese have an "insatiable" ... thirst for "face" and prestige.'

5 Ibid:144. It is interesting to note that Singapore abolished trial by jury in a large class of cases in 1960 and trial by jury was completely abolished in 1969; Anthony Woodiwiss, *Globalisation, Human Rights and Labour Law in Pacific Asia,* Cambridge, Cambridge University Press, 1998, p. 233.

6 Lee devotes a number of pages to describing his secret meetings with the leader of the communists in Singapore in the later 1950s: see further ibid, pp. 278-89. Also see pp. 357-61.

7 Patten denies that 'Hong Kongers had been politically lobotomised...' (as they did have a keen interests in politics), but successive administrations made the political judgement which led them to conclude that Hong Kong was not at that time quite right yet for democracy; Patten, ibid:24.

8 Lee Kuan Yew tells of an episode in 1955 when he threatened to seek *habeas corpus* to gain the release of a Chinese communist, Liew Yit Fun. Liew was however then deported from Singapore to China by the British authorities. In a sense, the threat of *habeas corpus* backfired on Lee in this case.

9 See further, R. Tomasic, 'Company Law and the Limits of the Rule of Law in China,' (1995) *Australian Journal of Corporate Law* 4, p. 470.

10 It is interesting to note recent statements to this effect by former PRC Premier, Li Peng, speaking as the Chair of the National People's Congress when he said that:

> An important fundamental strategy for administration is to rule the country by law. The people's will and the [party's] will should be written into law through legal procedures for all the organizations in the country, including the [party] itself, to observe. In this way we can avoid repeating past mistakes. *South China Morning Post*, December 1, 1998, p. 17.

11 See for example, D. Saunders and S. Oldfield, 'Lyonnais sees peg cast aside by 2000,' *South China Morning Post* 1 December 1998, p. 1 (Business Post).

12 See further R. Tomasic, 'Globalization and the Transformation of Commercial and Legal Practice in the Asia Pacific: Opportunities and Challenges for Australian Commercial Lawyers and their Clients,' (1997), *Corporate and Business Law Journal* 10, pp. 69-100. Also see generally R. Tomasic and B. Kamarul, 'Citizenship, Corporations and Globalisation in Asia: An Exploratory Analysis,' (1999) *The Flinders Journal of Law Reform* 3/1, pp. 75-96, and R. Tomasic and B. Kamarul, 'The Rule of Law and Corporate Insolvency in Six Asian Legal Systems,' (1998) *The Canterbury Law Review* 7, pp. 157-70. Also see

W. Twining, *Globalisation and Legal Theory*, London, Butterworths, 2000.

13 Some other works which come to mind include studies of international arbitration by Bryant Garth and Yves Dezalay, John Braithwaite's work on international intellectual property law reform and others: See further J. Braithwaite and P. Drahos, *Global Business Regulation*, Cambridge, Cambridge University Press, 2000.

14 See further R. Tomasic, *Sociology of Law*, London, Sage, 1985.

15 Ibid:152. In this regard, see further C. Jones, 'Capitalism, Globalization and Rule of Law: An Alternative Trajectory of Legal Change in China,' (1994) *Social and Legal Studies* 3, p. 195.

16 The other members of the research team were Kam Kamarul, Kui Hua Wang, Angus Francis, and Kate Reid. However, either Roman Tomasic or Peter Little were present at all interviews. Roman Tomasic undertook interviews in the PRC, Taiwan, Hong Kong, and Singapore; whilst Peter Little undertook interviews in Singapore, Malaysia, and Indonesia.

17 See further Wang Weiguo, 'Adopting Corporate Rescue Regimes in China: A Comparative Survey,' (1998) *Australian Journal of Corporate Law* 9, pp. 234-62; and R. Tomasic, 'Insolvency Law Principles and the Draft Bankruptcy Law of the People's Republic of China,' (1998) *Australian Journal of Corporate Law* 9, pp. 211-33.

18 Ibid, pp. 218-22. See further J. Hoff (and G.J. Churchill, editor) *Indonesian Bankruptcy Law*, Indonesian Law and Practice Series: 2, PT Tatanusa, Jakarta, 1999.

19 See further T. Lindsey, *Indonesia: Law and Society*, Sydney, The Federation Press, 1999; and V. Taylor (ed.), *Asian Laws through Australian Eyes*, Sydney, LBC Information Services 1997.

20 For a more detailed discussion of this report, see A.H.Y. Chen, 'Law, Development and the Typology of Legal Systems', (1999-2000) *Journal of Chinese and Comparative Law* 4/1-2, pp. 30-49.

REFERENCES

Henderson, I. (1998) 'Bank bids to reign in hedge funds,' *The Australian*, 22 November 1998, p. 1.

Hoff, J. and G.J. Churchill (eds) (1999) *Indonesian Bankruptcy Law*, Indonesian Law and Practice Series: 2, Jakarta: PT Tatanusa.

Jones, C. (1994) 'Capitalism, Globalization and Rule of Law: An Alternative Trajectory of Legal Change in China,' *Social and Legal Studies* 3, p. 195.

Lee Kuan Yew (1998) *The Singapore Story*. Singapore: Prentice Hall.

Lindsey, T. (1999) *Indonesia: Law and Society*. Sydney: The Federation Press.

Lingle, C. (1998) 'Turning the tables on Lee Kuan Yew,' *The Australian Financial Review*, 29 October 1998, p. 23.

Patten, C. (1998) *East and West: The Last Governor of Hong Kong on Power, Freedom and the Future*. London: Macmillan.

Pistor, Katharina and P. Wellons (1997) *Symposium on the Role of Law and Legal Institutions in Asian Economic Development 1960-1995*, ADB report, October. (See now this title published by Oxford University Press, New York, 1999).

Robertson, R. (1990) 'Mapping the Global Condition: Globalization as the Central Concept,' in: M. Featherstone (ed.) *Global Culture: Nationalism, Globalization and Modernity*. Sage: London.

Rodan, G. (1998) 'Turning the tables on Lee Kuan Yew,' *The Australian Financial Review*, 29 October 1998, p. 23.

Saunders, D. and S. Oldfield 'Lyonnais sees peg cast aside by 2000,' *South China Morning Post*, 1 December 1998 at p. 1 (Business Post).

South China Morning Post, 1 December 1998.

Taylor, V. (ed.) (1997) *Asian Laws through Australian Eyes*. Sydney: LBC Information Services.

Tomasic, R. (1985) *Sociology of Law*. London: Sage.

– (1995) 'Company Law and the Limits of the Rule of Law in China,' *Australian Journal of Corporate Law* 4, p. 470.

– (1997) 'Globalization and the Transformation of Commercial and Legal Practice in the Asia Pacific: Opportunities and Challenges for Australian Commercial Lawyers and their Clients,' *Corporate and Business Law Journal* 10, pp. 69-100.

– (1998) 'Insolvency Law Principles and the Draft Bankruptcy Law of the People's Republic of China,' (1998) 9 *Australian Journal of Corporate Law*, pp. 211-33.

Tomasic, R. and B. Kamarul (1998) 'The Rule of Law and Corporate Insolvency in Six Asian Legal Systems,' *The Canterbury Law Review* 7, pp. 157-70.

– (1999) 'Citizenship, Corporations and Globalisation in Asia: An Exploratory Analysis,' *The Flinders Journal of Law Reform* 3/1, pp. 75-96.

Tomasic, Roman and Peter Little (eds) (1997) *Insolvency Law and Practice in Asia*. Hong Kong: FT Law and Tax, pp. 48-9.

Wang Weiguo (1998) 'Adopting Corporate Rescue Regimes in China: A Comparative Survey,' *Australian Journal of Corporate Law* 9, pp. 234-62.

Waters, M. (1995) *Globalisation*. London: Routledge.

Woodiwiss, Anthony (1998) *Globalisation, Human Rights and Labour Law in Pacific Asia.* Cambridge: Cambridge University Press.